MINISTERIAL PRIESTHOOD

MINISTERIAL PRIESTHOOD
CHAPTERS
(PRELIMINARY TO A STUDY OF
THE ORDINAL) ON THE RATIONALE
OF MINISTRY AND THE MEANING
OF CHRISTIAN PRIESTHOOD

BY R. C. MOBERLY, D.D.
SOMETIME REGIUS PROFESSOR OF PASTORAL THEOLOGY IN THE
UNIVERSITY OF OXFORD, CANON OF CHRIST CHURCH

WIPF & STOCK · Eugene, Oregon

Wipf and Stock Publishers
199 W 8th Ave, Suite 3
Eugene, OR 97401

Ministerial Priesthood
Chapters (Preliminary to a Study of the Ordinal)
on the Rationale of Ministry and the Meaning
of Christian Priesthood
By Moberly, R. C.
Softcover ISBN-13: 978-1-6667-3395-2
Hardcover ISBN-13: 978-1-6667-2929-0
eBook ISBN-13: 978-1-6667-2930-6
Publication date 8/12/2021
Previously published by Longmans, Green, & Co., 1910

This edition is a scanned facsimile of
the original edition published in 1910

PREFACE TO SECOND EDITION

I HAVE taken the opportunity of a fresh issue to modify a sentence on p. xiii, which seemed to put false emphasis on the word 'details'; I have accepted corrections in the notes on pp. 115, 225; and have added a very few words of further comment on pp. 32, 108, 228.

It might possibly be wise to say no more. Yet I am, on the whole, encouraged to try to elucidate a little further the meaning of some positions which have been specially criticized.

The first of these turns upon the word 'presuppositions,' as used in the Preface. It seemed to be supposed, on some sides, that I began by asking to have certain presuppositions granted, before and apart from any examination of evidence, on the ground that, unless this concession were made, the evidence would of itself be inadequate for my purpose. Nothing could be further from the truth. I was led to mention presuppositions at all, not for the sake of an argument which I wished myself to prop up, but because of the intimacy of their connection with the position which I wished to refute. I was impressed with the extent to which the conclusions (as I thought, the mistaken conclusions) of others were modified by (what I thought to be very disputable) presuppositions. In particular, I wished to draw attention to the strength of the unconscious presuppositions of those who (sometimes) suppose themselves to be without presuppositions at all. And then, in connection with this thought of their unacknowledged, and often illegitimate, weight in the arguments of those whom I was criticising, I added some observations—which plainly were too short and incidental for their purpose—upon the proper place of presuppositions in thought.

Under the circumstances, I will venture to add a few more words on this point. But before doing so I must insist, in the plainest way, that whether I have been able to analyze this relation with more success, or with less, my own book stands or falls, not according to my success or failure in this analysis, but according to its own attempt to give an intelligent, rational, and judicial marshalling and interpretation of the evidence of the actual historical facts.

I ask, and have asked, for nothing but what is severely rational. But then I must point out, that a great deal of what may be rightly called presupposition is, whether we like it or no, an absolute *sine qua non* for rational intelligence. The claim to be unprejudiced, in the exaggerated form in which it is in the present generation popular, is, on analysis really incompatible with reason. For prejudice indeed in the sense of wilful self-blinding, or tampering (whether more or less) with intellectual conscience, I have not one word of apology. But so far as the word 'prejudice' may be capable of being understood as referring to that antecedent content of mind and character which, in fact, largely affects a man's reception of evidence, it is intellectually indispensable for any power of apprehending truth at all. The whole antecedent content of mind and character constitutes, of necessity, a mental mould, into which evidence is not unaffected by entering; and makes a natural, or quasi-instinctive, capacity of insight, of some kinds, or in some directions, rather than others. This mental content, the result of all previous experience, constitutes a man's capacity of rational assimilation. It is his trained insight, which he should be at once using and correcting by use—but using at least as freely as correcting. It is not in spite of certainties already reached, but by their help, that new truth is to be seen; even though the insight of truth may itself react upon them; and they always are ready to be modified in the interest of truth.

In saying this, I am not offering an apology, as if for a certain pardonable suspension or modification of rational process. On the contrary, I am describing rational process itself. It is precisely this which constitutes its character as rational.

There are those who claim to have no previous convictions; and there are those who recognize what they have only, in effect, to hold a brief against them, or try to be as if they had them not. I do not believe that either of these mental conditions is ideally right for insight into truth. The attempt to put previous experience wholly aside, is really an attempt to decide upon imperfect evidence; for both the previous experience in itself, and the coherence of the new data with the previous experience, were legitimate elements in the total evidence. To put previous convictions aside, just in proportion as it is done with approximate completeness, is to produce a decision unfairly weighted in the direction of paradox. The attempt at fairness, too superficially made, has become a bias more or less profound, towards contradicting, rather than conforming with, the presuppositions of antecedent experience. On the other hand, a mind that was really like a sheet of blank paper would have no power of insight into anything at all. The conditions of knowledge and judgement being what they are, a thoughtful man does well to be conscious of the extent to which his conclusions upon any given evidence are conditioned by (even when they modify) his preassumptions; and should endeavour rather to scrutinize, to justify, or to correct, his preassumptions than to deny that he has them.

Whereas, then, there is a kind of 'prejudice' which is inseparable from any power of reasonable apprehension, I would urge that the claim to be 'wholly unprejudiced' should be modified by a conception—if not humbler, at all events more complex and truthful—as to the necessary conditions of thinking; that instead of claiming to be wholly unbiassed, the mind that wishes to be scrupulously fair should rather acknowledge, and accept, and consciously scrutinize the bias which it cannot be without.

It hardly ought to be necessary, at the present time, to be seriously insisting on principles like these; but since it seems still sometimes to be assumed that absence of presuppositions is the right mental condition for impartial appreciation of evidence, I must submit instead, first, that this is not a real possibility at all; and secondly, that, if it were, it would not be a right condition for apprehending truth. The condition required for truly weighing evidence is to approach it with the right and not the wrong presuppositions. I wish so far to shift the inquiry from the application of first principles to the first principles themselves. Of course I believe in fact that my own first principles — such, e. g. as belief in God, in the Incarnation, in the Holy Spirit, in a Church with divinely-appointed ministries and sacraments—are true. But that is not at all my point. My point is that the conclusions to be reached so largely consist of necessary applications of such first principles, that it is the first principles themselves which most need to be examined; because it is only in the light of these that the things which are to them subordinate and accessory can themselves be rightly discerned. I am not asking to have my presuppositions blindly assumed. I am asking to have the place and importance of presuppositions recognized; and so to have the presuppositions, as such, deliberately and on both sides, cross-examined.

I know that to some readers the plea of my preface has meant no more than an avowal of incapacity for fair-minded appreciation of evidence. Would it be wrong to suggest that such readers are still under the dominion of a very crudely objective conception of thought? I cannot help thinking that we are likely, in the future, to be more accustomed to the other way of putting it. Perhaps our critics in the future will be, in their turn, no less confident—perhaps no less one-sided —in insisting that the simplest of propositions can be made only by a person; and that the consciousness of the person who makes the proposition is of necessity a determining ingredient in the meaning, to him, of the proposition which he makes. After all, even the proposition 'two and two make four' is mere meaningless sound except as the apprehension of an apprehending mind; there may be many different *nuances* of meaning in the statement that 'it is wise to be virtuous'; whilst the words, 'I believe in God,' are capable of as many degrees of significance as there are varying capacities of personal consciousness. But at least I think I may plead that there is, in any act of personal thought or judgement, a personal factor which is both legitimate and necessary; and that the place and meaning of the personal factor is ignored overmuch by those who aim at fairness in too off-hand a way.

Our central convictions necessarily colour all our thought. They would do so, to a large extent, even if they were irrational 'prejudices.' They do so not the less, but much the more, when they are themselves the conscious outcome of all in us that is most deeply rational, most largely and vitally conversant with real truth. As long as I doubt whether to believe in God or no, the phenomena of primitive religion or the presence of pain in the world may seem to be presumptions against God's existence. But from the moment when belief in God has become the primal certainty of my being, all problems about savage religion, or pain, or sin, can only be raised in the light of the vital certainty that God is God above all. As long as I stand in doubt whether the Incarnation is really true, I may be utterly perplexed or incredulous about the Gospel miracles; but from the moment when the Incarnation is to me the crowning illumination of all philosophical or theological thought, the evidence about miracles can only be examined—nay, can only be stated or seen—in the light of the basal certainty of the Incarnation[1].

Such problems are really only incidents in a larger question—into which indeed they enter as ingredients, but which can only be decided as a whole. If viewed persistently in isolation, they cannot be adequately viewed at all. And in a somewhat similar manner it is true that a critical examination of texts, however valuable, is only a part, not the whole, of the theologian's access to the meaning of that living reality, which is portrayed for us in the New Testament alike by historic action and recorded word—but by neither nor both together in absolute completeness, just for this essential reason, that living reality is always more than any of its possible expressions in word or act.

It may be that the conception of the living

---

[1] Those who have read *Divine Immanence*, by the Rev. J. R. Illingworth, in connexion with his Bampton Lectures on 'Personality,' will understand how infinitely larger is the range of thought to which I refer, than it would be at all within my own power to express.

Church, as realized in Christian experience, could hardly, apart from Christian experience, have been deduced with infallible certainty from a verbal exposition of St. Paul. But Christian experience, as a whole, is a real part of our insight into the meaning of the Scriptures upon which the experience itself is based. There may be such a thing as true insight into the Theology of the Person of Christ, with its meanings and corollaries, which is mirrored in, which illuminates brightly as nothing else illuminates, and brings into full coherence and harmony, yet is not itself absolutely deducible from, the words of apostolic exposition. When I am perfectly certain of my belief in God, I *must* construe all the evidence, which might before have been ambiguous, in the light of this, which is now my primal certainty. When I am perfectly certain of my belief in a divinely ordered Church, I am right in taking my certainty with me to the interpretation of passages, which might otherwise, perhaps, have been explicable without it. If indeed the passages in question were incompatible with it, I should have to modify my conception to suit the passages; but if they without it are so far ambiguous, I do certainly right to interpret them by it. I am not now either explaining or arguing on behalf of the conception itself. I am only contending that it ought to be examined —and that upon the widest possible grounds— before I can be in a position to make my exegesis complete. Supposing for one moment that the conception is true, and that those to whom it has been among the most transparent of certainties have been dealing with spiritual fact and not spiritual fancy, then it would necessarily follow that exegesis which explains St. Paul's mystical teaching on the subject of the Church without reference to it—on the ground that his language can be explained apart from it—would be, as exegesis, misleading.

It is this which exegesis has to bear in mind. The separate texts are always merely parts of a whole. And it is in the light of the whole that alone they can, as parts, be truly understood. Suppose that the questions at issue are such as these: Was the method of the working of the Pentecostal spirit in the world, i. e. was the method of Christ's Church detached and individual, or corporate? Again, Was the corporate Church organized on the basis of private consent, or of Christ-descended apostolic authority? If I claim to approach the examination of texts bearing on these questions in the light of the historical idea of the Church throughout the ages, it is to be remembered that the historical idea of the Church is not an *a priori* imagination drawn out of my inner consciousness; it is itself the actual product in history of the very evidence, as a whole, of which I am invited to try and cross-examine some detached parts.

It ought hardly, perhaps, to be necessary to be pleading for the legitimacy of a principle of interpretation to which all evolutionary thought bears emphatic witness. If evolutionary thought has taught us anything, it has taught us not to exclude the end, *ex hypothesi*, where we want to understand the true nature of the beginning, but rather to recognize to how large an extent the beginning finds its true interpretation in the end.

But though evolution bears its witness to the intellectual method, this is no simple case of evolution. We are dealing not merely with a growth, but with a growth divinely guided and inspired. If the Church, articulate and harmonious, with its outward expression of ministry and sacraments, is now, or has ever been, a theological verity, it must have been a theological verity when apostles wrote. If the Church is a necessary corollary of the doctrine of the Incarnation, and the necessary expression of the doctrine of the Holy Ghost (and if not it would not be in place as an article of the Creed), then it was so on and from the day of Pentecost with a truth as true essentially as at any point since. If you were dealing with the writings of private, uninspired individuals, it might be a tenable position to say that they did not actually mean this great reality (though they say things strangely akin to it), because this great reality, though real, was as yet not realized in their consciousness to the full. But this is not an adequate form of statement in reference to the canonical writings of inspired apostles. Even if it were held (paradoxically, as it appears to me) that St. Paul, when he wrote to the Corinthians or Ephesians, had not yet grasped the theological conception of the Church; yet even so, on any tenable theory of inspiration or the doctrine of the Holy Spirit, you would have to say that the theological conception of the Church was, even without his knowledge, the real, though latent, truth behind the conception which he had.

Of course it is possible that we may be mistaken, more or less, in the form or proportion of our theological conceptions; and that it is just these which themselves most need to be corrected. This is precisely the sort of possibility to which I desire that Christian thought should be keenly alive. That theological preconceptions, as such, should tyrannize over the interpretation of the text, is the last thing for which I should plead. But I cannot do less than put it that the historic theology comes with me to the text, if not simply as a voice of authoritative interpretation, yet as a hypothesis which offers to interpret; and a hypothesis which has at least a presumption in its favour. By all means let any one approach, if he will, with alternative hypotheses also. There must be many, in fact, who do so approach, with tentative hypotheses half-formed, and with a view to deciding between rival hypotheses. If the question were asked, Which hypothesis interprets and illumines the evidence as a whole? I should be quite fearless as to the ultimate answer. But it must be remembered that no answer can be accepted as adequate which does not interpret and illumine the evidence as a whole. If, for example, half a dozen passages be examined in connexion with the question of apostolic authority, and of these *a*, *b*, and *c*, by themselves, can be almost, if not quite, as easily interpreted without it, *d* and *e* certainly suggest it, but not imperiously, while *f* is difficult to account for on any other hypothesis, what would the legitimate conclusion be? That because the numerical majority of the passages could stand without it, therefore it is to be rejected as, at best, not proven? On the contrary, the conclusion, on such data, ought to be that the hypothesis was in fact necessary to bring the entire six passages into a single harmony. And if the hypothesis thus necessary as hypothesis was itself also, as belief, the historical sequel and outcome of the apostolic age as a whole, it would at once be reasonably adopted—at the very least provisionally—as a true constitutive principle. I am not suggesting that the above is at all a true numerical statement about the passages which could be cited. Rather I am putting (on a somewhat extreme supposition) an illustration of the true and false methods of inference.

When we are charged with reading later meanings, unhistorically, into the earlier language of apostles, I am not sure that the charge comes really to more than this—that we are reading the part in the light of the whole, and using the direct outcome of the guided words and guided actions of the apostolic Church, as a whole, to light up the possible ambiguity of isolated incidents or texts.

I have acknowledged, as of course, that this, the true method of interpretation, may be (like all truths) overpressed; that is, that current assumptions as to the outcome of apostolic teaching, which themselves are open to correction, may be asserted too crudely as of overruling authority. But if it is therefore urged as the safer course that the exegetic theologian should keep his exegesis wholly apart from his theology, and interpret each passage severely by itself, it may be enough to reply that our object is—not safety, as safety, but the richest fullness of truth. And if the modern reaction towards stringency of verbal exegesis has been, in the main, a healthy one, it may still be asked, cannot it also go, and has it not gone, too far? too often mistaking its own somewhat limited methods for a measure of the richness of truth; isolating overmuch the several strands and aspects of a great complex living reality, and paring down each one to the lowest level of meaning of which, when separately cross-examined, it has seemed to be capable?

But I pass on to a distinct, though partly kindred, set of criticisms. From a good many different sides the language has been censured which speaks of the Church and the kingdom as properly identical. Convinced as I am that this is the true method of speech and thought on the subject, I can yet largely agree with that which the critics mean, while pointedly demurring to their conclusions. The objections are such as these: (1) whatever precise definition of the Church may be chosen, it will not in fact be conterminous with the kingdom. It will include some whom the kingdom will not include; and will exclude some who will not be excluded from the kingdom. And more than this, (2) it is urged that the Church and the kingdom are hardly words *in pari materia* at all; that 'the Church' is properly an 'extensive' word, having decernible limitations, just because its significance is in the outward sphere, so that (whatever be taken as the dividing line) it is humanly possible to distinguish those who are without from those who are within; but that 'the kingdom' signifies not an area at all, but an influence, a character, a spirit.

Now I entirely agree with the positive meaning of both these objections. The kingdom is the spirit. It is more properly defined by its central life than by the tracing of external lines of delimitation. Moreover, no Church on earth, however delimited, will or can be in fact conterminous with the kingdom which will be hereafter. What then? It was wrong to speak of them as identical? Not at all. The denial of identity will lead us much further astray than the assertion; though no doubt either assertion or denial need some explaining. Whilst we admit that no Church order ever has been, in fact, the perfect expression of the spirit, the question really is whether there is such a thing as a *right* Church order, the truly authorized and proper mode of expression of the spirit — in comparison with which all alternative forms of Church organization are, so far, definitely wrong; or whether it follows from what has been allowed that all outward organizations, as such, may be—I do not say equally desirable, equally historical, or equally expedient, but at least in ultimate rationale of principle equally indifferent or (what is the same thing) equally right. If neither Romanism, Anglicanism, nor Dissent is (in fact) exclusively spiritual, while there is spiritual, faith and life to be found within each of them, the conclusion is popularly drawn that true Christianity is in such sense an inward thing, that it is a mistake to imagine that it has any 'proper' or 'right' expression in outward order. This conclusion certainly does not follow—'Salvation is of the Jews.' It is at least possible that one form of outward order may be, as outward order, really right—however, alas! imperfectly spiritualized; and that the others, though not incompatible with spiritual life, may be nevertheless, in respect of their departure from the right outward order, really wrong. It is this which is the contention of my second chapter.

But it will of course be observed that if I say that a Presbyterian, a Lutheran, or a Methodist is, so far, in his departure from the ministry and sacraments of the Church, really wrong—which I mean to say without reserve—it does not follow that I am allowing them no position or possibilities at all. On the contrary, I not only admit in the abstract that there may be spiritual Christianity among those bodies, but as I come to know individual Christians among them, it is much more than possible that I shall be brought to own, with all reverence, that they are immeasurably nearer to the Spirit of Christ than I. Christianity to be real must be really personal. The height of privilege is the height of responsibility. No man of candid mind, who has himself been brought up in the midst of exceptional privilege (whether political, social, or spiritual), can be unaccustomed to the complex attitude—which will to him be instinctive, though to outsiders it may sometimes seem inconsistent—of feeling, at one and the same moment, on the one side how great are his advantages, and how overwhelmingly sure his conviction of the priceless value of them; and yet, on the other, how far greater and better personally than himself are others, in all directions, who have them not. But greater and better though he honestly feels them to be, he will still feel that he has on his side an insight and a certainty which (it may be) is denied to them. He cannot, because he owns them so far his superiors (intellectually often as well as morally), belie the unfaltering insight which he feels it to be his privilege to possess; which would, he feels, make them, if he could but share it with them, such splendid champions and prophets of truth in the world; which ought to make him, who has it, so much better and more useful than he is! So the churchman, in his unfaltering certainty of the priceless privilege of churchmanship, is anything rather than arrogant or unappreciative of others. He does not condemn, or exclude, or in any way belittle them. But he would to God that he could open to them that insight in which God's providence—not any power or faithfulness of his own—has, in fact, nurtured him!

But this is not the only point which I wished to urge. For so far the language used has been consistent with a form of thought which, however personally appreciative towards them, would yet clearly rule that they were, as matter of definition, 'outside the Church.' Are they then definitely 'outside the Church'? or where is the line to be drawn which distinguishes 'within' from 'without'? I must answer that it is a mistake, from the point of view of theology, to suppose that a single line of absolute demarcation can be drawn at any point whatever, of such nature that all on the one side of it shall be absolutely within, and all on the other side absolutely without. The more our logical faculties demand such a line, the more does theological insight prohibit it. Beyond question the nearest approach to such a line is Baptism; and Baptism would in fact at once definitely include every single one of those whom we have mentioned. But it is certainly not without some reserve, and that in both directions, that even Baptism can be allowed to stand as the absolute distinction between those who are and those who are not within the borders of the Church of Christ. Baptism does really represent such a line, and is the symbol of it. The language that it *is* such a line is itself not untenable nor improper language. Yet he who by logical process draws from that language its mechanical conclusion, and takes it for an adequate statement of truth, will certainly be misled. For some purposes the conclusion follows, for others it does not. It follows for some outward purposes, and the outward purposes representatively are, and ideally ought to be, identical with the inward which they signify; but, for all that, the *absolute* identification cannot always be pressed between the outward which is representative, and the inward which is represented by it.

It is in fact important to recognize that there is no really absolute distinction between within and without. On the contrary, what is incompatible with an absolute line, there are *degrees of withinness*; and these not only many but manifold, varying not only in gradation but in kind. For instance, in the comparatively outward sphere, if the main line is between the unbaptized and the baptized, there is still a considerable difference, in respect of 'withinness,' between the merely baptized who practically renounce all Churches and Creeds, and the baptized who also are religious; again, between the religiously minded baptized, who repudiate the organization of the Church, and those who mean to be loyal as Church members; and again, between those who are and those who are not confirmed; and again, between those who, by their constant place in the congregation and work for the congregation, give practical reality to their membership and those who do not; and again, between those who never and those who occasionally communicate; and again, between those who communicate now and then and those who live, and depend on, the regular communicant life. And again, across all these distinctions or others like these, sometimes varying with them, sometimes in startling independence of them, are the distinctions, known to God rather than to men, which are less of outward action than of inward life. Thus every one would recognize that amongst those who are equally regular communicants, so far as outward habit is concerned, some may be immeasurably more 'within' than others; and conversely, that among those who seem to stand most aloof, some, in fact, are immeasurably less 'without' than others; that (if I may venture on a suggestive, though impossible, comparison) there are, as it were, more sets than one of concentric circles, in planes neither identical nor parallel; that 'withinness,' *in the fullest sense of all*, belongs only to those who are in the innermost circle alike of communicant outwardness and of inward communion; and that, apart from these, not only are there infinite grades of withoutness and withinness, but moreover almost every variety is possible of combination of what is within and without. Nay, even in respect to those who are, outwardly speaking, the most totally without, that is to say, the uninstructed and the unbaptized, it is, to say the least, very possible to imagine conditions under which even their withoutness would be rather apparent, economical, and symbolic, than spiritual or real.

St. Paul, if he saluted his converts as saints, or magnified the meaning of membership of the Church, did not suppose that they were all saintly alike. The full meaning of membership, 'I in them, and thou in me'; St. Paul's 'I live, yet not I but Christ liveth in me,' is *ideally* true of all. Actually, I suppose, it is true in a thousand thousand different gradations upon earth, so that while even among habitual Church communicants there are many degrees of withinness; conversely it may be that among the outermost circles, nay, or even altogether on the outside, we know not what possibilities the Spirit of God may discern; and such possibilities so discerned, are in fact spiritual realities,

There is another point upon which it may be well to say a few words of a somewhat similar kind. We do not admit that the episcopal constitution of the Church is a mere instance of an evolved result. We are not content to plead that there were circumstances in the apostolic age which not unnaturally tended towards episcopacy; and that therefore episcopacy may be recognized retrospectively as a not illegitimate development of apostolic circumstances. This, if it be true, is at all events an understatement of our case. Such a form of principle might perhaps not unfairly be invoked on behalf of the organization of the Church into provinces, and the whole system of archbishops, metropolitans, primates, and patriarchs; or even (how far fairly or not I do not here inquire) on behalf of a papacy in some sort or sense. But episcopacy is not, in any parallel sense, a gradual development of organization. Its connexion, in principle, with apostolate is too vital in character; its existence is at once too early and too widespread, not only as a form of Christian ministry, but as the symbol of Church unity and authority, and therefore as a foundation essential for the legitimacy, and for the due transmission, of all other ministries and sacraments in the Church, to be explained as a mere example of not illegitimate evolution.

On the other hand, that there is an element of growth about it few would deny. We do not of course contend that a threefold order of 'Bishops, Priests, and Deacons' was present to the consciousness of the apostolic Church in the early days in

Jerusalem; or was itself, like the pattern of the tabernacle in the wilderness, revealed to the apostles during the great forty days. It is only by the action of the apostles in the Pentecostal Church that we can at all discern 'the things concerning the kingdom of God' which they then heard; and the nature of their action in the matter of Church ministries is enough to preclude the idea of any antecedently revealed pattern of either episcopacy or presbyterate. Thus far, at least, I suppose that we should all of us echo the statement that 'Church order' is 'not a scheme delivered by the Lord to the apostles, and by the apostles to the Church [1].' But what we contend is not that it was 'a scheme,' but that it was 'a principle' delivered by the Lord to the apostles and by the apostles to the Church; a principle of which 'commission' was the essence; and of which apostolic transmission had become, not by some late or disputable conciliar development, but as the immediate outcome of the first half-century of Christian experience, and therefore of the apostolic work as a whole, the one orderly mode and guarantee. It is not contended that either apostolic transmission, or anything which can fairly be regarded as episcopacy, were thus recognized as universal or necessary conceptions in the first exuberant flush of the Church's Pentecostal experience. It is not denied that the channels which existed from the first, and were to be more

---

[1] The words are quoted from the concluding sentence of the defence of Dr. Hort's *Ecclesia*, published by Professor Armitage Robinson in the *Guardan* of March 9, 1898, p. 371.

and more explicitly recognized as the channels divinely appointed for indispensable order, were at first too freely and too richly overflowed to be formally distinguishable as channels. They were overflowed, naturally enough, under the conditions of a period which, while it was marked on the one hand by an effervescence of spiritual enthusiasm—attested for the time by miraculous manifestations, yet in its very nature and necessity transient—was on the other hand necessarily as yet incapable of understanding either the indispensable necessity, or the indispensable conditions, of a system of order guaranteed and continuous, throughout the life of a great historical community.

If we maintain that the Churches depended really from the first upon apostolic commission, and that the outcome of the apostolic age was a definite conception as to the principle of transmission of apostolic authority, as illustrated in one aspect by Clement of Rome and in another by Ignatius of Antioch, we certainly shall not doubt that it had been only by degrees, in the natural process of a living experience, that this principle became formal and explicit in the Christian consciousness, and therefore rigid in its expression as outward method or rule. If, for example, it was by St. Paul, and in dependence on St. Paul's apostolic authority, that presbyters were constituted in the churches of Asia Minor, we do not therefore suggest that during the many consecutive years of St. Paul's imprisonment in Caesarea and in Rome there never was, because there never could have been, under whatever necessity, any fresh accession either to the ranks of the presbyters or to the number of 'confirmed' and communicant Christians. This is just the wrong sort of emphasis to lay upon what was doubtless establishing itself as principle before it was yet crystallized as rule. We may indeed fairly say that presbyterate was derived from the apostles; that the recorded history, from the very first, shows us this principle in (as it were) instinctive operation; and that the apostolic age as a whole left it translated into the form of definite outward necessary usages which at once directly expressed and directly protected it. But we can hardly doubt that there was a period, while apostles were remote and the direct action of the Spirit was on all sides miraculously manifest, when consciousness as to limitations of outward method was not yet definite, and questions about the distinction of mediate or immediate exercise of apostolic government were neither asked nor answered. We do not deprecate a recognition of historical gradualness so obviously probable and lifelike as this. What we do deprecate is the inference which is apt to be drawn, that the explicit consciousness of such outward principles and rules of method (which we claim as the direct outcome of apostolic work, and as having, with whatever fringe of indefiniteness, underlain the recorded and instinctive action of apostles from the first) was still—when it *did* become explicit as necessary rule—mistaken, or not necessary, or not expressly apostolic and divine.

Our point, then, is not that there was no element of natural development about the grades or forms of ministry, but that the threefold order was the form which a certain divine and essential principle had already taken from the earliest moment at which it could be recognized as having any definite form at all; and that the principle once for all identified with this form of expression within the consciousness of the apostolic age, and incorporated into the fabric of the Church's being as its central guarantee alike of coherent unity and of spiritual life, is no longer practically separable from the Church's history, on the ground of any later exegetical theory that the history of the Church could as legitimately have been otherwise shaped. It is within the life and under the special care of the last surviving apostle; it is therefore from the time, and as the outcome, of the translation of the divine principle of ministry into living action through the working of the Spirit in the apostolic age as a whole, that episcopacy stands forth, not as a novel, still less as a merely accidental growth, but as original, fundamental, and essential to the unity, continuity, and spiritual security of the Church.

Does any one demur to so close a juxtaposition, in thought, of a definite outward with a spiritual infinite? So far from being a forced or unnatural paradox, this is the familiar condition of that concrete expression of spiritual things which, in this world, is necessary for their realization as spiritual. On every side we are met by definiteness, sharp, concrete, and material, which is none the less rightly definite in outline for us, because it eludes the effort of our thought to press it at all points fully home, but fringes off—sometimes quickly—into that infinite out of which it came and which it only existed to signify. Distinctness, fringing off into mystery, this is the very characteristic of things spiritual on earth. But because of the mystery which fringes it, to deny the distinctness — often the very sharp and peremptory outwardness—is not really so much to vindicate what is spiritual as to make it all unreal. There is all the difference in the world between a recognition that the definiteness, even of things most sharply definite, shades off by-and-by with blurred edges into indefiniteness; and a refusal, to whatever is ultimately (in that sense) indefinite, of any right or claim to be definite or peremptory anywhere.

I should like to refer, for the illustration of this thought, to a very memorable sermon preached by the Bishop of Rochester before the Church Congress of 1896, from which I have ventured to transcribe a few sentences.

'Our witness is primarily spiritual—we speak that we do know: . . . we testify to His work when on earth; to His work ascended, by the Spirit; to the facts of His grace; to the actual and living Church of His building; to the ascertained direction of His will. But it can only be imperfectly, tentatively, with certainty shading off fast into uncertainty and conjecture, that we give precise account of the how and why, the explanations and the limits' . . . 'even of the things that are known and seen.'

We may venture, perhaps, to borrow and apply to this thought of the Church and its ministry another sentence, and to say that their truth is 'a truth of spiritual fact, with all which that means of largeness, of elasticity, of undefinableness, by even necessary, and, much more, unnecessary, terms of human language and human logic.' Such a fact is bound to require, on our parts, a combination of obedience that is concretely practical with thought that is very speculatively patient; a tolerance of the gaps or difficulties which result to logic when the infinite is really represented by the finite. So the bishop broadly claims as a part of the duty of Christian thought 'not to know, as well as to know, to see truth shading off into the unknown, and not to be able exactly to draw a dividing line; to be exercised in the endurance of much ignorance and difficulty — without petulantly flying to the cheap solution that there is no definite truth to be known; to be thrown back upon ourselves, to ponder and consider and pray over the bearings which known truth may have beyond its plain contents.'

But because we cordially echo words such as these, are we therefore to give up all the language about the reality of an outward order expressive of the inward reality or the duty, as practical and binding, of corporate membership; or the legitimate rightness of one outward order rather than another; or the true correspondence between the outward and the inward; so that identity with the inward —identity, indeed, not consummated or absolute, yet ideal and essential—is the only real or adequate mode of statement of the proper value and significance of the outward order? Not at all. The clearest recognition that God's working is not simply conterminous with His appointed means does not make obedience to His appointed means less imperative; nor make the identity of His appointed means with that work which He works in them less real or less absolute to those who have faculties to understand His commands and His working. The identity is not less real to those who have faculties to apprehend it, because it does not work, as mere mechanism works, in blind indifference to a meaning and a power which act through it, indeed, and are imprinted upon it, and yet are not to be found within itself.

No sane Christian, be his definition of the Church what it may, dreams for a moment that every outward churchman will be saved, and no one who is not an outward Churchman. *Extra Ecclesiam nulla salus* has lost none of its meaning to an intelligent churchman; but it does not mean to him anything like this. He does not believe himself to be personally better than those whose Church privilege he knows to be far inferior to his own. He is sure indeed that, in outward practice and order, he is right and they—so far —are wrong. But those who are—so far—wrong in practice and inferior in privilege, may nevertheless be better in fact than himself and far fuller of the Spirit of Christ. If so, they will be found to be ultimately and essentially within the Church, which is the Body of Christ. The churchman who is spiritual at all has no question of this. Only when he is asked (as he is in fact asked every day) to draw as conclusion from this, the principle that no outward order has intrinsic correctness or proper value of its own, he refuses utterly. That is just the wrong conclusion. There is a right in these matters, and these good people, though so much better personally than we are, are nevertheless explicitly wrong *in this*. The outward does not, here and now, at all perfectly correspond with the inward. Of course it does not. But the inward has a proper outward, and the true meaning, and character, and significance, of its proper outward form, is to be (though absolutely now it is not so) not only representative of, but identical with, that inward meaning which it only exists to signify.

Perhaps many of those who instinctively would criticise most what has been said of the Church, would nevertheless themselves feel something very like it in relation to baptism. That is to say, they would feel on the one hand that there may be those not literally baptized, who yet, under various circumstances easily imaginable, might be as if they were baptized in God's sight; and on the other hand they would not for a moment admit, as the right conclusion from this, in practice or theory, that baptism was therefore immaterial. Rather their conclusion would be that baptism, though imperative and essential, and in all possible respects to be received and regarded as such, yet does not absolutely correspond, even while it is the one real and only correspondence in outward life, with that which it, and it only, exists to mean. There will be some, perhaps many, unbaptized who will be as regenerate; and some, perhaps many, baptized who will be as unregenerate; yet none the less, baptism is the true, and imperative, and only expression in this world of regenerateness. We admit no corollary which depreciates outward baptism, or, in cases that are normal and right, its proper identity with that with which we still say that it is properly identified; only we recognize, as of course, that the identity of outward with inward, even whilst it is the whole meaning and reality of the outward, is yet of necessity, in this world, preliminary, experimental, unconsummated.

Finally, I should admit that it may, to some minds, seem almost like a verbal question, whether when we estimate the relation between outward and inward, or between Church and kingdom, we should rather affirm their identity, while admitting the extent to which they are not identical; or deny their identity, while admitting that they ought to be, and will be, more and more identified. For my own part I can feel little doubt that the former mode of conception and of language is the more profoundly true, both to Scripture and to spiritual life.

I hope that in this last paragraph I may have come very visibly near to some of those who have criticized me. May I take occasion from it also to say how very near I am conscious of being, for almost all practical purposes, to those whom I have myself ventured to criticise? If I cannot but submit that the direction in which Bishop Lightfoot or Dr. Hort shape their rationale of the ultimate principle of Church unity and authority is the wrong, rather than the right, direction, it is, after all, to the region of ultimate principle that the criticism belongs. Perhaps I may say this freely as one who cannot reasonably be suspected of undervaluing the importance of ultimate principles. In the long run, indeed, they dominate absolutely the whole form and proportion of thought. But none the less, for almost all immediate practical purposes, whether in the parish and diocese, or in the study, it would have been nothing but an honour and a privilege to have been allowed to work in subordination to either of those great men; nor do I imagine that I should readily have yielded to any one in loyal admiration—had I ever been placed under them—for the Christian nobility of spirit which at all times animated their actual work, and government, in the Church.

PREFACE TO FIRST EDITION

Perhaps it may be convenient to say, first, that the following pages, though not serving as lectures in their present form, have largely grown out of lectures delivered in the Chapter House of Christ Church; and secondly that, as they here stand, they by no means correspond with their original design. They had been meant to form part of a much larger whole. The principal object of the whole would have been a study of the Anglican Ordinal, in the light of the Ordinal forms of the earlier Church. Various circumstances, however, have induced me to offer these pages by themselves, as a sort of introduction to such a study.

The first six of the following chapters were intended as an introduction to the whole. The inquiry into the meaning of 'priesthood' would have come at a much later point. It was meant to follow *after* some sketch of the steps of the gradual growth of the fully developed forms of the Sarum Ordinal, and to have formed one portion or aspect (no doubt the most crucial one) in a consideration of the meaning of the transition from the unreformed to the reformed Ordinal of the English Church.

The particular application to recent controversy of the principles reached in this inquiry about priesthood was, under the circumstances of the moment, inevitable. Being however less constructive, and more incidental and controversial in character, than the other chapters had been intended to be, it is added as an appendix rather than as a substantive part of the whole.

Perhaps, under all the circumstances, it is right for me to say in explicit language that I am perfectly conscious of having no claim, through any special learning, to write upon the subject. But valuable beyond words as the special learning of the expert is, I must still believe that in discussions of this kind there is ample room for those who may only hope to deal in an intelligent way with comparatively ordinary data of knowledge, as well as for those who can advance the data of knowledge by exceptional learning of their own. At all events, it is in the former of these two characters, and in the strength of this belief as to its place and value, that I have ventured to speak at all.

I am conscious, however, that this very disclaimer, necessary as it may be in itself, makes it the more incumbent on me to say a few words in explanation of the extent to which I have ventured to criticize others, in some cases even those whose learning is monumental; most of all the late Bishop of Durham, Bishop Lightfoot. Believing, however, as I do that his famous utterance upon the Christian ministry has been upon the whole very misleading, it was impossible for me not to attempt to deal with it directly. Upon the face of it I believe that I am entitled to claim that the essay must be confessed to be ambiguous. For it is quite obvious that inferences, which the Bishop himself repudiated were on all sides largely drawn from it, alike by those who welcomed and those who criticized it, and it is at all events not equally obvious that the inferences were not, as inferences, legitimately drawn. It can hardly be denied then that the essay failed to express perfectly what the Bishop himself had in mind. But if so, I am entitled to press the question, why? Bishop Lightfoot did not lack the power of lucid exposition. Why did his essay seem to say what he did not mean? The very fact of the ambiguity requires some explanation. Where does the explanation lie?

In the answer to this question I believe will be found the true key to the criticism of the essay itself. The fault is not, of course, in Bishop Lightfoot's learning. If it were, there would be need of a critic singularly unlike the present writer to say so. But the fault lies rather in a sphere which was less distinctively the sphere of Bishop Lightfoot's unrivalled eminence. It lies in the mental presuppositions, the unchallenged assumptions, the hypotheses or postulates with which he approaches the examination of the evidence. There are flaws in these which will, I believe, account both for the superficial ambiguity (which is obvious), and also for what I, at least, must endeavour to represent as the really unsatisfactory character of his argument upon the evidence.

I should like to formulate some half-dozen propositions, several of them of an abstract character, which seem to belong to what I may call the unconscious substructure of the Bishop's essay. Thus:

Ends are greater than means, and means exist for ends; therefore whatever belongs to the category of means can in no case be rightly regarded as essential. Again: The outward represents the inward, and the inward which is represented is far higher than the outward, which represents it; therefore while the inward is essentially necessary for the reality of the outward, the outward is only conventionally necessary for the reality of the inward. Again: The literal and real meaning of the word sacrifice and priesthood is that which they bore in the Old Testament; by this all other applications of the words must be measured and judged. Again: If ministry is representative of the Body as a whole, then the Body as a whole, and every member thereof, must implicitly possess the right to minister. Again: A corporate or universal priesthood and a divinely and exclusively specialized priesthood are mutually incompatible ideas. Again: It will follow as a corollary that if there is for convenience a separated ministry, it cannot be matter of any crucial moment whether the ministerial authority of new ministers grows by a sort of evolution out of the life of the general Church Body, or is devolved ministerially through the action only of those who themselves have been similarly accredited as ministers before. Again: The Church is, in the first instance, a plurality of individual units, and by aggregation of these it becomes, in the second instance, subordinately, and as it were accidentally, an articulated unity.

I do not say that other propositions similar to these might not also be formulated, but these are what occur to my own mind. Nor of course do I mean that these assumptions are in any way peculiar to Bishop Lightfoot. On the contrary, it is the more important to notice them, just because they are the characteristic assumptions of many minds, both of theological writers and of the general public. Meanwhile, if it would be perhaps too much to say in sweeping fashion that every one of these propositions is absolutely false, at least it may safely be said that even the best and truest among them would require much careful interpretation and guarding before it could be safely accepted as true. And most of them on examination would have to be rejected altogether.

Of course I do not suggest that principles such as these are to be found asserted as principles, *totidem verbis*, in Bishop Lightfoot's essay on the Ministry. Had they been explicitly asserted they would have been less dangerous. Moreover, in order to be explicitly asserted they would have had to be consciously recognized, and so recognized they would have been cross-examined by the Bishop, and under cross-examination they could not but have been seriously modified. But I do believe that, though without explicit recognition, every one of these principles is—if unconsciously, only so much the more absolutely—taken for granted throughout the essay, as a secure assumption beyond reach of question or argument, as a fundamental hypothesis, as an axiomatic postulate.

At this moment I am not concerned to scrutinize them further. To a considerable extent at least they will be found to be scrutinized in the following pages. But I should like to suggest that there could hardly be an instance which would justify with more striking completeness the singular wisdom of the method of Hooker's argument in the *Ecclesiastical Polity*, when he devotes no less than four entire books, before reaching the apparent subjects of dispute, to the preliminary task of scrutinizing the underlying assumptions or mental postulates with which his antagonists approached the handling of the evidence that was before them; and, on the other hand, of slowly building up and explaining and justifying the counter-postulates which he, on his side, desired and claimed the right to use.

To me it seems always a congenial task, and I believe that it is very generally a necessary one, to dwell upon the supreme importance, for the insight of real understanding, of the underlying postulates or principles which ordinarily precede conscious argument. Principles of this kind are indeed indispensable. But though they cannot be dispensed with, it is most desirable that they should be examined—most desirable that they should be criticized. Such criticism, it is to be hoped, will often, not unimportantly, modify them. But the evidence cannot be approached without them. Examination of evidence, without postulates, would be profitless,—if it were possible. It is mere delusion to suppose that, in the absence of constitutive first principles, a study of details will lead to exceptionally unbiassed, or indeed even to intelligent conclusions at all. The cogency of evidence—nay, its whole value, and even meaning—depends absolutely on the mental convictions with which we approach it.

Thus, to take a leading example : If I am really convinced, in heart and conscience, that 'miracles never happened,' I shall of course so view the evidence, not legitimately only but inevitably, as to reconstruct it, if need be from beginning to end, upon the principles of the modern humanitarian theology. But if I am really convinced, in heart and conscience, that Jesus Christ is the incarnation and manifestation of the eternal God, then what we call 'miracles' will be to me little less than an inherent necessity of thought, a consequence, necessary and natural, of that central reality of 'nature' which a real absence of 'supernatural' powers would almost if not quite belie.

It is idle to pretend to approach the evidence in detail with *neither* conviction, or to build up conviction on such a point only out of the evidence in detail. The central convictions themselves, which are part, as it were, of the very structure of the personal consciousness, will be the result of the widest possible range of experience, and intelligent reflection, and habitual character; and the meaning of the particular evidence will depend almost wholly upon its relation to the central personal convictions. The very same events will be to one personality a positive experience of God's love, and to another a proof that there is neither love nor God. If I endeavour so to confine the range of my life's consciousness as to deduce a ruling principle on the highest questions from the particular evidence taken alone, the result will be, not that I shall succeed in doing so,—that is impossible; but that my ruling principle will be a sort of paradox reached by way of accident, instead of being itself the true outcome of reasonable thought. But if, as I must submit, everything in a matter of this kind — even the meaning of the evidence—depends upon the mental presuppositions with which the evidence is approached, it is necessary to plead for a more explicit recognition of this most important principle of truth.

Unhappily we are not quite unaccustomed even to that extreme *reductio ad absurdum* of the principle of (so-called) 'impartiality,' which would refrain from inculcating upon children the fundamental truths of God and man—in order that they may find them out 'impartially' for themselves! There is only one hypothesis which would save such a course from fatuity; and that is the hypothesis that the truths of the Creed are themselves unimportant conjectures upon subjects neither known at all nor at all necessary to be known. And this no doubt is what the advocates of such a course do in fact, either explicitly or unconsciously, hold. But suppose for a single moment that the truths of the Christian Creed are what they claim to be; and it would be *at least* as reasonable to leave children to shape out their own unguided experience as to principles about 'picking and stealing, evil-speaking, lying and slandering, temperance, soberness and chastity,' as about sin, and atonement, and love, the revelation of the fatherhood of God in the incarnate life of Jesus Christ, or the transfiguring of personality by the presence and the power of the Holy Ghost.

But to put out of sight what is mere extravagance of paradox, there are instances of a somewhat similar principle far more moderate in kind, which perhaps will come nearer home. No doubt immense service has been done in this generation by the detailed work of exegetical scholars; and especially by work in which, and for which, those scholars laid aside, as far as possible, for a time and for a purpose, the directive influence of their own theological preconceptions. But it is only up to a certain point that this is either possible or desirable; and it may be doubted whether prevailing fashions of thought do not exaggerate the scope and power of work which is conducted upon this basis. Such work is corrective, not creative; it cross-examines most valuably, but it cannot really construct. If it puts its presuppositions out of sight in order to make inquiries which shall test and correct them, it may be said to assume the presuppositions themselves, as well as the cross-examining purpose, as the very motive for putting them momentarily out of sight; and undoubtedly, as it puts them aside only in order to test them, so having tested (perhaps corrected) them in various particulars, it must fall back upon them again. It is the presuppositions themselves (as corrected, no doubt, or even perhaps remodelled, by particular criticism, but it is certainly not particular criticism, as taken apart from presuppositions) which can be called really illuminative. It is the old ideas, commonplaces of the thought and faith of the Church, to which insight belongs. Their expression may be modified by criticism. But criticism can neither supplant nor dispense with them.

I am pleading that the interpretation of the

text of the New Testament should be throughout theological as well as exegetical; or rather that theological beliefs should be recognized as legitimately present in, and for, the exegetical processes. Of course it is true that the theological beliefs themselves have their basis also in the text of the New Testament. But just as every action done by Christ, or every word spoken by His lips, requires for its perfect apprehension the realization of the Person whose word or act it was; so the theological truths which we have gathered (so far at least as we have rightly gathered them) from meditation (say) upon the Gospel of St. John,—ought really to be present as a necessary, and determining, quality of the thought with which we apprehend the real significance of historical details in the Acts or the Epistles. If, for a purpose, the words of Christ are often taken as if they were 'the words of any other man,' it will at least be recognized that something of their fullness is left aside so long as that hypothesis is maintained. It is a method legitimate, for a purpose, as method; but it is not the condition upon which the completest apprehension is possible.

Now I cannot help suggesting that it is a somewhat characteristic temptation of careful textual interpreters to try to work what are called the historical or exegetical methods, as if it were possible that they should yield their best results apart from the light of the truths of dogmatic theology. Something perhaps of this tendency we recognize even where we might little have expected it. It would be hard to find a scholar of graver or more solid judgement than Dr. Hort. Often there is upon his words the touch of a living and illuminating enthusiasm. Yet even Dr. Hort appears sometimes so to interpret the history as if the narrative detail of historical passages could yield their fullest meaning apart from the doctrinal verities which underlie, and find partial expression in, historical detail: as if, that is, the true exegesis of Church history could be non-theological. This comes most clearly into view when he draws negative conclusions from his text, and offers, by them, to correct traditional belief. If, for example, by this method, he claims to show that the Apostles received from our Lord no authority to govern in the Church; that there were no 'ecclesiae' as a result of St. Paul's first missionary journey in Europe; that a διάκονος had nothing to do with teaching; or that the connexion between 'laying on of hands' and 'ordination to ministry' was rather accidental than important; is he not, so far, misunderstanding the scope of his own method, and carrying it into exactly the kind of conclusions which it is inherently unable to bear? The full evidence for or against such principles as these can never be found in a textual exegesis from which theology, as such, is excluded by hypothesis.

It may be said, perhaps, that I am pleading for what would be both retrograde and perilous; that I am asking to go back from a scientific to an *a priori* method of interpreting history. It is true that I am asking to go back from an exaggeration of the so-called scientific method, to so much as was true in the method described, or misdescribed as *a priori*. That this (like every conceivable method) is liable to abuse, I have no doubt whatever. I should admit also that the abuse of it is the besetting sin of whatever is artificial or narrow in ecclesiastical professionalism; and therefore that it is in this direction that the temper which is before all things orthodox and dutiful is most characteristically liable, when not perfectly balanced, to be betrayed into mistake. Nevertheless, I must still plead that the reading of history in which great vital facts, like the Incarnate Life, or the nature and meaning of the Church of Christ, are contained, does and must always so essentially depend upon the fundamental convictions of the reader, that for the adequate interpretation of the written history correct mental presuppositions and principles are as indispensable as is a scholarly fidelity to the letter of the text. Spiritual narrative, as well as spiritual philosophy, is for the seeing eye and for the hearing ear; which means that something else is needed for discernment of their truth than the merely intellectual impartiality of the secular scholar or historian. I do not really need to plead for reading in the light of mental presupposition; for I am convinced that it is impossible to read otherwise: but inasmuch as the whole effect of the reading will depend upon the quality of the presuppositions, whether they be true or whether they be false, I do plead that, instead of being covered up and ignored, or denied, these should themselves be most carefully measured and informed. To read with wholly erroneous presuppositions is (unless they be abandoned) necessarily to end in a perverse conclusion; whilst so to ignore the place of the presuppositions as to affect to read with none at all—even if all perversity be avoided—is almost to ensure an element, at least, of accident or of paradox in the result.

To return, however, to the contents of the following pages. I should like to say that the question of the relation in general between 'inward' and 'outward,' in this world of body and soul, which I have tried explicitly to raise in the second chapter, appears to me to be the fundamental question of the book. I may have been quite unsuccessful in the attempt to throw any useful light upon this relation; but if so, I would only say the more emphatically, that inasmuch as it is this which certainly, if not obviously, lies at the root of an immense amount of apparent discrepancy of thought upon all sacramental or quasi-sacramental subjects, it is exactly this which in a very special and urgent sense stands in need of true and wise treatment. Perhaps there could hardly be a greater boon than a treatment of this subject which should be philosophically and theologically adequate.

The first part of this volume deals with what appears to be an excessive depreciation of the outward, upon the Protestant side. The later part deals rather with the counter-tendency, with which Romanism has more and more identified itself, to overstate the outward. The one seems to me so to subordinate, as really to sacrifice, the outward to the inward. The other more and more merges inward in outward. But if outward can have no reality save as outward of an inward, it is no less true that inward can have no expression, and therefore in this world at least cannot realise itself after all, save in and through outward. The truth is, in this respect, delicately balanced: and neither the one nor the other strikes the balance of truth.

What I have been led to say upon the subject was primarily the outcome of an attempt to criticize such imperfect conceptions as are to be found perhaps at their best in Bishop Lightfoot's essay. But I could not but feel that the principles which had been gradually emerging out of this attempt to criticize an exaggeration upon the side of protestantism, were themselves the very principles upon which to determine the controversies which have more lately developed themselves upon the opposite side. The clue was ready at hand by which to discern between what was true and what was merely formal or distorted in theories as to the reality of Christian priesthood. And certainly anything like insight into the reality of Christian priesthood seemed to carry with itself the real refutation of all Roman attempts to invalidate the priesthood of the Anglican Church. Such attempts have been kaleidoscopic and shifting enough. But below all such surface variations, the true issue, I am convinced, will ultimately turn upon no superficial logic or technical details, but upon the profounder discernment of the answer to the question, 'What does Christian priesthood really mean?'

The main thought of the second (which is the most cardinal) portion of the essay on Priesthood (ch. vii) is of course not new. Striking expression was given to it, some years ago, by the Rev. J. R.

Illingworth. It is worked upon in considerable detail by Dr Milligan. But neither of these writers was using it exactly as the key to the true interpretation of Priesthood. Indeed, it is rather, perhaps, a matter of surprise that there have not been more endeavours than there have to expound the doctrine of priesthood, as a whole, upon what may be called the distinctively Anglican hypothesis, which is also, I believe, the inclusive and balanced truth. Meanwhile, if the exposition of this seventh chapter should commend itself, on its own grounds, to any of those who may read it, I should certainly venture to suggest that (as the Appendix has endeavoured to show) this is also the true standpoint from which to view the various controversies that have been raised both about Anglican priesthood, and about the true basis and standing of Anglicanism.

There is only this further to add: that it is certainly not in any blindness as to their immense inadequacy, in manifold directions, that I have nevertheless convinced myself that I do right, under existing circumstances, in commending these pages to the judgement of the Church; not certainly without abundant cause for misgiving, yet in hope that (with whatever qualifications or corrections) the real effort of their thought will be found to be 'according to the proportion of the faith,'—'the faith which was once for all delivered unto the saints,'—'the faith which is in Christ Jesus[1].'

CHRIST CHURCH,
Feast of St Michael and All Angels 1897.

---

[1] Rom. xii. 6, Jude 3; 1 Tim. iii. 13.

CONTENTS

CHAPTER I.

THE NATURE OF CHURCH UNITY.

    PAGE

Conceptions of Church ministry are found to be dependent upon conceptions of Church Unity 1

Is the 'unity' of the Creed a gradual result of secular uniting, or a dominant and necessary principle of religion? . . . 2

Different ideas or forms of unity—unity of accidental circumstances—unity developing into a practical ideal—unity as a philosophical conception—unity as a theological verity These are not really antithetical, but combined in the Church. and no one of them is untrue except so far as it is used to deny the truth of the others 3

Dr. Hatch's Bampton Lectures Their apparent effort so to press the lower as to discredit the higher conceptions of unity Arguments from Hebrews x. 25, Jude 18, Hermas, Barnabas, and Ignatius 10

What is the real outcome of the passages? . . . 19

Note upon 'The Christian Ecclesia' by the Rev. Dr. Hort, late Margaret Professor in the University of Cambridge . . 22

CHAPTER II.

THE RELATION BETWEEN INWARD AND OUTWARD.

Is, then, the unity only 'spiritual'? Relation between spirit and body. The apostolic Church corporate and organized—witness of excommunication—St. Paul's struggle for corporate unity 30

It is in proportion to failure that the inner idea and its outward expression are discordant or antithetical. The Church

militant and the Kingdom triumphant are the same Church The saint in imperfection, or in beatitude, is one personality. Spirit does not supersede body; but body is the method of spirit; and spirit is the meaning of body 36
    The place of the bodily and outward misconceived by Bishop Lightfoot—and the character of Church unity. The mistaken antithesis of Montanism. Ignatius and Tertullian. Dr. Hatch and Montanism. The same misconception lies at the root of 'Quakerism,' and is part of the instinct of modern Puritanism . 43
    Ends and means—'inherent' value of means. Distinction between 'essential' and 'of the essence.' Divine use and moral indispensableness of *media*. 56

CHAPTER III.

THE RELATION BETWEEN MINISTRY AND LAITY

If 'means,' as the methods of God's condescension, are 'essential,' in what sense is ministry an indispensable means? Is it a real intermediary between God and His people? . . 64
    The Church is a 'body': the body means not some, but all: but the body performs specific actions through specific organs. The Bampton Lectures for 1868—Canon Gore—Dr. Milligan. Fallacy of the inference that if the empowered organ represents all, all must have the power to represent . 65
    The distinction, nevertheless, wholly missed by Dr. Hatch —his meaning otherwise a noble one—and by Bishop Lightfoot. Their use of Tertullian. Tertullian's misconception a necessary result of his Montanism. Origen—Clement of Alexandria. Bishop Lightfoot's use of them illegitimate. Their real position that of every rational 'high Churchman.' Irenaeus and Justin Martyr 73
    Church people in general have a real relation to ordination: but ministers, if *representatives*, are not *delegates*. Fallacy of the word 89
    On the other hand, ministerial distinction, whatever else it may be, does not of itself alter personal character, or essential conditions of right and wrong. There is a real priestly character and obligation which is shared by all. The development of 'vicarious' ideas of priestly capacity and separateness —due more to spiritual indolence of laity than to spiritual ambition of ministry. Canon Gore and Dr. Liddon on the universal priesthood. Spiritual dignity of a 'layman' . . 91

CHAPTER IV.

THE BASIS OF MINISTRY—DIVINE COMMISSION.

Authority to minister in spiritual things must rest upon reality of commission—not from men but from God. The only practical question is, How is this divine commission conferred? . . . 100

I. Is it through merely individual inspiration? practically, rather than abstractly, incredible antecedent improbabilities the case of Old Testament prophecy: the case of St. Paul · the *Didache* Would the method be credible now, even if it had been true then? 105

II. Is it through Church appointment by any—or no—outward ministry? Involves denial of the whole ministerial and sacramental principle but ultimately must be determined by Church history. Cannot rationally emerge as a new principle in the later centuries 110

III. The principle of apostolic succession, as principle—the 23rd Article in exact accord with it. Enormous strength of the witness of Clement of Rome. Importance of the issue . . 113

The real issue never recognized by Bishop Lightfoot. Contradictory indications of his meaning. Is ministerial authority evolved or devolved? The question turns historically upon the origin of the episcopate 117

Apostolic succession a question, in each generation, of the *present* rather than of the *past* It is distinguishable in abstract principle from episcopacy, but not in practice, *if episcopacy be right*. 123

CHAPTER V.

GRADATIONS OF MINISTRY IN THE NEW TESTAMENT.

I. Apostolate. Dependent on personal mission from Jesus Christ. The case of St. Paul. Its awful authority—neither based upon, nor merged in, the mutual love of the apostle and his flock. Apostolate the basis and background of everything in the Church 126

II. Diaconate. Its secular work—its spiritual character. The secular aspect apt to be exaggerated 136

III. Presbyterate. No notice of its institution The names 'bishop' and 'presbyter' interchangeable. Ruling—teaching —indications of deeper mysteries—solemn pastoral care. A *local* leadership, but always assuming the background of apostolate 140

IV Apostolic men or delegates. The case of St. James—in the first instance personal and unique. He 'personifies' the

CONTENTS

Church of Jerusalem   The case of Timotheus and Titus; ruling, teaching, control over services and teachers; jurisdiction over the whole Church, including presbyters or bishops. The connexion between authority and ordination in the case of Timotheus 146

V. Prophets. Who are they?—Acts xiii. 1 seqq.; 1 Cor. xii.-xiv. three inferences from the picture in 1 Cor. xiv.: Ephes iv. Prophecy a divine endowment rather than a ministerial office; but a natural (perhaps necessary) qualification for the higher possibilities of ministry 158
Recapitulation of results 167

CHAPTER VI.

GRADATIONS OF MINISTRY IN SUB-APOSTOLIC TIMES.

I. The *Didache*—its Jewish character and questionable authority—its picture of Church ministry   Conception of the 'apostolic background'; its likeness—and unlikeness—to the New Testament. Limited insight of the writers . . . 170

II. Clement of Rome   Authority and character of his letter   What has become of the 'prophets'? In relation to ministry, at all events, they have no place at all   Has the apostolic background disappeared?   Clement's own position really episcopal   Indications in the letter that 'presbyters' (in the ordinary sense) are not ultimately supreme . . 179

III. Ignatian letters—their witness to unity   This unity sacramental, ministerial unity, represented by the bishop, the symbol and seal of it   Vagueness of Ignatian witness to episcopacy in any aspect but this one. Episcopal references in the letter to Rome . . 190

IV. The letter of Polycarp   Its silence about episcopate   Its episcopal character 200

V. Hermas. Unity of the Church. Ministerial distinctions. 'Bishops' quite discernible; yet perhaps verbally included within the title 'presbyters.' The prophets in Hermas. Hermas' own position as prophet—his date; if *temp.* Pius, episcopacy is assumed; if *temp.* Clement, his indications important as supplementing Clement's letter 206

Summary   Was the episcopal background of the second century newly evolved, or lineally descended from the 'apostolic background'?   The former view irreconcilable with Clement's doctrine of apostolic succession, as well as with Ignatius. Both Polycarp and Hermas really on the same side . . . 215

CHAPTER VII.

WHAT IS PRIESTHOOD IN THE CHURCH OF CHRIST?

I.

The counter-exaggerations of the sixteenth century, Roman and Puritan, reach their climax on this subject . . . **220**

The unreformed conception. Its popular exaggeration part of what the Reformers had to deal with The Sarum Pontifical—its ancient prayers. Proportion of their teaching altered by development of ceremonial actions—development all in one direction—disproportioned results The Council of Trent—its caution—yet failure to restore proportion . . **223**

The Anglican Reformation—retention of the priestly title. Significance of this. Bishop Lightfoot's mistaken relation to the terms *sacerdotium* and *sacrificium* **234**

II.

These words only properly intelligible in the Person of Jesus Christ. Not Calvary alone, but the eternal presentation of Himself in heaven (as 'the living One' who 'was dead') is the consummation of His sacrifice Analogy of the Levitical law **243**

I. What is sacrifice in Him? Not inherently suffering, but rather that which becomes suffering under human circumstances. It is Divine Love, within conditions of sin Its outward necessity crucifixion ; its inward, and atoning, reality, infinite love. The outward is not separable from the inward, it is merely the inward in utterance **246**

II. What Christ is, the Church must be. She is priestly by outward enactment, in the Eucharist, which is her ceremonial identification with the Atoning Sacrifice . inwardly, through the correlative reality, in her, of the spirit of sacrifice, the self-expenditure of Divine Love **251**

III. The priesthood of the ministry is the priesthood of the Church specialized and personified in certain representative instruments—outwardly as authorized enacters and leaders of Eucharistic worship—inwardly as set to embody personally the spirit of priestly sacrifice, which is love . . . **257**

The outward fails in reality after all, except so far as it is the outward of the inward. No account of priesthood can be adequate which rests in terms of ceremonial enactment only . **260**

III.

These two aspects of Christian ministry have never rightly been separated. Why the 'sacrificial' language is not more explicit in the New Testament. All the conceptions essential to it shown to be there They are involved in the doctrine of the Atonement. Acts xx. St. Paul. The Epistle to the Hebrews 263

Corroboration of this view of Scripture from the *Didache*, Clement of Rome, Ignatius, Justin Martyr, and others. Bishop Lightfoot misled by false antitheses 272

IV.

The Anglican position Restoration of true proportion of outward and inward. Priestly executive privilege, and pastoral self-devotion, two aspects of one reality. Acts xx. and the Ordinal. No perfection claimed for the Anglican Ordinal; but it is a real recovery of the scriptural—and the true—relation 283

Reply to two objections :—1. 'That pastoral devotion, however necessary, is a wholly distinct thing from priesthood.' It is not so verbally, if the priesthood is the title of the *whole* office; it is not so essentially, because the priest who is in no sense pastor is inadequate as priest 2. 'That even though pastoral devotion inhere in fullness of priesthood, yet definitions and formulae can move only in the sphere of *outward* distinctions.' Fallacy involved in defining by distinctive outwardnesses, illustrated by the case of a viceroy. The Church should be always on her guard against this very tendency to externalize; and nowhere more importantly than in the language of her Ordinal . , ... 290

APPENDIX

UPON THE RECENT ROMAN CONTROVERSY AS TO THE VALIDITY OF ANGLICAN ORDERS

Technical questions of validity turn rather upon the ceremonial outwardness than the inner meaning of priesthood. Four requirements of outward technicality—apostolic succession, intention, laying on of hands, and prayer 301

The real question turns upon the Roman claim to have priesthood and intention exclusively defined in her own sense. It is manifest that Anglicanism challenges the correctness of

lvi   CONTENTS

                                                                    PAGE
Roman definitions and proportions. No argument possible between disputants on the assumption that one of them has been throughout, and is, infallible Almost all Roman argument based ultimately on the assumption that Rome is infallible . . 305
 Character of the efforts of recent writers.
 I M. Dalbus. His striking admissions; his strangely inadequate reasons for an adverse decision . 311
 II. M. Duchesne Criticism of Dalbus Character of the position really occupied by MM Dalbus and Duchesne. Their helplessness 316
 III M. Boudinhon, No. 1, answers M. Dalbus His argument about intention; warning to M. Duchesne . . 320
 IV M. Boudinhon, No 2, constructs a new argument to prove the Anglican 'forms' inadequate; three fallacious assumptions underlying his major premiss, his curious conclusions; new position about intention . . 325
 V. M Delasge His criticism on the controversy, disallows the objections; would recognize Anglican orders as valid, though irregular General position of the argument . 334
 VI. The Papal intervention; expectations and possibilities, pathos of the result, the Encyclical; character and effect of its claims . . . 338
 VII The Bull, its decision, its argument, takes apparently two objections (*a*) to 'form,' (*b*) to 'intention.' Both reducible to intention only, and to the two simple assumptions—1. Rome is infallible; 2. Rome has divine right to implicit and universal obedience. No argument outside these assumptions . 343
 The Anglican position neither understood nor affected at all. If Rome be not infallible, the entire Roman argument collapses 351
 Grave prospect on the side of Romanism. Its self-identification with mechanical externality. Character and function of the Anglican Church 353

INDEX 355

MINISTERIAL PRIESTHOOD

CHAPTER I

THE NATURE OF CHURCH UNITY

THE basis of a true understanding of Church ministry is a true understanding of the Church. The Church is likened to a body; her ministers to certain specific organs or members of the body[1]. If, in the material body, one member differs from, or is related to, another, these mutual differences, or relations, at once serve to explain, and receive explanation from, the unity of the body as a single articulated whole. So when we inquire into the rationale of Church ministries, we are inquiring into the principle of the differentiation of functions within a single unity. If there are differences of ministries, if ministry, as a whole, is different from laity, these differences at once illustrate, and depend upon, the unity of that whole in which, and for which, they exist. It is a fundamental truth that the differentiation is a differentiation of, and within, unity. If then we are to reach an intelligent view of the nature of the differentiation, we must begin with an intelligent view of the nature of the unity. Till there is some agreement as to the meaning of Church unity, a discussion of

---

[1] Cf. Romans xii. 4-8 with 1 Cor. xii. 12-30.

the rationale of Church ministry would be a discussion in the air.

That the question of the nature of the unity of the Church is no merely speculative but the necessary practical basis of an intelligent theory of Church ministry, is sufficiently illustrated by a comparison of two of the more recent expositions of ministry. Dr. Hatch and Canon Gore, however otherwise they may differ, are alike in this. Each begins his explanation of ministerial organization by a theory of the nature and being of the Church. No doubt the conclusions of the two writers differ widely. But the conclusion reached by either writer in respect of ministry is in sufficiently accurate correspondence with the theory from which either sets out as to the character of the Church, and the meaning of the organization which protects and expresses her unity.

It is not the fact of the unity which is in question. The words of the Nicene Creed, 'I believe in one Catholic and Apostolic Church,' contain an assertion of unity which would not be challenged on either side. But it may be worth while to distinguish some of the different ideas which such acknowledgement of unity may represent. In what sense is it part of the Christian Creed that the Church is *One*?

The most obvious distinction to draw is between unity acquired by degrees from below, and unity revealed as inherent from above. Take the two cases in their simplest and barest forms. In the first case certain historical conditions tend towards the realization of unity as a fact; and out of the fact of unity is developed the idea. In the second case the unity is first in idea, a necessary element in the meaning of the life of the Church, and remains, as such, equally fundamental and constant, whether it is more, or is less, realized in fact.

The first of these two appears, in its origin at least, to be a purely accidental unity. If this is the true account of the unity of the Church, then in the first instance there was no such thing, either in fact or idea, as Church unity; but Christians were merely individual units, whom pressure of circumstances drove more and more to coalesce into a society, until by degrees the idea of the society became a leading idea of the Christian life. If this is historically true, then the idea of the society, exactly so far as it became among Christians religiously dominant or peremptory, is convicted of being a false idea. For dominant or peremptory in the sphere of conscience is just what a politic convenience, so evolved, has no right to become.

No doubt, however, it is true that in any society, however accidentally evolved, when it once has reached self-consciousness as a society, the maintenance of the social conception becomes a sort of instinctive necessity of self-preservation. Even therefore the merely politic method of association tends to produce an ideal of unity, which, as ideal, does constrain the imagination, even if it has no right to command the conscience. The history of the society is human, is in origin accidental: but the ideal, when produced, outstrips and ignores the accidental origin. Such an ideal, so produced, may be less, or more, noble and inspiring. But it has no right to claim to be transcendental, essential, divine. Trade guilds in the older, and trades unions in the newer, world, may serve perhaps as examples of such unity, coalescing, at first, out of separateness, and yet afterwards (in some cases) speaking to separateness with the prophet-like tones of an ideal which may claim to be obeyed.

But even in associations purely human and politic it is the case, quite as often as not, that the coalescing is not accidental in kind, that the idea comes first, and that the association which follows, follows only as a realization, more or less complete, of the formative idea. To say that an association is deliberately formed, is to say that the idea precedes the act. It is recognized that if an idea is to be made dominant in the imaginations and characters of men, the effective way to propagate an idea is to organize a society. Without the brotherhood of a living society it is useless, it seems, to preach either political or social, either moral or religious, ideals. Political clubs, Christian (or other) social unions, temperance or white cross societies, attest on all sides the efficacy of the corporate method of giving life to ideas, the essential dependence (as perhaps we may venture to say) of the inward life upon the outward organism, of spirit (under this world's conditions) upon body. To suggest that the Church is an association parallel with these, though for a higher or more inclusive purpose, would be indeed to make it, in its origin as association, on the level of the merely human and politic; but it would be by no means identical, as interpretation of history, with the theory that Christians, as individual units, gradually coalesced under pressure of circumstances into corporate life, and, out of union, acquired the conception of unity.

We have then, so far, two quite distinguishable forms of the theory of Church unity as being, in the main, human and politic.

But by degrees we recognize that our thought is challenged by conceptions which go beyond these. There rises, more or less explicitly, the consciousness that men, after all, however much we have learned to regard them instinctively as individuals, are neither quite so distinct, nor so separately complete, as they seemed. From the φύσει πολιτικόν of Aristotle down to the scientific formula 'solidarity of humanity,' or the overt efforts or latent instincts of modern socialism, there is a gathering witness to the fact that unity in humanity is no merely politic uniting, that there is a sense in which unity is an ultimate and necessary predicate of humanity, a truth which is not inconsistent with, but which lies back behind, individual separateness. The man is not exclusively himself. Even in the conditions of his own individuality, he too is, to an unknown and indefinite extent, the product of the lives and minds of others; nor is there anything which he can do, or be, or say, which begins and ends wholly in himself. With and for others he is blest; with and for others he suffers, as others, inextricably, suffer or are blest with him. The most selfish, the most separate, really stands only to an infinitesimal degree, alone. Nay, it is only in relation to others that he is himself in any adequate sense. Not in abstraction, or isolation, but in communion, lies (it may be) the very meaning of personality itself. As such conceptions as these assert themselves in human consciousness, whether from the metaphysical, or the scientific, or the practical moral side, they can hardly fail to affect, and that profoundly, the meaning of the idea of the unity of the Church. For whatever may be the failures of Church history, it is plain that, by the very nature of her being, the Church, in idea at least, intends and aspires to be universally inclusive. If any are left out or sundered from the Church, it is not from the narrowness of the basis on which the Church is conceived. In her own conception at least the Church is Catholic. Even on the most individualistic theory of the Church, it would be admitted that she ought ideally to include all individuals. Her ideal basis is as wide as humanity. Now, however little the conception of the mutual interdependence or solidarity of humanity might affect the idea of an association framed for some highly specialized and narrow purpose, it can hardly fail to give a new depth of meaning to an association which, even without it, and on any showing, was anyhow—just so far as it realized its own ideal —not a specific corporation *within* humanity, but the corporately articulated unity of humanity itself, and that, just in the widest inclusiveness, just for the highest possibilities, of which human being is capable. Beyond then the merely politic conceptions of the meaning of Church unity, there rises what may be distinguished perhaps as the philosophic conception—based upon the demonstrable incompleteness of the individual life, and appealing to the intellectual imagination with all the grandeur of an eternal principle, which can wait for its realization with majestic patience, just because—before realization or without it—its own ideal truth remains immovable

It is plain, of course, that behind the philosophical conception there remains the theological. Thus far at least the theological conception does not differ from the philosophical, that there is nothing in the philosophical which is not in the theological. But theology has something further to add as to the origin and nature of the unity which, in their different ways, both philosophy and science have recognised. To her, all being is ultimately, not an abstract personification, but a Personal Unity. The unity which the Church represents is the Unity of God. It is true therefore of the Church, in the highest conceivable sense, that her unity is not to be understood as a growth which begins from below, and gradually coalesces: her unity is not the crown of an evolution which starts from disunion; the Church is one in idea whether she is one in fact or not, her ideal unity from the first is inherent, transcendental, divine she is one essentially, as and because God is One.

In an age whose Trinitarian thought is so superficial as to run, at many points, into Tritheism, it may be that even the appeal to the unity of God has lost part of its meaning. The unity of God is not an accidental, it is much more than a merely arithmetical, unity. It is not merely the negation of dualism It is the unity of all-comprehensiveness It is the unity of inherent self-completeness. The unity is a positive, a necessary, an inherent quality of the essence. To doubt the unity, would be to deny the essence, of Deity. But it is an unity which must not be stated only in abstract terms. It is a living unity, a moral unity, nay, it *is* goodness, it *is* life It is no more capable of plurality than are the idea of moral goodness or the idea of Life; the meaning of either of which is not amplified, but in an instant altered, limited, and degraded by being expressed in the plural.

An unity so complete, an unity which cannot even be viewed from without, is necessarily only in part capable of expression. Words do but indicate, they can never compass it. It is plain, however, neither words nor thought can be even approximately adequate to the truth, which ignore the scriptural conception of the Spirit as the constituting and realizing of unity, or the revelation of the Spirit as Love.

The expression of unity, in this transcendental sense, as the meaning of the life of the Church, is in Scripture direct and complete. It is there as ideal, not implicit only but expressed, not in the early aspirations of the Church only, but in that which was divinely set before the Church, before as yet the Church had begun to be. It may be desirable to quote in full the concluding words of the great High Priestly Prayer of our Lord Jesus Christ, wherein the exposition and aspiration of His work are summed up, at the close of the last evening before He died: 'As Thou didst send Me into the world, even so sent I them into the world. And for their sakes I sanctify Myself, that they themselves also may be sanctified in truth. Neither for these only do I pray, but for them also that believe on Me through their word; *that they may all be one . even as Thou, Father, art in Me, and I in Thee, that they also may be in Us;* that the world may believe that Thou didst send Me. And the glory which Thou hast given Me I have given unto them; *that they may be one, even as We are one; I in them, and Thou in Me, that they may be perfected into one;* that the world may know that Thou didst send Me, and lovedst them, even as Thou lovedst Me. Father, that which Thou hast given Me, I will that, where I am, they also may be with Me, that they may behold My glory, which Thou hast given Me: for Thou lovedst Me before the foundation of the world. O righteous Father, the world knew Thee not, but I knew Thee; and these knew that Thou didst send Me; and I made known unto them Thy Name, and will make it known; that the love wherewith Thou lovedst Me may be in them, and I in them¹.' If any of us should feel that there are points at which we imperfectly understand these words, that is certainly not a reason for explaining away so much as we do understand. Plainly at least they set forth, from the beginning, unity,—the transcendental unity, the divine unity,—as the ideal meaning of the society which Christ came to found; and which, when He was gone, should remain to the end, as His temple, and the representation of His Person, on earth.

With this ideal, as set forth in Christ's consummating prayer, we take the practical appeal of the Apostle to members of the Church: 'I therefore, the prisoner in the Lord, beseech you to walk worthily of the calling wherewith ye were called, with all lowliness and meekness, with long-suffering, forbearing one another in love; giving diligence to keep the unity of the Spirit in the bond of peace. There is one Body, and one Spirit, even as also ye were called in one hope of your calling; one Lord, one Faith, one Baptism, one God and Father of all, who is over all, and through all, and in all².'

It may seem at first sight superfluous to pause at this point and ask which of these views of unity we are ourselves to accept as the meaning of the unity of the Church. Yet it is worth while, if only that we may observe to how very small an extent the different views are really exclusive of each other. It is plain that the theological conception simply absorbs, while it transcends, the philosophical. How far is it inconsistent with the politic? If by the 'politic' view of Church unity should be meant (1) that there were various conditions observable in the world eighteen centuries and a half ago which tended towards and facilitated the corporate organization of Christians; or (2) that the method adopted by the Apostles for the spread of Christian doctrine was, as a matter of history, the corporate method; that from the first they went everywhere proclaiming a 'kingdom,' enrolling 'members' into it, and organizing for it officers, discipline, and government; or

---

¹ St. John xvii. 18-26.   ² Eph. iv. 1-6.

(3) that the more Christians realized their corporate coherence as a matter of fact, so much the more paramount, even to the natural instinct of Christians, did the corporate ideal become; then it is plain that the higher view of unity as a theological doctrine is not traversed by such a politic view as this in any particular whatever. Things such as these, as matters of historical study, are as interesting upon the theological, as upon any other, theory of the unity of the Church.

If at the beginning of the Christian era historians can trace, as one (so to speak) of the characteristics of the social atmosphere, a striking 'tendency towards the formation of associations[1]'; this, as an element in the general *Praeparatio Evangelica*, will be no less significant to the Christian theologian, than it would be to any one who should, by its help, desire to explain away the divine conception of the Church. Meanwhile that the Apostolic method of propagating Christianity was as observed from the outside—whatever might be their own inner theory about the method—parallel, in its main features, with that of other moral and religious societies, is not open to question. Every organization framed among men for the spreading of an idea, illustrates *pro tanto*, and is illustrated by, the method of the preaching of the Gospel on earth. Whatever the description may, or may not, leave unsaid, undoubtedly the Christian Church can be truly described as an organized 'association for personal holiness.' It will be observed therefore that such human or politic accounts of Church unity only begin to be in conflict with the deeper theological theory, if or when they are used for the express purpose of superseding or contradicting that theory. The antithesis between the two is neither necessary nor natural; it is an artificial antithesis. To the theologian, these more external and secular aspects of the growth of the Church are not in any sense untrue,

[1] *The Organization of the Early Christian Churches*, by Dr Hatch, p. 26. The Bampton Lectures for 1880.

but they are most incomplete: in much the same sense in which we should most of us regard as valuable, so far as it went, but ludicrously inadequate, any explanation of man's being which should be content to describe him by a chemical analysis of the elements, or a history of the development, of his body. So long as any such explanation of man ignores entirely the question whether the body is all, or whether there is any meaning—transcending, even if interpreting, body—in such words as 'soul' or 'spirit,' we may simply smile at the immense inadequacy. But if, whether tacitly or deliberately, the explanation is in fact in any measure made use of, to deny, or to discredit, the ideas 'soul' or 'spirit'; or, at the least, to suggest that soul and spirit are ideas so remote and incommensurable, that the chemical body cannot be the expression of them, nor they the animating reality which constitutes and interprets the true meaning of the body; we should most of us instinctively feel, in the presence of such an assumption, much as the theologian feels if, tacitly or openly, the secular conditions of the development of the Church are used to discredit the idea of her transcendental unity; or at least to suggest that, whether as facts or ideas, her unity on the one hand, and her organization on the other, are, and must be, mutually incommensurable and unrelated.

Now it seems to me hardly doubtful that the opening positions of Dr. Hatch's Bampton Lectures would, to the great majority of readers, distinctly convey the impression that the writer meant so to use the 'politic' and 'voluntary' as to deny, first the original or inherent existence, and therefore in the last resort the ultimate rightfulness, of the claim of the 'transcendental' or 'peremptory' theory of Church unity, as a doctrine which must be realized in Christian practice. In the first lecture, sketching beforehand his intended work, he says of it, 'We shall see those to whom the Word of Life was preached gradually coalescing into societies[1].' In his synopsis

[1] p. 21.

he sums the opening thoughts of his second lecture thus: 'There was a general tendency in the early centuries of the Christian era towards the formation of associations, and especially of religious associations. It was consequently natural that the early converts to Christianity should combine together: the tendency to do so was fostered by the Apostles and their successors, and at last, though not at first, became universal[1].' In the second lecture itself he says 'Such an aggregation does not appear to have invariably followed belief. There were many who stood apart; and there were many reasons for their doing so[2]' 'The chief purpose' of the Ignatian Epistles, he says, 'seems to be to urge those who called themselves Christians to become, or to continue to be, or to be more zealously than before, members of the associations of which the bishops were the head[3].' From certain passages in the Ignatian Epistles, he says, 'it is clear' (1) that 'there were Christians' in the cities addressed 'who did not come to the general assembly or recognize the authority of the bishop, presbyters, and deacons'; (2) that 'this separation from the assembly and its officers went to the extent of having separate eucharists', and (3) 'consequently, that attachment to the organization of which the bishop was the head was not yet universally recognized as a primary duty of the Christian life[4].' It is difficult to see what is meant in all this, unless it be, by dwelling on the natural and secular genesis of the Church, and especially by this insistence upon passages which are supposed to carry the conclusion that external unity was not a primary Christian idea, to throw at least more or less of discredit and doubt over any theological postulate of essential unity.

I do not forget that Dr. Hatch was endeavouring to explain the 'organization of the Christian Churches' without so much as 'touching' the 'Christian faith.' 'With

[1] p. xx. [2] p 29. [3] p 30.
[4] In a note (10) on p 30.

doctrine, and with the beliefs which underlie doctrine,' he refuses to be concerned[1]. But I must say at once that the attempt to explain Church organization or ministry without reference to Christian doctrine or belief appears to me to be an obviously impossible task. I have in mind moreover a phrase which I have marked by italics, which makes it difficult to say precisely how much he himself intended in this part of his argument. Speaking of the subapostolic insistence upon Church unity, he says: 'We consequently find that the union of believers in associations had to be preached, *if not as an article of the Christian faith*, at least as an element of Christian practice[2]. But this very sentence suggests to me a remark which I should have anyhow to press in reference to the passages quoted above. He hints here, somewhat uncertainly, at a possible contrast between the requirements, on the one hand, of the Christian faith, and the attainment, on the other, of the Christian practice. Was there then such a contrast, or was there not? If, or so far as, it can be shown that there was still in apostolic or subapostolic days some tendency on the part of some individuals on the fringe of Christ's Church to try to be 'Christians' without necessarily being 'Churchmen,' was this, or was this not, really compatible with the essential and inherent nature of Christianity? This is the very first question which ought, upon the hypothesis, to be raised. And this is just the question which he has not raised at all. When he says, 'There were many who stood apart: and there were many reasons for their doing so,' the first thing we want to be told is 'were there ever any who were *allowed to* stand apart? were there, or could there have been, any *lawful or adequate* reasons for their doing so?' He adds, 'A man might wish to be Christ's disciple and yet shrink

[1] Lect. ii. p. 23.
[2] Lect. ii. p. 29. Is the verbal implication in these words to the effect that as 'faith' it was already accepted, but as 'practice' it still needed to be preached? or is it that, though as 'practice' it was desirable, yet it was *not* to be preached as an article of faith?

from hating father and mother and wife and children and brethren and sisters, yea and his own life also.' Of course he might. But Dr. Hatch does not say a word as to whether he might *legitimately* so wish. Still less does he make a point of reminding us that in these very words which he is in fact quoting, Christ Himself had laid down, long before subapostolic times, that upon such conditions a man 'cannot be My disciple.'

Are we then, upon the other hand, to understand that it is admitted by Dr. Hatch that all lax exceptions were necessarily disloyal and untrue to the Christian ideal? Is there no suggestion that the instances quoted are, or may be, indications of an earlier Christian ideal which was gradually superseded by a later? Is it assumed that evasion of Churchmanship was of course, and always, faultiness of Christianity? In whichever way we may choose to interpret his thought, the point is that this is the question which Dr. Hatch does not raise. But we cannot tell, without raising it, how to interpret the passages which he adduces And it must be added that unless he means at least in part to suggest that the Christian ideal might at first have dispensed with Church membership, it is difficult to understand the emphasis which he lays upon the matter at all. If lapsing from effective membership was *ipso facto* Christian failure, and was, so far, like any other lapsing into worldliness or self-indulgence, the few passages which indicate that there were Christians who so failed are of no importance at all as illustrating any process of 'gradual coalescing' into corporate life: they show only that the requirements of corporate Christianity were from the first irksome to the flesh, and that the necessary coherence of the Church, though from the first an indispensable element in the Christian ideal, was yet in the earliest years of Christian experience less completely inwrought into the universal Christian consciousness than it very speedily became.

Such a view as this of the meaning of the passages is

completely borne out, when we turn to examine the passages themselves. Dr. Hatch quotes from five writers altogether—two within, and three without, the canon of Scripture. The New Testament writers are the author of the Epistle to the Hebrews and St Jude. Take these first. The crucial words in the Epistle to the Hebrews are these, 'not forsaking the assembling of ourselves together, *as the custom of some is*[1].' Now it may be very difficult to draw from these words any exact historical inference as to the extent of the erroneous 'custom,' but what is perfectly certain upon the passage as a whole, is that this 'custom' of 'some'—whatever it amounted to—involves, to the mind of the writer, a total failure to discern the necessary bearing of Christian faith upon practical life. He has been expounding with elaborate care, in the light of the Levitical sacrifices which led up towards it, the nature of the great Christian sacrifice, which was the culmination of the work of the incarnate Redeemer, and was therefore cardinal to the whole system and meaning of a Christian believer's life. From the doctrine of the Atonement it absolutely follows, to him, that the Christian life is a life which is perpetually being presented—with the presenting of the Blood of Jesus—into the holiest place, in and through the way of His consecrated flesh, and this truth of doctrine, exhibited upon the side of practical life, involves at least these two practical consequences. First, it involves the perpetual consecration of the individual life, with discipline and purifying of the individual conscience. And secondly, since the relation to the Blood of Jesus, through His flesh, is a common, not a private relation, and the great appointed act of communion therewith is a social act,—is the act, is the life, of the brotherhood (the union, not of each with Him severally, but of all with Him corporately, of each therefore necessarily with each, just as truly as of each with Him), it follows that there is also involved both the witness of a corporate worship, and

[1] Hebrews x. 25.

the emulation of a mutual devotion and service of love[1]. The 'some' who do not perceive this have never caught the real significance of the doctrine of Atonement, or its bearing upon personal life. Such seems to be the meaning of the passage. Whether the 'some' were many or were few, the one thing which seems to come out with perfect clearness is that they were fundamentally and altogether wrong.

But if the bearing of the passage to the Hebrews is sufficiently unmistakable, in St. Jude there is no reserve at all[2]. The most bigoted ecclesiastic could hardly denounce schism in more scathing or unsparing language. 'These are they who make separations, sensual, having not the Spirit.' The whole epistle is an eloquent one, and a terrible, in denunciation. But it might be quoted just as reasonably to show that there was room for profligacy, as for disunion, in the Church of the Apostles. In a sense perhaps neither assertion might be literally false. Yet either would be—and on St. Jude's evidence, at least, would be *equally*—the essential contradiction of the truth.

To these two singularly unfortunate passages of Scripture there are added references to three uncanonical writers. First there are five passages in the Shepherd of Hermas, and one in the Epistle of Barnabas. The passages of Hermas are all very similar, and all very slight. What seems to be contemplated in them is neither, on

---

[1] The passage runs thus :—
'Having therefore, brethren, boldness to enter into the holy place by the Blood of Jesus, by the way which He dedicated for us, a new and living way, through the veil, that is to say, His flesh; and having a great priest over the house of God; let us draw near with a true heart in fulness of faith, having our hearts sprinkled from an evil conscience, and our body washed with pure water: let us hold fast the confession of our hope that it waver not; for he is faithful that promised: and let us consider one another to provoke unto love and good works; not forsaking the assembling of ourselves together, as the custom of some is, but exhorting one another; and so much the more, as ye see the day drawing nigh' Hebrews x. 19-25.

[2] Jude 18-20.

the one hand, a view of Christianity which ever was, or could have been, in itself the right view; nor yet, on the other, any deliberately reasoned or consistently completed form of schism from the Church, but rather a certain spirit of worldliness among baptized Christians, which made them wish overmuch, as far as their daily routine was concerned, to live on as part of the secular social life which was going on round them (and which was of course, in fact, a heathen life), instead of fearlessly devoting themselves, out and out, to the comparative unworldliness of the social life and social burthen[1] of the Christian brethren. But here again, as in the Scripture, this desire to stand, whether more or less, apart, is consistently condemned as incompatible with the Christian calling. So to be worldly and separate is to desert the truth, to be sundered from the saints, to be valueless unsightly stones, left out of the fabric of the temple of Christ. It is to be self-approved, and therefore self-blinded, undisciplined, unloving, unspiritual.

The passage in the Epistle of Barnabas is just similar to these. It is a reproof of the selfishness of isolation from the efforts of what ought to be a corporate life. But it is evident that the isolation thought of is, not a rival theory of Church life, but an ordinary piece of moral indolence or cowardice[2]. Such an impulse towards worldliness is of

---

[1] The same verb occurs in every case: οἱ ἐγνωκότες τὴν ἀλήθειαν, μὴ ἐπιμείναντες δὲ ἐν αὐτῇ μηδὲ κολλώμενοι τοῖς ἁγίοις, Vis. iii. 6. οἱ ἐν ταῖς πραγματείαις ἐμπεφυρμένοι καὶ μὴ κολλώμενοι τοῖς ἁγίοις, Sim. viii. 8. ὑψηλόφρονες ἐγένοντο, καὶ κατέλιπον τὴν ἀλήθειαν, καὶ οὐκ ἐκολλήθησαν τοῖς δικαίοις, ἀλλὰ μετὰ τῶν ἐθνῶν συνέζησαν, Sim. viii. 9. οἱ ἐν ταῖς πραγματείαις ταῖς ποικίλαις ἐμπεφυρμένοι . . . οὐ κολλῶνται τοῖς δούλοις τοῦ Θεοῦ . . . οἱ δὲ πλούσιοι δυσκόλως κολλῶνται τοῖς δούλοις τοῦ Θεοῦ, Sim. ix. 20. μὴ κολλώμενοι τοῖς δούλοις τοῦ Θεοῦ, ἀλλὰ μονάζοντες ἀπολλύουσι τὰς ἑαυτῶν ψυχάς, Sim ix. 26. Compare Clem Rom. 1 Cor xlvi γέγραπται γάρ· Κολλᾶσθε τοῖς ἁγίοις, ὅτι οἱ κολλώμενοι αὐτοῖς ἁγιασθήσονται Cp. also below, ch. vi. p. 206.

[2] Φύγωμεν ἀπὸ πάσης ματαιότητος, μισήσωμεν τελείως τὰ ἔργα τῆς πονηρᾶς ὁδοῦ μὴ καθ' ἑαυτοὺς ἐνδύνοντες μονάζετε ὡς ἤδη δεδικαιωμένοι, ἀλλ' ἐπὶ τὸ αὐτὸ συνερχόμενοι συνζητεῖτε περὶ τοῦ κοινῇ συμφέροντος. λέγει γὰρ ἡ γραφή· Οὐαὶ οἱ συνετοὶ ἑαυτοῖς καὶ ἐνώπιον ἑαυτῶν ἐπιστήμονες. γενώμεθα πνευματικοί, γενώμεθα ναὸς τέλειος τῷ Θεῷ, Barn. iv. 10, 11.

course perfectly natural. It is hardly conceivable that it should have been absent. Yet the references to it are not such as to suggest that it was largely prevalent in the Christian communities; still less that it represented any such obstinate instinct or deep-seated conviction of disapproval as we might expect to find, if the principle of organised unity were itself only gradually gaining possession of the minds of those who had been Christians individually *before* they constituted a Christian Church.

What these writers really feel is that there were men who did not make their Christian life sufficiently a life of mutual service. They did not understand the extent to which mutual interdependence and corporate self-sacrifice were to be the necessary expression of the Christian spirit. If this lesson was quickly learned as far as the mere external conformity went, and if few Churchmen of later days would doubt that the Church is corporate, it must perhaps still be owned that the reality of mutual service, as expressive of Christianity, is almost as far from being fully realized in an age which takes the corporate theory for granted, as it could have been in any earlier form of Church experience.

The last witness is the Ignatian Epistles. Now here no doubt we are met with an insistence upon the doctrine and duty of unity, which if upon one side it may be quoted as an emphatic witness to the ecclesiastical idea, pours itself out withal in strains of such vehement earnestness as naturally to suggest, upon the other side, that both the duty and the doctrine of unity seemed in some way to the mind of the Bishop of Antioch to be seriously challenged and brought into peril. This in itself is a condition of things which is hardly compatible either with the earlier indications of the Epistle to the Hebrews, or St. Jude, or with the vaguer moral reproof of Hermas. Decisive as their language in its own way is, it must have been differently conceived if they had been thinking, not of a secular looseness of membership, but of a deliberate separation, of theory and practice, from the Church; no longer that is of a separatist tendency, but of an organized schism. It is this no doubt which explains the earnestness of the language of Ignatius. In his case, but in his case only, it is fair to infer the presence of an imminent peril of disunion. To recognize the community ordered under bishop, priests, and deacons, and to refuse it; to substitute an alternative practice based on an alternative theory; to institute private Eucharists over against the Episcopal Eucharist; this, if connected in any way with earlier tendencies, is at least an audaciously new development of them. This is no conservative protest against a novel conception of uniting, but rather a novel audacity of separation from the familiar methods of the unity of the Church. It is a revolt against the community itself. And so it is regarded by St. Ignatius, as a question not between one or another complexion of Christianity, but between the true and the false, between reality and pretence, between being Christians in fact, or only in name [1].

There is one point more. 'After the subapostolic age,' writes Dr Hatch, 'these exhortations cease. The tendency to association has become a fixed habit [2].' How shall we best represent the meaning of such truth as these words express? Perhaps in some such statement as this. The unity of the Church was, from the first, a necessary theological principle, and was, as such, put into practice from the first to the utmost extent that circumstances would allow. But this principle (a) was not in every case present, as axiomatic, to the conscience of average Christians, and (b) was in various exceptional cases, for moral or other reasons, imperfectly realized in practice. As, however, the mind of Christians realized the principle, as principle, more sweepingly, the results reached were (a) that the external organization, as such, became more essentially a matter of course, and (b) that, in proportion as it was matter of course externally, the real meaning of the principle expressed by

[1] μὴ μόνον καλεῖσθαι Χριστιανοῖς ἀλλὰ καὶ εἶναι, Magn. IV.   [2] p. 30.

it sank in moral value. Secularity of mind—which no age of the Church has yet uprooted—instead of prompting men (as at first) to hold loosely to the conception of corporate life, led them rather, in accepting, to materialize and degrade it. They learned to separate its right to theoretical acceptance from its claim on the moral life. If they had shrunk from it while it pinched them, they learned how to explain, in accepting, it, so that it should cease to pinch. Worldliness, instead of refusing, adopted and interpreted it. Thenceforward the idea was, to Christian consciousness, fundamental. There might be schisms and heresies and false views as to what *was* the Body: there might be secular emphasis upon the external organization merely as external and organized; but doubt as to whether the Christian Church carried necessarily a corporate life or no, which had meant from the first a hopelessly inadequate grasp of Christian truth, could not, even as a misconception, survive the earliest forms of Christian consciousness. Church unity, just because it could not but be universal and imperative, found a way of becoming external and unexacting. The corporate idea (it may be said) had to be unduly carnalized, just because it could not be denied. Such perversion does not discredit—it bears witness to the truth of—the perverted principle; just as Ananias and Sapphira bore witness to the truth of the ideal which they dishonoured. However perverted in practice, the idea at least, as idea, was beyond all challenge.

It has seemed worth while, in deference to the prestige of Dr. Hatch's name and memory, to glance at these passages [1]: but it is, in truth, characteristic of the more

---

[1] The argument is lightly treated by Canon Gore, *The Church and the Ministry*, p. 53. 'This mode of conceiving the progress of Christianity is in direct violation of the evidence. The only evidence produced for the supposed first stage which preceded obligatory association consists in the fact that the earliest Church teachers found it necessary to preach the duty of association "if not as an article of the Christian faith, at least as an element of Christian practice." This is evidenced by the warning in the Epistle to the Hebrews against forsaking the Christian assemblies; by St. Jude's denunciation of those who "separate themselves"; by the passages in the Shepherd of Hermas about

paradoxical side of Dr. Hatch's mind that they should have been adduced at all as evidence to prove that the idea of Church unity was an aftergrowth The two things which the passages most clearly prove are (1) that any infringement of corporate unity was sternly denounced, from absolutely the earliest times of all, as incompatible with a true Christianity; and (2) that the Church contained, in respect of this (as, indeed, of the fundamental requirements of the moral law), some unworthy and ignorant members. There is in them absolutely nothing whatever to justify the statement that they show Christians 'gradually coalescing into societies.' To say, in reference to them, that the apostles 'fostered' a 'tendency' towards combination which was 'natural' to early Christians—however true— is to describe the apostles' work by an under-statement so immense as to have the effect of a very positive misstatement. To say that this tendency 'at last, though not at first, became universal,' is to make a statement which, for its purpose, has hardly even a consistent meaning. In the sense in which it was not universal at first, that is, in the literal, historical sense, Church unity never has been perfectly realized at all. In the sense in which it was universal at last, that is, in the doctrinal and ideal sense, it never could be, and has never been, less than universal.

The distinction here made is one which it is necessary to insist upon positively. 'I believe one Catholic and Apostolic Church' is no statement about the accidents of history, but a profession of essential doctrine. If it were a statement only about the *de facto* history of the Church, it would be more than difficult to subscribe it as true. Can I look abroad and find the unity of the Church as a historical

those who "have separated themselves" and so "lose their own souls." What do such utterances really go to prove? A separatist tendency on the part of *those who had been Christians*—a sin of schism, denounced like any other sin. But the idea is nowhere discernible that every Christian was not, as such, a member of the Church, bound to the obligations of membership Schism is a sin in Scripture as really as in Ignatius' letters.'

phenomenon? To explain the meaning of her unity as the *de facto* realization in history of a natural secular tendency would be only the preliminary to discovering that the word 'unity' was in fact a mistake. If this is the nature of its meaning in the Creed, the Creed would be both safer and truer without it. It is just because its meaning is not of this character, because, whether realised or unrealized, its truth remains inherent, ideal, immutable; because the unity which it represents, whether more perfectly or less, is the essential unity of the One God, that this doctrine of the uniqueness and unity of the Church could stand as a necessary element in the truth from the very beginning; and that it must remain to the end inseparable, by inherent necessity, from the Christian Creed.

NOTE.

IN reference to the subject of the first chapter, and to Dr. Hatch's contention, I should like to refer, with great satisfaction, to much of the exposition contained in *The Christian Ecclesia* by Dr. Hort, the late Margaret Professor at Cambridge. To me at least it appears that Dr. Hatch's position is completely destroyed by statements such as are represented in the following quotations [1].

St. Paul 'goes on to warn them [the Corinthians] against the natural abuse of these gifts, the self-assertion fostered by glibness and knowingness, and the consequent spirit of schism or division, the very contradiction of the idea of an Ecclesia. The habit of seeming to know all about most things, and of being able to talk glibly about most things, would naturally tend to an excess of individuality, and a diminished sense of corporate responsibilities. This fact supplies, under many different forms, the main drift of 1 Corinthians. Never losing his cordial appreciation of the Corinthian endowments, St. Paul is practically teaching throughout that a truly Christian life is of necessity the life of membership in a body [2]. . . . Again he points out [3] that the party factions which rent the Ecclesia, while they seemed to be in honour of venerated names, were in reality only a puffing up of each man against his neighbour.'. . . 'Then comes the familiar 13th chapter on love, which in the light of St. Paul's idea of the Ecclesia we can see to be no digression, this gift of the Spirit being incomparably more essential to its life than any of the gifts which caught men's attention [4].'. . . 'Almost the whole Epistle [to the Romans] is governed by the thought which was filling St. Paul's mind at this time, the relation of Jew and Gentile, the place of both in the counsels of God, and the peaceful inclusion of both in the same brotherhood [5].'. . 'The apparently ethical teaching of chapters xii and xiii is really for the most part on the principles of Christian

---

[1] Which might be almost indefinitely multiplied.   [2] p. 129.
[3] In ch. iv. 6, p. 130.   [4] p. 132.   [5] p. 133.

fellowship.'. . . . 'The xvth and parts of the xvith chapter illustrate historically, as other chapters had done doctrinally, St. Paul's yearnings for the unity of all Christians of East and West[1].' To all such teaching he represents the Ephesians as the theological climax 'Here, at last, *for the first time in the Acts and Epistles*[2], we have "the Ecclesia" spoken of in the sense of the one universal Ecclesia, and it comes more from the theological than from the historical side; i. e. less from the actual circumstances of the actual Christian communities than from a development of thoughts respecting the place and office of the Son of God: His Headship was felt to involve the unity of all those who were united to Him. On the other hand, it is a serious misunderstanding of these Epistles to suppose, as is sometimes done, that the Ecclesia here spoken of is an Ecclesia wholly in the heavens, not formed of human beings[3].' With this last sentence may be compared the following: 'Membership of a local Ecclesia was obviously visible and external, and we have no evidence that St. Paul regarded membership of the universal Ecclesia as invisible, and exclusively spiritual, and as shared by only a limited number of the members of the external Ecclesiae, those, namely, whom God had chosen out of the great mass and ordained to life, of those whose faith in Christ was a genuine and true faith. What very plausible grounds could be urged for this distinction, was to be seen in later generations; but it seems to me incompatible with any reasonable interpretation of St Paul's words[4].'

Of the similitude of the Body he says: 'In Ephesians the image is extended to embrace all Christians, and the change is not improbably connected with the clear setting forth of the relation of the Body to its Head which now first comes before us. . . . The comparison of men in society to the members of a body was of course not new. With the Stoics in particular it was much in vogue. What was distinctively Christian was

---

[1] p. 134.
[2] I venture to italicize these words, in order to draw attention to the fact that Dr. Hort is speaking of the exposition of Ephesians—not as the first Christian realization of the idea of unity, but as the first scriptural insistence upon its theological significance *since the teaching of our Lord Himself, as recorded in the Gospels.*
[3] p. 148.
[4] p. 169

the faith in the One baptizing and life-giving Spirit, the one uniting body of Christ, the one all-working, all-inspiring God [1].'

And of the marriage similitude: 'Again, the unity of the Ecclesia finds prominent expression in various language used by St. Paul on the relation of husband and wife. . . . St. Paul's primary object in these twelve verses is to expound marriage, not to expound the Ecclesia: but it is no less plain from his manner of writing that the thought of the Ecclesia in its various higher relations was filling his mind at the time, and making him rejoice to have this opportunity of pouring out something of the truth which seemed to have revealed itself to him. If we are to interpret "mystery" in the difficult 32nd verse, as apparently we ought to do, by St. Paul's usage, i. e. take it as a Divine age-long secret only now at last disclosed, he wished to say that the meaning of that primary institution of human society, though proclaimed in dark words at the beginning of history, could not be truly known till its heavenly archetype was revealed, even the relation of Christ and the Ecclesia [2].'

The loftiest passage of all is an admirable statement (which unfortunately does not appear to be made cardinal to the thought throughout the volume) from the sermon preached in Emmanuel College Chapel [pp. 272-3]. '*One Body, One Spirit.* Each implies the other. In the religious life of men the Bible knows nothing of the Spirit floating, as it were, detached and unclothed. The operation of the Spirit is in the life and harmony of the parts and particles of the body in which, so to speak, it resides. And conversely a society of men deserves the name of a body in the scriptural sense in proportion as it becomes a perfect vehicle and instrument of the Spirit.'

But striking as much of this teaching appears to be, I must be allowed to comment, on the other hand, on what looks like a somewhat determined refusal on Dr. Hort's part to allow his own arguments to carry him the whole way to their own theological and practical conclusions.

In spite of the glowing emphasis which his language reaches at times about the inward ideal of the unity of the body, it may be permissible to doubt whether he can be said to have stated, with any adequacy, the true relation between this inward ideal

[1] pp. 146, 147. [2] pp. 150-152.

which he recognizes and the organization on earth of a visible Church. I would call attention in particular to the following quotations, which I have grouped together, and I cannot but very seriously question that which appears to be their outcome on the whole. In the first of them it is not so much perhaps the things said, as the apparent drift of the things said, which will raise doubts: 'At first the oneness of the Ecclesia is a visible fact due simply to its limitation to the one city of Jerusalem. Presently it enlarges and includes all the Holy Land, becoming ideally conterminous with the Jewish Ecclesia But at length discipleship on a large scale springs up at Antioch, and so we have a new Ecclesia. By various words and acts the community of purpose and interests between the two Ecclesiae is maintained; but they remain two. Presently the Ecclesia of Antioch, under the guidance of the Holy Spirit speaking through one or more prophets, sets apart Barnabas and Paul and sends them forth beyond Taurus to preach the gospel. They go first to the Jews of the Dispersion, but have at last to turn to the Gentiles. On their way home they recognize or constitute Ecclesiae of their converts in the several cities and choose for them elders. Thus there is a multiplication of single Ecclesiae. We need not trace the process further. We find St. Paul cultivating the friendliest relations beween these different bodies, and sometimes in language grouping together those of a single region; but we do not find him establishing or noticing any formal connexion between those of one region or between all generally. He does however work sedulously to counteract the imminent danger of a specially deadly schism, viz. between the Ecclesiae of Judaea (as he calls them) and the Ecclesiae of the Gentile world. When the danger of that schism had been averted, he is able to feel that the Ecclesia is indeed One. Finally, in Ephesians, and partly Colossians, he does from his Roman habitation not only set forth emphatically the unity of the whole body, but expatiate in mystic language on its spiritual relation to its unseen Head, catching up and carrying on the language of prophets about the ancient Israel as the bride of Jehovah, and suggest that this one Ecclesia, now sealed as one by the creating of the two peoples into one, is God's primary agent in His ever-expanding counsels towards mankind [1]'.

[1] pp. 227, 228.

It is very difficult to be sure how much is meant, or implied, in this refusal to see St. Paul either 'establishing or noticing any formal connexion' between the different Churches. And the difficulty is by no means diminished when we take this first passage in connexion with another, which is not easy to follow, either as to its main thought, or as to the extent to which its main thought may perhaps be qualified (perhaps in more than one possible direction) by the final sentence: 'We have been detained a long time by the importance of the whole teaching of "Ephesians" on the Ecclesia, and especially of the idea now first definitely expressed of the whole Ecclesia as One. Before leaving this subject, however, it is important to notice that not a word in the Epistle exhibits the One Ecclesia as made up of many Ecclesiae. To each local Ecclesia St. Paul has ascribed a corresponding unity of its own; each is a body of Christ and a sanctuary of God; but there is no grouping of them into partial wholes or into one great whole. The members which make up the One Ecclesia are not communities but individual men. The One Ecclesia includes all members of all partial Ecclesiae; but its relations to them all are direct, not mediate. It is true that, as we have seen, St. Paul anxiously promoted friendly intercourse and sympathy between the scattered Ecclesiae; but the unity of the universal Ecclesia as he contemplated it does not belong to this region: it is a truth of theology and of religion, not a fact of what we call ecclesiastical politics. To recognize this is quite consistent with the fullest appreciation of aspirations after an external ecclesiastical unity which have played so great and beneficial a part in the inner and outer movements of subsequent ages. At every turn we are constrained to feel that we can learn to good effect from the apostolic age only by studying its principles and ideals, not by copying its precedents[1].'

In this passage he appears to be drawing distinctions which are hardly intelligible, and to be drawing them almost for the express purpose of avoiding acceptance of the unity of the Church as a really dominant idea. How can the One Ecclesia be made up of all the members of the many Ecclesiae, and yet not be made up of the many Ecclesiae? If he were speaking of denominations in the modern sense, which are doctrinally discordant, and if he

---

[1] p. 168.

intended to sacrifice all idea of external unity, the distinction might be intelligible. But when the difference of 'Churches' is local only—not of doctrine, nor of organization, at all; and when all alike are dependent upon Apostles, and the Apostles are not discordant, but are the focus and symbol of the one indivisable Church, is there any real meaning left in the distinction?

Again, the distinction between a truth of theology and a fact in the region of ecclesiastical politics is, no doubt, for many purposes, a real distinction; yet it passes almost at once into a meaning and use which are not real. That which is a truth of theology may be most imperfectly realized in ecclesiastical fact; but, however imperfectly realized, it is nevertheless an ecclesiastical fact—it has its place, that is, a rightful and necessary place, in the region of outward things; and any mode of speech or thought which should seem to imply that it does not belong to the region of outward things, or that it is not properly to be looked for there, would be, so far, misleading. To put it in another way, a 'study' of principles or ideals is, no doubt, possible which makes no attempt to realize them: but how can you attempt to realize them—how, that is, can you study them to any effect, study them with the character as well as with the abstracted intellect, without aspiring to translate them into practical outwardness? No principle is really alive which is not already on the way to realization in fact. On the other hand, no fact in the region of ecclesiastical politics, nor suggested moral or inference from such fact, can be other than tentative or partial, unless or until it is seen as the embodiment of a theological principle. Only essential principles of the theology of the Incarnation are, to the Christian intellect, really sure or luminous truths.

There is a paragraph, again, in the sermon at Bishop Westcott's consecration, which repeats the same somewhat puzzling denial of a 'unity of Churches,' even while asserting that the unity of the Church is universal: 'The foundation of the teaching now poured forth by the Apostle to the beloved Ephesian Church of his own founding, and doubtless to other Churches of the same region, is laid in high mysteries of theology, the eternal purpose according to which God unrolled the course of the ages, with the coming of Jesus as Christ as their central event, and the summing-up of all heavenly and earthly things in Him. That universal primacy of being ascribed to Him suggests His Headship in relation to the Church as His Body. Presently unity is ascribed to the Church from another side; not indeed a unity such as was sought after in later centuries, the unity of many separate Churches, but the unity created by the abolition of the middle wall of partition between Jew and Gentile in the new Christian society, a unity answering to the sum of mankind. Thus the Church was the visible symbol of the newly revealed largeness of God's purposes towards the human race, as well as the primary instrument for carring them into effect. Its very existence, it seems to be hinted in the doxology which closes this part of the Epistle, was a warrant for believing that God's whole counsel was not even yet made known.' There is much throughout this sermon which is of very stirring character. And yet even at the end of this sermon it must be said that it is not at all easy to determine what is the exact relation which the mind of the author intends between the inner or ideal unity, and the necessary outward and secular organization, of the Church.

All these passages are coloured by the ruling, early in the volume, to which, in the light of my second chapter, I cannot but directly demur : 'Since Augustine's time the Kingdom of Heaven and the Kingdom of God, of which we read so often in the Gospels, has been simply identified with the Christian Ecclesia. This is a not unnatural deduction from some of our Lord's sayings on this subject taken by themselves, but it cannot, I think, hold its ground when the whole range of His teaching about it is comprehensively examined. We may speak of the Ecclesia as the visible representative of the Kingdom of God, or as the primary instrument of its sway, or under other analogous forms of language. But we are not justified in identifying the one with the other, so as to be able to apply directly to the Ecclesia whatever is said in the Gospels about the Kingdom of Heaven or of God [1]'

In spite, therefore, of the stirring character of many passages in *The Christian Ecclesia*, and of the great authority which is inseparable from Dr. Hort's writings, I hope it will not seem presumptuous to suggest that the volume, in its total effect, still lends itself more than enough (on what is, after all, a very

[1] p. 19

important point of Christian intelligence) to what may be called the temper of theological hesitation and reserve. Under certain conditions there may be, it is true, an important place and function for the hesitating and balanced mind on questions of theology. But after all, it is not unseasonable at the present time to insist that this is only a condition of preliminary discipline. It is, after all, conviction, not balance, it is enthusiasm, not reserve; it is theological insight, not theological hesitation; it is the discernment (even, indeed, in things that are outward and practical) of essential principles of the theology of the Incarnation, which—all perils and pitfalls notwithstanding—is the true illumination and glory of the theologian.

Much of what Dr. Hort says in the earlier part of the volume about the representative character of the apostleship[1], and (as I must venture to think) all that he *ought* to mean by it, will I hope be satisfied by the principle insisted on in the 3rd chapter below. But I must suggest that he makes in some passages a somewhat serious misapplication of the legitimate 'argument from silence[2]'; and when he asserts that there is 'no trace in Scripture of a formal commission of authority for government from Christ Himself[3] [to the Apostles]'; or distinguishes in them (by what is surely, in reference to the circumstances, an unreal antithesis) 'a claim to deference rather than a right to be obeyed[4]', or describes their exercise of 'powers of administration' as 'not the result of an authority claimed by them but of a voluntary entrusting of the responsibility to the Apostles by the rest[5]', or when he says, of the laying on of hands for ordination, that 'as the New Testament tells us no more than what has been already mentioned, it can hardly be likely that any essential principle was held to be involved in it[6],' I hope that I may be forgiven for suggesting that he is in such wise attempting to read history apart from presuppositions, as in fact to read it with negative presuppositions of a seriously misleading kind.

[1] See pp 30, 33, 47, 52, &c. [2] pp. 95, 201, 202
[3] p. 84   [4] p. 85.   [5] p. 47.   [6] p 216.

CHAPTER II

THE RELATION BETWEEN INWARD AND OUTWARD

IT will not improbably occur to the minds of some who have in the main agreed with what has hitherto been said, that the real drift of the argument is towards—not a principle of unity, expressing itself in the organization of a visible Church, but rather an invisible unity, independent of, and indifferent to, all external appearance of disunion. Unity, it may be said?—Yes, indeed. But this unity, by the very terms already used, is distinguished as spiritual not mechanical, as ideal not externalized—as lying behind diversity, as unifying diversity, as therefore implying, nay, requiring, the diversity which it unifies; certainly not as incompatible with it. It is the 'unity of the spirit': and unity of spirit is made real, not in proportion as it is expressed by—rather as it is frankly contrasted with—unity of body.

It seems to be therefore worth while, if the conception of what we mean by unity is to be, after all, consistent and practical, to examine more fully this question as to the true relation between the outward and the inward, between the ideal and the real, in the Church of our Lord Jesus Christ.

Now it is undoubtedly true that, in one sense, the unifying, even as ideal, implies a diversity. but the diversity so implied is only a diversity of subjects—a variety of personalities agreeing in one—a diversity sufficient to constitute agreement—certainly not a diversity implying, or consisting in, disagreement. Putting aside, however, this merely abstract form of argument, it still always remains that, in this matter, the ideal and the realization are, to say the least, distinguishable. It is true, moreover, that even upon the very best and most sanguine interpretation, the realization always has halted behind, never has attained, indeed under human conditions as we know them is never likely to attain, its own ideal. In this sense we may truly say that the external and the ideal never have been, never on earth are likely to be, identified. To this extent we are with those who discern that the ideal unity lies behind, and is so far compatible with, that it is not overthrown by, a great deal of *de facto* diversity. But does it therefore follow that the expectation of, or the insistence upon, external unity of organization, is from the point of view of the ideal unity, either mistaken or indifferent? Or, if there be an externally coherent unity, in some relation to the ideal unity, what is the proper nature of this relation? These are the two questions to which, in the present chapter, I desire to attempt to give an intelligible answer.

It cannot but occur to us in the first place that the contrast between unity of spirit, and unity of body, is not scriptural. 'One Spirit; therefore not one Body' says the argument. 'One Body and one Spirit' says the Scripture. Nor, apart from dogmatic phrases, can there be any doubt that, in the history which the New Testament records, the Apostles did enrol Christians into a Body, which at least aimed at unity; and did make most explicit provision for their corporate government and discipline. The very existence of apostolic authority—a background which is never absent from the Church of the New Testament—is in fact a striking witness to unity, both of fact and idea. The practical relation of St. Paul to the corporate life and discipline of the Church at Corinth will occur to every one. It has indeed been often pointed out that there could hardly be a stronger witness to the conception of external and corporate unity than is implied in the very idea of excommunication The extreme Christian penalty, a penalty which transcended all penalties known to the experience of the world, was expulsion. Expulsion from what? From the unity of a visible Church? or from the invisible unity of a Church which existed as ideal only? It might truly be urged in answer that the terror of excommunication lay really in this; that whatever the immediate form of the penalty, its ultimate significance implied the invisible and ideal exclusion. Most true: the visible unity expressed and represented something much greater than itself. But it is quite impossible to deny that that which immediately signified the invisible exclusion was a literal exclusion from a very visible body. The ideal unity was so immediately represented by the visible, that exclusion from the visible human unity carried with it at once all the terror of a Divine exclusion from the invisible and ideal[1]. Excommunication which did *not* mean exclusion from external relations in a body visible and organized, is a form of penalty which certainly never has been, and was never likely to be, tried.

But if this thought is familiar, it may be doubted whether, in relation to the question of external order, sufficient weight is usually attached to what may perhaps without exaggeration be called the lifelong struggle of St. Paul on behalf of the corporate unity of the Church. Many aspects of his struggle with the Judaizing Christians are most familiar. Is it as familiar as it deserves to be in this aspect, as a life and death struggle against the principle of an externally divided Christianity? Upon the gravity indeed of the struggle there is little need to dwell.

From the days of the first serious controversy at Antioch, from the first great victorious field-day at the council of Jerusalem, we pass on in thought to the conflicts of his subsequent work in Gentile cities; we watch him followed with the deadly enmity of Judaistic emissaries—Jews no

[1] See note, p 63

doubt (as he was himself a Jew) but believing, 'Christian' Jews[1]—who dog his steps with implacable hostility from city to city, denouncing his teaching, denying his apostleship, traducing his character; and in his own language of unsparing denunciation we read the appalling nature of their enmity towards him. Or we think of the politic side of St. Paul's great conception of a collection of offerings throughout the Gentile Churches for the Jewish Christians[2]; we watch at one time his eager hopefulness, at another, the depth of his misgivings, about this great peace-offering from Gentile to Judaic Christianity, his hope as culminating in words of triumphant anticipation to the Corinthians[3]; his anxiety, as when he appeals for the prayers of the Roman Church[4] that the saints in Jerusalem may accept the offering for which he had worked so long. And when the crisis comes, we know how grave the peril in Jerusalem—not from Mosaic only but from Christian Jews—was felt and was found to be. And what, after all, is it all about? It may be worth while, from our present point of view, to consider how simply this great anxiety of his life might have been composed, if the things which he had to urge about unity of Spirit could have frankly dispensed with unity of Body, or such doctrinal agreement as is necessary for unity of Body; if he had felt it consistent with Christianity to recognize two types of faith, and two organizations of Christians, who while agreeing in most of the articles of the Christian creed, should yet agree to differ in certain important conceptions of practical life, and be, as Christians, content to remain distinct. If he could so have interpreted his own insistence upon One Lord, One Faith, One Baptism; if he could so have understood the One Body, and the One Bread, as to allow of a Judaic Church over against the Gentile, and a Gentile

---

[1] Acts xv. 1, 2 sqq; cp 2 Cor. x. 10; xi. 5, 12-15 sqq.; Gal. i. 7, 8; ii 4; iv 17; v. 2-12; vi 12, 17
[2] Acts xxiv 17. [3] 2 Cor iv 12-15. [4] Rom xv. 26-33.

Church over against the Judaic, the Judaic Church believing in Jesus Christ very nearly as the Apostles had believed in Him in the early Pentecostal days, that is, with a full observance of the law and a practical ignoring of Gentiles, the Gentile Church believing in Jesus Christ equally, but with a more Catholic inclusiveness of conception, and without any specific reference to Judaism,—how would the sting have been taken out of a struggle which was to St. Paul, in fact, as a lifelong martyrdom, how simply might the great controversy which shook the Apostolic Church have been—not composed so much as avoided altogether from the first!

It seems then to be clear that the idea of a unity which was in such sense transcendental as to dispense with the necessity of any outward expression of its ideal in the form of a practically organized and disciplined union, is an idea which never presented itself to the minds of Apostles at all. On the contrary, the more transcendental their conception of the Divine unity of the Church, so much the more did it follow, as a matter of course, that the Church which expressed that unity, must be, if divinely then also humanly, if in Spirit then in Body, if inwardly and invisibly then visibly and outwardly, One[1]. It is true of course that the

[1] The following passage from Dr. Milligan (*The Resurrection of our Lord*, pp 199-202) is quoted by Canon Gore Its enthusiasm is so directly to the present purpose that I cannot but transcribe it 'If it be the duty of the Church to represent her Lord among men, and if she faithfully performs that duty, it follows by an absolutely irresistible necessity that the unity exhibited in His Person must appear in her. She must not only be one, but visibly one in some distinct and appreciable sense—in such a sense that men shall not need to be told of it, but shall themselves see and acknowledge that her unity is real No doubt such unity may be, and is, consistent with great variety—with variety in the dogmatic expression of Christian truth, in regulations for Christian government, in forms of Christian worship, and in the exhibition of Christian life It is unnecessary to speak of these things now Variety and the right to differ have many advocates We have rather at present to think of unity and the obligation to agree As regards these, it can hardly be denied that the Church of our time is flagrantly and disastrously at fault The spectacle presented by her to the world is in direct and palpable contradiction to the unity of the Person of her Lord, and she

Divine ideal of unity did not disappear because the outward expression corresponded with it imperfectly: and the thought of Judaic Christianity (even though St. Paul's great effort was so far successful) may serve still as a reminder how imperfectly, even from the first, the ideal was realized. but it was the case, as emphatically then as afterwards—and as always—that the way to make spiritual ideas real, is to give them expression of reality in bodily life The bodily expression may, and will, be inadequate· there will always be a contrast—discernible at least, too often deplorable — between its meaning and itself· but even so, underneath whatever weight of failure, until it traitorously disowns its own significance, the imperfect outward will represent, will aspire towards, will actually in a measure express, that

would at once discover its sinfulness were she not too exclusively occupied with the thought of positive action on the world, instead of remembering that her primary and most important duty is to afford to the world a visible representation of her exalted Head In all her branches, indeed, the beauty of unity is enthusiastically talked of by her members, and not a few are never weary of describing the precious ointment in which the Psalmist beheld a symbol of the unity of Israel Others, again, alive to the uselessness of talking where there is no corresponding reality, seek comfort in the thought that beneath all the divisions of the Church there is a unity which she did not make, and which she cannot unmake. Yet, surely, in the light of the truth now before us, we may well ask whether either the talking or the suggested comfort brings us nearer a solution of our difficulties The one is so meaningless that the very lips which utter it might be expected to refuse their office The other is true, although, according as it is used, it may either be a stimulus to amendment, or a pious platitude; and generally it is the latter But neither words about the beauty of unity, nor the fact of an invisible unity, avail to help us What the Church ought to possess is a unity which the eye can see If she is to be a witness to her Risen Lord, she must do more than talk of unity, more than console herself with the hope that the world will not forget the invisible bond by which it is pled that all her members are bound together into one. Visible unity in one form or another is an essential mark of her faithfulness . . The world will never be converted by a disunited Church Even Bible circulation and missionary exertion upon the largest scale will be powerless to convert it, unless they are accompanied by the strength which unity alone can give. Let the Church of Christ once feel, in any measure corresponding to its importance, that she is the representative of the Risen Lord, and she will no longer be satisfied with mere outward action She will see that her first and most imperative duty is to heal herself, that she may be able to heal others also.

perfect ideal which is waiting still to gain, in outward expression, its consummation of reality.

There is, and there will be, a contrast. Often it will seem almost immeasurable. Thus it is that in the New Testament we seem to recognize two, more than distinguishable, pictures: and men may perhaps be excused if sometimes there has seemed to them to be little correspondence between the two. On the one hand, there is the living community of the Church, visible, militant, humanly organized, and subject to all the conditions and experiences of a secular organization of most imperfect humanities: on the other, there is the Kingdom of Heaven, without spot or flaw, transcendent, ideal, the perfection of holiness, the heavenly Bride, the Body of Christ. It would be impossible to deny that (however different their mode of presentment may be) each of these conceptions is, in the pages of the New Testament, most familiar. But what is the true relation between the one and the other? Will any one say that it is a relation merely of contrast? Or will it be said that the relation is so far one of likeness as well as of contrast, that the Church, though it never attains, is at least always aspiring after, and working towards, the ideal of the Kingdom? that the Church—though essentially different—is yet a sort of representation, clumsily executed indeed, and in rough material, of an idea which is never realized by it? that the relation therefore between the Church and the Kingdom may be not unaptly compared to that between an artist's finished sculpture, and the inspiring vision, which it at once reveals, and yet fails to attain? It seems to me that this, even though in part true, is nevertheless a comparison quite inadequate to the truth. For it altogether omits the crucial fact, that the Church is, even on earth, through experience which includes real failures and fractures, still growing, and will (though not under present conditions) so grow as to realize actually and perfectly the whole ideal character of the Kingdom of God. If the artist's sculpture were only the present stage of a work which, through all vicissitudes, would never cease to grow on and on, until it was actually the ideal vision, then and then only would it afford a true measure of comparison.

The Church militant does not merely *represent* the Church triumphant. The Church on earth will not be abolished and ended in order that the Kingdom of Heaven may take its place. But the Church which Christ founded on earth, which from Pentecost onwards, under all its failures and wickednesses, has yet been really the temple on earth of the Spirit,—the Church disciplined, purified, perfected,—shall be found to *be* the Kingdom; the Kingdom of Heaven is already, in the Church, among men. Scripture, which knows so well both the Church and the Kingdom, knows nothing of any antithesis between the two. The 'Kingdom of Heaven' was the phrase under which the first announcement of the Church was made. The parables which portray the growth of the Church, even under human and secular conditions, even with reference, the most express, to the necessary presence and working of evil, not only round about but within the life of the Church, are the 'parables of the Kingdom.' Yet the full and characteristic picture of the Kingdom is not reached till the vision of the twenty-first chapter of the Revelation of St. John.

After all, then, for all our admission of the actual difference—too often the terrible contrast—between the Church as it practically is, and the ideal beauty of the Kingdom, we must claim that the proper relation between these two is not a relation of contrast, not even a relation of resemblance, but is, in underlying and ultimate reality (if the paradox of the phrase may be allowed), the relation of identity

There is an illustration which seems to me to make this very clear—an illustration more pertinent by far than that of the ideal and the attainment. It is the illustration of the continuous personality of an individual saint. What is the relation between Simon Bar-Jona, the affectionate but presumptuous disciple—St. Peter, the leader of the Apostles, the pillar of the Church, who yet (on one occasion) could be 'condemned[1]'—and St. Peter, as we may reverently try to conceive of him, throned, crowned, glorified, in the glory of his LORD, in heaven? Difference there is indeed, no question—more than we can measure. Yet no vastness of difference impairs the far deeper truth, that they are one and the same. The rash Simon was not destroyed that St. Peter might be created in his stead. But the enthusiast became the saint—with imperfection, and the saint, with imperfection, became the saint in glory. Look backward in retrospect from the beatified saint; and he, even himself, *was*—Andrew's brother Simon. Look back in retrospect from the consummated Kingdom; and it, even itself, *was*—the visible, humanly organized, struggling, imperfect, society of the Church. As, to scripture language, the individual Christian is, from the first, a 'saint'; so, to scripture language, that is, to the language of the divinest truth, the struggling organization and polity of the Church is, from the first—even when to us such words seem almost terrifying—all that the ideal vision of the Kingdom is.

There is another way in which this illustration will be helpful for our present purpose. *Why* does Scripture —that is, why does Truth—call a sinful man a saint? or a very human society the Kingdom of God? Not certainly as denying the humanness, or the sin; but because, in those whom God is drawing and perfecting, even the true fact of sin is not the truest fact of the character. Sinful and human they truly are: but they *more truly* are that which, by God's grace, they are even now becoming. There are grades of truth truth more essential, and truth more accidental; truth more external, and truth

---

[1] κατεγνωσμένος, Gal. ii. 11.

more profound, a more transient, and a truer, truth. So with man, in the bodily life. What is he? It is the simple truth that he is flesh and blood. It is also true that he is a spiritual being. He is Spirit, of Spirit, by Spirit, for Spirit. Even while the lesser and the lower continues true, the higher is the truer truth. That man is spirit, is a deeper, more inclusive, more permanent, *truer* truth than that man is body. In comparison with this truth, the truth that he is body (though true) is as an untruth. It is a downright untruth, whenever or wherever, in greater measure or less, it is taken as contradicting, or impairing, or obscuring the truth that he is Spirit. Thus St. Paul does not hesitate roundly to deny the truth of it—'Ye are not in the flesh, but in the Spirit, if so be that the Spirit of God dwelleth in you'—denying it, of course, in the context of his thought, with absolute truth; even though the proposition that the Roman converts were in the flesh might seem to be, in itself, one of the most undeniable of propositions. Of course this is an inversion of the verdict of natural sense. If natural sense would say, Man's bodiliness is the fundamental certainty, man's spirituality is only more or less probable, there is another point of view to which man's spirituality is so the one overmastering truth, that even his bodily existence is only a truth so far as it is an incident, or condition, or expression, of his spiritual being. As method of Spirit, it is true, and its truth is just this—to be method or channel of Spirit.

Such is the case of the individual man, he is obviously bodily, he is transcendently spiritual. His bodily life is no mere type, or representation of his spiritual; it *is* spiritual life, expanding, controlling, developing under bodily conditions. The real meaning of the bodily life is its spiritual meaning. The bodily is spiritual.

And conversely, the spiritual is bodily. Even when he is recognized as essentially spiritual, yet his spiritual being has no avenue, no expression, no method, other than the bodily; insomuch that, if he is not spiritual in and through the body, he cannot be spiritual at all. Is he then bodily or spiritual? He is both; and yet not separately, nor yet equally both. If his bodily being seems to be the primary truth, yet, on experience, the truth of his spiritual being is so absorbing, so inclusive, that his bodily being is but vehicle, is but utterance, of the spiritual; and the ultimate reality even of his bodily being is only what it is spiritually. He is body indeed, and is spirit. Yet this is not a permanent dualism, not a rivalry of two ultimate truths, balanced over against one another, while remaining in themselves unrelated. More exactly, he is Spirit—in, and through, Body.

Just so it is with the Church. The visible Body *is* the spiritual Church—is so really, even while it most imperfectly is; as the living man (in himself too truly a sinner), while he is, at the best, only most inchoately and imperfectly, yet to the eye of the Almighty Truth, which sees the blossom in the bud, the fruit in the seed, the end in the beginning, is truly, because he is truly becoming, a saint[1]. In external truth, the most primary, the most obvious to the eye, the Church is a human society, with experience chequered like the experience of human societies; in its inner reality, it is the presence and the working, here and now, of the leaven of the Spirit; it does not represent—but it *is*—the Kingdom of God upon earth. The real meaning of all the bodily organism and working of the Church is the spiritual meaning. Whatever is not expression of Spirit is failure. And conversely, here as everywhere, the working of the Spirit must be looked for in and through organisms which are bodily. In the world of our

---

[1] The expression of Clement of Alexandria is striking· Οὕτω τὸ πιστεῦσαι μόνον καὶ ἀναγεννηθῆναι τελείωσίς ἐστιν ἐν ζωῇ· οὐ γάρ ποτε ἀσθενεῖ ὁ Θεός. Ὡς γὰρ τὸ θέλημα αὐτοῦ ἔργον ἐστί, καὶ τοῦτο κόσμος ὀνομάζεται οὕτως καὶ τὸ βούλημα αὐτοῦ ἀνθρώπων ἐστὶ σωτηρία, καὶ τοῦτο ᾽Εκκλησία κέκληται. Οἶδεν οὖν οὓς κέκληκεν, οὓς σέσωκεν· κέκληκεν δὲ ἅμα καὶ σέσωκεν, Paedag. 1. p. 114. Cp the Augustinian phrases, 'Tales nos amat Deus, *quales futuri sumus*, non quales sumus ... Per [fidem] perveniemus ad speciem, *ut tales amet, quales amat ut simus*, non quales odit quia sumus,' de Tim 1 21.

experience at least, body, rightly understood, means spirit: neither is there any working of the spirit which is not through body. The visible body then, of the Church, is real, and its outward process and history, as body—the history (so to speak) of its chemical analysis, or the history of its material development—are real: yet the truth of these is as untrue, in comparison with the overmastering truth of its spiritual reality, which alone gives, even to these, their real significance. and even the very truth of these becomes a downright untruth, in so far as it ever is used, in greater measure or less, to contradict, or impair, or disguise the truth of its essential being as Spirit. So worse than idle is it—so positively misleading—to try to analyze the material history (so to speak) of the body of the Church, as if it were an explanation of what the Church is. It would be as profitable for the chemist or the anatomist, as such, to pronounce upon the ultimate meaning of the being of man.

It will be observed that what has now been insisted upon is the full, and (in a sense) the balanced statement of a truth which has two aspects. It is fatal to the understanding of the being of man either to deny that he is bodily, or to deny that he is spiritual; either to deny that the meaning of the bodily is its spiritual meaning, or to deny that the method of the spirit is through body. I speak of this as *in a sense* a balanced statement, because the balance is not precisely equal. If in a sense it is true that the body and the spirit are, as predicated of man, both equally true; it is, as already explained, a truth deeper and truer to deny that the truths are ultimately equal. They are not balanced: the one gradually disappears in the other. Yet, for present purposes at least, they stand out against one another as mutually indispensable aspects of one complex truth. For any real understanding of the Church, or its ministries and sacraments, it will be found, in like manner, indispensable to realize to the full the two aspects of this truth and their mutual relation.

What has been said enables us to insist, with the utmost possible emphasis, upon the essential character of the Church as Spirit. If the spiritual work of the Church has instruments, organs, ordinances, if these have an existence which may be described as mechanical and material, yet their entire reality of meaning and character is spiritual. 'It is the Spirit that quickeneth; the flesh profiteth nothing · the words that I have spoken unto you are Spirit, and are Life[1].' The whole reality is Spirit If any of those who are inclined to protest against external ordinances lay all their stress upon this principle, we desire on our part to lay it down with an emphasis so sweeping that they may find it impossible to say it more sweepingly than we. If they demur to the idea that there can be any absolute value or reality in formal practices—including in this phrase the whole sacramental or ministerial system—we too echo every such word to the very uttermost, we sympathize to the full; nay, we lay down this principle for ourselves, and build upon it as an indispensable foundation of truth. There is no true meaning or reality whatever but Spirit Only just as, in man's life, the Spirit, which alone is the essential meaning and reality of human life, must have expression through bodily organs and actions; and the over-mastering truth of Spirit does not diminish the truth, in its subordinate place and degree, of body: so in the life of the Church, the very reality of the Spirit cannot but express itself through definite methods and processes; which orderly forms and methods, so far from having in themselves any absolute reality or value, only exist for this, in order that they may be— only are real after all just so far as they really are—not formal realities, arithmetical, ponderable, measurable, but reflexions, expressions, activities of Living Spirit. The Spirit is the meaning of the Body, the Body is the utterance of the Spirit. The Body is not therefore an unfortunate condescension, an accidental and regrettable necessity.

[1] John vi. 63.

However gross it may be apart from its animating meaning; yet as vehicle of Spirit, which is its true function, it rises to the full dignity of that which it expresses, nay, it no longer merely expresses, in its true essence already it may be said to *be* Spirit. It is an error, somewhat Manichaean in character, to treat Body, the Body of Spirit, as mere condescension. The Body of Christ, whether Personal or Mystical, is what Christ is, in respect of dignity. 'A body didst thou prepare for Me[1]' is a word which has true significance in reference to the Body of the Church.

It is from this point of view that we cannot but criticize the opening position of Bishop Lightfoot's famous essay upon the 'Christian Ministry.' He insists, truly in the main, upon the Church's essential existence as spiritual. But he uses this truth to deny the reality of her proper existence as bodily; and then, being forced to deal with her existence as bodily, he treats it, not (in analogy with every experience of this world, an experience consummated and consecrated in the Incarnation for ever), as the living, proper method and utterance of Spirit, but as a lower, politic, condescending, accidental necessity: not as something to be identified with, interpreted by, more and more absorbed into, but rather as to be contrasted with, and (if it were possible) disowned by, its own spiritual meaning. He contrasts the ideal and the actual of the Church · not, as in any age he well might do, on the ground that in the Church as it is, the outward order expresses its own animating Spirit so imperfectly, but because its Spirit is expressed in any outward order at all[2]. It is

[1] Hebrews x. 5
[2] Bishop Lightfoot's essay opens thus 'The kingdom of Christ, not being a kingdom of this world, is not limited by the restrictions which fetter other societies, political or religious It is in the fullest sense free, comprehensive, universal. It displays this character, not only in the acceptance of all comers who seek admission, irrespective of race or caste or sex, but also in the instruction and treatment of those who are already its members. It has no sacred days or seasons, no special sanctuaries, because every

necessary, with all respect, to insist that this position cannot be either philosophically or theologically maintained. Accepting for the moment the imagery which the word 'ideal' suggests (though I have tried already to show

time and every place alike are holy Above all it has no sacerdotal system. It interposes no sacrificial tribe or class between God and man, by whose intervention alone God is reconciled and man forgiven. Each individual member holds personal communion with the Divine Head. To Him immediately he is responsible, and from Him directly he obtains pardon and draws strength.

'It is most important that we should keep this ideal definitely in view, and I have therefore stated it as broadly as possible Yet the broad statement, if allowed to stand alone, would suggest a false impression, or at least would convey only a half truth. It must be evident that no society of men could hold together without officers, without rules, without institutions of any kind; and the Church of Christ is not exempt from this universal law. The conception in short is strictly an *ideal*, which we must ever hold before our eyes, which should inspire and interpret ecclesiastical polity, but which nevertheless cannot supersede the necessary wants of human society, and, if crudely and hastily applied, will lead only to signal failure As appointed days and set places are indispensable to her efficiency, so also the Church could not fulfil the purposes for which she exists without rulers and teachers, without a ministry of reconciliation, in short, without an order of men who may in some sense be designated a priesthood '

And two pages later he writes 'This then is the Christian ideal; a holy season extending the whole year round—a temple confined only by the limits of the habitable world—a priesthood coextensive with the human race.

'Strict loyalty to this conception *was not held incompatible with* practical measures of organization. As the Church grew in numbers, as new and heterogeneous elements were added, as the early fervour of devotion cooled and strange forms of disorder sprang up, *it became necessary to provide for the emergency* by fixed rules, and definite officers. The community of goods, by which the infant Church had attempted to give effect to the idea of an universal brotherhood, must very soon have been abandoned under the pressure of circumstances. The celebration of the first day in the week at once, the institution of annual festivals afterwards, *were seen to be necessary to* stimulate and direct the devotion of the believers The appointment of definite places of meeting in the earliest days, the erection of special buildings for worship at a later date, *were found indispensable to* the working of the Church But the Apostles never lost sight of the idea in their teaching. They proclaimed loudly that "God dwelleth not in temples made by hands." They indignantly denounced those who "observed days and months, and seasons and years." This language is not satisfied by supposing that they condemned only the temple worship in the one case, that they reprobated only Jewish sabbaths and new moons in the other. It was against the false principle that they waged war; the principle which

that for the purpose this imagery is inadequate), we must certainly insist, with the utmost emphasis, that the ideal would be, not a Church without holy times and holy places, without ministries or sacraments, without order or expression, without (in a word) all that we have hitherto tried to express by 'body'; but a Church whose entire outward expression as 'body' did at every point simply express, and perfectly correspond to, its spiritual import; a Church whose outward order so perfectly revealed and expressed, that it could, not untruly, be said to *be*, Spirit

The analogy with the individual is still the most instructive analogy. An ideally spiritually man is not a man without body; but a man whose whole bodily life is a perfect expression of spirit. Nor indeed is there any form of expression, other than the bodily life, by which, under any conditions intelligible to us, the most perfectly spiritual man could act, speak, or live spiritually at all.

It is, then, the greatest possible mistake to imagine that if the Church on earth could for one moment be ideally spiritual, special seasons, or places, or ordinances, or ministries, or sacraments, would, in that atmosphere of perfect spirituality, dwindle into comparative insignificance. On the contrary, being, as they would by hypothesis be, the perfectly undimmed and faultless expression of the highest spiritual possibilities, they

exalted the means into an end, and gave an absolute intrinsic value to subordinate aids and expedients These aids and expedients, for his own sake and for the good of the society to which he belonged, a Christian could not afford to hold lightly or to neglect But they were no part of the *essence* of God's message to man in the Gospel; they must not be allowed to obscure the idea of Christian worship

'So it was also with the Christian priesthood. For communicating instruction and for preserving public order, for conducting religious worship and for dispensing social charities, *it became necessary to* appoint special officers.'

The italics in this second passage (except the word *essence*) are mine. They illustrate the Bishop's conception of external expression or method as an unfortunately inevitable necessity of condescension.

would be—not merged but accentuated, not obscured but illumined; they would be more conspicuous, more dominant, more profound and august in their reality than they are in any form of the Church that now is

Now this opening position of Bishop Lightfoot's may be said to be the basis of his whole conception of ministry. and this one criticism, if accepted, as I must submit that it needs to be accepted, would affect the entire balance of his argument

There is another criticism also, which belongs rather to the argument of the first than of the present chapter, which is to be made upon the opening pages of the essay. It will be observed that Bishop Lightfoot's initial statement of the ideal reality of the Christian Church is conceived in a wholly individualistic form 'Each individual member holds personal communion with the Divine Head.' This is the keynote. Everything else is more or less an 'economy' subordinate to this Practical measures of organization were only 'not held incompatible with' an ideal, to which, as it seems, humanity as a collective term—'man'—was never a corporate unity at all. Each individual severally, and therefore (as it were, by accidental consequence) all—this is what the ideal seems to mean Again I must submit that the other mode of thought, viz. humanity, as a total unity—in Adam, or in Christ—and therefore each individual as an item within the total unity, would be, whether philosophically or theologically, a conception far more vitally true Of course either aspect of the thought will ultimately, in a sense, imply and include the other. But the inferences which follow from the one or the other mode of statement, in respect of the meaning of corporate unity in the Church, and the dignity, in a spiritual reference, of articulated order and coherence of mutual relation, will be almost immeasurably different.

It seems, then, that there is a disproportion in Bishop Lightfoot's initial position; and that the disproportion is in the direction of so magnifying the inward and spiritual meaning as to undervalue the outward and bodily expression of the Church. If so, this may be said to be a very restrained and gentle form of a tendency of mind which has been not unfamiliar in Church history, and which has more than once been carried, with unrestrained logic, to destructive practical conclusions. Unbalanced insistence upon the spiritual, to the prejudice of the bodily, pressed home with a fierceness more relentless than spiritual, we recognise it as the animating temper of Montanism. Montanism would be in any case too directly relevant to the present purpose to be passed over altogether in silence: and the language which has been recently used about it, on some sides, makes it the more imperative to refer to it. From being a mere heresy, it has come to be spoken of as though it were the conservative retention of a more original conception and practice of Church life—almost as though the Catholic Church were the heretic, and only Montanism truly orthodox[1].

[1] These words may not unfairly describe the tone of various Church writers upon the subject. Dr. Hatch's statement upon the subject is in part quoted below, p 51 sqq The extreme conclusion is itself formulated in the *Expositor*, third series, vol. v p 231 (March 1887), by Professor Rendal Harris: 'The few surviving notes which we have with regard to the Montanists would have told us the whole story, if we had been willing to read them, without the prejudice and persistent misunderstanding which we have inherited from the Church of the second century Even now, with the master-key in his hand, Dr. Sanday does not seem to see that the only legitimate conclusion from his admissions is that Montanism was primitive Christianity.

When Dr Sanday goes on to say, "there was an *element* of conservatism in it," he seems to me to altogether understate the case, and to take his key out of the lock and throw it back again into the swamp from which a good genius had fetched it Sound in morals (for no one now believes the ridiculous and contradictory scandals with which they were besmeared), and pure in faith (for even the Catholics admitted their orthodoxy), inspired in utterance and expression (perhaps even to a fault), their only error is found in discipline; *that is, in their continuity with primitive times* It is no reproach to them that, in their desire to save the Church, they themselves became cast away on the rocks of the new organization St. Paul might have suffered the same if he had been the junior of Ignatius instead of his predecessor.' I quote this passage as somewhat significant in its place in the discussion in the *Expositor*, but it is not upon the position of Professor Rendal Harris that I intended to comment in the text

I have no wish to speak with any impatience of this altered conception of the spiritual aspirations of Montanism. But if it may, in some respects, be discerning and instructive, I cannot doubt that it is ill-balanced; and that, like all exaggerated statements of truth, it leads speedily to error. The positive truth which Tertullian desired to emphasize, in his somewhat scornful attack upon the authority of the organized Church, is a truth which is always necessary and important The essence of the Church is the Personal Presence of the Spirit. Upon this truth, in this form, it is impossible to insist too emphatically. 'Ecclesia proprie et principaliter ipse est Spiritus, in quo est Trinitas unius Divinitatis Pater et Filius et Spiritus Sanctus' But Tertullian does not rest here. From this positive he infers a negative—the very negative which, as has been argued above, it does *not* contain. He infers that *therefore* the Church, in respect of its visible organization and officers, is not the proper Body of the Spirit. He draws, on the contrary, an antithesis between the one and the other If the Church is the Spirit, it follows, to him, that the episcopate is not the mouthpiece or government of the Church. If the episcopate is accepted, the Church is no longer the Spirit. It is either 'Ecclesia Episcoporum' or 'Ecclesia Spiritus[1].' They stand in antithesis as alternatives. To choose either is to lose the other. This is not merely a complaint that the bishops were in fact too often unspiritual. It is a repudiation of the episcopal system, as antithetical to spirituality.

Now it is necessary in the first place to insist unreservedly, in exact accordance with the position already stated, that this is altogether a false antithesis: and that while Tertullian's main positive is a truth immovable and of priceless value, his negative inference is an exaggeration and an untruth. This being clear, it is of interest to ask what leads him into exaggerating? Montanism is

[1] De Pudic., xxi. fin. (p. 574).

characterized by Bishop Lightfoot as being in this regard 'a rebound from the aggressive tyranny of hierarchical assumption.' The 'extravagant claims' which provoked this 'strong spiritualist reaction[1]' he recognizes principally in the 'Ignatian letters' on behalf of Catholicism and in the Clementine writers in the interests of Ebionism. Now it may be perfectly true that in the generations which followed the Ignatian letters there was an exaggeration of the external organization of the Church, and an overstatement of its intrinsic value. It may be perfectly true that the correlative 'spiritual' exaggeration of Montanism was provoked by natural and, to a certain extent, healthy reaction. How far Ignatius would himself be responsible for this, whether his own letters were unbalanced and misleading or not, is a question for our present purpose of minor importance. That his own mind or language was untrue would certainly not follow from an admission of the fact that it was the occasion of untruth in others. That when he pleaded for unity with the bishops everywhere and always, his words were ardent words, fired with a genuine fervour of enthusiasm, is obvious. That he dwelt upon the truth which was aflame within him, without staying simultaneously to relate it in exact proportion with all other aspects of the truth, is certain.

But all these qualities, it is to be remembered, are consistent with divine truth. One and all, they are characteristic of the mind and writing of St. Paul. Truth, which is many-sided, cannot wholly be conveyed at once. The insistence, at one moment, upon one side of truth only, even to the extent of apparent paradox, and with the apparent effect of confounding the advance towards truth of minds which, having no touch of illumining moral ardour, were just rationally balanced and nothing more, belongs to the familiar methods of the teaching of Jesus Christ Himself. That St. Paul's doctrine of justification by faith

[1] Lightfoot, p 237, Hatch, p. 122.

was the occasion of Antinomian extravagance in others is patent even on the evidence of the pages of the New Testament. Vehement as the appeals of St. Ignatius are, and in this—the true scriptural—manner one-sided, it may yet be doubted whether they contain anything which is in itself untrue.

We justly complain of one-sidedness, and call it error, in Tertullian: not because he enlarges, with ardour, upon his side of the truth, but because he so uses his truth as to deny the truth which is its proper complement. If Ignatius misused his insistence upon episcopal order, to deny that the essence of the Church was the presence of the Living Spirit, we should at once convict him of an error, similar in kind, but more serious than that of Tertullian. It would be more serious for this reason: because of the two mutually supplementary truths—the Ignatian truth of outward order, the Tertullianist truth of inward spirit; we can have not a moment's hesitation in asserting that the spiritual truth is the deeper, the more transcendent, the one which ultimately, in a sense, includes and absorbs the other. But it absorbs it—not by abolishing or denying, but by establishing, informing, characterizing it with itself. Though Spirit be higher than Body, yet Body also is true; and Spirit is through Body. Now Tertullian so affirms Spirit, as to deny Body. Ignatius, fervent as is his vindication of Body, never uses it for the denial—never tends towards denial, or in any sense under-valuing—of Spirit. Still whatever may be said in this way about St. Ignatius himself, it may be admitted, if the admission is desired, that his letters were calculated to produce, in the popular mind of ordinary Christians, an excessive idea of the formal and (as it were) independent value of external order; calculated, at least in the sense, and to at least the extent, in which St. Paul's letters were calculated to suggest to the 'unlearned and unstable' a new opening for Antinomian excess.

Dr. Hatch, when he comes to Montanism, introduces

it thus: 'Then came a profound reaction. Against the growing tendency towards that state of things which afterwards firmly established itself, and which ever since has been the normal state of almost all Christian Churches, some communities, first of Asia Minor, then of Africa, then of Italy, raised a vigorous and, for a time, a successful protest. They reasserted the place of spiritual gifts as contrasted with official rule. They maintained that the revelation of Christ through the Spirit was not a temporary phenomenon of apostolic days, but a constant fact of Christian life. They combined with this the preaching of a higher morality than that which was tending to become current.' I quote these words because (apart from the apparent implication that real discipline and government, as from above, was only a growing novelty in the Church) they strike a note which will come home to every Christian as of deep and enduring value. But unfortunately even these words describe, more literally than they appear to do, the vice as well as the virtue of the spiritual protest. To protest, on behalf of spiritual Christianity, against every touch of *formalism* in official rule, is a necessity of every generation of the Church. But to protest against 'official rule' is to protest in fact against the conditions divinely and inextricably attached to every movement of life within human experience.

Further on Dr. Hatch writes: 'In theological as in other wars the tendency is to cry "Vae victis!" and to assume that the defeated are always in the wrong. But a careful survey of the evidence leads to the conclusion that, in its view of the relation of ecclesiastical office to the Christian life, the Montanism, as it was called, which Tertullian defended, was theoretically in the right, though its theory had become in practice impossible. It did not make sufficient allowance for changed and changing circumstances. It was a beating of the wings of pietism against the iron bars of organization. It was the first, though not the last rebellion of the religious sentiment against official religion¹.' There is so much, both in these words and in the pages from which they are quoted, with which it is impossible not to feel a strong underlying sympathy of sentiment, that it may seem to be the more invidious, but perhaps is in truth the better worth while, to try to distinguish in them what is said in due proportion and what is not. Perhaps the 'Vae victis' warning is most serviceable to us in the form of a reminder that while no form of false theory is wholly without truth, it is sometimes the case that the amount of truth in theories which the Church has justly repudiated as a whole is at once very large and very important. But what is really meant by saying that Tertullian's 'spirituality' was theoretically right, yet in practice impossible? To admit that it was in practice impossible is at least to impair the sense in which it could be pronounced theoretically right. An ideal which is out of relation with possibility is likely to be an ideal misconceived. The thought appears to be like that of Bishop Lightfoot's opening paragraphs—as though outwardness were, even in this world, an unfortunate condescension, diplomatically necessary, instead of being the inevitable condition, to inwardness. Any way the practical necessity is admitted in fact. But it would have been better and truer to have laid it down, not as a degrading concession, but as a divinely ordered principle of life, that in this world the expression of Spirit is Body, and that inward unity is revealed and lives in the harmony of visible union

The last sentence quoted will carry us a little further. I must insist again that when Dr. Hatch speaks of the rebellion of 'religious sentiment against official

---

[1] In the page which intervenes between these two quotations Dr Hatch represents the Montanist theory and claim about Church organization as if it did not differ from the Catholic Church *at all* except in its view of cases of emergency; claiming in the absence of clergy, and then only, an extreme and exceptional possibility of lay ministry This may be true in the main; and it certainly fairly represents one well-known passage. But the phrase 'non ecclesia numerus Episcoporum' implies really much more than this.

religion' he is bound to mean, not official religion *simpliciter*, but 'officialism in religion,' or whatever other phrase would imply that the 'official' has *unduly* asserted itself to the prejudice of the 'spiritual' character of religion. With this correction I have already agreed that the statement may very probably represent a historical truth about Montanism and Tertullian. With rich allusiveness Dr. Hatch speaks of it as 'the first, though not the last' such protest. Here again, with the statement of fact and with the sentiment which lies behind the statement, every serious Christian will be in eager accord. Indeed, it is important to insist that, as long as human frailty remains in the Church and her ministries, the spiritual protest which asserted itself (and went astray) in Montanism will continue to be urgently needed In every age of the Church human imperfectness, in its use even of the simplest and the sacredest forms, tends naturally, more or less, towards mechanical formalism. Therefore human imperfectness always keeps, and will keep, alive the necessity for earnest protest against mechanical adherence to form. On some sides, and in some ages, the whole fabric of Christian faith and worship has seemed to become such a lifeless weight of formalism that spiritually minded men might well be excused if their indignant protest on behalf of spiritual life took the shape of unrelenting attack upon forms which had seemed to have become irremediably formal. It may be true, perhaps, that there is no age, nor place, in which the protest is not needed. Yet it is a protest which too easily overreaches itself. And in fact the protest, if made against not formalism only but form (however provoked and therefore in individuals morally excusable), is really a demand for conditions of spiritual life which are literally and absolutely impossible. There is much in the feeling which underlies Dr. Hatch's sympathetic and interesting pages about Montanism that is really attractive. So far as this spirit of Montanism is a reaction against mechanical officialism, it will have high place and value in the Christian character just as long as man is imperfect. Yet even in this particular—without going into any question either of its more audacious claims about the possession and utterance of the Holy Ghost or of its Puritan conception of discipline—we must take leave still to maintain that the instinct of the Catholic Church which rejected Montanism was the instinct of abiding truth.

The protest which in the ancient world is so far identified with the name of Tertullian is at least as familiar in the modern world as in the ancient. Probably it comes out for us into strongest prominence in the history of Quakerism But the doctrine which is most characteristic of the Society of Friends does in fact lie at the root, not only of a very large part of pious non-conformity in many denominations, but also of the critical and separatist tendency which is so very familiar a characteristic, in our parochial congregations, of many even of those who do conform. Certainly we do not need to speak of this at all less sympathetically than either of Montanism or of Dr. Hatch's conception of Montanism. It is perhaps the first instinct of a piety which, while genuine, is inexperienced and ill-informed, to try to realize its new-found earnestness, not by means of, but in contrast with, the traditionally received expressions of piety. The man who, living in the midst of Christian traditions and customs, wakes up for the first time to a real sense of personal religion, does often, not quite unnaturally, identify the whole fabric of Christian traditions in the practice of which he himself had religiously slumbered, with the slumber in which he had practised them; and seems to himself to find, in his very revolt against tradionally orthodox faith and practice, a pledge of his personal reality. With all this instinct, as with the Montanist spirit in its best form, it is possible to feel a great deal of sympathy.

Nevertheless the reactionary protest is extravagant,

and the practical outcome of its extravagance is in a high degree desolating and destructive. To get rid of form is of course impossible The attempt to do so ends really in the substitution of such forms as seem to be least like forms—forms, that is, the most unintelligent and uninspiring—in the place of those which are most venerable, and which, if they had been richly animated, not swept away, by the newly inflowing tide of spiritual life, would have been found to be the most significant, the most edifying, and the most abiding. For a while indeed the new piety lives on in spite of its isolation from Christian history and its poverty of outward expressiveness. But the fire which sustains the first enthusiasts does not sustain their successors: there is lack of fuel to replenish it, lack of historical continuity, lack of adequate expressiveness or authority of form: in the long run spirit corresponds with body, as body with spirit; and those who have tried to cut loose from what seemed to them merely outward, find more and more, in fact, that in losing reality of body they have been losing reality of spirit too.

Take the words in which Canon Curteis describes the central aspiration which animated the thought of George Fox: 'His first great doctrine is this (and it is also the doctrine of the Catholic Church); that the visible and outwardly organized Church, with all her hierarchy, her canons, her ritual, her creeds, her sacraments, is nothing more than the shell (as it were) of the living creature, the scaffolding of the real building, the means and not the end, the casket and not the jewel[1].' Without staying to consider whether every one of these four metaphorical parallels will hold, it is worth while to say that the obvious meaning which they are endeavouring to express is one with which we cannot too cordially sympathize. God the Holy Spirit—the Spirit of the Incarnate Son, who is the Revelation of the Father—is the end, the reality, the essence, the life of the Church.

[1] 'The Church and Dissent' Bampton Lectures for 1871, pp. 258, 259.

Everything outward is outward, and the outward, at best, is the mere expression of the inward. But no insistence on this truth will get rid of the necessity—nay the sanctity—if not inherent, yet real, of the expressing outward. Nay, the more profoundly the one central truth is grasped, so much the more august, and profound, because really and utterly spiritual, will be felt to be whatever belongs to the due and authorized representation or conveyal of that one supreme inward reality, which is God Himself. Whether it be urged by Montanist, or Quaker, or Plymouth brother, or any other variety of pious Nonconformist or over-scrupulous Churchman, the antithesis between spirit and body—true as it is for certain purposes, and up to a certain point—breaks down utterly and disastrously when pushed on to the point, not only of significant distinction, but of real antagonism. The disavowal of body will not hold of the Body of the Church, at least until it holds of the body of the individual saint.

The passage from Canon Curteis expressly contrasts 'means' with 'end,' and this phrase of his, at least, we may unreservedly adopt. The same distinction occurs in the early pages of Bishop Lightfoot's essay. After conceding the practical necessity of external organization and ordinances, the Bishop argues that 'the Apostles never lost sight of' an ideal to which these were foreign. 'They proclaimed loudly that "God dwelleth not in temples made by hands." They indignantly denounced those who "observed days and months and seasons and years" This language is not satisfied by supposing that they condemned only the temple worship in the one case, that they reprobated only Jewish sabbaths and new moons in the other. It was against the false principle that they waged war; the principle which exalted the means into an end, and gave an absolute intrinsic value to subordinate aids and expedients. These aids and expedients, for his own sake and for the good of the society to which he belonged, a Christian could not afford to hold lightly or neglect But they were no part of the *essence* of God's message to man in the Gospel: they must not be allowed to obscure the idea of Christian worship[1].'

Now we should desire to protest as strongly as Bishop Lightfoot or any one could do, against any confusion of means with ends; or against giving to methods, however divinely appointed, what could be *in strictness* called an 'absolute' or 'intrinsic value.' These last phrases, however, would require to be carefully discriminated; for though the value of such methods belongs to them wholly and only as they truly represent, and by Divine Grace are empowered to convey, a spiritual which is not themselves; yet when they do so truly represent and convey, the language of Scripture (which comes nearer after all to the living truth than do the distinctions either of science or of logic) speaks of them absolutely as 'being' that which, in the particular relation, they are made in effect to be. There is therefore a sense, and a supremely true one—even though it be distinct from either logical or scientific exactness —in which, under circumstances, their value may be called inherent, and even 'absolute': just as 'body,' whenever regarded (by impossible abstractness of logic) as *mere* body, means, in strictness of the term, 'not Spirit'; and yet, in proportion as Body attains its true meaning, behold its animating character, its vivifying reality, after all, therefore, its essential meaning—simply *is* Spirit.

That Bishop Lightfoot completely ignored this distinction is obvious, not only from the general use which he makes of the thought of this passage, but, in the passage itself, from the sudden introduction—where we should have expected such a word as 'methods' in the sense just indicated—of the alternative and very depreciatory phrase 'subordinate aids and expedients.' Neither 'aids' (to what?) nor 'expedients,' are adequate words;

[1] p. 182.

but the word 'subordinate' begs the whole question at once, and begs it in the wrong sense. The clause should rather run, 'the principle which exalted the means into an end *per se*, or gave any value (*apart from* the Spirit expressed by them) to methods whose one real meaning was the Spirit they expressed.' It could not *then* have been added that the Christian's respect for such methods[1] was based upon considerations which appear to be regarded as human and politic; though the phrase 'for his own sake and for the good of the society to which he belonged' is capable of expressing a sanction far more august than the text appears to intend.

'But,' Bishop Lightfoot adds — though not to be despised or neglected—'they were no part of the *essence* of God's message to man in the Gospel.' Now upon this phrase I have two comments to make. First, I have tried already to make clear a sense in which I should submit that all Christians must agree in saying that neither ministries nor sacraments can properly be called the essence, or even a part of the essence, of the Life of the Church. The 'Spirit of the Incarnate' alone is the essential Life of the Church. But to deny that 'methods,' taken in their detail, are, properly, even a 'part of' the essence of the Church's Living Being, is one thing; to deny that they are even a part of 'God's message to man in the Gospel' is another. This second phrase, which is the one used by Bishop Lightfoot, appears to be a much vaguer one, and might well be considered to include not only the theological exposition of what is the *essentia* of the Church's Life, but also such precepts or practices as are, in the Gospel Revelation, prescribed to man, with a view

---

[1] It is to be remembered that at this stage of the argument the word 'methods' would have to contain any methods, however divinely commanded, simply as being methods. Whether there are any divinely ordered methods or not, or, if any, what methods are ordered divinely, is an inquiry not yet opened. What is here said by the Bishop is said of methods or means simply because they are such; and, as such, belong to the world of outward and visible ordinances.

to the Life of the Church. If so, whatever is part of the divinely ordained method, is part of the essence of 'God's message to man in the Gospel'

But there is another consideration of some value, based upon the practical difference of meaning between the noun 'essence' and the adjective 'essential.' If I am asked, are ordinances part of the '*essentia*' of the Church's being, I may well hesitate: there is a sense in which they are; and there is a sense in which they are not. If I am asked, are ordinances essential to the Church's life, I can have no hesitation at all. Most assuredly they are. But they may be indispensable conditions of the essence; the appointed—conceivably even the only possible— methods of the essence; in the second instance, therefore, in their practical working, by God's will identified with the essence · and yet, after all, so distinguishable from the essence, that I might hesitate to assert that they 'were' the essence itself. Nor, in that case, would the phrase 'part of the essence' help me. In the sense in which I should shrink from calling them 'the essence,' I could not possibly admit that they were 'part of the essence'; for God is not divisible into parts. But though there be this hesitation about the word 'essence,' the meaning practically borne by the adjective 'essential' does not correspond to this. It does not mean, in effect, 'constituting the essentia,' but 'indispensable'—as condition or otherwise—with a view to the essentia; which is precisely the meaning which we pointedly retain at the very moment when (it may be) we let the word 'essence' go. Canon Gore, in his criticism of the passage, assumes outright, that when Bishop Lightfoot denies that methods are any 'part of the essence' he intends to assert that they are non-essential[1].' In reference to the practical course of the argument, this assumption is perhaps not unreasonable.

---

[1] Appendix A, p. 355 'He is not, of course, using *essence* in any metaphysical sense, but in such sense as that what is essential is equivalent to what is necessary.' The distinctions of this Appendix are very valuable.

Yet, since Bishop Lightfoot's statement is in the former shape, and not the latter, I would prefer to suggest that, not having the distinction before his mind, he passes (at most), by imperceptible and unconscious transition, from his actual statement, which thus far is tenable, to an untenable meaning, which appears to be, but is not, practically identical with his statement. Moreover, he does not altogether so pass. It may well be that he would not actually have used the word non-essential. But if so, the ambiguity which remains between the two forms of thought is not otherwise than characteristic of an essay which has notoriously been open to so much doubtful and mistaken interpretation.

Now, having drawn this distinction, and insisted that ordinances, whether asserted or denied to be 'of the essence' of the Church's Life (either of which methods of speech is tenable), are at all events 'essential,' in the sense of being God's own appointed and imperative conditions and methods of the essence, it becomes necessary for us still to ask in what sense this 'essential' necessity is asserted. Is the necessity, in every conceivable case, self-acting and absolute? Is it incapable of exception? The question is enough to carry the answer; and the answer is thoroughly familiar. They are essential in the sense that, in so far as we are commanded by God to use them, we have no power of dispensing with the use of them, or of obtaining, otherwise than by the use of them, the gifts which God has bidden us find in and through their use. So far, at least, the old instance of Naaman's leprosy is strictly applicable. If God prescribed the use of Jordan water, the use of Jordan water became by God's command, as, on the one hand, efficacious with the efficacy of almightiness, so, on the other, indispensable with the necessity of God. If God has ordained Christian ordinances, then Christian ordinances have become—just in proportion as He has laid them upon us—both 'essential,' and (though in a secondary sense) even 'intrinsically' efficacious. As it would have been obviously futile for Naaman to have drawn a distinction, either, in respect of his own duty, between bathing in Jordan on the one side, and obeying God on the other, or, in respect of his own blessing, between bathing in Jordan on the one side, and recovery from leprosy on the other, for in either case, when God had spoken, the distinction had absolutely ceased to be,—so, in respect of Christian ordinances, *if or in so far as they are divinely ordained*, it would be futile, and even meaningless, for a Christian to try, as it were, to cut in either between such ordinances, spiritually used, on the one hand, and, on the other, Christian homage of faith, or obedience, or love ; or between such ordinances, spiritually used, on the one hand, and, on the other, the very richness of the presence and life of the Spirit of Jesus Christ. It is the old distinction. If God is not in any way bound to His own appointed methods of grace, yet we are. Outside His appointed 'media' of whatever kind — ministries, sacraments, ordinances — He can work, if He will, as divinely as within them. He can cleanse with Abana, or with Pharpar, or with nothing, as effectually as with Jordan. But that is nothing to us, if He has bidden us to wash in Jordan. So, if there are, in His Church, divinely prescribed ministries and ordinances, the consideration that He is not bound to ministries and ordinances, even though it be true, becomes nothing — but a snare — to us. It may serve indeed somewhat to the lowliness of our thoughts ; it may abash us from the presumption of even imagining, at any time, anything like a judgement of others, whose case before God is known to Him, not to us. But used as a guide to our own conception or conduct, it could have no effect, expect to mislead

The necessity, then, which is asserted (contingently upon there being Divine ministries, &c., at all) is a necessity not simply self-acting, like the operations of a physical quality; it is a necessity, not of a material but of a moral kind, a necessity which, by its inherent character as moral, cannot but have real relations to varying conditions of understanding and of opportunity; a necessity which appeals alike to our belief and our obedience, with a moral power indefinitely the greater, just because it is *not* either in all cases literally universal, or in any case visibly demonstrable.

The gradations, the exceptions, are not for us to define. The fact that they exist modifies the sharp logic of our abstract theory of necessity: it holds us back, even in thought, from the concrete judgement of individuals. But it does not alter, in the least, the moral obligation which rests upon us who understand, to make clear to ourselves, and to those to whom we can make clear, what belief and obedience require—of them and of us. To those who have eyes to see and hearts to understand, the dutiful use of Divine 'methods' (if any such there be) is a necessity 'essential' to obedience, and to faith It is a necessity, like all moral necessities, not stupidly inexorable, but characterized and informed by the inherent attribute of equity.[1] It is a necessity which itself is part of the revelation of God—so far as God is revealed. It is a necessity therefore, not of blind law, as the order to Naaman first seemed to be, but of the Supreme perfection of Wisdom and Equity, as the order to Naaman was. It is part of the wisdom of the Spirit to understand the necessity —what it is, and what it is not. It is a necessity, in so far, at least, as there is insight to discern its necessity, not

---

[1] It is interesting in this reference to contrast the position of Hooker and his opponents in reference to the necessity of Baptism. Both were dealing with the fact of the existence of 'equitable' exceptions. The opponents said, Because equity requires the admission of exceptions, therefore the necessity of Baptism is an untenable doctrine. Hooker, reversing the argument, replied, Because equity is inherent, as of course, in the 'necessity' of a Divine command to intellect or character, therefore the only objection to the doctrine of the necessity of Baptism falls to the ground. Equitable interpretation, in his view, is not a qualification, far less the negation, but rather an inalienable attribute or element, of a moral necessity.

to enable God, but to authorize and to enable us. To discern and to characterize the necessity aright, is to determine the question, not so much of Divine possibility as of Divine revelation, and therefore of human validity and obedience. We want to know, not within what limits God *can* work, but by what methods He has revealed that He does; and therefore wherein and whereby we ourselves may, dutifully and securely, meet and find Him, and live and grow into Him, in Spirit and in Truth.

NOTE, p. 32.

THE visible exclusion none the less expresses the invisible—and finds its whole meaning and terror in expressing it—even though it is not only distinct from it, but in ultimate motive even contrasted with it. It is inflicted in order that the invisible (which it immediately expresses) may *not* be incurred.

CHAPTER III

THE RELATION BETWEEN MINISTRY AND LAITY

THE discussion in the last chapter was quite general in kind. It referred to 'media' as such. It was only hypothetically assumed that there are such things as divinely ordered 'media' in the Church of Christ. To any specific method or ordinance there was no reference at all. An attempt was made, however, to vindicate the idea of such divinely ordered media; to maintain their necessity as essential to the valid security — of the rendering of human faith and service upon the one hand—of the receiving of Divine grace upon the other; and to relate this doctrine of 'essential means' with the unmeasured freedom of the goodness of God. Such means in truth are no limiting of the goodness of God: they are a defining to man, in terms humanly intelligible, of the methods by which his access, and his blessing, may securely be realized, while they emphasize, in this defining, the reality of man's corporate life, as brotherhood At no point, at no moment, are they a substitute for service spiritual and personal· but they say, Combine to render your spiritual service *thus* *thus* believe· and *thus* do, individually alike and corporately: for thus God is pledged to receive you, and to enrich They are a reaching out of infiniteness to finiteness, an accommodation of the invisible to the visible; they are (since to our senses the invisible and the infinite mean the indefinite and the uncertain) a condescension of heaven to conditions of earth; an anticipation — in terms of faith, yet in circumstances of material life — of the interpenetration of Humanity with Deity. Their apparent limitation constitutes, to us, being such as we are, their definiteness, and their security; the sure certainty of their comfort, the glory of their condescension.

But the subject more immediately before us is not sacramental ordinances in general, but in particular the rationale of an apostolic ministry. Now any serious discussion of ministry may seem to imply, and the preface to our Ordinal expressly asserts, alike the perpetuity and the necessity of ministerial order within the Church. Assuming, then, in the light of the last chapter, the *fact* of the necessity, it is important to ask what, and how much, is meant by asserting that it is necessary. What is the relation that results between this Ministry and either the Body as a whole, or the Laity, if the Laity be regarded apart? How much is contained, or implied, in the principle of an indispensable ministry?

Would it mean that, in the Church of Christ, which is the very home of Divine privilege and perpetual possibility of access to God, this access and these privileges are committed not to the Body of the Church as a whole, but only to a few—a caste, or a class, through whom, and through whom only, all others, as outsiders, must be content to have their mediated access? Is our ministerial order, in this sense, a sanctified intermediary, higher in official status, nearer in Divine intimacy, holier in the sanctity of personal life, and, as such, set to stand and to mediate, between the mere *plebs Christiana* and their God? Is the immediate possibility of access of all human spirits to the Father of Spirits, through the Person of Jesus Christ, either denied in it, or in any way qualified?

It is, I conceive, matter of quite capital importance that those who consider the meaning of Christian ministry should raise clearly, and fully answer, this question to themselves. The question, as just put, contains phrases tenable and untenable; but almost all of them, whether untenable or tenable, would require to be carefully discriminated before the answer given would be clearly intelligible. It would be comparatively easy to answer the question with a negative, and the simple 'no' would be, no doubt, much nearer to the truth than a simple 'yes.' But a simple 'no' after all neither illumines, nor explains, anything at all. Moreover, it would probably deny much truth as well as untruth. To make then our answering position really clear, it is desirable to express it rather more fully, in the form of certain principles, which appear to be fundamental to an understanding of what is properly meant by any assertion, on the part of Churchmen, of the indispensableness of consecrated 'order.'

I. First, then, the Church is, in Scripture language, a Temple and a Body. It is the Body of Christ. It is the Temple of the Holy Ghost. The truth which is expressed under either image is that its inner life is the Presence of the Spirit; and that the outer fabric of its articulated corporate movement and growth is but essentially the expression of a Presence, the Body of a Spirit. What then, exactly, is this spiritual Body; and of whom does it consist? Most emphatically we reply, that it consists of, and means, not in any way the clergy as such, but the whole corporation or Church of Christ; into which Christian Baptism primarily admits: in which, by laying on of hands, members pass to full exercise of that spiritual franchise or privilege of Divine citizenship (in real sense, even, of Divine priesthood), to the whole of which, from the moment of Baptism, they already possessed an inherent and implicit right. The spiritual privilege, the Divine access, the life of, and with, and by, and unto God, are essentially the possession of all, not of some; of the whole Body, primarily, as a whole (for the corporate life precedes and transcends the individual); of individuals, as they are true members of the Body, not as they are members to whom this function, or that, in the organism of the Body, is assigned. The language in which Scripture insists on this principle of the oneness of the total Body, and of the necessity of the total Body for oneness, is reiterated and emphatic· 'For even as we have many members in one body, and all the members have not the same office; so we, who are many, are one body in Christ, and severally members one of another[1].' 'For as the body is one and hath many members, and all the members of the one body, being many, are one body; so also is Christ[2]' In both passages, and with

[1] Romans xii. 4.
[2] 1 Cor. xii. 12. The passage goes on· 'For in one Spirit were we all baptized into one Body, whether Jews or Greeks, whether bond or free; and were all made to drink of one Spirit For the body is not one member, but many. If the foot shall say, Because I am not the hand, I am not of the body; is it therefore not of the body? . And if they were all one member, where were the body? But now they are many members, but one body. And whether one member suffereth, all the members suffer with it; or one member is honoured, all the members rejoice with it. Now ye are the Body of Christ, and severally members thereof. And God hath set some in the Church, first apostles, secondly prophets, thirdly teachers, then miracles, then gifts of healings, helps, governments, divers kinds of tongues. Are all apostles? are all prophets? are all teachers? are all workers of miracles? have all gifts of healings? do all speak with tongues? do all interpret? But desire earnestly the greater gifts. And a still more excellent way show I unto you. If I speak with the tongues of men and of angels, but have not love, I am become sounding brass, or a clanging cymbal,' &c, &c Take with this Eph. iv. 11-16 'And He gave some to be apostles; and some, prophets; and some, evangelists; and some, pastors and teachers; for the perfecting of the saints, unto the work of ministering, unto the building up of the Body of Christ till we all attain unto the unity of the faith, and of the knowledge of the Son of God, unto a fullgrown man, unto the measure of the stature of the fulness of Christ; that we may be no longer children, tossed to and fro and carried about with every wind of doctrine, by the sleight of men, in craftiness, after the wiles of error; but speaking truth in love, may grow up in all things into Him, which is the Head, even Christ; from whom all the Body fitly framed and knit together through that which every joint supplieth, according to the working in due measure of each several part, maketh the increase of the Body unto the building up of itself in love' And 1 Pet ii. 4, 5: 'Unto whom coming, a living stone, rejected indeed of men, but with God elect, precious, ye also, as living stones, are built up a spiritual house, to be a holy priesthood, to offer up spiritual sacrifices, acceptable to God through Jesus Christ.' And 9, 10: 'But ye are an elect race, a royal priesthood, a holy nation, a people

great fullness in the latter of them, the principle is expressly applied to the thought of differences of function, and of dignity of function, in the body, which, despite all difference of function and apparent dignity, is none the less itself one coherent unity of parts which are mutually dependent, severally incomplete.

II. If the Body is not some, but all; and the powers and gifts inherent in the life of the Body are the powers and gifts which, so far, belong to all; and the Spirit which is the Body's life, is the Spirit of all; what is the relation of ministers specifically ordained, to this total life and power of the total Body? Clearly they are not intermediaries between the Body and its life. They do not confer life on the Body, in whole or in part. But they are organs of the Body, through which the life, inherent in the total Body, expresses itself in particular functions of detail. They are organs of the whole Body, working organically for the whole Body, specifically representative for specific purposes and processes of the power of the life, which is the life of the whole body, not the life of some of its organs. 'They are for public purposes the organs of the Body's life; but the great life itself, the great deposit of the spiritual life remains in the Body at large[1].' This is the truth, which gives a touch of enthusiasm to much of the language of the fifth of Dr. Hatch's Bampton Lectures, an enthusiasm with which, so far as it really rests upon this truth, it is impossible not to sympathize. But it is important to distinguish this truth most sharply from an inference which it does not contain. We therefore explicitly lay down

III. The fact that the organs represent, and live by, the life of the whole body, does not mean that the rest of the body can dispense with the organs. If any

for God's own possession, that ye may show forth the excellencies of Him who called you out of darkness into His marvellous light which in time past were no people, but now are the people of God which had not obtained mercy, but now have obtained mercy'

[1] Bampton Lectures, 1868 Lect ii. p 60

organs are missing, it does not follow that all the rest of the body put together can discharge the special functions which the missing organs were made to discharge. A body however otherwise complete cannot see without eyes, hear without ears, or run a race without legs. Still less does it follow, because the eye (say) is an organ of the whole body, living and seeing by, and not apart from, the body's life, that therefore any and every other member of the body severally has the same functional power as the eye for seeing. Nor again does it follow, because the life of the eye is the life of the body, specialized for a particular functional purpose, that therefore its sight-capacity is conferred upon the eye at the will or by the act of the body. Neither any other member in detail, nor the body as a whole, conferred upon the eye its capacity of seeing, or can transfer that capacity to any other organ, or can itself in any other way exercise the capacity of vision, if it should lose the eye The eye is but an organ of the body by which the body sees, the hand is but an organ of the body by which the body strikes. But the body did not confer upon hand or eye their capacity of striking or of seeing for the body. It is therefore abundantly plain that, whatever may be true upon other grounds, it most certainly is not contained as a logical inference within the principle that Church ministers are organs of the life of the Body of the Church, and not intermediaries between the Body and Life; that therefore the rest of the Body, even all put together—much less than any and every individual member of it—is already *de jure* a minister, or that the authority of the ministers to minister is derived from, or is conferred by, the mere will or act of the Body

For the fuller illustration of this distinction and its consequences, I may be allowed to refer to the entire argument of my father's Bampton Lectures[1]. It is there

[1] *Administration of the Holy Spirit*, by the late Bishop of Salisbury; the Bampton Lectures for 1868, pp. 60, 61.

stated directly as follows · 'The analogy so much presented to us in Holy Scripture, of the natural body of a man, can hardly, as it seems to me, be pressed too far in its strong and close bearing upon my present point One vitality diffused over the whole, special organs for special services of general and indispensable use, all needful for each, each needful for all; — does not the likeness seem to fit in every particular, showing by an example of which every one of us is fully capable of judging how "the whole" spiritual "body fitly framed together, and compacted by means of every joint of the supply, according to the working in the measure of each several part, maketh the growth of the body unto the building up of itself in love?" The strength and health of the whole natural body is needed to enable each separate member and limb, each bodily organ and faculty, to discharge its own proper functions successfully; and yet no one of these separate members or organs derives its own peculiar functions nor the power to exercise them in the first place from that strength and health. The nervous sensibility helpful to the eye as the organ of sight, or to the ear as the organ of hearing, or to the other organs for the discharge of their respective offices, is diffused over the whole body; yet not only do these organs not derive their peculiar powers from that diffused sensibility, but if the organs themselves be from any cause inoperative, no such diffused sensibility can restore them. The body is absolutely blind, if the eye cannot see, and entirely deaf if the ear cannot hear. The case appears to be closely, I might say singularly, parallel to that of the spiritual body, and may very justly, as it does most forcibly, illustrate the case of a priesthood, strictly representative in its own proper being, yet receiving personal designation and powers, not by original derivation from the body which it represents, or continual reference to it, but by perpetual succession from a divine source and spring of authorizing grace.'

The thought thus expressed appears to be exactly

reflected by Canon Gore, when he is speaking of the relation of ministry, as such, to the Body as a whole: 'It is an abuse of the sacerdotal conception, if it is supposed that the priesthood exists to celebrate sacrifices or acts of worship in the place of the body of the people or as their substitute..... The ministry is no more one of vicarious action than it is one of exclusive knowledge or exclusive spiritual relation to God. What is the truth then? It is that the Church is one body. The free approach to God in the Sonship and Priesthood of Christ belongs to men as members of "one body," and this one body has different organs through which the functions of its life find expression, as it was differentiated by the act and appointment of Him who created it. The reception, for instance, of Eucharistic grace, the approach to God in Eucharistic sacrifice, are functions of the whole body. "*We* bless the cup of blessing," "*we* break the bread," says St. Paul, speaking for the community; "*we* offer," "*we* present," is the language of the liturgies. But the ministry is the organ—the necessary organ—of these functions. It is the hand which offers and distributes; it is the voice which consecrates and pleads. And the whole body can no more dispense with its services than the natural body can grasp or speak without the instrumentality of hand or tongue. Thus the ministry is the instrument as well as the symbol of the Church's unity, and no man can share her fellowship except in acceptance of its offices [1].'

It is a cognate thought which is in Dr. Milligan's mind

[1] *The Church and the Ministry*, pp. 85, 86. I refrain from quoting, but must make reference to, a similar passage on pp. 93, 94, which substitutes a Christianly corporate, for Bishop Lightfoot's individualistic, basis of Church polity (see above, p. 46): 'Each Christian has in his own personal life a perfect freedom of access. But he has this because he belongs to the one body.... The individual life can receive this fellowship with God only through membership in the one body and by dependence upon social sacraments of regeneration, of confirmation, of communion, of absolution—of which ordained ministers are the appointed instruments. A fundamental principle of Christianity is that of social dependence.'

when he says, of the prophetical office of the Church, 'It may, for the sake of order, be distributed through appropriate members; but primarily it belongs to the Church as a whole, the life of Christ in His prophetical office being first her life, and her life then pervading and animating any particular persons through whom the work of prophesying is performed[1].' It is hardly necessary, at this point, to canvass the precise meaning or adequacy of the phrase 'for the sake of order.' Dr. Milligan is engaged rather in vindicating the priority of the corporate life and powers of the Church than in distinguishing the exact nature or sanction of the authority of those who, ministerially, exercise her powers. And it is plain, I imagine, that his thought, even when emphasizing most the priority of the collective Church, never, as if by necessary logic, infers that ministerial authority must needs be either conferred by those who themselves have it not, or implicitly possessed, *de jure*, by all Christians alike.

It would not be very good logic to confound the universal with the distributive 'all.' If 'all Englishmen,' i e universally, the total nation, could abolish rights of property, it does not follow that 'all Englishmen,' i e. distributively, any one who is English, has authority to abolish property; nor, if the rights of 'all Englishmen,' i. e. universally, are, for certain purposes, representatively exercised by the sovereign, does it follow either historically that the sovereign was appointed by popular vote, or even that there *could* not be such a thing as a sacred succession and Divine right to be king.

The distinction, then, between these two thoughts, the thought on the one hand that the ministry represents the whole Body, and (under whatever sanction) wields, ministerially, authority and powers which, in idea and in truth, inherently belong to the collective life of the Body as a whole; and the thought, on the other hand, that every member of the Body is equally of right a minister,

[1] *The Ascension of our Lord*, p. 236, cp also pp. 222, 223, 229, &c

or that, if there be a distinctive right to minister, it is conferred by the voice of the Body simply, *without* authorizing or enabling empowerment of directly and distinctly *Divine* ordaining, is a distinction of absolutely vital importance for the understanding of the rationale of ministry.

This distinction, however, is one which, for whatever reason, is not before the mind either of Dr. Hatch or of Bishop Lightfoot at all. I said just now that it was impossible not to sympathize with the generous warmth which seems to underlie much of Dr. Hatch's language upon the priestly character of the Church as a whole. But it was not easy to quote language which would express this without *ipso facto* implying that, in the original and ideal Church, one and all had the implicit right of ministering alike in sacred things; an idea which, I venture to think, even the New Testament alone is sufficient to disprove[1]. I may now however venture to quote some of his sentences, strongly commending the one half of his meaning, whilst as strongly protesting against the ambiguous inclusion (as I must hold) of untruth in the other half. 'In those early days—before the doors of admission were thrown wide open, before children were ordinarily baptized and men grew up from their earliest years as members of a Christian society, before Christianity had become a fashionable religion and gathered into its net fish "of every kind," both good and bad—the mere membership of a Christian Church was in itself a strong presumption of the possession of high spiritual qualifications. The Christian was in a sense which has often since been rather a satire than a metaphor, a "member of Christ," a "king and priest unto God." The whole body of Christians was upon a level; "all ye are brethren." The distinctions which St. Paul makes between Christians are based not upon

---

[1] Cp. e. g. Acts xiv. 23; xx. 28; 1 Cor. xii. 29; to say nothing of the pastoral Epistles.

office, but upon varieties of spiritual power.¹' Again: 'There was a vivid sense, which in later times was necessarily weakened, that every form of the manifestation of the religious life is a gift of God—a χάρισμα, or direct operation of the Divine Spirit upon the soul. Now while this sense of the diffusion of spiritual gifts was so vivid, it was impossible that there should be the same sense of distinction between officers and non-officers which afterwards came to exist. Organization was a less important fact than it afterwards became².' Upon the exaltation of the ideal of the lay life, which clearly ennobles these passages, I shall have something to add presently. Meanwhile, Dr Hatch, after speaking of the growth of Church organization (in the second instance as he thinks, and in exaggerated form), goes on: 'Then came a profound reaction³' (i. e. Montanism). 'They' (Montanists) 'reasserted the place of spiritual gifts as contrasted with official rule⁴.' 'The view which he (Tertullian) took of the nature of office in the Church was that it does not, as such, confer any powers upon its holders which are not possessed by the other members of the community⁵.' 'The fact of the existence of Montanism, and of its considerable success, strongly confirms the general inferences which are drawn from other evidence, that Church officers were originally regarded as existing for the good government of the community and for the general management of its affairs: *that the difference between Church officers and other baptized persons was one of status and degree: that quoad the spiritual life, the two classes were on the same footing:* and that the functions which the officers performed were such as, apart from the question of order⁶, might be performed by any member of the community⁷.'

¹ p. 121. ² p. 122. ³ p. 122. ⁴ p. 123. ⁵ p. 124.
⁶ i. e. no doubt, orderliness, τάξις, 'propter ecclesiae honorem'; not technically 'Ordo' or 'Orders.' It is like Bishop Lightfoot's phrase 'has *for convenience* entrusted'; see below, p. 76
⁷ p. 125

I have italicized two of these clauses because (as will presently appear) they are as admirable upon the principles advocated in these pages as upon Dr. Hatch's own. But it is the final clause which shows what Dr. Hatch's distinctive position really is. He proceeds in the same lecture to exhibit in part, and give the explanation of, the very real and serious disproportion in the way of over-statement of ministerial distinction and power which has been only too familiar in some parts of Church history; and he concludes it in words whose solemnity of feeling and aspiration we can re-echo with hardly the less of sympathy because we are convinced that they are exegetically misconceived: 'But in earlier times there was a grander faith. For the kingdom of God was a kingdom of priests. Not only the "four and twenty elders" before the throne but the innumerable souls of the sanctified upon whom "the second death had no power" were "kings and priests unto God." Only in that high sense was priesthood predicable of Christian men. For the shadow had passed; the Reality had come; the one High Priest of Christianity was Christ [1].'

It will be remembered that the thought which is still immediately before us is the thought of ministers, as organs of the whole Body, specialized for certain particular functions, which are necessary for the life of the whole, in function, so far, distinct, not dependent simply upon any act or will of the whole for their functional empowerment and authority; yet being none the less, even in their most distinct functional activity, organs representative and expressive of the living capacity or inherent prerogative of the whole. Now when, with this leading thought, we turn to Bishop Lightfoot's essay, it is impossible not to be struck with the extent to which this thought, if he admitted it, would modify large sections of his argument. The last twenty-five pages of the essay he devotes to discussing and exposing 'Sacerdotalism.'

[1] p. 142.

It would be quite premature to enter upon any discussion of that word here. But this is perhaps the time to notice that, at least in large part, sacerdotalism seems to Bishop Lightfoot to mean, or at all events (amongst other things) to imply, the precise contradictory of our present principle —the doctrine that 'sacerdotal ministry' is *not* representative of, but is something exclusive and apart from, the life of the Body as a whole. He sets the two ideas, of sacerdotalism on the one hand and representative ministry on the other, in sharp antithesis, as alternatives. An account of ministry (however otherwise 'sacerdotal'), which began by insisting on the harmony of the two, as a position fundamental for understanding the rationale of ministry, would cause at once the larger part of his argument to fall as irrelevant to the ground.

Thus he says (speaking of what he regards as an earlier and purer ministerial conception), 'Hitherto the sacerdotal view of the Christian ministry has *not been held apart from* a distinct recognition of the sacerdotal functions of the *whole Christian body*. The minister is thus regarded as a priest, because he is *the mouthpiece, the representative of a priestly race*[1]. . . . So long as this important aspect is kept in view, so long as the *priesthood of the ministry is regarded as springing from the priesthood of the whole body*, the teaching of the Apostles has not been directly violated.' It will be observed that these two sentences (and particularly the phrases which I have italicized), though capable of misinterpretation, would stand as the natural expression of the very view which has been maintained above. But that, to Bishop Lightfoot, they contain and mean the very thing which has been protested against above, is clear from the sentence which in his paragraph intervenes between the two. It is this. 'Such appears to be the conception of Tertullian, who speaks of the clergy as separate from the laity *only* because the Church *in the exercise of her prerogative* has *for convenience* entrusted to them the

[1] *Philippians*, p. 256. The italics throughout these sentences are mine.

performance of certain sacerdotal functions belonging properly to the whole congregation, and of Origen, who giving a moral and spiritual interpretation to the sacerdotal office, considers the priesthood of the clergy to differ from the priesthood of the laity only in degree, in so far as the former devote their time and their thoughts more entirely to God than the latter.'

Of Tertullian and Origen I will speak a little further presently. Meanwhile compare the way in which the two sentences quoted below are written by Bishop Lightfoot together, as if they were but two ways of conveying practically the same thing. After having said, 'In such cases (viz. the weekly alms, oblations, prayers, thanksgivings, &c) the congregation was represented by its minister, who thus acted as its mouthpiece and was said to "present the offerings" to God: so the expression is used in the Epistle of St. Clement of Rome: but in itself it involves no sacerdotal view;' he adds these two sentences: 'This ancient father regards the sacrifice or offering as the act of the whole Church performed through its presbyters. The minister is a priest in the same sense only in which each individual member of the congregation is a priest[1].' It is difficult to see on what ground the Bishop makes the assertion of the latter sentence at all, except on the assumption that it is identical with that of the earlier. But this at least it certainly is not. Even the earlier assertion, though true, is not capable of being deduced from the phrase (to which he refers) in Clem. ad Cor. 44.

One more sentence may be quoted: 'The point to be noticed at present is this; that the offering of the Eucharist, being regarded as the one special act of sacrifice and appearing externally to the eye as the act of the officiating minister, might well lead to the minister being called a priest and then being thought a priest in some exclusive sense, where the religious bias was in

[1] p. 260.

this direction and as soon as the true position of the minister as the representative of the congregation was lost sight of[1].' Here, it will be observed, the idea of 'representing the congregation' is in express terms made directly antithetical to the idea of an official priesthood, a priesthood, that is, appertaining to the ministers more than to other individual members of the congregation. This is precisely the confusion of which we complain. That a 'representative' priesthood (which we strongly assert) implies, in a real sense, the priestly character of the Church as a whole, we should altogether insist: that it implies that any other members of the Church than her ordained ministers are authorized to stand as the Church's representative *personae*, in order to exercise ministerially the functions by which expression is given to her priestly character, we both repudiate as inference, and also deny in fact.

That Tertullian, as especially in the well-known passage, quoted both by Bishop Lightfoot and Dr. Hatch, went too far in the direction of this false inference, may be admitted[2]; that in so doing he rather overstated a

[1] p 261.
[2] *De Exhort. Cast* vii 'Vani erimus si putaverimus quod sacerdotibus non liceat, laicis licere Nonne et laici sacerdotes sumus? Scriptum est Regnum quoque nos et sacerdotes Deo et Patri suo fecit Differentiam inter ordinem et plebem constituit ecclesiae auctoritas et honor per ordinis consessum sanctificatus Adeo ubi ecclesiastici ordinis non est consessus, et offers et tinguis et sacerdos es tibi solus. Sed ubi tres, ecclesia est, licet laici. . . . Igitur si habes ius sacerdotis in temetipso ubi necesse est, habeas oportet etiam disciplinam sacerdotis, ubi necesse est habere ius sacerdotis. Digamus tinguis? digamus offers? quanto magis laico digamo capitale erit agere pro sacerdote, cum ipsi sacerdoti digamo facto auferatur agere sacerdotem.'
These are the words which have been held to be so capital I have been content to take them in their ordinary interpretation : but must own that their meaning does not seem to me so absolutely clear 'Sacerdos es *tibi solus*' seems to represent a very different thought from any right, under supposed necessity, to minister congregationally It sounds more like what any modern High Churchman would say of a Christian secluded from all access to Church ordinances It will be said no doubt that the 'et offers et tinguis' exclude such an interpretation. Perhaps they do but it does not seem to me at all impossible that a writer, who can be so rhetorical as Tertullian, would express himself

truth than stated what was wholly an untruth[1], is implied in the position as set forth above: that he should have, just in this way, overstated his truth, seems to be the most natural consequence in the world from his admitted Montanism; from the imperfect perception of the relation between 'outward' and 'inward' which is a basis of Montanism; and from the attitude of conscious depreciation of the sacredness of external order, and even of protesting opposition against it, into which his Montanism necessarily drew him[2]. It is difficult to

thus, without meaning necessarily more than that 'your own prayers and spiritual communings take the place of preaching, praising, baptizing, confirming, communicating—everything whatever.' Such a rhetoric, and the precise form it here takes, would be made all the more probable, because there would anyhow be a limited sense in which both the 'offers' and the 'tinguis' might seem to be literally predicable of occasions in domestic lay life: the 'tinguis' as representing the ultimate possibility 'si necesse est' of baptizing, the 'offers' as not wholly inapplicable to the habitual reception in private of the sacrament reserved. After all, it is Tertullian who says, *de Baptismo*, 17, 'Alioquin [sc. salvo Ecclesiae honore] etiam laicis ius est [sc. dandi baptismum]'; and again, it is Tertullian who writes of the Christian wife of a heathen man (*ad Uxorem*, II. v.), 'non magiae aliquid videberis operari? non sciet maritus quid secreto ante omnem cibum gustes? et si sciverit panem, non illum credit esse qui dicitur? Et haec, ignorans quisque rationem, simpliciter sustinebit? sine gemitu? sine suspicione panis an veneni?' Such a familiar possibility as these words contemplate must form part of the atmosphere through which we distinguish the meaning of Tertullian. I am not suggesting, however, that Tertullian is here so much speaking, directly and literally, either of Baptism *in extremis*, or of private self-communicating; but rather that, in a passage which is primarily rhetorical, the possibility of these two things enters in, partly to give a sense of justification to, partly to determine the precise form of, the rhetorical phrases.

It will be understood that these remarks affect the meaning of Tertullian's apparent assumption that a layman, as such, was admittedly capable of administering sacraments. They affect it particularly as evidence of contemporary custom or thought. But they do not affect the use which Tertullian makes of the assumption, whatever the assumption itself may mean. He undoubtedly uses it for the purpose of wiping out all real distinction between ministry and laity, and reducing it to a mere arrangement of ecclesiastical orderliness. It is curious to see how he helps himself herein by the word 'priests,' and the quotation from Rev. v. 10. The word 'priest' lent itself to this ambiguity, as the words 'apostle,' 'bishop,' 'presbyter,' 'deacon,' had never done.

[1] In the sense explained in chapter ii. p. 50.

[2] Cp., as in the last chapter, p. 48, the distinction drawn between the 'ecclesia episcoporum' and the 'ecclesia spiritus,' in the *de Pudicitia*, xxi.

see how, under these conditions, he *could* have dwelt upon the 'universal priesthood'—as he does to noble and valuable purpose—without shaping it in just this false way. That Bishop Lightfoot should put aside the fact that the treatise was written by Tertullian the *Montanist*[1], as a fact of no importance to the character of his evidence, is astonishing[2]: it would have been impossible, if Bishop Lightfoot himself had had his eyes fixed on the truth, that it is not the 'scriptural doctrine of an universal priesthood' (which 'was common ground to [Tertullian] himself and his opponents'), but rather the perverted statement and misuse of this doctrine (which was to a Montanist practically inevitable), that really stands in any antithesis against the 'sacerdotal view of the Christian ministry.' To Tertullian's own characteristic assertion of this view, under other circumstances, the Bishop himself draws sufficient attention[3].

Before leaving Tertullian it may be well to call explicit attention to the fact that the references to him have unavoidably mixed up two questions that are really distinct. Our proper subject at present is the distinction

---

[1] Cp also the opening of the *de Monogamia* 'Haeretici nuptias auferunt, Psychici ingerunt . . . Psychicis non recipientibus spiritum ea quae sunt spiritus non placent Ita dum quae sunt spiritus non placent, ea quae sunt carnis placebunt, ut contraria spiritui Caro inquit adversus spiritum concupiscit, et spiritus adversus carnem' Here 'Psychici' means 'Churchmen,' as opposed to the 'Paracletus,' i e 'Montanus'
Cp. Canon Gore, p. 206, note 1, for a proof of the fact that the treatise is Montanistic.

[2] For a far juster view of what is involved in the Montanism of Tertullian, see Canon Gore, p. 204 sqq.

[3] e. g. the *de Praescr. Haeret*, xli. . 'Inprimis quis catechumenus, quis fidelis, incertum est . . . simplicitatem volunt esse prostrationem disciplinae . . . ante sunt perfecti catechumeni quam edocti . . . . Ordinationes eorum temerariae, leves, inconstantes . . . . Nusquam facilius proficitur quam in castris rebellium, ubi ipsum esse illic, promereri est Itaque alius hodie Episcopus, cras alius · hodie Diaconus, qui cras Lector hodie Presbyter qui cras Laicus, nam et Laicis sacerdotalia munera iniungunt;' i e to Tertullian, *the Catholic Churchman*, 'carelessness about sacerdotal distinctions' had been, in Canon Gore's phrase, 'the very characteristic of heretical bodies.'

and mutual relation between ministers and laymen. Tertullian's language has combined this with the further question of the titles 'priest' and 'priesthood.' But if it is impossible to examine the evidence about the first question without being partly drawn into the second, it will help clearness of thought to insist that the second is only here incidentally touched, because it cannot be wholly disentangled from the other. We are as yet only directly concerned with the relation, in Christ's Church, between ministers (whatever they may be called) and those who are not ministers.

When we turn to Origen, there seems no reason for admitting any exaggeration at all. The fact that in some contexts he speaks of 'priests' in the ordinary ministerial sense is not cancelled, nor even affected in the slightest degree, by the fact that in other contexts, where he is not discussing the regulated order of this world, but looking onwards to the spiritual consummation of all things, he finds the true spiritual counterpart of the Levites, the Priests, the High Priest of the Levitical covenant, not so much in the ministerial grades of Christian 'Order'—however real, or even exclusive for their appointed purposes—but in the degrees of devotion and nearness to God in the inward spiritual life. What reverent Churchman would decline to do the same? What Christian in his senses would suppose, either on the one hand that the orderly precedence of Bishops, Priests, Deacons, Lay people in the Church on earth, carries a similar precedence of souls in Heaven: or that the fact that it does not, constitutes any argument at all against such grades of ecclesiastical office on earth? 'The last shall be first, and the first last.' Spiritually it may well be, that he who was but a pauper shall be found as a bishop, and he who was held in high reverence on earth as theologian, and bishop, and saint, never cease from praising, if he be but admitted as the poorest and the lowest. What spiritual mind ever failed to dwell on such a truth? But

F

if a theologian should dwell on it ever so much, it would be grotesque to infer that he thereby denied the sacred character of 'Order' on earth. There is, then, no warrant for saying, with Bishop Lightfoot, that 'in all these passages Origen has taken spiritual enlightenment and not sacerdotal office *to be the Christian counterpart* to the Aaronic priesthood' For the words which I have italicized it would be perfectly right to substitute 'the ultimate spiritual counterpart' · and then the sentence would no longer make Origen contradict himself, by implying that he ever denied the existence of *a* counterpart to Aaronic priesthood in the ministry of the Christian Church.[1]

[1] When expounding Levitical ordinances of priesthood in reference to Christian ministry, Origen is apt to mark the transition by substituting 'sacerdos Ecclesiae' or 'sacerdos Domini' for the simple 'sacerdos.' So e. g. in the passage *in Levit* Hom V. iv. (Delarue, vol. ii p. 208): 'Discant sacerdotes Domini, qui ecclesiis praesunt, quia pars eis data est cum his quorum delicta repropitiaverint Quid autem est repropitiare delictum? Si assumseris peccatorem, et monendo, hortando, docendo, instruendo, adduxeris eum ad poenitentiam . . . si ergo talis fueris sacerdos, et talis fuerit doctrina tua . . . . intelligant ergo sacerdotes Domini . . . . sciant se in nullo alio partem habituros apud Deum, nisi in eo quod offerunt pro peccatis id est, quod a via peccati converterint peccatores' No doubt all this passage may be said to be primarily metaphorical—in the sense, at least, that he is interpreting Leviticus, and that he starts from the Levitical text, to find analogies to its meaning elsewhere: but at least one of the most familiar analogies is that of the ministry of the Church For a different analogy see *in Levit*. Hom. II. iv (p 190) '*In morali autem loco* potest pontifex iste sensus pietatis et religionis videri, qui in nobis per orationes et obsecrationes quas Deo fundimus velut quodam sacerdotio fungitur'; where the Levitical High Priest corresponds to the spiritual element in a man.

He is passing however beyond the region of mere metaphor or analogy when he says, Hom V iii (p 207) · 'Consequens enim est ut secundum imaginem eius qui sacerdotium Ecclesiae dedit, etiam ministri et sacerdotes Ecclesiae peccata populi accipiant, et ipsi imitantes magistrum remissionem peccatorum populo tribuant. Debent ergo et ipsi Ecclesiae sacerdotes ita perfecti esse, et in officiis semper sacerdotalibus eruditi, ut . . .' Or again, when he is speaking of penitence in the Church of Christ 'Est adhuc et septima, licet dura et laboriosa, per poenitentiam remissio peccatorum, cum lavat peccator in lacrymis stratum suum, et fiunt ei lacrymae suae panes die ac nocte, et cum non erubescit sacerdoti Domini indicare peccatum suum et quaerere medicinam . . . in quo impletur et illud quod Jacobus Apostolus dicit· Si quis autem infirmatur, vocet presbyteros Ecclesiae, et imponant ei manus, ungentes eum oleo in nomine Domini, et **oratio fidei salvabit infirmum, et si in peccatis fuerit, remittentur ei.'** Hom. II.

What Bishop Lightfoot should have said here of Origen, is illustrated by what he does in part say of Clement of Alexandria. He quotes from Clement the following sentence:[1] 'It is possible for men even now, by exercising themselves in the commandments of the Lord, and by living a perfect gnostic life in obedience to the Gospel, to be inscribed in the roll of the Apostles. Such men are genuine presbyters of the Church and true deacons of the will of God, if they practise and teach the things of the Lord, being not indeed ordained by men, nor considered righteous because they are presbyters, but enrolled in the presbytery because they are righteous; and though here on earth they may not be honoured with a chief seat, yet shall they sit on the four and twenty thrones judging the people.' The Bishop goes on: 'It is quite consistent with this truly spiritual view, that he should elsewhere recognize the presbyter, the deacon, and the layman, as distinct orders.' Consistent? of course it is consistent. The 'truly spiritual view,' which entirely coincides with what I understand Origen to mean, seems to be precisely what Mr Keble—amongst ten thousand others — would have said But neither

---

iv (p 191). Here the simple 'sacerdoti' might have been explained as mere metaphor · but the 'sacerdoti Domini' is not so much a metaphor as a title. (This, at least, must be capable of being referred directly to 'presbyters' and will therefore qualify any too great breadth of generalization as to the reference of 'sacerdos' or 'sacerdos ecclesiae' to 'bishops,' in early writings See Bishop Taylor on *Episcopacy*, end of § 27, vol. vii p 113) It is difficult to see on what grounds Bishop Lightfoot asserts (p. 256 note) that in Origen's opinion the confessor to the penitent need not be an ordained minister. He is referring to Hom. in Ps. xxxvii. 6 (p. 688), where all that Origen does is to advise the penitent to choose a really skilled 'physician' as his confessor. Such advice cannot possibly prove that he might choose a layman. Canon Gore's reference to the passage seems to correspond with it far more exactly. It is, he says, a 'strong exhortation to confession, which is to be private or public at the confessor's discretion.' Canon Gore adds a reference to Hom. V. xii. (p. 214), where the unworthy priest 'non est sacerdos nec potest sacerdos nominari.' Does Origen here mean more than we should all join in saying, if, apart from questions of technical validity, we were contrasting the 'true' and the 'nominal' priest?

[1] *Strom.* VI. xiii. p. 793.

Mr Keble would have said it, nor Clement of Alexandria, if they had felt any doubt about the divine commission of the ministry on earth. It is precisely those to whom this, as a fact in Christ's Church, is most completely a matter of course, beyond all reach of denial or misunderstanding, who can most naturally, and do most freely, pass beyond the definite fact into those more indefinite spiritual analogies,[1] of which, to them, the fact is full. Whilst, then, the clear apprehension of the fact is, of course, consistent with this 'spiritual' application of the fact, it is to be observed, on the other hand, that the terms in which the fact is spiritually applied would be quite inconsistent with any uncertainty as to the truth of the fact. 'It is possible for men even now'—'such men are genuine presbyters of the Church and true deacons of the will of God'—'being not indeed ordained by men nor considered righteous because they are presbyters'—'though here on earth they may not be honoured with a chief seat' —these phrases unmistakably imply that there was, in

---

[1] Take the following stanzas from *The Christian Year* (Wednesday before Easter):—

'Nor deem, who to that bliss aspire,
Must win their way through blood and fire.
The writhings of a wounded heart
Are fiercer than a foeman's dart
Oft in Life's stillest shade reclining,
In Desolation unrepining,
Without a hope on earth to find
A mirror in an answering mind,
Meek souls there are, who little dream
Their daily strife an Angel's theme,
Or that the rod they take so calm
Shall prove in Heaven a martyr's palm.

'And there are souls that seem to dwell
Above this earth—so rich a spell
Floats round their steps, where'er they move,
From hopes fulfilled and mutual love
Such, if on high their thoughts are set,
Nor in the stream the source forget,
If prompt to quit the bliss they know,
Following the Lamb where'er He go,
By purest pleasures unbeguiled
To idolize or wife or child,
Such wedded souls our God shall own
For faultless virgins round His throne'

Who could have written these lines except on the basis of a vivid realization, first of all, of the meaning and blessedness of literal virginity, and literal martyrdom? or what would be thought of a commentator who should adduce them to prove that the words 'virgin' and 'martyr' had, to Mr Keble, *only* a 'spiritual' significance?

the visible Church, a regularly constituted and authorized order of ministry, and that the men here spoken of did *not* belong to it; and that to call them presbyters, &c., however spiritually and invisibly true, was to the obvious sense, and in the outward order, a paradox[1], challenging attention as such[2].

This truth requires no further emphasizing. If it did, it would find it in the phrase at the beginning of the chapter, in which Clement says that it is possible for pious Christians to be 'inscribed on the roll of the Apostles[3].' It is quite plain here that he starts from the ordinary sense of the word Apostles. They, he says, did not become Apostles (I quote Canon Gore's translation) 'because they were chosen for some special peculiarity of nature, for Judas was chosen with them; but they were capable of becoming Apostles on being chosen by Him who foresaw even how they would end.' Thus it is that personal fitness is ultimately more than outward election. Thus Matthias, who did *not* share their election, when he shows himself worthy, takes the place of Judas. And thus (he goes on) it is possible for men of holy life, &c to be enrolled in the chosen body of the Apostles The transition from Matthias who was 'numbered with the eleven' in one sense, to those who may be numbered with the twelve in another sense, is curious· but the general meaning is plain It is, if possible, even clearer when he speaks of Apostles than

[1] But less *sharp* as paradox when πρεσβύτεροι and διάκονοι, though bearing a technical sense, were not yet exclusively technical. 'Church elders and true servants' is still a large part of what the words say to the ear

[2] In the very same chapter Clement gives expression to this underlying assumption which his language all along has implied, descending from the spiritual analogy to the external earthly fact: ἐπεὶ καὶ αἱ ἐνταῦθα κατὰ τὴν Ἐκκλησίαν προκοπαί, ἐπισκόπων, πρεσβυτέρων, διακόνων, μιμήματα, οἶμαι, ἀγγελικῆς δόξης, κἀκείνης τῆς οἰκονομίας τυγχάνουσιν, . . ἐν νεφέλαις τούτους ἀρθέντας γράφει ὁ Ἀπόστολος, διακονήσειν μὲν τὰ πρῶτα, ἔπειτα ἐγκαταταγῆναι τῷ πρεσβυτερίῳ κατὰ προκοπὴν δόξης (δόξα γὰρ δόξης διαφέρει) ἄχρις ἂν εἰς τέλειον ἄνδρα αὐξήσωσιν

[3] Or 'included within the election (ἐγγραφῆναι εἰς τὴν ἐκλογὴν) of the apostles.'

when he speaks of presbyters that he is declaring, as apparent paradox, the spiritual possibility, that those who officially and ministerially rank as lowest in Christ's Church on earth, may be, before God, on an equality with even the highest of the highest in Heaven. Would any one argue from this that Clement did not believe in the earthly apostolate at all? His exposition does not weaken for a moment—it emphatically presupposes—the reality of that hierarchy on earth from which the whole thought starts.

To Clement the Bishop comes from Irenaeus, and to Irenaeus from Justin Martyr. The Bishop's immediate object is to show that sacerdotal terminology does not, in all these writers, belong properly to Christian ministry. But as the crucial passage from Tertullian has shown us, this thought is closely interwoven with another, viz. that Christian ministry (under whatever title) is not the exclusive right of the ordained. It is in pursuance of the second of these thoughts, not of the first (which I have not yet properly reached), that I have been following his quotations—from Tertullian backwards—here. It may be conceded at once that neither Irenaeus nor Justin call Christian ministers 'priests.' But will any one venture to claim that the line of ministerial distinction between ministers and laymen is in the least blurred by either of them? Indeed, it is not a little curious that it is not until the nominal identification of 'ministry' and 'priesthood' is complete that there is any symptom of uncertainty as to the distinction between ministry and laity; and that, when it appears, it appears as it were in dependence on the priestly nomenclature, and shelters itself under the possible ambiguity of the word ἱερεύς. Not that the doubt rises really from this ambiguity. Rather it rises out of the pseudo-antithesis between 'ecclesia episcoporum' and 'ecclesia Spiritus' which is a characteristic of Montanism. But having arisen it shelters itself for the moment under the 'kingdom and priests'—the βασιλείαν καὶ ἱερεῖς—of Rev. v. 10.

But however possible it might be in the time of Tertullian to slur in this way the distinction—fi t between ministerial and universal 'priesthood,' and so, by consequence from this, between ministry and laity altogether, the real principle of the matter had in fact been settled long before, when the *title* 'priest' was still used only tentatively, partially, and semimetaphorically of the Christian celebrant. For from the passages of Justin Martyr three points of teaching very clearly emerge: first, that the Jewish sacrifices and priesthood being rejected as unreal, the reality of priesthood and sacrifice belonged only to the Christian Church; secondly, that the overt and ceremonial presentment of this priestly sacrifice in the Christian Church was to be found in the Eucharistic celebration, which is the fulfilment of the prophecy of Malachi; and thirdly, that this Eucharistic 'sacrifice' was not 'offered' by any miscellaneous Christians at random, but that he who was head of the Christian body stood as the celebrant, and that distribution was made by the hands of deacons. In thus sweeping in unhesitatingly the whole Christian people as the real 'high priestly race,' while he finds the ministerial exercise of the Church's high priesthood in the Eucharist, and assumes that the Eucharist is celebrated by ministerial hands, Justin has really beforehand covered all the ground. Though the word 'priest' is not yet used as a title for the Christian minister; though when it comes to be used, half a century later, as a familiar title, it can be made to serve as cover for an attack on the ministry of the Church; yet in fact Justin has really given beforehand—and perhaps all the more simply and naturally just because the word 'priest' has none as yet of the associations of a mere title—something like the true rationale and the true distinction (within the inclusive priesthood of the Christian Church Body), at once of the priesthood of the Christian layman, and of the priesthood of the Christian minister. He greatly fortifies our characteristic position that the minister is so the representative of the community that what he does they do, and what they do they do through him; but where is any word or hint to imply (what would really be required for the Bishop's argument) that what they corporately did through the act of their president they *could* equally do through any member whatever? While we cordially concede that Justin bears witness to the truth that the Christian people, as contrasted with the Jewish priests, possess the true and abiding priesthood upon earth; we must still insist that Justin knows nothing of any ministerial exercise of this priesthood, save in and through the act of those who are authorized to stand as the ministers and instruments of the priesthood of the Church.[1]

[1] *Dialogus cum Tryphone*, 116, 117, p. 209: Οὕτως ἡμεῖς ... ἀρχιερατικὸν τὸ ἀληθινὸν γένος ἐσμὲν τοῦ Θεοῦ, ὡς καὶ αὐτὸς ὁ Θεὸς μαρτυρεῖ, εἰπὼν ὅτι ἐν παντὶ τόπῳ ἐν τοῖς ἔθνεσι θυσίας εὐαρέστους αὐτῷ καὶ καθαρὰς προσφέροντες. οὐ δέχεται δὲ παρ' οὐδενὸς θυσίας ὁ Θεὸς εἰ μὴ διὰ τῶν ἱερέων αὐτοῦ.
Πάντας οὖν οἱ διὰ [Qy.? πάσας οὖν διὰ] τοῦ ὀνόματος τούτου θυσίας ἃς παρέδωκεν Ἰησοῦς ὁ Χριστὸς γίνεσθαι, τουτέστιν ἐπὶ τῇ εὐχαριστίᾳ τοῦ ἄρτου καὶ τοῦ ποτηρίου, τὰς ἐν παντὶ τόπῳ τῆς γῆς γινομένας ὑπὸ τῶν Χριστιανῶν προλαβὼν ὁ Θεὸς, μαρτυρεῖ εὐαρέστους ὑπάρχειν αὐτῷ· τὰς δὲ ὑφ' ὑμῶν [i e the Jews] καὶ δι' ἐκείνων ὑμῶν τῶν ἱερέων γινομένας ἀπαναίνεται, λέγων, καὶ τὰς θυσίας ὑμῶν οὐ προσδέξομαι ἐκ τῶν χειρῶν ὑμῶν διότι ἀπὸ ἀνατολῆς ἡλίου ἕως δυσμῶν τὸ ὄνομά μου δεδόξασται, λέγει, ἐν τοῖς ἔθνεσιν· ὑμεῖς δὲ βεβηλοῦτε αὐτὸ ...
... ὅτι μενοῦν καὶ εὐχαὶ καὶ εὐχαριστίαι ὑπὸ τῶν ἀξίων γινόμεναι τέλειαι μόναι καὶ εὐάρεστοί εἰσι τῷ Θεῷ θυσίαι καὶ αὐτός φημι. ταῦτα γὰρ μόνα καὶ Χριστιανοὶ παρέλαβον ποιεῖν, καὶ ἐπ' ἀναμνήσει δὲ τῆς τροφῆς αὐτῶν ξηρᾶς τε καὶ ὑγρᾶς, ἐν ᾗ καὶ τοῦ πάθους ὃ πέπονθε δι' αὐτοῦ ὁ Θεὸς τοῦ Θεοῦ μέμνηται [Qy.? ὁ υἱὸς τοῦ Θεοῦ μέμνηται]

Apologia, i. 65-67 (p. 82): Ἡμεῖς δὲ . . τὸν πεπεισμένον . . ἐπὶ τοὺς λεγομένους ἀδελφοὺς ἄγομεν . . . κοινὰς εὐχὰς ποιησόμενοι . . ὅπως καταξιωθῶμεν . . . ἀλλήλους φιλήματι ἀσπαζόμεθα . . ἔπειτα προσφέρεται τῷ προεστῶτι τῶν ἀδελφῶν ἄρτος καὶ ποτήριον ὕδατος καὶ κράματος, καὶ οὗτος λαβὼν αἶνον καὶ δόξαν . . . ἀναπέμπει· καὶ εὐχαριστίαν . . . ποιεῖται· οὗ συντελέσαντος τὰς εὐχὰς καὶ τὴν εὐχαριστίαν, πᾶς ὁ παρὼν λαὸς ἐπευφημεῖ λέγων ἀμήν. . . . εὐχαριστήσαντος δὲ τοῦ προεστῶτος, καὶ ἐπευφημήσαντος παντὸς τοῦ λαοῦ, οἱ καλούμενοι παρ' ἡμῖν διάκονοι διδόασιν ἑκάστῳ . . . [Then follows an account of the Institution by Jesus Christ]· Ἡμεῖς δὲ μετὰ ταῦτα λοιπὸν ἀεὶ τούτων ἀλλήλους ἀναμιμνήσκομεν . . ἐπὶ πᾶσί τε οἷς προσφερόμεθα, εὐλογοῦμεν τὸν . . . . καὶ τῇ τοῦ ἡλίου λεγομένῃ ἡμέρᾳ . . . τὰ ἀπομνημονεύματα τῶν ἀποστόλων . . . ἀναγινώσκεται . . . εἶτα παυσαμένου τοῦ ἀναγινώσκοντος, ὁ προεστὼς διὰ λόγου τὴν νουθεσίαν καὶ πρόκλησιν τῆς τῶν καλῶν τούτων μιμήσεως ποιεῖται. ἔπειτα ἀνιστάμεθα κοινῇ πάντες, καὶ εὐχὰς πέμπομεν· καὶ ὡς προέφημεν, παυσα-

It has been necessary to dwell at some length upon this principle—that the ministry is at once the true representative, and yet neither the accidental representative nor the mere delegate or nominee, of the total Christian body—because its truth has been so seriously obscured. But whilst we emphatically deny that mere popular appointment can constitute a minister, or that distinction of ministers is mere matter of politic convenience, it is true of course that even considerations of politic convenience bear, in their own way, witness that the Divine ordinance of ministers is (like other ordinances of God) no arbitrary superfluity, but the Divine consecration of a natural and secular need. Moreover, though that which constitutes men Christ's ministers, is (as we shall see) a solemn setting apart, not by merely human but by Divine methods and sanctions, it is true at the same time that, in such things as electing and presenting for Ordination, the general Church body has a responsible work of preparing for and concurring with the Divine act. Though ministerial appointment is certainly not human in place of being Divine, yet neither is it Divine quite apart from being human also The Church as a whole has its selecting and consentient voice; and even what is most distinctively Divine in ordination is still conferred *through* the Church. So far as the general or lay voice is concerned, the circumstances of popular election and public approbation have at many times in the Church presented to view much more emphatically than they nowadays do the aspect of the priesthood as representative of the congregation. It might perhaps be

μένων ἡμῶν τῆς εὐχῆς ἄρτος προσφέρεται καὶ οἶνος καὶ ὕδωρ· καὶ ὁ προεστὼς εὐχὰς ὁμοίως καὶ εὐχαριστίας ὅση δύναμις αὐτῷ ἀναπέμπει, καὶ ὁ λαὸς ἐπευφημεῖ λέγων τὸ ἀμήν. καὶ ἡ διάδοσις καὶ ἡ μετάληψις ἀπὸ τῶν εὐχαριστηθέντων ἐκάστῳ γίνεται, καὶ τοῖς οὐ παροῦσι διὰ τῶν διακόνων πέμπεται. οἱ εὐποροῦντες δὲ καὶ βουλόμενοι κατὰ προαίρεσιν ἕκαστος τὴν ἑαυτοῦ ὃ βούλεται δίδωσι· καὶ τὸ συλλεγόμενον παρὰ τῷ προεστῶτι ἀποτίθεται, καὶ αὐτὸς ἐπικουρεῖ ὀρφανοῖς τε καὶ χήραις, καὶ τοῖς διὰ νόσον ἢ δι' ἄλλην αἰτίαν λειπομένοις, καὶ τοῖς ἐν δεσμοῖς οὖσι, καὶ τοῖς παρεπιδήμοις οὖσι ξένοις, καὶ ἁπλῶς πᾶσι τοῖς ἐν χρείᾳ οὖσι κηδεμὼν γίνεται.

wished that this aspect might be more emphasized amongst ourselves. But the clear witness to it in the forms of the Ordinal, whether unreformed or reformed, has never been lost[1]; and the idea which is expressed by it is of value too permanent to be overthrown even by attempts made from time to time to exalt it into the constitutive reality of Ordination

Now in this sense it is possible that a very limited acceptance may be granted to the word 'delegate,' which is used more than once by Bishop Lightfoot as if it were synonymous with 'representative.' But how risky a word it is at the best, and how naturally it misleads into the wrong inference, is clearly shown by the use which the Bishop makes of it. After recalling the *representative* character of the minister's function, he goes on: 'He is a priest, as the mouthpiece, the delegate[2], of a priestly race. His acts are not his own, but the acts of the congregation. *Hence too it will follow that,* viewed on this side as on the other, his function cannot be absolute and indispensable. It may be a general rule, it may be *under ordinary circumstances a practically universal law,* that the highest acts of congregational worship shall be performed through the principal officers of the congregation. But an emergency may arise when the spirit and not the letter must decide. The Christian ideal will then interpose and interpret our duty. *The higher ordinance of the universal priesthood will overrule* all special limitations. *The layman will assume functions* which are *otherwise restricted* to the ordained minister[3].'

This paragraph appears to combine two somewhat inconsistent lines of thought. The first runs thus. The layman is inherently a priest: and the universal priest-

[1] See more fully in Canon Gore's *Church and the Ministry,* pp. 100-104.
[2] Cp p 180: 'The priestly tribe held this peculiar relation to God only as the *representatives* of the whole nation As *delegates* of the people, they offered sacrifice and made atonement.' On which see Gore, p. 72, note.
[3] *Philippians,* p. 266. The italics are mine.

hood is a 'higher ordinance' than the ministerial. It is therefore *essentially lawful* for the layman to perform all priestly functions; even though this essential and 'higher' right may ordinarily submit, on lower grounds of convenience and expediency, to restriction. The second runs thus. Inasmuch as he has never received any commission which would warrant his doing so, it is *essentially unlawful* for the layman to minister. Nevertheless extreme emergencies may so over-ride all law as to make it spiritually right sometimes to do even what is, as long as law holds at all, positively and peremptorily forbidden. This second position has its own very obvious questions—and dangers. Still I do not care at present to argue the second position, provided it is kept quite distinct from the first. As to the first, I can only repeat my protest against the falsity of the logic which would tacitly assume it, as if it were contained, as inference, within the truth that the actions of the priest are not his own, but corporate actions, which he has been authorized to perform as the representative *persona* of the Church.

For some time past we have been engaged practically in protest against an overstatement, which would ultimately merge all distinction, so far as concerns any special character, or graces or powers for ministerial authorization or capacity, between ministry and laity. Before leaving the subject it is necessary also to protest against exaggeration of the opposite kind. If we are not unaccustomed to theological theory which explains the reality of ministerial commission overmuch away, Christian history has perhaps been even more accustomed to another disproportion, which first falsely enhanced, and then falsely conceived and explained, and so both in theory and practice spoiled, the distinction between lay and clerical life. The priest and the layman do not differ ultimately in kind, as far as their personal prerogatives of spiritual life are concerned. The distinction is of ministerial authority, not of individual privilege. Even the technical word 'character' as applied to ministry lends itself easily to mistake. If we assert that Holy Order confers 'character,' or that 'character' is 'indelible,' character in the current sense of the word, the total moral quality of the individual man, is exactly what we do not mean. That which in himself he is in personal moral quality or capacity before God, is exactly what is unchanged; he is neither better nor worse in personal value than he was before. The 'character' which is conferred, and is indelible, is a status, inherently involving capacities, duties, responsibilities of ministerial life, yet separable from and, in a sense, external to the secret character of the personal self, however much the inner self may be indirectly disciplined or conditioned by it—for good or for evil[1]. The priesthood of the layman is no merely verbal concession. It is a doctrine of importance, essential (as we shall see when the time comes for discussing 'priesthood') for a due understanding of the priesthood of the ministry. It was said above that Tertullian pushes this thought into overstatement. But what he pushes by overstatement into error is in itself truth. Thus in the opening of the passage whose conclusion was criticized just now, he argues with perfect truth that there can be but one standard of moral and spiritual life for members of the Body of Christ: in no case one for the priest, and another for the layman. Differences there may of course be in circumstances, and in such expediency as is dependent on circumstances. But what is essentially right or wrong for either, is so of necessity for both. Both alike—apart from empowerment for active exercise of representative ministerial functions on

---

[1] Of course the self is very largely conditioned by its reception and use of the ministerial—as of every other responsible—gift. As the self is identified more and more with the ministry and its possibilities, the distinction between the two becomes one rather of logic than of fact: while in the bad priest, still authorized as priest, the contrast may be increasingly terrible. But all these things belong rather to the consequential results, than to the direct content, of the divine gift of ministry, regarded as a gift of 'indelible character' once for all conferred.

behalf of the Body—are, in the private inner life of the Spirit, consecrated Kings and Priests to God. 'Vani erimus, si putaverimus quod sacerdotibus non liceat laicis licere Nonne et laici sacerdotes sumus? Scriptum est Regnum quoque nos et sacerdotes Deo et Patri suo fecit [1].' There is no shadow of exaggeration here.

But such a conception as this has no doubt been largely obscured, and the notion has been widespread, that a priest, as compared with a layman, had in his own personal life a more intimate relation with God, a deeper intensity of spiritual privilege, a higher standard and necessity of holiness. In proportion as it became a familiar conception that the priest was altogether on a different level of holiness, the idea of the priesthood as *representative* of all in the corporate service of God, acquired (not quite unnaturally) a further and very perilous development,—small at first in appearance but ultimately revolutionizing the whole idea; and the priesthood was conceived of as working with God *vicariously* on behalf of all. That the priest was holy, while the layman was not; that the priest performed God's service in the layman's stead; that the priest propitiated God on the layman's behalf; that, when the layman's time came, the priest could come in and make right his relation with God—here was indeed a distorted development of ministerial theory. To what causes is such a development due? Something no doubt is to be allowed for pretensions, through ambitious motives, on behalf of the clergy. But these, if lay Christianity had maintained its true standard, would by themselves, at the most, have had comparatively little effect. The true cause is to be sought far more on the lay than on the clerical side.

Bishop Lightfoot connects its early beginnings with the large preponderance of imperfectly Christianized Gentile

---

[1] Cp. Jerome's well-known 'Sacerdotium laici id est baptisma'; and Canon Mason on Confirmation as especially symbolized by *unction* in *The Relation of Confirmation to Baptism*, p. 11.

feeling, still characterized largely by Gentile—that is practically by Pagan—modes of instinct. 'It is,' he says, 'to Gentile feeling that this development must be ascribed. For the heathen familiar with auguries, lustrations, sacrifices, and depending on the intervention of some priest for all the manifold religious rites of the state, the club, and the family, the sacerdotal functions must have occupied a far larger space in the affairs of every-day life than for the Jew of the dispersion, who of necessity dispensed, and had no scruple at dispensing, with priestly ministrations from one year's end to another[1].' But in large part, after all, the explanation needs no special knowledge of accidental historical conditions. It is to be found in the natural slackness of semi-religious life. If, to the natural instinct of the laity, a claim to superior dignity in ministerial life is, as dignity, wholly unwelcome; it is nevertheless true that the idea of a *vicarious* service or holiness of ministers (though it be in truth the most supremely exaggerated form of ministerial dignity) is to the carnal lay instinct strangely agreeable. The Divine consecration of lay life—such consecration as is implied, for instance, as part of the inherent meaning of Christianity in Christ's Church, in every line of the First Epistle of St. John—seems like an intolerable strain to the natural sense. Every natural instinct of spiritual indolence is flattered and soothed by a practice which, tacitly remitting true religious consistency to the professional minister, seems to justify for lay life an inferior standard of holiness.

In this context we cordially welcome every word in which—putting aside, of course, the question of authority to stand forward and represent the congregation by public functions of ministry—Dr. Hatch makes protest on behalf of the underlying spiritual equality of lay and clerical life[2]. On this point at least there need be no discordant voice. The distinction drawn by Bishop Lightfoot (though

[1] *Philippians*, p. 259.   [2] See above, pp. 73-75.

he follows it by an inadmissible corollary) is fully echoed by Canon Gore and Dr. Liddon. 'The minister's function, says the Bishop, 'is representative without being vicarial.' 'The chief of the ideas commonly associated with sacerdotalism, which it is important to repudiate'— so writes Canon Gore—'is that of a *vicarious* priesthood. It is contrary to the true spirit of the Christian religion to introduce the notion of a class inside the Church who are in a closer spiritual relationship to God than their fellows "If a monk falls," says St. Jerome, "a priest shall pray for him; but who shall pray for a priest who has fallen?" Such an expression construed literally would imply a closer relation to God in the priest than in the consecrated layman, and such a conception is beyond a doubt alien to the spirit of Christianity[1].' 'So far as there is gradation in the efficacy of prayers, it is the result not of official position but of growing sanctity and strengthening faith. It is an abuse of the sacerdotal conception, if it is supposed that the priesthood exists to celebrate sacrifices or acts of worship in the place of the body of the people or as their substitute. This conception had, no doubt, attached itself to the "massing priests" of the Middle Ages. The priest had come to be regarded as an individual who held, in virtue of his ordination, the prerogative of offering sacrifices which could win God's gifts. . . . Now this distorted sort of conception is one which the religious indolence of most men, in co-operation with the ambition for power in "spiritual" persons, is always tending to make possible. It is not only possible to believe in a vicarious priesthood of sacrifice, but also in a vicarious office of preaching, which releases the laity from the obligation to make efforts of spiritual apprehension on their own account. But in either case the conception is an unchristian one. The ministry is no more one of vicarious action than it is one of exclusive knowledge or exclusive

[1] p. 84.

spiritual relation to God. . . . The difference between clergy and laity "is not a difference in kind" but in function[1].' I have purposely placed this sentence last because in it Canon Gore is quoting from Dr. Liddon; and Dr. Liddon's words are so directly to our purpose that it is desirable to quote from them a little more fully.

'Certainly,' Dr. Liddon writes[2], 'if Christian laymen would only believe with all their hearts that they are really priests, we should very soon escape from some of the difficulties which vex the Church of Christ. For it would then be seen that in the Christian Church the difference between clergy and laity is only a difference of the degree in which certain spiritual powers are conferred; that it is not a difference of kind. Spiritual endowments are given to the Christian layman with one purpose, to the Christian minister with another: the object of the first is personal, that of the second is corporate. . . . The Christian layman of early days was thus, in his inmost life, penetrated through and through by the sacerdotal idea, spiritualized and transfigured as it was by the Gospel. Hence it was no difficulty to him that this idea should have its public representatives in the body of the Church, or that certain reserved duties should be discharged by Divine appointment, but on behalf of the whole body, by these representatives. The priestly institute in the public Christian body was the natural extension of the priesthood which the lay Christian exercised within himself; and the secret life of the conscience was in harmony with the outward organization of the Church. . . . Where there is no recognition of the priesthood of every Christian soul, the sense of an unintelligible mysticism, if not of an unbearable imposture, will be provoked when spiritual powers are

---

[1] That is to say, of course, not in kind, *apart from* functional capacity; not in kind except just so far as distinctive authority to represent the Church by public performance of her corporate functions, of itself constitutes, in a limited sense, a difference of kind.

University Sermons, Second Series, sermon x on 'Sacerdotalism,' pp 198, 199.

claimed for the benefit of the whole body by the serving officers of the Christian Church. But if this can be changed; if the temple of the layman's soul can be again made a scene of spiritual worship, he will no longer fear lest the ministerial order should confiscate individual liberty. The one priesthood will be felt to be the natural extension and correlative of the other[1].'

Perhaps it may be remarked in conclusion that it is only in the light of considerations like these that we see the full mischief of that mischievous current phrase 'going into the Church,' when what is meant is 'receiving Holy Order within the Church.' Many phrases, though on analysis untrue or absurd, are yet harmless in effect. Others, however innocently used by the individuals who use them, none the less spread a poison of untruth in the air. It is difficult to measure the contribution to untruth, and, though very indirectly, to moral and spiritual laxity, which is rendered by such a phrase, so long as it remains in possession of men's lips and minds. It is, regarded in itself, a most noxious untruth;—and if it is not a lie on the part of those who utter it, there is only so much

[1] Cp the following passage from Dr Milligan, *Ascension*, pp 245-6: 'As in the fundamental vision of [the Revelation of St. John] we are taught that Christ exalted in glory is a Priest, . . . so we are taught that in Him all His people are also priests They have been made "to be a kingdom, to be priests unto His God and Father," and the white robes which they wear throughout the book are the robes of priests. The idea of priestly function cannot be separated from the Christian Church. All the Lord's people are priests. . . . Let the priestliness of the whole Church, *not that of any particular class within her*, be brought prominently forward ; let it appear that the very object of insisting upon the Church's priestliness is to restore to the Christian laity that sense of their responsibility and privilege of which Protestantism, hardly less than Romanism, has practically deprived them.' We need make only two slight criticisms on this language, and none on its general meaning. ' All the Lord's people are priests,' though true, is not true in quite the same sense in which the whole Church is priestly ; and the phrase which I have italicized should rather run, ' Let the priestliness of the whole Church, *and of any particular class within her only in reference to, and as expressive of, the priestliness of the whole.*' The 'not' of the text may well mean no more than this (as frequently in Scripture, e. g ' I will have mercy and not sacrifice,' &c.), but it is open to misconception. The relation between a ' priestly Church ' and priests ordained within the Church, is discussed more fully below in chapter vii.

the more reason for denouncing it as a lie successfully imposed on men's language, by him whose purpose it only too insidiously helps.

The word laity, on the other hand, is a far nobler word than people imagine. It is apt to be thought of as a merely negative term. The 'layman' is one who is *not* a clergyman, or (in other contexts) *not* a medical man, *not* a lawyer, *not*, in this or that, an expert. He is a 'mere' layman; and a layman is a mere 'not.' But to Israel of old, to be 'the People' of God was the height of positive privilege· and to be a layman means to be a member of 'the People'—not as in modern phrase contrasted with privilege, nobility, government, &c., but as in the mouth of a devout Israelite,—'the People,' ὁ λαός—in contrast with the nations, the Gentiles, the heathen. It is the word of most positive spiritual privilege, the glory of covenanted access to and intimacy with God.

CHAPTER IV

THE BASIS OF MINISTRY—DIVINE COMMISSION

WE think, then, of ministry, not as a holy intermediary, wielding powers peculiar and inherent, because it is Spirit-endowed on behalf of those who are not. But Christian ministry is the instrument which represents the whole Spirit-endowed Body of the Church; and yet withal is itself so Spirit-endowed as to have the right and the power to represent instrumentally. The immense exaltation—and requirement—of lay Christianity, which in respect of its own dignity cannot be exaggerated, in no way detracts from the distinctive dignity of the duties which belong to ministerial function, or from the solemn significance of separation to ministry.

Upon the dignity of Christian ministry, as dignity, there is no occasion now to enlarge. At least we have behind us all that is implied in the exegesis of the 3rd chapter of 2 Corinthians. At least the 'ministration of the Spirit,' the 'ministration of righteousness' does still, in its true significance, outdazzle that which was in itself too dazzling for the eye of man to endure But leaving thoughts like these, or the meaning of them, we turn next in order to the other thought, that of the meaning of separation to ministry, and the ideas involved in, or necessary for, that

If, then, we insist that some, and not all, have the right, as organs and instruments, to represent the Church, and wield ministerially the powers that are inherent in her, of what nature is that which makes such ministerial distinction between the few and the many? Of the answer to this question, at least so long as it is in an abstract form, there can be no doubt The work is God's work, and the authority to undertake it must be God's authority. Even if we should hold that nothing is required except a popular approval, the 'call' of the Church or of a congregation, or, more simply still, a man's own inner sense of capacity and of inclination, yet even these, if they are to have the semblance of adequate warrant for a life of ministry, must be conceived of as the immediate methods through which God appoints and enables. The first and most cardinal principle, then, for a ministry which can possibly claim to be valid or authorised, is adequacy of commission; that is, commission understood to proceed from God

This principle is in Scripture abundantly expressed and illustrated. To pass by all lessons derivable from the Old Testament ministry (which might be validly urged in support of this principle, however much we believed that the Levitical distinctions of ministry had themselves no counterpart whatever in the Church of Christ); to omit even the broader emphasis upon the principle in such passages as the denunciation of the prophets who were *not* sent in the 28th of Jeremiah, or the 'Here am I, send me,' following upon the 'Lo, this hath touched thy tongue,' of the 6th of Isaiah; it emerges as a principle no less cardinal in the Church of the New Testament. Compare our Lord's commission to the twelve, 'As the Father hath sent Me, even so send I you,' with the argument of Romans x., 'How then shall they call on Him in whom they have not believed? and how shall they believe in Him whom they have not heard? and how shall they hear without a preacher? and how shall they preach, except they be sent? even as it is written, How beautiful are the feet of them that bring glad tidings of good things!'

Our Lord's words base the 'sending' of Apostles upon

His own 'sending.' This sending, or commission, regarded (along with human capacity of sympathy) as an essential principle of priesthood, even in the Person of Christ, is the basis of the argument in the 5th chapter to the Hebrews: 'Every high priest, being taken from among men, is appointed for men in things pertaining to God, that he may offer both gifts and sacrifices for sins who can bear gently with the ignorant and erring, for that he himself also is compassed with infirmity, and by reason thereof is bound, as for the people, so also for himself, to offer for sins. And no man taketh the honour unto himself, but when he is called of God, even as was Aaron. So Christ also glorified not Himself to be made a high priest, but He that spake unto Him, Thou art My Son, this day have I begotten Thee: as He saith also in another place, Thou art a priest forever after the order of Melchizedek.' And again, that these words, because they apply to Christ, do not therefore apply to every Christian in the same sense, is clear from 2 Cor. ii.-v. amongst other places: 'Thanks be unto God, which . . . maketh manifest through us the savour of His knowledge in every place. . . And who is sufficient for these things? . . . Such confidence have we through Christ to Godward, not that we are sufficient of ourselves to account anything as from ourselves; but our sufficiency is from God; who also made us sufficient as ministers of a new covenant; not of the letter, but of the Spirit; for the letter killeth, but the Spirit giveth life. . . Therefore seeing we have this ministry, even as we obtained mercy, we faint not; . . . but we have this treasure in earthen vessels, that the exceeding greatness of the power may be of God, and not from ourselves; . . . wherefore we faint not; . . . all things are of God, who reconciled us to Himself through Christ, and gave unto us the ministry of reconciliation; . . . we are ambassadors therefore on behalf of Christ, as though God were intreating you by us[1].' It will be observed that,

[1] Cf. Rom. xii. 6-8; 1 Cor. xii. 29, Eph. iv. 11, &c.

in these passages, the sense of Divine commission is the backbone of ministry; partly in the more negative sense that, without it, no man durst presume to exercise ministerial functions at all, partly in the more positive sense, that to those who have it, it alone, that is to say the overshadowing consciousness of Divine command, Divine companionship, Divine empowering, constitutes all the reality of what they do, and is to them all their courage and their strength. In other words, any aspiration to ministry in Christ's Church, or attempt to discharge its duties, however otherwise well-intentioned, would be a daring presumption at the first, and in practice a disastrous weakness, in proportion as it was lacking in adequate ground to believe in its own definitely, validly, divinely received authority to minister

'Even so send I you'—nothing short of this can bear the strain of ministry 'When He had said this,' the text of St. John proceeds at once, 'He breathed on them and saith unto them, "Receive ye the Holy Ghost."' I am not now discussing these words as a formula in the Ordinal; but looking at them in a more general way, it is plain that valid authority to minister (whatever the methods which convey or assure it) means such gift of Spirit as enables—by Divine warrant and in Divine power—to a real 'ministration of the Spirit.' If the first point to lay down is that authority to minister must be felt to come to the individual soul from God, the second is that the differentiating character and essential meaning of ministry is 'Spirit.' This essential 'Spirit,' character of ministry, and its dependence alike for its valid inception, and for its maintenance throughout, upon 'Spirit,' receives careful expression in the address in our Ordinal to all candidates for priesthood. 'Forasmuch then as your Office is both of so great excellency, and of so great difficulty, ye see with how great care and study ye ought to apply yourselves, as well that ye may show yourselves dutiful and thankful unto that Lord who hath placed you in so high a dignity, as also to beware, that neither you yourselves offend, nor be occasion that others offend. Howbeit, ye cannot have a mind and will thereto of yourselves; for that will and ability is given of God alone: therefore ye ought, and have need, to pray earnestly for His Holy Spirit. . . . You will continually pray to God the Father, by the mediation of our only Saviour Jesus Christ, for the heavenly assistance of the Holy Ghost.' That the Ordinal subsequently purports to convey an exceedingly solemn *charisma* of the Holy Spirit, and that this solemn *charisma* for ministry is conceived of as constituting the essential distinction and capacity of ministerial life, is of course, upon the face of the service, obvious.

I am not now discussing the Ordinal in itself, only glancing at its coherence in this matter with the scriptural principle that Divine commission, whose constitutive character is endowment of 'Spirit,' is the one warrant for, and the one strength of, any form of self sufficing or independent Church ministry. But it may be worth while to emphasize this particular point of view by quoting the striking expression of it in words which will be widely accepted as authoritative.

'Now, besides that the power and authority delivered with those words is itself χάρισμα, a gracious donation which the Spirit of God doth bestow, we may most assuredly persuade ourselves that the hand which imposeth upon us the function of our ministry doth under the same form of words so tie itself thereunto, that he which receiveth the burden is thereby for ever warranted to have the Spirit with him and in him for his assistance, aid, countenance, and support in whatsoever he faithfully doth to discharge duty. Knowing therefore that when we take ordination we also receive the presence of the Holy Ghost, partly to guide, direct, and strengthen us in all our ways, and partly to assume unto itself for the more authority those actions that appertain to our place and calling, can our ears admit such a speech uttered in the reverend performance of that solemnity, or can we at any time renew the memory and enter into serious cogitation thereof but with much admiration and joy? Remove what these "foolish" words do imply, and what hath the ministry of God besides wherein to glory? Whereas now, forasmuch as the Holy Ghost which our Saviour in His first ordinations gave doth no less concur with spiritual vocations throughout all ages, than the Spirit which God derived from Moses to them that assisted him in his government did descend from them to their successors in like authority and place, we have for the least and meanest duties performed by virtue of ministerial power, that to dignify, grace, and authorize them, which no other offices on earth can challenge. Whether we preach, pray, baptize, communicate, condemn, give absolution, or whatsoever, as disposers of God's mysteries, our words, judgements, acts, and deeds, are not ours but the Holy Ghost's. Enough, if unfeignedly and in heart we did believe it, enough to banish whatsoever may justly be thought corrupt, either in bestowing, or in using, or in esteeming the same otherwise than is meet. For profanely to bestow, or loosely to use, or vilely to esteem of the Holy Ghost we all in show and profession abhor[1].'

Now in everything that has hitherto been said, or quoted, on the subject, it has been clearly implied that commission, to be commission in any sufficient meaning of the term, must be commissioned not from below but from above. Only as it is clearly understood to be from above—from God essentially and not man—can it spiritually authorize or empower; however much such authorizing may be accompanied by, or even may require, as a regular preliminary, acclamation or acceptance from below. It never can be conferred by those who have not authority to confer it. Even on the extreme supposition that either popular choice or individual impulse were the sufficient witness and method of God's appointment, it would still be God's act and not the popular voice, God's

[1] Hooker's *Eccl. Pol.*, Bk V. lxxvii. § 8. p. 462.

inspiration and not the individual's response thereto, which conveyed the authority. No doubt the use or sanction of processes like these might be very unlike the method of God's dealing with men in His Church. They might be a very extreme instance of the old maxim *Vox populi vox Dei*. But it would still be only as *vox Dei* that the *vox populi* could be supposed to suffice.

The one idea, then, which is altogether incompatible with the passages quoted is the idea that the difference between ministry and laity is a difference merely of secular or politic convenience. Even on the extremest form of anti-ecclesiastical theory I must venture to repeat that the belief that the congregation could constitute a minister must mean a belief that that which speaks through the choice of the congregation is God's voice; that it is Himself pronouncing and appointing through this particular means. The idea of a secular appointment *as secular*, a distinction of convenience drawn on the basis of convenience, without reference to the Divine purpose, or consciousness of being instrumental to a Divine Act, is the one idea which may be regarded as wholly untenable. It is not too much to say that any theory of ministry such as this stands condemned beforehand as an impossibility.

But if this be put wholly aside, there remain, it seems, three alternative forms which the idea of a Divine designation might take. First, there is the view that Divine appointment manifests itself solely within the individual conscience of a man who is called, because he feels that he is called, by God to minister. Secondly, there is the view that the witness in the individual conscience must be accompanied by appointment on the part of the general Church body, or some adequate portion of it, but without reference to any particular 'ministerial' method or continuity, of transmission. Church appointment to ministry, on this view, is not to be dispensed with. But the Church is in no way bound. She can provide herself ministers and instruments wherever, or however, she thinks fit. And, thirdly, there is the familiar Church view that none can be held to be divinely commissioned until he has received commission on earth from those who themselves had received authority to commission from such as held it in like manner before them; that is, when the matter is pressed home, that valid ministerial authority depends, upon its earthward side, upon continuous transmission from the Apostles of Jesus Christ.

It seems to me worth while to consider these alternatives to some extent separately. As to the first alternative, I am hardly perhaps concerned to deny so much its abstract possibility, as its practical possibility under Church conditions. At the least, I am persuaded that the presumption against its credibleness in any particular case is for practical purposes overwhelming. The principle that inward acts through outward, grace through means of grace, Spirit through Body, is a principle which in the great vital fact of the Incarnation seems to have received its full and final consecration; and thenceforward to abide for ever, as what may truly be called at once an essential principle, and a revealed law, of the life of Christ's Church. The principle requires, first of all, and finds its expression in, the fact of the organization, or Body, of the Church of Christ. But that the Church should be an organized Body at all, and yet that this principle should be set aside in a matter of importance quite cardinal to the entire administration of the Church, is, to the theology of the Incarnation, nearly inconceivable. If the principle of the consecration of the material and the outward has no place in the public authorization of ministers to minister in spiritual things, the entire method which pervades the life of Christ's Church, the whole rationale of the sacramental system, is *pro tanto* invalidated. Baptism by water, Communion in Bread and Wine, cease to be of one piece with the entire revelation of the religion of the Incarnate, and become rather isolated and fragmentary observances, imposed upon an obedience which is no longer intelligent.

In spite however of considerations like these, there are still three points, I imagine, which might be urged in support of the theory. These are, first the precedent of the Old Testament prophets, in the light e. g. of Amos vii. or Jeremiah i., secondly, the precedent of St. Paul, according to his own determined insistence in Galatians i. and ii.; and thirdly, the picture of the Christian prophets as portrayed in the *Didache*.

If appeal is made to the precedent of Old Testament prophecy, it must be answered that the very contrast of the Old Testament bears emphatic witness, in this matter, to the character of the New. Broadly, in the old dispensation, the material and the spiritual were still kept apart—the spiritual being still, itself, symbolically rather than directly spiritual. But in the new covenant all reality is spiritual; the material is nothing but the direct expression of spirit. Thus in the Old Testament it may perhaps be said that the formal regularity of the outward or material is represented by the hereditary priesthood; the transcendency of the spiritual inward by the occasional and variable inspiration of prophets. In the New Testament these two principles coalesce. The ministry is not of hereditary descent, but of personal vocation: its outwardness lacks full reality except it be the outward of an inward, the representation of a Spirit; yet its succession is not casual but orderly, not inscrutable but through regularity and solemnity of method. In this it exactly accords with all the fundamental methods of the earthly revelation of the kingdom of heaven.

If appeal be made to the instance of St. Paul, and his claim in the Epistle to the Galatians, it must be answered that the very case of St. Paul, in proportion as it was exceptional, bears exceptional witness to the strength of the principle contended for. That spiritual reality was not, in the kingdom of heaven, to supersede, but rather to be guaranteed by, outward form, is a principle made sufficiently clear in the normal Church processes: but it is stamped with greater emphasis still in a few instances which are abnormal. The principle that Spirit-baptism was not to be without water, is never enforced quite so strongly as when Cornelius and his companions, even after they had first (for special reasons) received the presence of the Holy Ghost— a presence made manifest by miracle—were nevertheless ordered to be baptized. So the principle that commission to ministry is by laying on of hands, while it is illustrated, comparatively incidentally, by the positive instances recorded in the New Testament, is nowhere made quite so emphatic as when St. Paul, with Barnabas—after his Divine call, his mission to the Gentiles and his courageous preaching, and with all his sense of vocation to apostleship direct from Jesus Christ personally—yet with fasting and prayer, is set apart by the laying on of hands of his brother 'prophets,' for the great missionary work to which the Holy Ghost was calling him. Such exceptional instances emphasize most strongly the place which was to belong to the 'outward' in the Church of Christ.[1]

But it may be said that even if individual inspiration be not the regular mode of appointment to ministry, yet it may validly stand side by side with a ministry of more regular method. Does not the *Didache*, it may be asked, show clearly that it did so at the first? and if at first, why not now, if men really feel themselves to be inspired? I am not prepared to admit, on the authority of the *Didache*, that it was so at the first. But of that there will be occasion to speak by-and-by. Meanwhile, even supposing that this premiss were granted, I should deny the *sequitur*. Whatever there may be supposed on any side to be, either of abstract possibility or of actual evidence, for a merely supernatural setting apart in the earliest days—and there are the gravest doubts about either, even apart from the great improbability constituted by the

[1] See Note, p. 125.

case of St. Paul—I shall submit that not even the supposition that it existed then, would carry us any material distance towards a belief in its credibleness now. If it be granted, for the sake of argument, that the prophets of the *Didache* were unordained men, who superseded the ordained in the highest functions of their ministry; yet I should certainly not allow the principle to pass unchallenged, in abstract form, that what God did then He might at any time do. Some things which of old He praised, or commanded, or did, became, in the process of His development of man, inherently incredible and impossible. If we cannot say as much as this of a Divine, but non-ministerial, ordination to ministry, it would none the less be doubtful whether there could be evidence adequate to convince us, in any individual case, that He had so ordained. God does not contradict His own revelation of Himself. Direct interposition of the kind supposed might with perfect consistency be conceived of as a consolidation of the infantine, and yet as a dissolution of the organized, Church. In proportion as Church order is apprehended as itself a part of the revelation of the character of God, a great change comes over the evidence which should convince us that it has been overruled by the act of God. The presumption against such overruling becomes by degrees so enormous that it is open to question whether—say in the nineteenth century, any conceivable evidence would be adequate to rebut it. Evidence after all, if offered, can only be valid as evidence if it has a certain relation of admissibleness to the fundamental convictions of the apprehending mind. There are cases in which any amount of apparent evidence would be felt to be delusive, and that even in proportion to its very appearance of convincingness. On such a ground some minds—on their own essential hypothesis consistently enough—reject beforehand any conceivable evidence for miracle. On such a ground a Christian, with the highest intellectual cogency, condemns before examination, as manifestly contradictory and immoral, anything which tends to prove that God Himself could perpetrate wickedness, or the visit of an angel warrant, to a Christian conscience, the sacrificial murder of a son[1].

It is certain that nothing is more apt to be manifestly self-deceiving than the fancies of a man's own brain about himself or his own inspiration. If, then, we are challenged to believe in an Ordination which is merely supernatural on any evidence which could be produced from a man's inner consciousness, we should justly say that all the conditions are conspicuously wanting, which, in respect of such a claim as that, would make even evidence reasonably credible. And if his personal claims should seem to be vindicated by external corroborations, even to a miraculous sign made manifest in the heavens, it is at least an open question, on New Testament principles, whether the whole should not be treated far rather as an inscrutable delusion than as a veritable sign from God.

This thought will, I believe, be further fortified by the considerations which immediately follow. I pass then to the second of the three alternatives, the idea (which forms a large element in the unexpressed thought of many who do not give form to it) that the voice of God's designation to ministry is to be recognized in the act of the appointing Church, but without any limitation whatever in respect of such matters as ministerial succession or sacramental method. The whole is a matter of unfettered and indefinite discretion, on the part of the corporate Church, or some portion thereof. Here is a position which is felt to be eminently plausible. It sounds as if it loyally believed in the Church. It sounds as if it magnified

---

[1] It was in reference to Abraham's obedience in the sacrifice of Isaac that this argument was made by Dr. Mozley an abiding possession of the Christian intellect. See *Ruling Ideas in Early Ages*, particularly the second Lecture. Perhaps I may be excused for mentioning that, some years ago, I had occasion to discuss (on the basis of this argument of Dr. Mozley's) the abstract proposition 'what God has once done God may at any time do,' in relation to the Levirate law, and the marriageableness of a sister-in-law. The proposition looks axiomatic—but only till it is examined.

the spiritual principle. It seems at first sight to withhold nothing but technicalities, involved and obscure, while conceding to the full everything that could possibly be asked upon the side of what is spiritual or real.

But let us distinguish a little further what, on this view, is held, and what is denied. It is admitted that there must be a sort of setting apart by the act of the Church: but it is not admitted that there are any special instruments in the Church through whom alone she is to act ministerially in setting apart, or any specific sacramental method according to which (through such instruments or otherwise) she is, in dutifulness, compelled to act. Observe then, in the form of this statement, what is really denied. It is a denial, not, as was supposed, of some insignificant or remote details; it is a denial of the ministerial principle itself. The very point of the ministerial principle is this, that whilst it is always the corporate Church which acts through its representative instruments, it is only through instruments, empowered to represent, that the corporate Church does act. To claim, in this case (upon which every possible act, ministerial or sacramental, depends), that the Church may act through any one, any how, is not merely to give up a certain musty ecclesiastical prejudice about the detail of ministerial succession; it is to make all ministry unmeaning everywhere.

It is certainly relevant to urge against such a view that it does not square with the analogy of the relation, in the human body, between the general corporate power and the organs specifically endowed, which was dwelt upon in the last chapter; and the analogy is not without weight, however little, as mere analogy, it can be conclusive. There is also against it a much more formidable weight of presumption from all that has been urged about the ministerial principle, and the sacramental relation between outward and inward in the principles of the theology of the Incarnation, and therefore in the experience of the Church of Christ. But after all it is mainly a question of history.

The true answer to it will lie in an examination of the methods of Ordination to ministry in Christ's Church from the day of Pentecost onwards; an examination which, for the present, it is necessary to defer. If the theory be true as theory, it is on the field of history that it must establish itself. It must show that the supposed necessity of episcopal laying on of hands came in, as an aftergrowth, upon an earlier simplicity. If it cannot make good its place in history during the early centuries of the Church, it is useless to ask us to accept it as theoretically true.

It is impossible at this point to enter seriously upon a discussion which belongs rather to another branch of the subject—the question as to methods of ordaining: but perhaps I may say at once (as this volume does not reach the further subject) that there does not seem to me to be a *prima facie* case in history for the theory that is before us. It is true that a discussion of methods would have to examine a few cases alleged to show (*a*) that the ordinary practice of laying on of hands was in some cases varied, at least in respect of its literal detail; and (*b*) that it was in some instances performed by non-episcopal presbyters[1]. But for the present purpose it is to be observed that such variations as these, even if they were established, would show indeed that an unexpected latitude had been, in rare cases, allowed in the sacramental administration of Ordination: but they would not tend at all to show that Ordination was regarded as otherwise than a sacramental act; or could be conveyed sacramentally except by instruments ministerially empowered to convey it. Even the claim of Tertullian that every layman is a priest *in posse*, and may so act in case of necessity (whatever its merits or demerits may be), would not carry us far towards supposing either that, necessity apart, every layman has the same right as a priest to minister in sacred things, or that the distinction which makes one man

[1] They are alleged by Dr. Hatch, Bampton Lectures, pp. 133, 134; and discussed by Canon Gore, Appendices B and E of *The Church and the Ministry*.

'priest' or 'bishop,' and another not, is a distinction which can be conferred, apart from all sacramental method or representative spiritual authority, by the mere designation of lay Church members.

I return, then, to the traditional view as to the 'ministerial' transmission of ministry and I conceive that it is a matter of some importance to emphasize this principle, in its abstract form, as principle, quite apart from, and prior to, any more particular questions, either as to degrees or distinctions of ministry, or as to methods in detail by which ministerial authority is conveyed. It is precisely this which appears to be done in the 23rd of our Articles, and done in exactly right order. The question as to the *method* of 'Consecration of Archbishops and Bishops, and Ordering of Priests and Deacons' as represented by the Ordinal of the reign of King Edward VI., is not reached till the 36th Article. But long before any reference to the method of the Ordinal—which carries with it the threefold distinction of Order—the principle in the abstract form is correctly laid down. 'It is not lawful for any man to take upon him the office of public preaching, or ministering the Sacraments in the Congregation, before he be lawfully called and sent (*vocatus et missus*) to execute the same. And those we ought to judge lawfully called and sent, which be chosen and called to this work by men who have public authority given unto them in the Congregation, to call and send Ministers into the Lord's vineyard.' It is possible that it may be contended—and if so, we need not be greatly concerned to deny—that the phraseology of this Article may have been in part determined, not indeed by a desire expressly to endorse (which is not at all probable), but by a certain unwillingness to be explicit in condemning, under the then existing circumstances, the system of the Continental Protestants. But whether there be in the language any such side reference, or no, it is none the less clear that what results is a statement of principle in precise accord with the proportion of truth It is the principle in the abstract. Those only are duly commissioned who have received commission from such, before them, as were themselves commissioned to commission others.

Now while we have the principle before us just in this form, it is desirable to call attention, as emphatically as possible, to the exceeding strength with which it is insisted upon in the letter of the Church of Rome to the Church of Corinth, written within the first century, which bears the name of St. Clement. It is of course to be understood that we have not yet come, either to distinctions of orders of ministry, or to the question of exact methods of ordaining; but that (whatever there may be to be said about these) ministerial office depends upon orderly transmission from those empowered to transmit the authority to ordain, that is upon a real apostolic succession, is maintained by St. Clement as strongly as it is possible for man to maintain it. The whole passage, from the 37th chapter to the 44th, absolutely depends upon it. He appeals to the orderliness of an army, and the absolute necessity of military obedience, for order: 'All cannot be captains or generals, but all are arranged, from the emperor downwards, in a completely articulated hierarchical system. So it is with the body and its members, in the language of St. Paul to the Corinthians. And such must be the unity of the Body of Christ—based upon mutual submission, dependence, subordination. Self-assertion and pride are the characteristics of fools. There is order everywhere—order of place, times, persons—as the sacrifices of old had appointed places and times; and high priest, priests, levites, people, their distinct and co-ordinate offices. Everything, then, and every one in place and order. God sent forth Christ. Christ sent forth His Apostles. The Apostles, from their converts, constituted bishops and deacons. So Moses of old established a graduated hierarchy, and silenced the voice of jealousy against the priesthood by the blossoming rod of Aaron laid up in the ark of God. In parallel-wise the Apostles, foreseeing the jealousies which should arise about ministerial office (ἐπὶ τοῦ ὀνόματος τῆς ἐπισκοπῆς), did not merely, as has been said, constitute bishops and deacons, but afterwards also made provision, in case of their decease, for a continuous succession of ministerial office. Those, then, who have once been duly constituted ministers, either by Apostles, or by other faithful men after them, with the consent of the whole Church, can never justly be deposed from the ministry which they have so long and blamelessly exercised. Such deposition of men who without scandal or irreverence have exercised the presbyteral office, and offered the gifts of the Church, would involve the Church in grave sin[1].' Such in brief paraphrase is the substance of what is urged in these seven chapters. Now however much it may be questioned whether St. Clement's letter bears witness for or against the presence of episcopacy in Rome or in Corinth, or in both; I must submit that it would be difficult to find a stronger assertion than this, of the principle that ministerial office is an outward and orderly institution, dependent for its validity upon transmission, continuous and authorized, from the Apostles, whose own commission was direct from Jesus Christ.

Whether bishops, priests, and deacons are or are

[1] The paraphrase, as given above, is not greatly affected by the uncertainty of the word ἐπινομήν (?). Canon Gore translates it 'gave an additional injunction,' adding, with a query, or 'established a supervision.' Bishop Lightfoot adopts the reading ἐπιμονήν, and translates 'have given permanence to the office.' There is no doubt that Bishop Lightfoot's view of the phrase brings it into singularly exact accord with the context and its argument. The point in that case emphasized by the sentence would be that they provided *permanence* (cf. ἐπίμονος at the end of ch. 46) by means of *succession*. Nothing then could be more apt than the expression, just at that point, of the word permanence. But of course, even if it be unexpressed, the idea of permanence is implied in provision made for transmission of succession by the prescience of Apostles. [It has been pointed out to me that the Latin version discovered by Don Morin, with its 'legem dederunt,' is probably decisive in favour of ἐπινομήν. See the *Anecdota Maredsolana*, 1894.]

not scriptural or exclusive orders of ministry, is on its own grounds fair matter for argument; but antecedently to any such argument, I must submit that the principle in abstract form—that ministerial authority depends upon continuous transmission from the Apostles, through those to whom the Apostles transmitted the power to transmit—must be recognized as being, from the time of St. Clement onwards, a principle implanted in the consciousness of the Christian Church. When it is remembered in what position St. Clement stood, and with what tone and claim of authoritative remonstrance he wrote, as the 'persona' of the Church of Rome, to the Church of Corinth; and again to what date he and his writing belong, he himself in greater or less degree a companion of Apostles, and his letter written as early as the dying years of the first century, very little after —if after—the close of the life of St. John[1], the significance of this exceedingly strong assertion of the principle of apostolic succession in this earliest of authoritative post-apostolic writings becomes overwhelming indeed Not Ignatius himself is a stronger witness to 'apostolic succession' than is the Church of Rome in the person of St. Clement.

After what has been said, it will be evident that (to put this matter at the lowest) it becomes at least a question of crucial importance to determine whether Christian ministry does or does not depend upon such a continuity of devolution from Apostles as St. Clement describes. Must true ministerial 'character' be in all cases conferred from above? or may it sometimes, and with equal validity, be evolved from below? Is uninterrupted transmission from those who had the power to transmit a real essential? or can the Church originate, at any point, a new ministry

---

[1] The limits of the possible variation of date are not very wide. The year actually fixed by Bishop Lightfoot (and Dr. Salmon) is A.D. 96. Bishop Westcott is expressly of opinion that St. Clement's letter was written and sent while the Apostle *St. John was still living* at Ephesus. [*Speaker's Commentary*, Introd. to St John, p xxix.]

whose commission of authority should exceed or transcend what had been ministerially received? It is difficult to exaggerate the importance of this question, and of the answer which is to be made to it.

Now, strange to say, it is one of the principal complaints against Bishop Lightfoot's famous essay, that he appears to ignore this question altogether. He never really answers it: he never raises it · he shows no consciousness that there is any importance in it it never presents itself to his mind at all. That he does not intend to contradict the principle of St. Clement might possibly be inferred from the very ambiguity of the statements in the essay itself, and still more from the Bishop's repudiation of views about his own meaning which he found to be current But not even in demurring to mistaken views of his meaning does he ever put his finger upon our present point, or express his own judgment about it And meanwhile there are in the essay not a few statements which no one who had the question before his mind at all could possibly have made, unless it were with the purpose, which appears not to be the Bishop's purpose, of controverting the principle. Thus 'The episcopate properly so-called would seem to have been developed from the subordinate office. In other words, the episcopate was formed not out of the apostolic order by localization but out of the presbyteral by elevation[1].' 'If in some passages St. James is named by himself, in others he is omitted and the presbyters alone are mentioned. From this it may be inferred that though holding a position superior to the rest, he was still considered as a member of the presbytery, that he was in fact the head or president of the college[2].' 'Though remaining a member of the presbyteral council, he was singled out from the rest and placed in a position of superior responsibility[3].' St. Clement 'was rather the chief of the presbyters than the chief over the presbyters[4].' 'Even as late as the close of the second century the bishop

[1] p. 194. [2] p. 195. [3] p. 205. [4] p. 219.

of Alexandria was regarded as distinct and yet not distinct from the presbytery¹.' The bishop, 'though set over the presbyters, was still (after the lapse of centuries) regarded as in some sense one of them².' 'In the investigation just concluded I have endeavoured to trace the changes in the relative position of the first and second orders of the ministry, by which the power was gradually concentrated in the hands of the former. Such a development involves no new principle and must be regarded chiefly in its practical bearings It is plainly competent for the Church at any given time to entrust a particular office with larger powers, as the emergency may require³'

These passages are not quoted as necessarily erroneous (though the first and the last of them seem to approach so near to a contradiction of the principle of 'apostolic succession' that they could certainly not have been expressed in this way by any one who thought that it represented a truth of the least importance in the Church), but rather to illustrate the absence of the particular question from Bishop Lightfoot's mind. We may set against them if we will other passages, from the essay and elsewhere, which seem to carry us far in the opposite direction · such as, for example, these three 'If the preceding investigation be substantially correct, the threefold ministry can be traced to apostolic direction; and short of an express statement we can possess no better assurance of a Divine appointment, or at least a Divine sanction⁴. . . The result has been a confirmation of the statement in the English Ordinal: "It is evident unto all men diligently reading the Holy Scripture and ancient authors that from the Apostles' time there have been these orders of Ministers in Christ's Church, Bishops, Priests, and Deacons⁵." . . . We cannot afford to sacrifice any portion of the faith once delivered to the saints; we cannot surrender for any immediate advantages the threefold ministry which we have inherited from

---

¹ p. 224. ² p. 226. ³ p. 242. ⁴ p. 265.
⁵ *Dissertations on the Apostolic Age*, p. 243.

apostolic times, and which is the historic backbone of the Church¹.' But it will be observed that in the passages on this side, as in those on the other, the principle in the form in which we found it practically in St. Clement is never really raised or touched at all.

Even the statement that the episcopate was 'not formed out of the apostolic order by localization' may mean practically little more than that the office of the bishop was never wholly identical with that of the Apostles. Bishop Lightfoot, in denying this identity, almost seems to think that he is denying the current sense of 'apostolic succession²'; but in truth it may be doubted whether any of those who maintain succession would thereby intend identity³. The correlative statement that the episcopate was formed 'out of the presbyteral order by elevation' may be perfectly true, but does not necessarily affect the matter at all. The really crucial question is untouched by these words. It would still have to be asked 'formed by whom?' and 'on whose authority?' It may be urged that what Bishop Lightfoot says about the 'competence of the Church at any time to entrust a particular office with larger powers' shows that according to his view the episcopal authority was, in principle, rather originated by the general authority of the Church, than authoritatively devolved by the Apostles; and probably the words would, in strictness, contain this conclusion. And yet, upon the whole of the passages, it is greatly to be doubted whether this was in fact the Bishop's meaning; and it may certainly be said that, if he desired to

---

[1] *Dissertations on the Apostolic Age*, p. 246; so also on p. 244.

[2] 'It is not therefore to the Apostle that we must look for the prototype of the Bishop. How far indeed and in what sense the Bishop may be called a successor of the Apostles, will be a proper subject for consideration; but the succession at least does not consist in an identity of office,' p. 194.

[3] Both Dr. Liddon and Canon Gore make reference to the passage in which Bishop Pearson distinguishes, in the apostolic office and authority, the 'temporary and extra-ordinary' from the 'ordinary and permanent';— the former expiring with the Apostles, the latter perpetuated in the Episcopate. See *The Church and the Ministry*, p. 70, note 1.

take his stand upon this, as the ultimate basis of all ministry in the Church of Christ, the principle needed a much clearer statement and fuller justification, theological as well as historical, than he has attempted to give.

The question whether ministerial status is evolved or devolved only directly suggests itself in Bishop Lightfoot's essay in connexion with the episcopate. Presbyterate and diaconate would have been originally devolved by commission from Apostles as a matter of course. But attention can hardly be drawn too emphatically to what is, on a little consideration, the very obvious fact that, throughout the history of the Christian Church, presbyterate and diaconate have in fact been made wholly to depend upon episcopate. It is episcopate alone which has been understood to have received the power to transmit. It is episcopate alone which has in fact, at any time, conferred either presbyterate or diaconate. Now if the other orders depend upon episcopate, and if episcopate is itself, in its ultimate rationale, 'evolved from below,' then it follows that the basis of all these orders alike is *not* apostolic devolution or succession, but evolution out of the general spiritual life and consciousness of the Church.

Is it not a curious paradox? The Apostles ordained both presbyters and deacons, and provided (as St. Clement says) for their transmission to the after-ages. Devolution by succession, that is to say, was the apostolic principle, carefully prearranged. But the Apostles' principle was frustrated and their prevision and precaution nullified by the insertion of a new order, itself unauthorized apostolically, as that upon which the two others should depend for their very existence.

The only escape from the difficulty is to deny that episcopate has any separate existence at all. There is in fact, on this theory, no room for it. The Church is really presbyterian. Episcopate is either not distinguishable from presbyterate, or it is self-condemned in distinguishing itself. Episcopate may be just tolerated, so long as it is clearly understood that the bishop is not really different, in any essential particular whatever, from what every presbyter is. But the moment it is claimed that episcopate can do anything whatever that presbyterate cannot, episcopate becomes a false usurpation and delusion. In other words, episcopate, in the only sense in which it has ever been received or regarded anywhere, has been, and is, an accretion so deluding that it ought not to be tolerated.

Considering how entirely, if episcopacy be retained or believed in as having any reality at all, the rationale of ministerial office rests ultimately upon the decision between the devolution and the evolution of episcopate, it is quite extraordinary how completely the point of the question is ignored by Bishop Lightfoot. It is in this form that the question must be asked and answered. To this, the question whether the episcopal office is identical with the apostolical, or in what respects it differs, is an irrelevant detail. To this, again, all such evidence as goes to show that the episcopal presbyter was in some sense a presbyter still, though he was over the presbyters, is of no real importance whatever. That so much as this was at least in some sense true, even of an apostle and (in many ways) the leader among apostles, is emphasized for us by St. Peter when he claims to write as fellow-presbyter to presbyters[1]. So far is the theory of the presbytership of the bishop from militating in any way against the most stringent doctrine of apostolic succession, that this very doctrine, that the bishop is presbyter, was before the Reformation for a thousand years throughout the West, and is in the Roman Church to this day so habitually exaggerated, that it has become a settled and formal part of the Roman theological teaching, that there is no distinct 'order' of bishops at all[2]. If the bishop

---

[1] 1 Pet. v. 1; see below, ch. vi. p. 187, note 4.

[2] 'Quamvis unus sit sacerdotii ordo, non tamen unus est sacerdotum gradus' is the heading of qu. xxv. in cap. vii. p. II of the Tridentine

was 'set over' the presbyters, if St. Clement was 'chief' either 'over' or 'of' the presbyters, if St. James was 'singled out from the rest and placed' in a position of superior responsibility, the real question is *by whom, and through what method*, and *under what sanction*, were they so 'set' or 'singled' or 'placed'?

So long as no one presumes to exercise powers except they be within the four corners of the commission which he has formally received, the principle of apostolic succession is not violated. Thus it has been pointed out by Canon Gore[1] that if Apostles or their successors ordained in any place not a single episcopal presbyter, but a whole college of presbyters with episcopal commission and capacity, the principle would remain intact. Such a college of presbyters-in-episcopal-orders (to use modern phraseology) if they confirmed, or ordained, or consecrated diocesan bishops, would not be travelling outside the powers committed to them. It is the claim to originate (as it were) capacities for ministerial function which have not been expressly received, which denies the principle. Could John Wesley ordain? Could the American Church of the last century, without the intervention of bishops, have conferred episcopacy upon itself? Such as these are the questions which directly raise it. It is perfectly compatible with episcopate, which whilst authorized to wield the prerogatives of episcopate, remains also a presbyterate still. It is not compatible with episcopate purporting to be conferred by those who held no commission authorizing them to confer it[2].

Catech ad Paroch. The 'grades' of priesthood enumerated are (1) sacerdotes simpliciter, (2) episcopi or pontifices, (3) archiepiscopi or metropolitani, (4) patriarchae, (5) Romanus pontifex maximus, totius orbis terrarum pater et patriarcha.

[1] p 73.

[2] 'This is the Church principle that no ministry is valid which is assumed, which a man takes upon himself, or which is merely delegated to him from below. That ministerial act alone is valid which is covered by a ministerial commission received from above by succession from the Apostles. This is part of the great principle of tradition. . . . What heresy

There is another point which it may be worth while to put expressly. The theory of apostolic succession is one against which a prejudice is often raised by the form in which it is stated. Objectors object to it, or those who should be its defenders with a light heart surrender it, as though its chief purpose were to satisfy a certain craving for logical symmetry, or perhaps for the natural pride in an immemorial pedigree, by making dogmatic assertions, in themselves regarded as doubtful, perhaps even as impossible, as to the detail of events of a thousand or of fifteen hundred years ago. How can you tell, it is asked, or what can it matter, whether there was or was not a link missing in the chain, somewhere perhaps in the thirteenth—or in the third—century?

Now if any one wishes really to measure what is meant, he should raise the question not in the dim perspective of the past, but in the foreground of the immediate present. It is in respect of its own time that each generation has its practical concern in, and charge of, the principle. Those who speak lightly of what may have happened long ago, are they indifferent to the things which concern themselves? Would they accept as their bishop one who was is in the sphere of truth, a violation of the apostolic succession is in the tradition of the ministry. Here too there is a deposit handed down, an ecclesiastical trust transmitted; and its continuity is violated, whenever a man "takes any honour to himself" and assumes a function not committed to him. Judged in the light of the Church's mind as to the relation of the individual to the whole body, such an act takes a moral discolouring The individual of course who is guilty of the act may not incur the responsibility in any particular case through the absence of right knowledge, or from other causes which exempt from responsibility in whole or in part; but judged by an objective standard, the act has the moral discolouring of self-assertion The Church's doctrine of succession is thus of a piece with the whole idea of the Gospel revelation, as being the communication of a divine gift which must be received and cannot be originated,—received, moreover, through the channels of a visible and organic society; and the principle (this is what is here emphasized) lies at the last resort in the idea of succession rather than in the continuous existence of episcopal government—even though it should appear that this too is of apostolic origin, and that the Church, since the Apostles, has never conceived of itself as having any power to originate or interpolate a new office.' Ibid., pp. 74, 75

But see the whole passage, from p 69 onwards.

consecrated to episcopate by laymen? or receive absolution in their hour of anguish, or the eucharistic gifts in their highest worship, from one who had received his ordination at the hands only of the unordained? Belief in apostolic succession really means a belief that this has been a practical question to each generation severally in its turn, and that each generation severally has cared about, because it has believed in, the dutiful answer to the question. Those who care *now* that Ordination should be received from those only who have themselves received power to ordain, care really for all that apostolic succession means Certainly there was no foolish pride in dim remoteness of pedigree (though there was a deep sense of the religious value of authority duly received because lawfully transmitted), nor was there any mere craving for symmetry of logic, on the part of those who, within the first century of the Church, made the solemn remonstrance of the Roman with the Corinthian Christians turn upon the question of apostolic and continuous transmission of ministry.

Whether ministry received from Apostles is transmissible only through bishops, or through presbyters also, is no doubt a question of the utmost importance. But the theory of apostolic succession may be, in itself—and is—affirmed on both views alike.

The principle, in its abstract form, is quite capable of being detached from any theories about episcopacy. On the other hand, if episcopacy be, in any real sense, accepted, the principle of apostolical succession can no longer be kept in detachment from it. To a presbyterian theory of succession, episcopate (as was suggested above) would become something less tolerable, more positively erroneous, than any mere surplusage. If there are, and rightly are, bishops as the centres of Church government, then the principle of apostolical succession, however in the abstract distinguishable, must become in fact vitally identified with episcopal theory.

But for the present I have tried to speak rather of the

abstract principle. In respect of almost all that has been hitherto said, the constitution of the Church may be conceived of either as episcopal or presbyterian: but whatever it be, as far as concerns the forms or distinctions of Orders, I must submit that the evidence of the scriptural quotations given above, linked as they are to the subsequent course of Church history by the massive authority of the Church of Rome, speaking within the first century in the person of St. Clement, makes sufficiently clear to us the meaning of the principle, which since the days of St. Clement has never been successfully challenged in the Church; the principle, namely, that ministerial validity is provided for, on the human and material side, and in that sense is dependent upon, a continuity of orderly appointment and institution, received in each generation from those who themselves had been authorized to institute by the institution of those before them; that is, on analysis, by uninterrupted transmission of authority from the men whose own title to authority was that they too were 'Apostles,' 'sent' by Him who, even Himself, was 'sent' to be the Christ[1].

[1] The word Apostle is itself used of Him in Hebrews iii. 1.

NOTE, p. 108.

THOSE who, in protest against the idea that it was St. Paul's ordination to apostleship, would make least of the ceremony of Acts xiii. 3, can hardly, with reason, bring it down to the level of a service of benediction for a particular enterprise only. It seems anyhow to be unique in St. Paul's life, and to stand in marked relation with his entry upon formal apostolic work.

CHAPTER V

GRADATIONS OF MINISTRY IN THE NEW TESTAMENT

WHAT has been said hitherto has been said of the general idea of ministry. We pass now to what is really quite a different department,—the question of distinctions of ministerial office. Obviously we begin with the New Testament. What then is the evidence which meets us within the pages of the New Testament itself as to ministerial distinctions in the Church of Christ?

I. First and foremost, on every principle, stands the apostolate. The original basis of the apostolic distinction is found in the solemn selection by our Lord of twelve of His disciples, to whom He gave 'authority over unclean spirits, to cast them out, and to heal all manner of disease and all manner of sickness.' But this, however significant of their essential relation to Himself, and of the authority which should inhere, by virtue of that relation, in apostleship, is itself as yet only preliminary and tentative. For the full apostolate, in its Pentecostal sense, our Lord's personal training of His selected disciples would be gradual and complete. Whatever aspect such a fact may give to the subsequent apostolate of St. Matthias or St Paul[1], or whatever (in the

---

[1] But St Matthias was expressly chosen out 'of the men which have companied with us all the time that the Lord Jesus went in and went out among us, beginning from the baptism of John, unto the day that He was received up from us' (Acts i. 21); and even St. Paul connects his claim to apostleship expressly with the thought of having ' seen Jesus Christ our Lord' (1 Cor. ix. 1; xv. 8).

case of St. Paul at least) may have been the exceptional compensation for this gradual shaping of character under the hand of Christ, of the fact itself there can be no question whatever. It is perhaps not always remembered quite as clearly as it deserves to be that the real lessons in pastoral training within the New Testament are not to be found nearly so much in the so-called Pastoral Epistles, which are (by comparison) accidental and accessory, as in the four Gospels, in the history of the companionship of the chosen disciples with their Lord [1].

The apostolate then was already formed and fashioned for the Church before the Church began, at Pentecost, to be alive. Church without apostolate never existed for a moment. If it might be thought an exaggeration to say that the Church without the apostolate would be inconceivable; at all events it is true to say that from the Church as it is sketched in fact, whether in the early records or in the apocalyptic visions of the New Testament, the apostolate is altogether inseparable.

Of apostolate, the fundamental character and warrant is before us in the words already referred to, in St. John: 'Peace be unto you. . . . Peace be unto you: as the Father hath sent Me, even so send I you. And when He had said this, He breathed on them, and saith unto them, Receive ye the Holy Ghost: whosesoever sins ye forgive, they are forgiven unto them; and whosesoever sins ye retain, they are retained [2].'

[1] This is the thought which is worked out with so much valuable detail in Mr. Latham's *Pastor Pastorum*.

[2] John xx. 19-23. Dr. Hort, in reference to this passage, writes as follows.—[*Ecclesia*, pp 32-34.]

'Much stress is often laid on the supposed evidence afforded by the words of the evangelists that they [i. e. the words in Matt. xxviii. 16-20 and John xx. 19-23] were addressed exclusively to the Apostles. Dr. Westcott has shown how, when we look below the surface, indications are not wanting that others were not improbably likewise present, at all events on the

With the words of this awful commission we may set the record also of His parting utterances: 'These are My

occasion recorded by St. John, when his narrative is compared with that of St. Luke (xxiv. 33 ff).

'But in such a matter the mere fact that doubt is possible is a striking one. It is in truth difficult to separate these cases from the frequent omission of the evangelists to distinguish the Twelve from other disciples; a manner of language which, as we have seen, explains itself at once when we recognize how large a part discipleship played in the functions of the Twelve.

'Granting that it was probably to the Eleven that our Lord directly and principally spoke on both these occasions (and even to them alone when He spoke the words at the end of St. Matthew's Gospel), yet it still has to be considered in what capacity they were addressed by Him. If at the Last Supper, and during the discourses which followed, when the Twelve or Eleven were most completely secluded from all other disciples as well as from the unbelieving Jews, they represented the whole Ecclesia of the future, it is but natural to suppose that it was likewise as representatives of the whole Ecclesia of the future, whether associated with other disciples or not, that they had given to them those two assurances and charges of our Lord, about the receiving of the Holy Spirit and the remitting or retaining of sins (howsoever we understand these words), and about His universal authority in heaven and on earth, on the strength of which He bids them bring all the nations into discipleship, and assures them of His own presence with them all the days even to the consummation of the age.'

Dr. Hort's apparent drift is (1) to minimize the distinction between the Apostles and other Christians; and (2) to suggest that the charge in verses 21-23, if spoken 'directly and principally' to the Apostles, was not spoken to them in any exclusive sense: and it is apparently in reliance upon this that he afterwards says, 'There is indeed, as we have seen, no trace in Scripture of a formal commission of authority for government from Christ Himself [to the Apostles]' (p. 84). I cannot but submit that this is quite the wrong way of putting it. To say indeed that the commission of authority for government formally given to them was given to them not exclusively but representatively, that is, to them as representing the Church, and as ordained to exercise ministerially the authority of the Church, is the very view which the previous chapters have endeavoured to explain. So far as Dr. Hort is feeling after this, we shall fully sympathize with him. But this view, instead of denying, presupposes, and instead of explaining away, *bases itself upon, a real commission of authority* for government, delivered to the Apostles as representing the Church, and delivered to the Church to be administered through the Apostles—and through those after them who should in other generations be similarly 'sent.' Does Dr. Hort really mean that the Church was anarchical? or that the powers spoken of in the text could be exercised by, or through, any one? or that the ministerial distinction of Apostles, if it existed, depended upon anything else except the selection, and preparation, and commission of Jesus Christ? I cannot but submit that the view given in the previous chapters is what he ought to mean, and that he has no right to mean more. Upon this view it is not very material whether

words which I spake unto you, while I was yet with you, how that all things must needs be fulfilled, which are written in the law of Moses, and the prophets, and the psalms, concerning Me. Then opened He their mind, that they might understand the Scriptures; and He said unto them, Thus it is written, that the Christ should suffer, and rise again from the dead the third day; and that repentance and remission of sins should be preached in His name unto all the nations, beginning from Jerusalem. Ye are witnesses of these things. And behold, I send forth the promise of My Father upon you: but tarry ye in the city, until ye be clothed with power from on high[1].' 'All authority hath been given unto Me in heaven and on earth. Go ye therefore[2], and make disciples of all the nations, baptizing them into the Name of the Father and of the Son and of the Holy Ghost: teaching them to observe all things whatsoever I commanded you; and lo, I am with you alway, even unto the end of the world[3].' 'He was received up, after that He had given commandment through the Holy Ghost unto the Apostles whom He had chosen: to whom He also showed Himself alive after His passion by many proofs, appearing unto them by the space of forty days, and speaking the things concerning the kingdom of God: and, being assembled together with them, He

others besides the Apostles were present or no; though we certainly cannot suppose (in Dr. Hort's phrase) that such others were included 'directly' or 'principally' within the scope of Christ's words See more particularly Canon Gore, *The Church and the Ministry*, p 229, n 4.

It certainly would seem to be the truth *de facto*, that from the time when that commission was given (whether you like to say 'to the Apostles' o to the Church') (1) there was an order of men, distinguished as ἀπόστολοι who did in fact, both corporately and individually, exercise such a ministerial power of binding and loosing; and (2) that no others ever did so save as the 'Amen' to the Apostles—except in virtue of authority understoo be delegated and derived to them from Apostles.

[1] Luke xxiv. 44-49.
[2] For an (indirect) comment upon the word 'therefore' in this context, compare Milligan's *Ascension*, p. 198 sqq.
[3] Matt. xxviii. 18-20.

charged them not to depart from Jerusalem, but to wait for the promise of the Father, which, said He, ye heard from Me: for John indeed baptized with water; but ye shall be baptized with the Holy Ghost not many days hence. . . . Ye shall receive power, when the Holy Ghost is come upon you, and ye shall be My witnesses both in Jerusalem, and in all Judaea and Samaria, and unto the uttermost part of the earth[1].' The Apostles' understanding of these words receives no small illustration from St. Peter's argument after the death of Judas. 'For he was numbered among us, and received his portion in this ministry. . . . It is written in the book of Psalms, . . . His office let another take. Of the men therefore which have accompanied with us all the time that the Lord Jesus went in and went out among us, . . . of these must one become a witness[2] with us of His resurrection[3].'

It is to be remembered that the selection of St. Matthias is before the day of Pentecost. It has nothing therefore directly in common with the methods of the Pentecostal Church. What the Apostles actually did, pre-penticostally, was neither themselves altogether to appoint, nor wholly to leave it for a Divine intimation; but they put forward the two whom they believed to be likeliest, and then made appeal by prayer to their ascended Lord to determine between the two in casting of lots. It is not necessary for the present purpose to make any further comment upon the method. But whatever may be otherwise thought about it, this at least is plain; that we are here as far as possible from any conception which could have imagined apostleship as otherwise than a matter of most solemn and Divine 'sending.'

[1] Acts i. 2-5, 8.
[2] Compare the 'Ye are witnesses of these things' (Luke xxiv. 48) and 'Whereof we are witnesses' (Acts iii. 15).
[3] Acts i. 17-22.

One more case must be referred to expressly—that of St. Paul. Nothing can be clearer than his claim to be an Apostle, in the full sense, in the sense in which the Twelve were Apostles. He is hardly exactly a thirteenth, for we see him exercising no apostleship until after the death of St. James, the one Apostle whose death is solemnly recorded in Scripture. Of the relation between his exceptional appointment by Christ, and his receiving of a solemn laying-on of hands, I have already spoken[1], and of the emphatic witness thus given to the principle of external ordination. But it is quite certain that his claim to apostleship is based not upon the 'ordination' as such, but upon his unique vision of and mission from Jesus Christ.

It is certainly not that St Paul slurs the distinction or minimizes the office of apostleship 'God hath set some in the Church, first apostles, secondly prophets[2].' 'Are all apostles? are all prophets[3]?' 'How shall they hear without a preacher? and how shall they preach except they be sent[4]?' 'And who is sufficient for these things[5]?' 'Such confidence have we through Christ to Godward: not that we are sufficient of ourselves, to account anything as from ourselves; but our sufficiency is from God, who also made us sufficient as ministers of a new covenant[6].' These and other such phrases do not come from a man to whom apostleship was any tentative or human economy. But this is the man who asks, 'am I not free? am I not an apostle? have I not seen Jesus our Lord? are not ye my work in the Lord? If to others I am not an apostle, yet at least I am to you · for the seal of mine apostleship are ye in the Lord[7].' 'Truly the signs of an apostle were wrought among you in all patience, by signs and wonders and mighty works[8].' 'Paul, an apostle, not from men, neither through man, but through Jesus Christ...

---

[1] See above, p. 108. [2] 1 Cor. xii. 28 [3] 1 Cor xii 29.
[4] Rom. x. 15. [5] 2 Cor. ii. 16. [6] 2 Cor. iii 4-6.
[7] 1 Cor. ix. 1, 2. [8] 2 Cor xii. 12.

neither did I receive [the gospel] from man, nor was I taught it, but it came to me through revelation of Jesus Christ . . . but when it was the good pleasure of God, who separated me, even from my mother's womb, and called me through His grace, to reveal His Son in me, that I might preach Him among the Gentiles; immediately I conferred not with flesh and blood: neither went I up to Jerusalem to them which were apostles before me[1].' . . . 'Contrariwise, when they saw that I had been entrusted with the gospel of the uncircumcision, even as Peter with the gospel of the circumcision (for He that wrought for Peter unto the apostleship of the circumcision wrought for me also unto the Gentiles),' &c.[2]

It is the more important to be clear that St. Paul classes himself quite unreservedly with 'them which were Apostles before' him, because, with the records which are in fact before us, it is in the person of St. Paul rather than that of any or all others that we are enabled to see what apostleship practically meant

Not to dwell now upon the thought of its spiritual magnificence[3] or of its material disabilities[4], or of its fatherly yearning and self-sacrifice[5], or on other possible aspects, we shall feel that St Paul at least is clear about its inherent and (if need be) tremendous authority. 'Now some are puffed up, as though I were not coming to you. But I will come to you shortly, if the Lord will; and I will know, not the word of them which are puffed up, but the power. For the kingdom of God is not in word, but in power. What will ye? shall I come unto you with a rod, or in love and a spirit of meekness? .... For I verily, being absent in body but present in spirit, have already, as though I were present, judged him that hath so wrought this thing, in the name of our Lord Jesus, ye being gathered together, and my spirit, with the power of our Lord

---

[1] Gal. i. 1, 12, 15, 17. [2] Gal ii 7, 8. [3] As in 2 Cor. iii.
[4] As in 1 Cor. iv. 9-13; 2 Cor. xi; Col i 24, &c.
[5] As in 1 Cor. ix. 19-23; 2 Cor. vii.; xii. 14, &c.

Jesus, to deliver such a one unto Satan for the destruction of the flesh, that the spirit may be saved in the day of the Lord Jesus[1].' . . 'Yea, I beseech you, that I may not when present show courage with the confidence wherewith I count to be bold against some, which count of us as if we walked according to the flesh. For though we walk in the flesh, we do not war according to the flesh (for the weapons of our warfare are not of the flesh, but mighty before God to the casting down of strongholds[2]).' . . . 'For this cause I write these things while absent, that I may not when present deal sharply, according to the authority which the Lord gave me for building up, and not for casting down[3].'

It belongs to the nature of the New Testament record that this authority, of which St. Paul speaks so plainly, should be comparatively little dwelt upon except by St. Paul. But it is surely the very same tone which speaks in the Third Epistle of St. John· 'Therefore, if I come, I will bring to remembrance his works which he doeth, prating against us with wicked words[4].' For myself, I should add that the first four verses of 1 Pet. v. appear to be characteristically animated by the consciousness of an overruling authority which it is the very object of the Apostle so to waive at the moment as not even expressly to refer to it: and I must add that the same inherently tremendous power seems to receive an awful— if somewhat staggering — emphasis, in what I will not call the act of St. Peter, but the act of God in significantly awful relation with the person and ministry of St. Peter, in the scene of the death of Ananias and Sapphira.[5]

In this same connexion we might fairly appeal also to the thought of the disciplinary authority which St.

---

[1] 1 Cor. iv. 18 sqq.; v. 3, 4.   [2] 2 Cor. x. 2-4.
[3] 2 Cor. xiii. 10.   [4] 3 John 10.
[5] Acts v. 5, 6, 9. There is nothing even remotely approaching to a decision on St Peter's part to punish (as there is on St. Paul's part in 1 Cor. v.), much less to punish by death. He does not decree anything; he does but discern the awful working of the judgement of God.

Paul calls upon Timotheus and Titus to exercise: 'For there are many unruly men ... whose mouths must be stopped, ... for which cause reprove them sharply ... these things speak and exhort and reprove with all authority. Let no man despise thee[1].' If we be reminded that their authority is not strictly apostolical, this gives only an *à fortiori* character to the argument. Such authority as they have is simply derived to them from the apostolic authority of St. Paul: or does any one suppose that St. Paul recognized in them an authority independent of himself? No doubt such authority in them, in proportion as they are perfectly successful, will seem to be merged in the moral influence of a mutually devoted affection; but it is clear that St. Paul is thinking of an authority in them which (a) is not the less a real, even if it fails to become a 'moral,' authority; and (b) derives its origin and inherent rights, not from the 'spontaneous homage' towards them of the Christians of Ephesus or Crete, but from the commission they had ministerially received from himself.

It is of course perfectly consistent with all this profound reality of authority, and of power to vindicate the authority, that, as St Paul indicates in the last six verses of 2 Cor. x., the Apostles should exercise the greatest possible reserve in any exercise of authority over one another's converts · or again that the apostolic Church at Jerusalem, in restraining the pardonable zeal of its converts at Antioch, should studiously abstain from the use of merely authoritative language. It is also no doubt perfectly true that, in the ordinary relation between an Apostle and his converts, any sense of submission on the one side and jurisdiction on the other would be entirely merged in the far more obvious reality of mutual devotion. But the most passionate intensity of mutual loyalty between a king and his servants, or a master and his disciples, or a father and his sons, does not really qualify the fact that the master and the father and the king, in their

---

[1] Titus i. 10, 13; ii. 15. Compare 1 Tim. iv. 12, 14; v. 11, 17, 19, &c.

different ways and degrees, do, on analysis, hold authority too. It is not that authority is really merged in moral influence: both are present still in undiluted fullness: only, in the atmosphere of love, the antithesis between the two is dissolved[1].

On the whole, then, I must venture to submit the following proposition, if not as scientifically proved, yet at least as the natural outcome of what has been said; as a basis, then, which it is reasonable at least to accept provisionally and test by acceptance, viz. that, in the history and government and development of the Church, everything depends upon the apostolate, everything emanates from the apostolate; nothing comes into existence on a basis independent of the apostolate, the Apostolate is, throughout, the assumed condition which lies behind as the basis and background of everything. When it is said that everything emanates from apostolate, what is particularly meant in the present connection is that neither the perpetuation, in any form, of apostolate, nor the creation of any other ministerial offices, different from itself, could rest upon any other than an apostolic basis. And this indeed appears to be the one aspect

---

[1] I cannot therefore but deprecate, as a seriously misleading understatement, Dr Hort's mode of putting it, when after denying that the Apostles had received from Christ any formal authority for government, he goes on to say [p 84], 'But it is inconceivable that the moral authority with which they were thus clothed, and the uniqueness of their position and personal qualifications, should not in all these years have been accumulating upon them by the spontaneous homage of the Christians of Judaea, an ill-defined but lofty authority in matters of government and administration': and applying this to the question of Acts xv. about the Gentiles [p. 83]: 'A certain authority is thus implicitly claimed. There is no evidence that it was more than a moral authority; but that did not make it less real.' And again [p. 85]: 'Hence in the letter sent to Antioch the authority even of the Apostles, notwithstanding the fact that unlike the Jerusalem elders they exercised a function towards all Christians, was moral rather than formal; a claim to deference rather than a right to be obeyed.' No one need desire to deprecate anything that is here said about the reality of the moral authority in itself; but it is surely illegitimate so to use the 'moral,' as to deny that Apostles possessed any other possibility of, authority. Authority is not the less authority because it is fused in love

which is, for our present purpose, really important. We do not really need so much to explore exactly what Apostles, as Apostles, did. But we do need to conceive of apostolae as constituting, in the literal sense of the word, the universal and unvarying hypothesis underlying all ecclesiastical organization and life[1].

II. Proceeding chronologically, the first extension or variation of any kind which we meet with in the history of ministerial office, is the institution of deacons in Acts vi. Great attention is drawn in the narrative of the Acts to the new departure in Church ministry which this institution involves. It is presented as one of the great steps in the rapid process of the widening of the Church. The institution of the diaconate[2], with the circumstances which had necessitated it; the work and death of St. Stephen; the history of the conversion of Saul of Tarsus; the circumstances, first and last, of the baptism of Cornelius, and the defence of St. Peter; these are the great successive moments which separate the Church of the early pentecostal days from the Church of the apostolate of St. Paul.

[1] It is hardly necessary to discuss in this connexion the wider use of the word ἀπόστολος in the New Testament: for it is plain that the existence of a wider does not destroy the significance of the narrower application of the title. This possibility of ambiguous use is perfectly natural in the case of a word which did not cease to express its own etymological meaning because it was also acquiring, or had acquired, a special and technical sense The same is certainly true of the words πρεσβύτερος and διάκονος, perhaps even of χήρα. On the wider use of ἀπόστολος, see Lightfoot, *Galat*, p. 95 sqq.

[2] On the identity of the 'seven' with 'deacons' (which the instinct of the Church has never doubted), see Bishop Lightfoot's Essay, p. 186. He adds: 'The narrative in the Acts, if I mistake not, implies that the office thus created was entirely new. Some writers, however, have explained the incident as an extension to the Hellenists of an institution which already existed among the Hebrew Christians, and is implied in the "younger men" mentioned in an earlier part of St Luke's history (Acts v 6, 10). This view seems not only to be groundless in itself, but also to contradict the general tenor of the narrative. It would appear moreover, that the institution was not merely new within the Christian Church, but novel absolutely. . . . We may fairly presume that St. Luke dwells at such length on the establishment of the diaconate because he regards it as a novel creation.' Lightfoot, *l.c.*, p. 187

As to the conception of the office, two things are made very clear on the face of the history of its institution. The first, that 'the work primarily assigned to the deacons was the relief of the poor.' The second, that, by contrast with the apostolate itself, this work of diaconate was looked upon as comparatively external and secular. It was to release the apostolate from a ministry 'of tables'; and to enable them to be given more continually to 'prayer' and to 'the ministry of the word.' It is probable, however, that this aspect of the office has been somewhat exaggerated in the Christian idea—though hardly in the practice—of diaconate. Bishop Lightfoot points out the closeness of the connexion which naturally existed between these duties of diaconate and some of the most valuable of ministerial opportunities. 'Moving about freely among the poorer brethren and charged with the relief of their material wants, they would find opportunities of influence which were denied to the higher officers of the Church, who necessarily kept themselves more aloof. The devout zeal of a Stephen or a Philip would turn these opportunities to the best account; and thus, without ceasing to be dispensers of alms, they became also ministers of the word' [p. 188]. It may be doubted, however, whether this account, which describes the diaconate as affording opportunities of spiritual work to deacons who happened to be spiritually minded, does adequate justice to the spiritual side of diaconate itself. For it is to be remembered, first, that to be 'full of the Spirit and of wisdom' was among the qualifications to be required as preliminary to election to diaconate; secondly, that men elected upon that qualification, and presented to the Apostles for consecration to their work, were so consecrated by the very same method by which all other ministers were consecrated to distinctively Christian ministry; and thirdly, that from the very moment of that consecration, the actual work which we hear of as discharged by the deacons is work of most essentially spiritual character[1]. This last fact is

[1] So much so that it is, in fact, the deacon protomartyr who gives the

mentioned by Bishop Lightfoot: but he adds at once, 'still the work of teaching must be traced rather to the capacity of the individual officer than to the direct functions of the office.' Is this quite the right way of putting it? Would it not be in truer proportion to say that spiritual teaching and influence were always understood and intended to be elements in the office, to which spiritual men were spiritually set apart, even though they were so far incidental to an external duty rather than themselves primary, that diaconate still could stand contrasted in spiritual character with apostolate, and might even be blamelessly discharged where the direct work of teaching was quite subordinate?

Bishop Lightfoot appeals to the qualifications for diaconate as sketched by St. Paul in the First Epistle to Timothy[1]. It is true, no doubt, that there is a distinction observable even there between the qualifications for diaconate and for presbyterate; but the effect of Bishop Lightfoot's appeal to the passage is a good deal qualified when we remember to how large an extent *both* pictures, as there sketched, are pictures of the antecedent qualifications, in domestic and general life, of those who might become good deacons or presbyters, rather than descriptions of the life or work of those who have already entered upon office[2].

---

lead to the whole college of Apostles in the conception of the true catholicity of the Church. Compare also Acts viii. 5 sqq , and the account of Philip the Evangelist 'who was one of the seven,' and his four daughters 'which did prophesy,' in Acts xxi 8, 9

[1] 'St. Paul writing thirty years later, and stating the requirements of the diaconate, lays the stress mainly on those qualifications which would be most important in persons moving about from house to house and entrusted with the distribution of alms. While he requires that they shall hold the mystery of the faith in a pure conscience, in other words that they shall be sincere believers, he is not anxious, as in the case of the presbyters, to secure "aptness to teach," but demands especially that they shall be free from certain vicious habits, such as a love of gossiping and a greed of paltry gain, into which they might easily fall from the nature of their duties' [p. 188]. What, it may be asked, is exactly signified by the statement that those who have served well in the diaconate 'gain to themselves . . great boldness in the faith which is in Christ Jesus'? 1 Tim. iii. 13

[2] Thus Dr. Hort, accounting for the fact that 'we learn singularly little

The further references to diaconate in the New Testament are thus summed up by Bishop Lightfoot: 'From the mother Church of Jerusalem the institution spread to Gentile Christian brotherhoods. By the "helps"[1] in the First Epistle to the Corinthians (A.D. 57) and by the "ministration[2]" in the Epistle to the Romans (A.D. 58) the diaconate solely or chiefly seems to be intended; but besides these incidental allusions, the latter epistle bears more significant testimony to the general extension of the office. The strict seclusion of the female sex in Greece and in some Oriental countries necessarily debarred them from the ministrations of men: and to meet the want thus felt, it was found necessary at an early date to admit women to the diaconate. A woman-deacon belonging to the Church of Cenchreae is mentioned in the Epistle to the Romans[3]. As time advances, the diaconate becomes still more prominent. In the Philippian Church a few years later (about A.D. 62) the deacons take their rank after the presbyters, the two orders together constituting the

---

about the actual functions' of the ministers in these passages, says, 'Doubtless it was superfluous to mention either the precise functions or the qualifications needed for definitely discharging them. What was less obvious and more important was the danger lest official excellences of one kind or another should cloak the absence of Christian excellences. To St. Paul the representative character, so to speak, of those who had oversight in the Ecclesia, their conspicuous embodiment of what the Ecclesia itself was meant to show itself [on this see below, pp 258-260], was a more important thing than any acts or teachings by which their oversight could be formally exercised;' p. 195. None the less, he thinks himself at liberty to argue negatively, from the absence of any reference to teaching in the passage in 1 Tim. iii ; and considers that the whole facts are adequately met when he adds, 'On the other hand, we may safely say that it would have been contrary to the spirit of the apostolic age to *prohibit* all teaching on the part of any διάκονοι who had real capacity of that kind;' pp. 201, 202. It may be granted that 'teaching,' at least in any formal shape, was no part of the 'official' duty (in the strictest sense of the word official) of the seven as originally set apart. But there was that in diaconate which, from the very first, outran the merely external occasion of its institution. And, ever since St. Stephen himself, Christian instinct and practice has seen in it something more that a merely administrative office to which, in exceptional cases, the 'teacher's' influence was 'not forbidden.'

[1] 1 Cor. xii. 28. [2] Rom. xii. 7. [3] Rom. xvi. 1.

recognized ministry of the Christian society there[1]. Again passing over another interval of some years, we find St. Paul in the First Epistle to Timothy (about A.D. 66) giving express directions as to the qualifications of men-deacons and women-deaconesses alike[2]. From the tenor of his language it seems clear that in the Christian communities of proconsular Asia at all events the institution was so common that ministerial organization would be considered incomplete without it. On the other hand, we may perhaps infer from the instructions which he sends about the same time to Titus in Crete, that he did not consider it indispensable; for while he mentions having given direct orders to his delegate to appoint presbyters in every city, he is silent about a diaconate[3].'

It need only be added that the word διάκονος is itself a very general one; that it only gradually acquires any technical character (it is not used directly in Acts vi. at all), and that even when most accepted as a technical term it shows no sign of losing its general use[4].

III. The next variety of ecclesiastical office which we meet with is the presbyterate. In striking contrast with the diaconate, the presbyterate can hardly be said to be introduced at all. By a casual glimpse we see incidentally that there are Christian 'presbyters'; that is all. If to institute an order of deacons marked a step in development, it is evident that, to the mind of the historian of the Acts, the appointment of presbyters did not mark anything at all. It seems to have been too much of a matter of course to be even worth mentioning. It is indeed mentioned, as a simple historical fact, that in their first missionary journey in the provinces of Asia Minor, Paul and Barnabas made a point of constituting presbyters there in every city in which they had converts[5];

---

[1] Phil. i. 1.   [2] 1 Tim. iii. 8 sqq.   [3] p 189. See Tit i. 5 sqq.
[4] On the words διάκονος and διακονία see more fully Dr. Hort's *Ecclesia*, p. 202 sqq.
[5] 'And when they had appointed for them elders in every Church, and had

but that apart from, and before, the beginning of those missionary journeys presbyters were already a regular institution of the Christian Church in Jerusalem is disclosed only by an accidental phrase, when the disciples at Antioch, 'every man according to his ability, determined to send relief unto the brethren that dwelt in Judaea· which also they did, sending it to the elders by the hands of Barnabas and Saul[1]' So curiously unobtrusive is this phrase that, if the passage stood alone, we could hardly fail to understand that the word 'elders' was a word of general description, and that what it meant in particular was the 'Apostles'; but if the rest of the New Testament forbids such an explaining of the title away, we naturally fall back upon the supposition that officers under that title were already so much a matter of course in the Jewish communities and synagogues that a similar organization of the Christian brethren was a matter to be taken for granted

After these two passages we hear that those who were delegated from Antioch to the first Church council went 'up to Jerusalem unto the apostles and elders,' where they were received of 'the Church and the apostles and the elders[2]'; and (keeping to Jerusalem) that when St. Paul came up there for the last time he 'went in with us unto James, and all the elders were present.[3]' The book of the Acts gives us also the famous occasion when 'from Miletus he sent to Ephesus, and called to him the elders of the Church. And when they were come to him he said unto them ... Take heed unto yourselves and to all the flock, in the which the Holy Ghost hath made you bishops, to feed ($\pi o\iota\mu\alpha\acute{\iota}\nu\epsilon\iota\nu$) the Church of God, which He purchased with His own blood.[4]' If this passage from the Acts does not wholly

prayed with fasting, they commended them to the Lord, on whom they had believed' Acts xiv. 23.

[1] Acts xi. 29, 30.
[2] Acts xv. 2, 4; so also 22, 23 ('the Apostles and the elder brethren'); xvi. 4
[3] Acts xxi. 18.   [4] Acts xx. 17, 28

prove that the titles πρεσβύτεροι and ἐπίσκοποι were used interchangeably, on the ground that though the same men here bear both titles they might bear them in respect of different functions; and that the functions might be sometimes but not always united, so that not all 'presbyters' might be 'bishops' nor all 'bishops' 'presbyters'; it is hardly possible to maintain even this distinction in the passage at the beginning of the Epistle to Titus. He is not there speaking of specific individuals, who were (perhaps accidentally) both 'bishops' and 'presbyters'; he is speaking, without reference to individuals, of the office in the abstract, and describes it by either term indifferently. 'I left thee in Crete, that thou shouldst .. appoint elders in every city, as I gave thee charge; if any man is blameless . . . for the bishop must be blameless as God's steward.[1]' The absolute clearness of this passage rules for us the interpretation of the passages, clearly parallel to this, in the First Epistle to Timothy, and the meaning of the words ἐπισκοπή and ἐπίσκοπος as there used; and the comparison of these two passages together rules also the interpretation of 'the bishops and deacons' who are saluted by St. Paul in the opening of his Epistle to the Church at Philippi.

As to the meaning of presbyterate, and the character of the presbyter's work, it is plain from the pastoral epistles, first, that he must be a man of blameless life in all ordinary social relations: secondly, that he will have to be a ruler in the community—'if a man knoweth not how to rule his own house, how shall he take care of the Church of God[2]?' 'let the elders that rule well be counted worthy of double honour[3]·' thirdly, that he will have to be a teacher in religious things,—'the bishop' must be 'apt to teach[4]' .. 'the bishop must be . . . holding to

---

[1] Tit. i. 5-7 On the practical equivalence of the terms, however much they may express distinct ideas, reached through different associations and from different sides, see Dr. Sanday in the *Expositor* for 1887, p. 104.
[2] 1 Tim. iii. 5   [3] Ibid. v. 17.   [4] Ibid. iii. 2.

the faithful word which is according to the teaching that he may be able both to exhort in the sound doctrine, and to convict the gainsayers[1].' Let the elders that rule well be counted worthy of double honour, 'especially those who labour in the word and in teaching[2].' The 'especially' of this last passage has been interpreted as implying that to labour in the word and teaching was not a natural part of an elder's work. When, however, we put it in conjunction with the other two passages (the second of which, it is to be remembered, is the one in which the words 'presbyter' and 'bishop' are used synonymously), it would seem impossible to conclude more, at the most, than that there might, under some conditions, be presbyters who did but little teaching, though teaching was normally one of the principal duties of the office.

The 'ruling' and the 'teaching' are mentioned in the Pastoral Epistles in very general terms. But that they include leadership in, and responsibility for, the whole spiritual worship and spiritual life of the community, and that that responsibility and leadership were of the most solemn kind conceivable, is plainly shown in the passage in Acts xx. For the present, however, these deeper implications may be said to be rather below than upon the surface of the obvious evidence. More will be said below, in connexion with the exposition of 'priesthood,' as to the conceptions to be found by necessary implication in this place.

There are a certain number of other passages also, in which presbyterate (whether named or not) is plainly spoken of, the implications of which should be carefully considered. Such as, 'But we beseech you, brethren, to know them that labour among you, and are over you in the Lord, and admonish you; and to esteem them exceeding highly in love for their work's sake[3].' 'Obey them that have the rule over you, and submit to them: for they watch in behalf of your souls, as they that shall give account; that they

---

[1] Tit. i. 9.   [2] 1 Tim v 17.   [3] 1 Thess. v. 12, 13.

may do this with joy, and not with grief: for this were unprofitable for you¹.' 'Is any among you sick? Let him call for the elders of the Church, and let them pray over him, anointing him with oil in the name of the Lord: and the prayer of faith shall save him that is sick, and the Lord shall raise him up; and if he have committed sins, it shall be forgiven him. Confess your sins one to another, and pray one for another, that ye may be healed. The supplication of a righteous man availeth much in its working².' 'The elders therefore among you I exhort, who am a fellow-elder³, and a witness of the sufferings of Christ, who am also a partaker of the glory that shall be revealed: tend the flock of God which is among you, exercising the oversight, not of constraint, but willingly, according unto God; nor yet for filthy lucre, but of a ready mind; neither as lording it over the charge allotted to you, but making yourselves ensamples to the flock. And when the chief Shepherd shall be manifested, ye shall receive the crown of glory that fadeth not away⁴.'

Putting, then, passages such as these together, it appears that we may lay down these principles about the presbyters of the New Testament. *First*, the name πρεσβύτερος and the name ἐπίσκοπος are practically interchangeable. To say this is not to deny that they may, as no doubt they do, express different aspects of the office, or that the two expressions have different histories; but it means that, in New Testament language, the two ideas are so far identified in one Christian office that every 'bishop' might be called also a 'presbyter,' and every 'presbyter' might be called also a 'bishop.' *Secondly*, the πρεσβύτεροι (otherwise called ἐπίσκοποι) appear as the regular rulers and representatives of what may be called the domestic religious life of the Church in every place; that is to say, of any local body of the Christian brethren, as locally constituted and organized. Those who send gifts to

---
¹ Heb. xiii. 17.   ² Jas. v. 14-16.
³ Cf. also the opening of St. John's Second and Third Epistles.
⁴ 1 Pet. v. 1-4.

a local Church send them to the presbyters there. Those who go to visit a local Church present themselves to its presbyters. Those who write to a Church (if within the Church they specify any officers at all) address themselves primarily to the bishops, that is, to the presbyters. More particularly it comes out (often as it were incidentally) that to teach, to withstand error, to govern the life of the community, and to lead it by example, to admonish, to watch for souls, to anoint and pray over the sick, and lead the way to confession of sins, and generally, as shepherds[1], to tend and feed the flock, are among the scriptural characteristics of the presbyter's office. But, *thirdly*, we are also to observe that this local organization and leadership of 'bishops' or 'presbyters' never, within the New Testament at least, exhausts the conception of the completeness of the Christian Church anywhere, or its machinery, or authority, even for purposes of local and practical discipline. In other words, the local presbyterate is never anywhere, for a moment, independent or supreme. It is always itself under discipline. There is always an authority behind it and above it, unquestioned and supreme. Whatever we may have to say about diaconate or presbyterate, it is of primary importance to remember that, at least from end to end of the Acts and Epistles, the *background of apostolate is always assumed*. In time no doubt the Apostles must pass away. The question as to their apostolic supremacy, whether it, or any elements of it, are to be perpetuated, or on what terms, or by what means, must rise no doubt before the mind of the Church, and must receive somehow its settlement. But however inevitable this question might be, or however far-reaching in importance, my point at this moment is that, within the limits of the canonical writings, it has never yet

---

[1] Whatever may have been the leading idea of 'shepherds' in the Old Testament, at least in the Christian Church the word can never be dissociated from the meanings which were stamped on it for ever in the teaching of the 10th chapter of St. John.

been at all conclusively dealt with. It has hardly as yet fully risen. The apostolate still is everywhere assumed as a background to everything in the Church, a background still available, present and living. It appears to me that a great deal of disproportion is introduced into the inquiry into ministerial offices in Scripture, if anything is allowed, even for a moment, to obscure the significance of this primary fact.

IV. But although, naturally enough, in the earlier years apostolate stands as a matter of course behind everything, and although even up to the furthest limits of the apostolic writings, the problem of the disappearance of the apostolate seems still to remain imperfectly determined, it is also part of Church history, within the New Testament, that under the immediate shadow of apostolate there did begin to grow, not perhaps quite at first everywhere, nor (within St Paul's lifetime at least) more than tentatively, partially, gradually, something which stood between apostolate and presbyterate, having much apparently in common with either office; something therefore which, as apostolate faded gradually away, might not improbably perpetuate in the Catholic Church whatever was capable of being perpetuated of that apostolic background, out of which all other Christian ministries had proceeded, and in front of which, and under which, they had always worked.

The first example of this newly developing function is found in the position of 'James the Lord's brother' in the Church at Jerusalem. The points which we notice about it within the New Testament are these. *First*, that whatever it exactly is, or means, it dawns upon our perceptions very gradually. No attention whatever is attracted to it—any more than to the institution of presbyters at Jerusalem, of whom, as Bishop Lightfoot repeatedly insists (and we need have no quarrel with the insistence so far), St James both was, and continued to be, one, albeit the principal one. *Secondly*, that which thus gradually dawns upon us is that, for some reason or other, when the local Church at Jerusalem is referred to, it is apt to be represented by the name of St. James. His name, even by itself, seems to signify that Church. He seems to have become, in familiar and as it were unconscious usage, the veritable 'persona ecclesiae Heirosolymitanae.' Thus St. Peter, delivered from prison, leaves word before his flight, 'Tell those things unto James, and to the brethren[1].' 'Before that certain came from James, Peter did eat with the Gentiles[2].' 'The day following Paul went in with us unto James; and all the elders were present[3].'

Thirdly, so marked is this local eminence, that (whilst it seems to retain its contrast with the apostolate specially so called, in the very fact of being distinctively local) St. James appears by virtue of it to take a position, in the local Church of Jerusalem, not inferior in dignity to that of the Apostles themselves. This appears first on the very notable occasion of the Council of Jerusalem, where the order of proceedings strongly suggests that St. James occupied the position of chairman or president. The first part of the meeting, is seems, was difficult; there was a good deal of disputation. Then a strong speech and appeal from St. Peter secures a hearing, respectful and attentive (which till then it seems had not been possible), for the story of the wonderful facts which Paul and Barnabas had to present. Finally, St. James reviews what has passed, re-enforces the argument of St. Peter, and puts forward what we should call the draught of a practical resolution[4], which is forthwith adopted and becomes the decision of the Council. Such a view of St. James' relations to the Apostles is further enforced by the language of St. Paul in the second chapter to the Galatians. He is speaking of the Church of Jerusalem, of the strong tradition among Jewish Christians

---

[1] Acts xii. 17.   [2] Gal. ii. 12.   [3] Acts xxi 18.
[4] Διὸ ἐγὼ κρίνω is more than the language of a private member, hazarding an individual and unofficial resolution.

of circumcision and legal obligation, and of the apostolic authority upon which this tradition either did, or was supposed to, rest. But, he says, this very supreme authority in the Church of the Circumcision in Jerusalem itself accepted the Church of the Gentiles upon equal terms; and he expresses this by three names—'when they perceived the grace that was given unto me, James and Cephas and John, they who were reputed to be pillars, gave to me and Barnabas the right hand of fellowship, that we should go unto the Gentiles and they unto the circumcision.' On any interpretation this position of the name of St. James, along with St. Peter and St. John, *and before either of them*, is most remarkable. It is in the sequel to this passage that emissaries from Jerusalem are described as 'certain' who 'came from James.'

The *fourth* point to be noticed about St. James is that St. Paul appears somewhat pointedly to include him within the apostolic title. It is quite true that the existence of other passages in the New Testament where it is more than doubtful whether the word 'Apostle' can imply what we mean by apostolic rank, may seem somewhat to blunt the significance of this fact. The passage, however, is one in which a vague use of the term Apostle, even if elsewhere quite possible, would be irrelevant. The whole thought is emptied of its obvious meaning if St Paul is not using the word of a rank which, whether it contained twelve names or fifteen, or whatever precise number more, was at all events perfectly definite and exclusive. 'Other of the Apostles saw I none, save James the Lord's brother;' the importance of the protest is lost unless by 'Apostles' he means those whose position in the Church was regarded as on a level with his own: 'neither went I up to Jerusalem to them who were Apostles before me.' Whatever inference we may draw from this passage as to his own Divine call, and its relation—or lack of relation—to any external commission to apostleship, it is difficult to resist the conclusion that St. James is intended to be included within the limits of the apostolic name, not necessarily for every purpose whatever, but so far at least as to be set, in his own Church, upon the apostolic level of dignity[1].

Such are the facts which the New Testament supplies about the position of St. James at Jerusalem. Now what do these facts amount to? Bishop Lightfoot writes, 'James the Lord's brother alone, within the period compassed by the apostolic writings, can claim to be regarded as a bishop in the later and more special sense of the term.' Now this phrase, I own, seems to me to be going somewhat beyond the actual evidence of the Scripture. A bishop in the later sense of the term should mean a member of a well-defined and well-understood episcopal order. St. James' position in the New Testament would rather appear to be exceptional and personal. It will be observed that what the passages go to establish is the eminence in respect of position and dignity of this man, who, if he was (as he may have been) a presbyter and chief representative of presbyters, is nowhere actually himself styled 'presbyter' or 'bishop,' but is, somewhat pointedly, classed as an apostle. In respect of position and dignity, as standing first within the local Church, and personifying it in relation to those without—particulars just parallel with those which would be conceded of St. Clement at Rome—the evidence is complete. But there is otherwise no evidence as to the nature of his duties or capacities in respect of other members, whether ministers or laymen, within his Church. Moreover, when we consider on the one hand the place and the date at which we find this eminence established, as early as the Council of Jerusalem, and in Jerusalem itself; that is to say, at a time when the actual apostolate was in undiminished fullness of

---

[1] It is here assumed that 'James the Lord's brother,' is not identical with 'James the son of Alphaeus' who was one of the Twelve. Of course, if that identification be accepted, the case of St. James ceases to be relevant to the present argument. In that case, however, the picture of an Apostle 'localized,' and 'personifying' a local community, would become in another way instructive in reference to the transition from apostolate to episcopate.

vigour, and in the place of all others which was most completely within the view and the reach of the government of the Apostles themselves: and on the other hand the significance of the phrase which seems to be the distinctive title of the man, 'James the Lord's brother'; it is difficult not to feel that the position occupied by such a man, in such a place and at such a date, is a position of eminence, in its origin mainly personal, conceded to the nearness of his earthly relationship with the Lord Jesus Christ.

To call it mainly personal is not to imply that it was a mere dignity without official prerogatives or duties, but rather to suggest that St. James is not so much the primary instance of a certain official class, as an individual standing in a position which was at the time, and was meant to be, wholly exceptional. The very fact, no doubt, of this exceptional position of his indirectly afterwards suggested and led the way towards the existence of the official class; to which he therefore stands in the relation rather of an antecedent suggestion and pattern, than of the earliest specimen. This is perfectly consistent with pronouncing, upon a retrospective view, that he is to be reckoned as the first Bishop of Jerusalem. This was the unhesitating view of the second century: and from the point of view of subapostolic times, when episcopate had grown, with the fading of apostolate, into real and vital existence, was the absolutely true view. But it is one thing to say, looking back from fifty years after, 'We see now that James was in point of fact the first bishop, and on his death Symeon became the second;' it would be another thing for a historian to pronounce of James, in the early vigour of apostolic times, when as 'the Lord's brother' he held a position side by side with the Apostles which appeared to be wholly unique, that he is to be regarded as then being 'a bishop in the later sense of the term.'

These considerations seem to explain the fact that

whilst what may be retrospectively claimed as the first development of episcopate is found in the very centre of the apostolic Church, almost at the beginning of St. Paul's apostleship, it is not till St. Paul is consciously in sight of the close of his work that we meet even the tentative beginnings of anything like a machinery for the maintenance of apostolic government, through men who governed as apostolic deputies because Apostles themselves were out of reach. Even when we do find such officials, their position seems to be at first strangely uncertain, temporary, and experimental, in comparison with what St. James had already held nearly fifteen years earlier in Jerusalem.

The instances of apostolic deputies or delegates are, of course, Timotheus in the Church at Ephesus, and Titus in Crete. Here again the retrospective language may be amply justified which speaks afterwards of Timotheus and Titus as the first 'bishops' of Ephesus and of Crete respectively; and yet the position occupied by either at the time may not have been that exactly of a diocesan bishop. It cannot indeed possibly have been so, as long as each was primarily the representative of an absent but still living and governing Apostle. And this even apart from the question whether the position held locally by either was regarded by St Paul as more than temporary. On the other hand, however much it may then have been regarded as temporary[1]; however much either, for the time, may have been rather the instrument of an absent than the wielder of an inherent authority; yet if the necessities which they were set to meet in Crete or in Ephesus were permanent and progressive, while the Apostle whom they represented was as it were even now passing out of sight, the temporary mission might have quickly become a permanent one, with or without the purpose— we might almost say the consciousness—of any one

[1] But such passages as 2 Tim. iv. 9, 21, Tit. iii. 12, fall far short of establishing its temporary character.

concerned. Temporary however or permanent, the positions of Timotheus and Titus, as representing by deputy those functions of apostolate which could be and which needed to be discharged by deputy, throw a flood of light upon the necessary meaning of the 'episcopal' office now dimly beginning to exist, such as we do not gather at all from the case of St. James.

As a preliminary we may observe that there is, at this point, no indication whatever of anything like a special title for the position which these two representatives of the Apostle held. The word 'bishop' is unreservedly interchangeable with 'presbyter.' It is possible that the total absence of any title may be another indication that St. Paul's mind was not, even now, directly occupied with the thought of a permanent provision for the absence of apostolate. Nor need such absence of provision strike us really as strange if we remember that St. Paul, as he drew towards his death, was leaving behind him, no longer only in connexion with the Churches of the East, but already probably in personal presence amongst his own Churches in the provinces of Asia and Galatia, not less than three of the twelve Apostles, with St. John himself at their head. The real absence of Apostolate was not immediately in sight; and the expectation of an early second Advent was hardly yet dead. Before St. John passes away, the indefinite, tentative stage of the development of 'episcopacy' is over.

To return, however, to the functions of Timotheus and Titus, as evidenced by the Pastoral Epistles. The following points emerge First they were to exercise a general discipline over the community as a whole: 'These things write I unto thee, hoping to come unto thee shortly; but if I tarry long, that thou mayest know how men ought to behave themselves in the house of God[1]. . . . These things also command, that they may be without reproach[2]. . . .

---

[1] 1 Tim. iii. 14, 15.   [2] Ibid. v. 7.

Them that sin reprove in the sight of all, that the rest also may be in fear[1]. ... For this cause left I thee in Crete, that thou shouldest set in order the things that are wanting[2]. ... These things speak and exhort and reprove with all authority[3]. ... A man that is heretical after a first and second admonition refuse[4]. ... Let our people also learn to maintain good works[5].' Secondly, they were emphatically teachers of the people: 'I charge thee in the sight of God ... preach the word, be instant in season, out of season; reprove, rebuke, exhort, with all longsuffering and teaching[6]. ... These things command and teach[7]. ... Till I come, give heed to reading, to exhortation, to teaching[8]. ... Take heed to thyself and to thy teaching[9]. ... Do the work of an evangelist, fulfil thy ministry[10]. ... The Lord's servant must ... be gentle towards all, apt to teach, forbearing, in meekness correcting them that oppose themselves[11]. ... Speak thou the things which befit the sound doctrine, that aged men be ... that aged women likewise be ... the younger men likewise exhort to be ... exhort servants to be in subjection,' &c.[12]

Now these first two particulars, ruling in the community and teaching, are exactly the two which characterized the office of presbyters (or bishops); though it may not unnaturally occur to us that, even in respect of these two, what is meant by the ruling and the teaching appears to be something of wider scope and deeper responsibility in the case of the direct representatives of the Apostle than in that of the regular holders of the presbyteral office. Moreover, it is just in respect of these two that there is no fundamental distinction, no distinction other than that of width of horizon and ultimateness of responsibility, between the ordinary presbyteral office as sketched in 1 Tim. iii. or Titus i., and the work not only

---

[1] 1 Tim. v. 20.
[2] Titus i. 5.
[3] Ibid. ii. 15.
[4] Ibid. iii. 10.
[5] Ibid. iii. 14.
[6] 2 Tim. iv. 1, 2.
[7] 1 Tim. iv 11.
[8] Ibid. 13
[9] Ibid. 16.
[10] 2 Tim. iv. 5.
[11] 2 Tim. ii 24, 25
[12] Titus ii. 1-9.

of the later episcopate, but even of the very chiefest of the Apostles.

From these two we pass to two other particulars, less obviously characterizing presbytership as such, but still not inconsistent with it. These are, control over other teachers and their teaching, and control over the arrangement of the public worship of the community. The first is represented by 'I exhorted thee to tarry at Ephesus, that thou mightest charge certain men not to teach a different doctrine[1],' and 'there are many unruly men, vain talkers and deceivers, specially they of the circumcision, whose mouths must be stopped; men who overthrow whole houses, teaching things which they ought not, for filthy lucre's sake[2].' The second is implied in the passage, 'I exhort therefore first of all that supplications, prayers, intercessions, thanksgivings, be made for all men: for kings and all that are in high place; that . . . I desire therefore that the men pray in every place, lifting up holy hands, without wrath and disputing. In like manner that women adorn themselves in modest apparel, with shamefastness and sobriety. . . . Let a woman learn in quietness with all subjection. But I permit not a woman to teach[3].'

Finally, we meet with two more particulars, which bring the office of Titus and Timotheus into direct comparison and antithesis with that of ordinary presbyters. These are the exercise of jurisdiction over all other grades of Church ministers, as such: that is, in express terms, over bishops or presbyters, deacons, deaconesses, and widows; and secondly that which, in the light of all subsequent history, we not unnaturally think of as a climax, the responsibility of approving and the power of constituting fit persons to each of these several offices in the Church.

---

[1] 1 Tim. i 3.

[2] Titus i. 10, 11. Compare also what is said about those who teach a different doctrine in 1 Tim. vi. 3, and the refusal of a heretic in Titus iii. 10.

[3] 1 Tim. ii. 1-12.

The meaning of the somewhat ambiguous phrase 'Rebuke not an elder[1]' is determined later in the same chapter by the words 'Against an elder receive not an accusation, except at the mouth of two or three witnesses[2].' The other side is expressed in 'Let the elders that rule well be counted worthy of double honour[3]' For censure, as for commendation, the apostolic representative is to exercise judgement upon the official work of the presbyter. The same is implied, less directly, in all that is said about the other point, namely, selection and ordination of presbyters: 'I left thee in Crete that thou shouldest... appoint elders in every city, as I gave thee charge[4].' 'Lay hands hastily on no man[5];' 'the things which thou hast heard from me among many witnesses, the same commit thou to faithful men, who shall be able to teach others also[6];' and in the insistence upon qualifications which must be regarded as necessary in those who are to be admitted to the presbyteral (or episcopal) office: 'If a man seeketh the office of a bishop, he desireth a good work. The bishop therefore must be[7]...' These directions are addressed to both. It is only to Timotheus that the charge about the 'bishops' is followed by 'deacons in like manner must be ... women[8] in like manner must be ... Honour widows that are widows indeed. ... Let none be enrolled as a widow under threescore years old, having been ... but younger widows refuse[9].'

However tentative, then, or temporary the circumstances may be considered to be, Timotheus and Titus stand as the first instances of the deliberate delegation of the powers of an absent Apostle to men, not themselves entitled or ranked as Apostles, who nevertheless exercise not a little of the substantial authority and prerogatives of Apostles.

Before we pass from them, there is one other point which both its own importance, and the emphasis laid upon

---

[1] 1 Tim. v. 1.   [2] Ibid. 19.   [3] Ibid. 17.   [4] Titus i. 5.
[5] 1 Tim. v. 22.   [6] 2 Tim. ii. 2.   [7] 1 Tim iii. 1 sqq.
[8] i. e. presumably deaconesses.   [9] 1 Tim iii. 8, 11, and v. 3, 9, 11.

it by St. Paul, forbid us to pass over in silence. For whatever reason, it emerges directly only in the Epistles to Timotheus, which are in other ways also, as we have had occasion to notice, considerably fuller than that addressed to Titus. We observe then the way in which, throughout the letters to Timotheus, all that St. Paul has to urge about the discharge of official duties is interwoven with the ever-recurring appeal to Timotheus' own memory and consciousness of what we can only describe as official consecration. Timotheus is one who has received, by ministerial consecration, a solemn and sacred and responsible trust. At every turn he is reminded of this. Every exhortation to official duty is dependent upon this. It is not to any natural or ordinary motives, not to his ambition or his opportunities, or his interest in the Ephesians, or his sense of duty towards or his love for St. Paul, that St. Paul appeals. He does perpetually appeal — does earnestly conjure him—not by things like these, but by his own consciousness of an awful trust, solemnly and therefore exactingly laid upon him. It is a deposit ($\pi\alpha\rho\alpha\theta\eta\kappa\eta$): 'O Timothy, guard that which is committed unto thee[1]. . . . That good thing which was committed unto thee guard through the Holy Ghost which dwelleth in us[2].' It is a charge—$\pi\alpha\rho\alpha\gamma\gamma\epsilon\lambda\iota\alpha$. It is a gift of grace—a $\chi\alpha\rho\iota\sigma\mu\alpha$. It was conveyed by a solemn act of the Apostle and of the Church; an act in which the leading memories are the ceremonial laying-on of hands, and the attendant outpouring of prophetic inspiration[3]. "This charge ($\pi\alpha\rho\alpha\gamma\gamma\epsilon\lambda\iota\alpha$) I commit unto thee, my child Timothy, according to the prophecies which went before on thee[4]. . . . Neglect not the gift ($\chi\alpha\rho\iota\sigma\mu\alpha$) that is in thee, which was given thee by prophecy, with the laying-on of the hands of the presbytery[5]. . . . I put thee in remembrance that thou stir up

---

[1] 1 Tim. vi. 20 [2] 2 Tim. i. 14.
[3] Whether regarded as accompanying the consecrating ceremony, or as designating Timotheus beforehand for consecration See Hort's *Ecclesia*, p. 181.
[4] 1 Tim. i. 18. [5] 1 Tim. iv. 14.

the gift (χάρισμα) of God which is in thee through the laying-on of my hands[1].'

We have no means of knowing the detail of the processes of Timotheus' ordination to ministry. Had he been set apart, or ordained, as a presbyter before? Did he afterwards receive any further setting apart, or consecration, when he went to wield apostolic jurisdiction over presbyters? What ordination is it to which St. Paul so solemnly and repeatedly appeals? We have not the historical knowledge to answer these questions. So direct, however, appears to be the connexion between the ordination thus appealed to, and the special responsibilities and duties which St. Paul is calling on him to discharge, and which—by virtue of the ordination—he ought to feel himself both empowered and compelled to discharge without shrinking, effectively, that it seems almost impossible for us to deny or to doubt that the ordination in question, whenever, wherever, or however conferred, was one which, in the power of its commission, covered the whole ground of his office as apostolic representative at Ephesus. For this purpose the words of the appeal in the opening of the Second Epistle are very significant.[2] It is in respect of the snares which beset the path rather of a governing apostle than of a governed presbyter; it is as against timidity—timidity in the exercise of what ought to be Power, timidity in the administration of what, if it is on one side the spirit of Love, is no less directly the spirit of Discipline[3]—that St. Paul conjures Timotheus to remember his ordination, and to kindle its χάρισμα into living flame. In these words indeed, taken in themselves, there is nothing inconsistent with the simple presbyteral office. But we cannot consistently understand the courage, the

---

[1] 2 Tim. i. 6.
[2] 'Αναμιμνήσκω σε ἀναζωπυρεῖν τὸ χάρισμα τοῦ Θεοῦ, ὅ ἐστιν ἐν σοὶ διὰ τῆς ἐπιθέσεως τῶν χειρῶν μου· οὐ γὰρ ἔδωκεν ἡμῖν ὁ Θεὸς πνεῦμα δειλίας, ἀλλὰ δυνάμεως καὶ ἀγάπης καὶ σωφρονισμοῦ.
[3] This seems to be the proper meaning of the πνεῦμα σωφρονισμοῦ.

power, and the discipline which are spoken of here, except in the light of the contents of the First Epistle; except that is with the meaning and in the context in which in fact St. Paul was calling upon Timotheus for these very qualities.

It is not uninteresting to add as a detail that St. Paul applies to him also in these Epistles the designations both of 'deacon[1]' and 'evangelist.[2]' Both words no doubt are capable of being wholly untechnical. But it is also a possibility that Timotheus may have been either, or both, and that his higher functions may have been thought of rather as reinterpreting and reinforcing than as cancelling the lower.

V. Now, so far, all the offices which we have been studying—apostolate, diaconate, presbyterate, together with the indications or steps towards an exercise of quasi-apostolic jurisdiction and prerogative (whether wholly or in part) by men who were not actually Apostles—may be said to be homogeneous and progressive. They are, so to say, *in pari materia*. They supplement each other. They fall quite naturally into a harmonious, not to say hierarchical, relation with each other. There is no conflict of principle, no incongruity of kind. They are all unmistakably *offices* to which men are solemnly set apart, upon regular conditions, by orderly methods. They belong to the organization of a regularly constituted polity. Possibly it might be satisfactory to us if the evidence of the New Testament ended here. But on this subject, as on many others, Scripture evidence is a little less clean cut, it has rather more of indeterminate fringe, than we might, some of us, at first sight have desired. We pass on, then, to consider some other indications, not quite co-ordinate with these. Whether they can be properly described as indications of ministerial office may be open to argument. At the least they have a not unimportant bearing upon the

[1] 1 Tim. iv. 6.   [2] 2 Tim. iv. 5.

question of the conception of ministerial office in apostolic times.

In Acts xiii. 1 we read that there were in the Church at Antioch certain 'prophets and teachers.' Five names are specified, including those of Barnabas and Saul. We find these men 'ministering to the Lord (λειτουργούντων) and fasting.' 'The Holy Ghost' bids them set apart to Him Barnabas and Saul. This they do by fasting and prayer and laying on of hands, and forthwith the missionary journeys of the Apostle of the Gentiles begin. More questions than one may be raised upon this account. For the present we are only concerned with the one. What is the meaning of the 'prophets and teachers'? The indications which rise out of the passage itself are not clear. On the one hand, the prophets and teachers appear to stand, in spiritual place and importance, very high. They are, subject of course to the apostolate, which was not on the spot, the chief ministers and rulers of the Church at Antioch. To them comes the command of the Holy Ghost. They consecrate Barnabas and Saul for their special calling. On the other hand, that to which Barnbas and Saul are commissioned appears to be something beyond the scope of the ordinary work of prophets. For they are themselves prophets before they receive this special call and consecration. It is to be remembered, however, that whatever may be, in other aspects, the significance of this laying on of hands,[1] it is plain that it is not to it that St. Paul in thought refers the basis of his apostolate.[2] In this respect the contrast between St. Paul himself, and Timotheus, his apostolic delegate, is very marked. If we were to draw a conclusion upon the data which have been hitherto before us, I suppose that we should be inclined to infer that these men occupied the position officially of 'bishops' or 'presbyters,' but that their official position was enhanced by their possession of a special gift of inspired wisdom, the 'prophecy' of the

---

[1] See above, p. 108.   [2] Gal. 1. 1

New Testament.[1] But how far do other passages of the New Testament elucidate the position of the prophets?

There are two notable passages to be considered, 1 Cor. xii. and Eph. iv.[2] The chapter to the Corinthians is the first of three chapters which are primarily about spiritual endowments. They begin with what may be called a formal heading or title—'Now concerning spiritual gifts, brethren, I would not have you ignorant.[3]' They constitute a discourse upon πνευματικά. The leading thought of the discourse is the variety of the πνευματικά— the oneness of the πνεῦμα so variously manifested. There are diversities of χαρίσματα, diversities of διακονίαι, diversities of ἐνεργήματα; the instances specified are wisdom, knowledge, faith, healings, miracles, prophecy, discerning of spirits, kinds of tongues, interpretation of tongues; but diverse as these are, one Spirit is the fountain of them all. This is the thought which St. Paul proceeds to illustrate by the likeness of the many members in one body; and so returns once more to the diversity which he is illustrating: 'Are all apostles? are all prophets? are all teachers? are all workers of miracles? have all gifts of healings? do all speak with tongues? do all interpret? But desire earnestly the greater gifts. And a still more excellent way show I unto you'—namely, Love, which transcends

---

[1] They are called προφῆται καὶ διδάσκαλοι. Compare below, p. 208, on Hermas, *Vis.* iii. 5. If the phrase occurred *there*, I should not hesitate to suggest that the phrase might be literally translated 'prophetic presbyters.' The suggestion is that the same meaning is, even here, substantially true in fact, though not directly deducible from, nor allowable as a translation of, the words.

[2] It is not easy to get much assistance from the case of Agabus. He (with others) comes down from Judaea to Antioch (Acts xi. 27 sqq.); he comes down again from Judaea to Caesarea (Acts xxi. 10); and each time apparently in order to deliver predictions of coming events. [It is quite possible that similar predictiveness may be implied in the τὰς προαγούσας ἐπὶ σὲ προφητείας of 1 Tim. i. 18.] We are warned perhaps hereby against excluding prediction from the idea of New Testament 'prophecy'; but can draw little inference as to the position of these prophets. But the impression would rather be that they were 'gifted men,' than ruling officers.

[3] Περὶ δὲ τῶν πνευματικῶν, ἀδελφοί οὐ θέλω ὑμᾶς ἀγνοεῖν.

prophecy, mysteries, knowledge, faith, everything. Therefore 'follow after Love;—yet desire earnestly spiritual gifts, but rather that ye may prophesy.' Now the general course of the context as here exhibited would not lead us to suppose that the mind of St. Paul was at all occupied in this passage with grades of ministerial rank, but rather with the infinite variety of personal spiritual endowment. On the other hand, when at the end of the twelfth chapter he returns from the figure of the members in the body to the varieties of spiritual endowment in the Church, he begins his list with three words which sound like grades of ministry, and he appears to rank them in a deliberate order—'apostles, prophets, teachers.' Here at least, it may be contended, even if (as it were) by accident, he is speaking hierarchically: whether apostles, prophets, teachers can be made to correspond to the orders of apostles, presbyters, and deacons, or whether the unexpected enumeration of a new set of orders is to be taken as showing that neither the one nor the other form of hierarchy ought to be understood to have any stereotyped or exclusive or permanent character. To which again perhaps it might be replied that even in these three words he is not speaking really of hierarchical office, but of individual endowment[1] (he goes on at once to miracles, healings, tongues, &c.); or only at most, so far half-glancing at official distinctions as they correspond, or might be supposed to correspond, or to approximate towards corresponding, with certain familiar types of personal gifts and capacities. If apostolate was, in fact, exceptionally endowed with spiritual capacities (as it clearly was in the person of St. Paul), apostolate would stand naturally first as well in a list of endowments as of offices. The inspired insight of 'prophecy,' the 'gift' of teaching, whether especially possessed by appointed presbyters or no, might have a place in such a catalogue no less legitimate and

---

[1] It is hardly open to doubt that for himself, in his own person, he would have claimed *all* the seven specified gifts.

L

only less eminent than that of the apostolic inspiration. And this is in fact the position occupied by 'prophecy' in the early part of the chapter. It is one of a list of 'gifts' —preceded by 'faith,' 'healings,' 'miracles'; followed by 'discerning of spirits, speaking with tongues, interpretation of tongues.' Just so in the fourteenth chapter, which is the third and last of this discourse upon spiritual gifts, the idea of 'prophecy' seems to be as remote as possible from constituted office; it has rather (as we shall see) the merits, and the defects, of a personal endowment of genius or of inspiration.

Before going on to this fourteenth chapter, it may be well to have the verses from the Ephesians before us[1]. The leading thought of this passage is an earnest moral appeal, from the imprisoned Apostle, for the suppression of selfish individualism. 'Lowliness and meekness, long-suffering, forbearance, love,' this is the theme; and this he preaches in the name and for the sake of unity—'the unity of the Spirit': 'There is one Body and one Spirit . . . one Lord, one Faith, one Baptism,' &c. Then comes the thought of variety in unity—'unto each one of us was the grace given according to the measure of the gift of Christ. And He gave some to be apostles; and some prophets; and some evangelists; and some pastors and teachers: for the perfecting of the saints, unto the work of ministering, unto the building up of the body of Christ; till we all attain unto the unity of the faith,' &c. This passage is undoubtedly reminding of that to the Corinthians: probably it reminded the Apostle when he wrote, quite as much as it reminds us who read. But though the other passage in a sense is in this; and though this, like the other, seems to be speaking immediately of variety of 'gifts'; there can be little doubt that this passage carries the thought of special endowments much more directly than the other did, to the case of endowments for the work of distinctive ministries. The list, then, apparently ministerial, which emerges from this passage

[1] Eph iv. 1-16.

is this: apostles, prophets, evangelists, pastors and teachers. There is no reason for taking 'apostles' in any other than the usual sense. 'Pastors and teachers' would correspond, with perfect exactness (and the other two terms would not correspond), with the description of the local 'presbyters or bishops.' The appearance, then, of this passage is that it inserts between apostolate and presbyterate two other orders—prophets and evangelists. Are we, then, to find in the New Testament a graduation of five orders?

About evangelists we need trouble ourselves comparatively little. One of the chief characteristics of the presbyterate was that it was settled and local. The presbyters are the heads of a local community. *Quâ* presbyters, they are anything but travelling missionaries. Now 'evangelists' is no doubt a missionary term; and it is obvious that in the condition of Christianity in the time of St. Paul, the missionary officers were in no sense less important than the officers of settled communities. We may fairly assume that any duly authorized missionary ministers who were not apostles might be called evangelists. Timotheus, as we have seen, as apostolic delegate is exhorted to 'do the work of an evangelist[1]' Philip the Deacon, in the very phrase which says that he was 'one of the seven,' is entitled 'Philip the Evangelist[2].' It would be the simplest of suppositions to suppose that if a presbyter from any city became a missionary, he would, *quâ* missionary, be called 'evangelist', while evangelist would be the most direct and natural term for those who would have been presbyters if their work had been (as it was not) in a settled community. To find therefore 'evangelists' thus mentioned, and to find them, at such a date, inserted in mention between apostles and presbyters would be perfectly natural. Apostles no doubt would be thought of as characteristically non-local. That their non-local subordinates should be named with them (whether constituting an Order or not) before the local

[1] 2 Tim. iv. 5.   [2] Acts xxi 8.

officers of communities would in itself raise no difficulty or question at all. But how, we should desire to ask, did a man, did Philip, for instance, become an evangelist? We know how he had been made a deacon. Was there anything similar which conferred on him the status of evangelist? We may be little able to answer the question directly. But we are entitled, perhaps, to point to the total absence of any suggestion of anything like a solemn conferring of 'evangelist' status: and, in its absence, to add that the view of the word as rather the description of an employment than the title of an office, at least thoroughly agrees with its application in Scripture to 'Philip, one of the seven,' and to Timotheus, in his apostolic delegacy at Ephesus.

Once more then we return to 1 Cor. xiv. upon the question what was προφητεία and who were these highly honoured προφῆται? Now through the greater part of the chapter St. Paul is emphasizing the excellence of 'prophecy' in comparison with other spiritual endowments, and particularly with the gift of tongues. The whole passage implies that, even at that date, the special endowments were too often apt to be direct causes of disorder in the Church. It is a great insistence upon the paramount duty of *order*; and it is upon grounds which are closely allied to this, its edification and its orderliness, that, for the first twenty-five verses, the endowment of prophecy is by comparison so highly extolled. But in the last twelve or fifteen verses St. Paul turns the same preaching of subordination and orderliness round upon the προφῆται themselves. From what he says to them on this score, I would suggest three, as it seems to me, very pertinent inferences. First in the Church community at Corinth, as it then stood (and it is worth while in connexion with this to remember the evidence of the earlier chapters of the Epistle as to the extent of the prevalent anarchy, corruption, and unspirituality), it might, according to the showing of the passage, be quite naturally assumed that there would be a somewhat indefinite number of 'prophets' actually present in the congregation Sunday by Sunday 'When ye come together, each one hath a psalm, hath a teaching, hath a revelation . . . let the prophets speak by two or three, and let the others discern. But if a revelation be made to another sitting by, let the first keep silence For ye all can prophesy one by one.' It is of course quite impossible to suppose that the prophets, of whom an indefinite number might appear from any part of the ordinary Corinthian congregation any Sunday, could themselves be a superior and almost apostolic grade of hierarchical ministry. Secondly, the 'prophets' need to be sharply exhorted to restrain themselves, and in particular to be reminded that they are perfectly well able to do so if they like In other words, it is implied that though the gift may be quite real and divine, the possession of this gift was often accompanied by—nay not unnaturally had a tendency towards—a very self-deceiving and carnal lack of self-restraint. 'The spirits of the prophets are subject to the prophets; for God is not a God of confusion, but of peace; as in all the Churches of the saints. . . If any man thinketh himself to be a prophet, or spiritual, let him take knowledge of the things which I write unto you, that they are the commandment of the Lord. But if any man is ignorant, let him be ignorant Wherefore, my brethren, desire earnestly to prophesy, and forbid not to speak with tongues. But let all things be done decently and in order.' The third inference is that the whole matter of individual gifts of προφητεία, respectfully as St. Paul conceives of them in comparison with such other capacities as the 'kinds of tongues,' so far from being—either from the side of responsible ordination or from the side of Divine inspiration — an orderly guidance and government of the Church, whether local or Catholic, is rather itself a matter of constant anxiety to the rulers of the Church, having to be restrained by peremptory rule, because itself naturally tending to disorder.

So far the upshot of the evidence of these three

chapters to the Corinthians is fairly clear. They do appear to me to dispose of the idea that prophets as such were a dignified order of ministry, and to make it quite certain that προφητεία was rather an individual inspiration than a ministerial status, an inspiration which could be recognized as such even in the midst of a great deal of disorder and ignorance. To say this is not at all inconsistent with recognizing the pre-eminent honour which seems to attach to the 'prophets and teachers' as at Antioch[1], or to 'prophets' as ranking next to apostles in Eph. iv[2] But it is to be observed that if the word 'prophet' is itself quite a neutral word as far as formal office is concerned, expressing rather 'inspiration' than 'official character,' and, as such, is applicable alike to private Christians, or to the leaders and rulers[3] of Christian communities, or even to apostles[4], then it would become no longer a mere matter of conjecture, but an almost necessary inference, that, *when* prophets are spoken of as Church rulers, what is meant must be men who, being constituted as Church rulers, are also prophetically inspired, and not merely men who, because they are prophetically inspired, must therefore be taken *ipso facto*[5] as rulers in the Church.

[1] Observe how emphatically these men appear to be spoken of as the local leaders and rulers of a local community. 'Now there were at Antioch, in the Church that was there, prophets and teachers, Barnabas and Symeon,' &c

[2] It is just possible that in such passages as 1 Cor xii. 28 and Eph. iv. 11, we might be right in recognizing some, perhaps indirect, traces of what (in the retrospect at least with its sharper differentiation of ideas and of titles) we should call 'Apostolic men.' For these, wherever or however they were recognized at all, would be sure to be, in fact, προφῆται. This would at once explain the 'almost apostolic' position of some of the prophets.

I should like to say that I owe this and the following note to the kindness of a friend, to whom indeed I owe very much more than these,—or indeed than I can say.

[3] The προιστάμενοι, ἡγούμενοι, &c.

[4] As would seem to be clearly implied (if indeed the implication is needed, in 1 Cor. xiv. 18, 19.

[5] It is, however, probable enough that such possession of προφητεία, though certainly not *ipso facto* conferring the status of a ruler, may have been

We put then aside all idea of finding, in the prophets, an 'Order' correlative to apostles or presbyters; and, in doing so, recognize it as a matter no longer of vague possibility, but of the strongest presumption, that those prophets who are recognized in the Church as nearest to apostles—seeing that they cannot be an Order of prophets *as such*—would be found to be such regularly constituted leaders of settled congregations or of missionary enterprise, that is, such presbyters or evangelists, as by God's grace adorned their official status with a signal measure of divinely inspired wisdom.

The results, then, which emerge on the whole from an examination of scriptural data as to gradations of ministry, taken now in order not of chronology but of official importance, would appear to be these. First and foremost there is the background of apostolate, unquestioned, supreme, everywhere, itself based absolutely upon the principle, which its name expresses, of mission from Christ—καθὼς ἀπέσταλκέν με ὁ Πατὴρ κἀγὼ πέμπω ὑμᾶς. This is a new and exclusively *Christian* ministry. Secondly, there are unmistakable indications, though fragmentary, gradual, and uncompleted—at first in the person of a single individual under circumstances wholly special, and afterwards in the case of two companions of St. Paul whose cases were necessarily rather typical than singular—of a recognition of quasi-apostolic rank, jurisdiction, and prerogative in men, bearing as yet no distinctive title

an important qualification—if not, in many cases, a necessary prerequisite—for ordination to rulership. We can hardly doubt that all Apostles had the gift of 'prophecy.' 'Apostolic men,' at least, were hardly likely to be chosen without it. It is likely that προφητεία consisted largely in παράκλησις, or a 'gift for preaching.' Barnabas had been sent to Antioch (Acts xi. 22) apparently because of his power of παράκλησις in the Holy Ghost, and in faith. Does this phrase practically mean 'because he was a prophet'? He certainly was so in fact before Acts xiii. 1. By Acts xiv. 14 he is reckoned as, at least, an 'apostolic man.' It is likely enough that it was his eminence in 'prophecy' which qualified him for 'Apostolic' character. Again, when Timothy is exhorted πρόσεχε τῇ παρακλήσει (1 Tim. iv. 13), may not the phrase refer to his responsibilities as a preaching προφήτης?

whatever, who may, on the evidence, not unfairly be described as apostolic, while it is certain that they were not apostles.

Thirdly, we recognize, almost from the very beginning, the appointment of presbyters everywhere, as (under the apostolate) the established rulers, teachers, and representatives of the local communities of Christians. Such appointment, just mentioned by the historian in relation to the early Gentile Churches, seems not to be, in his eyes, in the case of the mother Church of Jerusalem, a fact either significant enough or novel enough to need to be recorded at all. In its origin it seems to be a Jewish ministry.

Fourthly, among the earliest incidents of the first expansion of the Christian Church in Jerusalem there is recorded, apparently as a new and significant step, the solemn institution of the diaconate. It may be added that there are some clear indications of the inclusion, under this title, of women; though with women, even more than with men [1], it is hard to distinguish between the 'officer' and the 'servant' aspect of ministry. The primary associations of this office are, apparently Hellenistic.

Fifthly, more or less cutting across these regularly constituted ministerial offices, there is a great variety of special spiritual graces or endowments in individual Church members—on the one hand fading off into what we should call merely personal capacities for illustrating good qualities of the Christian life, on the other hand culminating in what the first Christians recognised as an over-ruling inspiration, under the title 'prophecy.' But even of this, the highest form of personal endowment, we have to observe that, whilst, *first*, it might in some cases mean so much as to raise its possessor to almost apostolic prominence of dignity in the Church; yet, *secondly*, whatever its possessors might be, in status or dignity, their

---

[1] John Mark in Acts xiii. 5 is the Apostles' ὑπηρέτης The distinction seems wholly to be lost in the case of Church widows

endowment of 'prophecy' was matter rather of individual inspiration than of regular, constituted, Church machinery or order (the whole mention seems inconsistent with any idea that men were ecclesiastically ordained to be 'prophets'); and, *thirdly*, this inspiration, even when real, was compatible with—if not even conducive towards—such a letting go of the self and spiritual self-discipline as was already near of kin to disorder.

CHAPTER VI

GRADATIONS OF MINISTRY IN SUB-APOSTOLIC TIMES

If these be the indications within the New Testament, what do we find when we pass beyond the limits of the Canon?

Immense interest has been excited in recent years by the discovery of the Διδαχή, or Teaching of the Twelve Apostles; and to this for various reasons it will be convenient to make reference first. Of course such interest would largely attach to any newly discovered document which was generally supposed to go back in date as far as the first century. It has been in this case not a little enhanced by the new light which the *Didache* is supposed to throw upon sub-apostolic Church polity, and particularly upon the 'prophets' of the Corinthian and Ephesian Epistles. Before considering, however, what the *Didache* says, it is necessary to ask a little about the *Didache* itself, and the sort of authority with which it speaks. It would be beyond our scope to discuss all that is involved in such a question; but it will be well to point out certain positions which seem to have been made sufficiently clear in respect of it [1].

First, then, the *Didache*, whilst part of it appears to stand in the relation of an original to the seventh book

---

[1] It may be sufficient to make reference to Dr. Taylor, in his edition of the document itself; Dr. Salmon, in his *Introduction to the New Testament*, lect. xxvi.; and Canon Gore, in Appendix L. to *The Church and the Ministry*.

MINISTRY IN SUB-APOSTOLIC TIMES 171

of the *Apostolic Constitutions*, and (in some respects) to the passages in the Epistle of Barnabas which are parallel with it, is itself, as we have it, not an original document. It is Jewish in origin, not merely in the sense that it emanates from Palestinian Christianity, but that it has its source in non-Christian and prae-Christian Judaism. It is an altered and Christianized form of what was originally a Judaic manual, with no Christian reference at all, for the instruction of Gentile converts to Judaism Of course it follows from this that its date is at least twofold Even if we assume that the alterations were all made at once, at all events the date of the Christian adaptation is later than that of the original Jewish manual.

For the indications which justify this assertion I must refer to the authorities already quoted. But I may say that the view itself seems to account, as no other would, (*a*) for the language in the *Didache* about Baptism, which is natural if it is the Jewish view of the Baptism of proselytes, just Christianized in phraseology, but almost inconceivable as a Christian exposition of Baptism. and (*b*) for the strange ambiguity as to whether the Christian Eucharist is referred to, or not, in chapters 10 and 11. These chapters become intelligible enough if we accept them as being, in the first instance, simply Jewish benedictions over meals [1], whose character is only obscured not altered by their quasi-Eucharistic reference [2]. But as a 'liturgical' form of apostolic or sub-apostolic antiquity they are totally inconceivable.

[1] This indeed, on any showing, would almost certainly be their primary origin.
[2] See Gore, *loc. cit.*, particularly the following sentences:—
'Sabatier says truly: "Our document cannot but surprise those who read for the first time its liturgy of the Eucharist. We have here a form without analogy anywhere. It separates itself much less from the Jewish ritual than from the Christian." "It is an ordinary repast just touched by a breath of religious mysticism, such as is the outcome of the importance which belongs, in Jewish and Oriental idea, to repast taken in common." There is, in fact, nothing to recall to our mind our Lord's words in the institution of the Eucharist, of which, we must remark, we have the form given us in St. Paul's

Secondly, the *Didache* as a Christian document is not of very high authority. A Jewish manual veneered with Christianity could hardly be very authoritative in the Church. Moreover, apart from internal evidence, we know nothing of whence it emanates, or how; while there is no pretence at all that it issues from an Apostle, or a Church, or any other body authorized to pronounce among Christians. On the other hand, that either it, or at all events a great body of the teaching which it incorporates, was of considerable popularity in the early Church, seems to be clear. If we assume that the book as we have it is the one referred to by Eusebius and Athanasius[1], we must certainly admit its widespread popularity, whilst we explain as best we may in what sense Athanasius thought it of value, along with the *Shepherd of Hermas*, in the instruction of catechumens. But the assumption itself is at best uncertain. The vagueness in character of the title makes the identification insecure: and if it could be shown that the seventh book of the *Apostolic Constitutions* is an expansion, not directly of the *Didache*, but rather of a common form of sub-apostolic teaching about Christian morality, which the *Didache* in its own way embodies or represents, such a view would fit Athanasius' account at least as well as our *Didache*, and would probably fit the description of Eusebius better[2].

Epistle to the Corinthians—nothing to recall to us St. Paul's language about the significance of the Communion. It is a Jewish feast Christianized in a measure by the recognition of the Messiahship of Christ and the expectation of His second coming.'

[1] 'There is a writing mentioned by Eusebius (*H. E.* iii. 25) as τῶν ἀποστόλων αἱ λεγόμεναι διδαχαί; there is also a διδαχὴ καλουμένη τῶν ἀποστόλων which Athanasius (*Epist. Fest.* 39) classes among "the books not admitted into the canon, but appointed by the Fathers to be read to those who are just coming to us and desire to be instructed in the doctrine of godliness"; but it is difficult to feel certain whether these references are to the *Didache* as we have it.' Gore, p. 412. (See his references to Dr. Salmon.)

[2] Dr. Taylor (p. 72, cf. p. 112), while pointing out the familiarity of Barnabas and Justin Martyr with the subject-matter of the *Didache*, decides that both of them refer rather to an oral tradition of apostolic teaching (comparing Titus i. 9 ἀντεχόμενος τοῦ κατὰ τὴν διδαχὴν πιστοῦ λόγου) than to the written document. This would suggest that our *Didache* is but one representation of a certain

Thirdly, putting aside its Judaic, local, and unauthoritative character in the Church, it is in any case of the nature rather of a manual for the instruction of converts and lay beginners, than of anything like liturgical or authoritative direction to the officers of the Church. This consideration adds enormously to the improbability that chapters 9 and 10 can be meant as a liturgical direction; and yet the proviso at the end that the 'prophets' (as distinguished from others) are to be allowed to 'give thanks' at discretion, would at once make these forms, with all their immeasurable inadequacy, liturgically binding on all uninspired celebrants, if the chapters are, properly speaking, concerned with Eucharistic forms at all.

But even these immense deductions are far from destroying the interest of the picture which the *Didache* presents. If indeed the document be brought down to a much later date than that usually assigned to it, the interest will largely evaporate, for in that case it could give us only a picture of a heretical body in definite schism from the Church. Its conditions could not have existed in the Catholic Church at any time later than the earlier part of the second century. But as a picture, local and in some respects ignorant, of the Church of the first century, it is not only possible, but in many ways interesting and instructive. Our present concern is with the phenomena of the ministry of the Church. The points, then, which we actually find are as follows:—

1. There are two sets of what may be called ministers

body of popular teaching; and that references like those of Eusebius and Athanasius can only, at most, with great caution be taken as having any direct reference to our document. So far, however, as they are understood to refer to what is represented within our document, it will still be, in the nature of the case, almost inevitable to suppose that the serious commendations of fourth-century theologians must refer rather to the moral teaching of the 'Two Ways,' than to what is said about the sacraments or the ministry. It must be positively doubtful whether they referred at all to a document containing a representation of Christian ministry so incongruous, from the point of view of their own experience, as those of our *Didache* must have been. But if they did, at all events this part of the document must have been to them, in effect, wholly obsolete.

the first, Apostles, Prophets and (apparently) Teachers: the second, Bishops and Deacons.

2. Apostles and Prophets appear to become so by virtue of a Divine inspiration: Bishops and Deacons are regularly appointed by the Church.

3. The terms 'Apostles' and 'Prophets' are apparently interchangeable and synonymous [1].

4. Apostles or Prophets are non-local. Their perpetual itineracy is a characteristic as essential as their claim to be inspired. Nevertheless, the possibility is contemplated of the permanent local establishment, in some cases, of a prophet.

5. Bishops and Deacons are the local officers of settled communities.

6. The class of Apostles, or Prophets, is overrun with (more or less self-deceiving) impostors. Thus a large proportion of what is said about them consists of provisions for detecting 'false prophets.' Thus whoever stays more than one day in a place, or, at most, two; whoever takes away with him anything more than bread to last till his next resting-place; whoever asks for money—or for anything else; whoever, though he speak in the Spirit, is not Christlike in conduct; whoever does not do the things which he teaches; whoever, having ordered a 'table,' ventures himself to partake of it, is, *ipso facto*, an impostor.

7. On the other hand, Apostles or Prophets, *if genuine*, are regarded as supreme in the Church. Thus, they are

---

[1] No doubt this will be disputed. But it is clear, I think, that every apostle is regarded as 'prophetic', and the condemnation of an unreal apostle or an unreal prophet is, alike and equally, that he is a ψευδοπροφήτης. The antithesis to ψευδοπροφήτης is naturally προφήτης ἀληθινός. ('Ἀπὸ τῶν τρόπων γνωσθήσεται ὁ ψευδοπροφήτης καὶ ὁ προφήτης.) The word used throughout the passage is generally 'prophet.' Of apostles (if distinguished from prophets) *nothing* is said except that they must itinerate, and must not beg. Both these things are plainly true also of prophets. Throughout what is said of prophets in chapters xi. and xii., it is difficult not to feel that the mind of the writer has in view a class of men who are, to him, supreme and ultimate in the Church—the highest—not a subdivision of the highest, nor the highest but one.

to be received as the Lord, and not to be judged; they (unlike others) are to 'give thanks' according to forms which their own inspiration suggests; they are compared to the 'high priests,' and, as such, they are to receive the first-fruits of everything; while it is evidently considered that Bishops and Deacons are honoured by being said to share in the ministry, and to deserve a part in the honour, of the Prophets and Teachers.

8. The Bishops and Deacons are mentioned subordinately, but in express connexion with the weekly eucharistic sacrifice. That this may be duly offered Sunday by Sunday, every community must have its own 'Bishops and Deacons'; 'for they also minister the service (λειτουργοῦσι τὴν λειτουργίαν) of the Prophets and Teachers.' This last phrase seems to imply (what the whole spirit of the context would lead us to expect) that the 'Bishops' would be superseded in the Eucharistic sacrifice, whenever a genuine 'Apostle' or 'Prophet', was present; though, as said above, it is greatly to be doubted whether the reference of the earlier chapters (9 and 10) is, except improperly, confusedly, and nominally, to the Christian Eucharist

When we begin to comment upon this picture, we shall feel, in the first place, that many of the leading features in the conception of Church polity are not at all unlike those which were familiar to us in the New Testament. The *Didache* carries some of them a little further, and exhibits what we can recognize as a period of transition, but with a singular absence of insight into the underlying principles of either past or future. Just as in Scripture, the word ἐπίσκοπος plainly means what we mean not by 'bishop' but by 'presbyter'; just as in Scripture, these bishops (or presbyters) constitute, with the deacons, the settled ministries of all local communities; just as in Scripture, these local communities, with their regularly appointed (as distinct from irregularly inspired) 'bishops and deacons' are not self-sufficing or independent. The communities stand, and their officers govern and minister, in the face of, and in dependence upon, a background of higher authority, which, as non-local, represents the apostolic government of the Catholic Church. So far, the conditions are singularly like those of the New Testament.

But what is this background of catholic, overruling, authority? Is it, as in the New Testament, the apostolate? It still retains the name of apostolate; but it is very obviously not the apostolate of the Twelve. Meanwhile its apostles hold that title interchangeably with the title 'prophets,' and the conception of the 'prophecy' of the 'prophets,' though in some respects altered and developed, is in its main features singularly like that of the Epistle to the Corinthians. It is altered by having become more formulated and more dignified; and, for this purpose, having dropped off what we may call its own fringe of more subordinate manifestations. Thus while St. Paul expects an indefinite number of the local Corinthian congregation to be prophets more or less, the *Didache* knows no prophets except the apostolically itinerating dignitaries. Meanwhile the office of these, regarded as a development from 1 Cor. xii. or Ephes. iv. is a development which emphasizes, most forcibly of all, these two things, both already familiar in the New Testament; first, the character of the prophetic gift as irregular, though inspired, rather than as an orderly function of calculable and constituted polity; and secondly, as a matter of history, its conspicuous and enormous abuse—an abuse so striking that we can hardly think of it as less than a positive demonstration of the inherent tendency of the original 'prophecy' to run towards abuse. It is difficult to read the *Didache*, and not to feel, that while prophets or apostles must have been a numerous class in the Church, an apostle who could be accepted as a genuine prophet must have been rare and difficult to find: rather, in point of fact, a cherished ideal than a familiar phenomenon.

Now it is just at this point that we feel that, like as

the facts of Church polity in the *Didache* seem at first sight to be to those of the New Testament, there has nevertheless come over these facts such a change as transforms seeming likeness into essential contrast. Behind the regularly constituted presbyters and deacons there seems at first sight to be the old apostolic background. But behold! this background of apostolate is like a ghost. It is rather an idea than a fact It is becoming more and more (though it clings—perhaps even *because* it clings so tight—to the old form and title), not only an unreality, but an imposture. There may be a core somewhere still of really apostolic and prophetic reality. But, so far as the evidence of the *Didache* goes, it is involved and rapidly disappearing in a cloud of illusory vagueness. The fact of this, as fact, cannot be said to escape the mind of the Christian writers of the *Didache*. But the significance of it escapes them totally. They have no conception as to the points in which the old apostolate was, and those in which it was not, to live on in the Church. The idea of apostolate in the *Didache* is a sort of rambling representation of Catholicity, non-local before all things, and august primarily by virtue of a direct endowment of special inspiration. But in fact it is certain that such a special gift of inspiration, if it was true of the real apostolate, was never its main or constitutive essence, and it is plain on the face of the *Didache*, that apostolate, so conceived, is a dying thing; justly dying, because it is a form, and an illusory form, not a reality. It has an outward resemblance to the old apostolate, an outward appearance of perpetuating it. But of the true perpetuation of apostolical authority under conditions of a Church organized for permanence of constitutional life in the world; of the system which was both suggested and begun in the case of St. James, rehearsed in the persons of Timotheus and Titus, brought to completeness under St. John in Asia Minor in that representative embodiment, at once of apostolicity and of unity, which has been known, ever since St. John, under the distinctive title of 'episcopacy';—of this the *Didache* knows nothing. Or, if it has heard of any such thing at all, the *Didache* misconceives it, fancying that as St. John may have settled at Ephesus without forfeiting apostleship, so elsewhere an apostolically commissioned governing bishop is to be explained as a prophet exceptionally permitted to desist from itinerating. At all events it seems to me quite as likely that the localized prophet, whom the *Didache* rather inconsistently recognizes, was really a 'bishop' whom the *Didache* imperfectly understood, as to suppose that the *Didache* is ecclesiastically right in its representation of the status and character of its prophets, and that such prophets, so portrayed, did in the second instance, by the act of settling, become bishops in the sense of St. Ignatius or St. John.

After all, whatever we may think of these or other details in the *Didache*, it is necessary to remember, first, that it is in no case a particularly intelligent or authoritative interpreter of the ecclesiastical phenomena which it reflects, and secondly, that the phenomena, even as phenomena, could only appear to be, as the *Didache* portrays them, within the limits of the Catholic Church, at a time when the Apostles themselves, though few perhaps and remote, had not as yet completely died away; and when therefore the true substitute for the original background of apostolate, which itself solidified gradually under apostolic direction and appointment, was by no means as yet fully organized, still less fully understood, through the length and breadth of the Church.

It is necessary to emphasize this character of the *Didache*, as we pass from it to such evidence as the letters of Clement and Ignatius[1]. There is simply no comparison at

---

[1] It seems hardly worth while to speak in any detail of the Epistle of Barnabas, which may, in point of date, rank with or even before the *Didache* or the Roman letter; because it gives so little indication upon the points in

all between it and them in respect of authority. The letter of St. Clement, itself within the first century of our era, is the formal remonstrance of the Church of imperial Rome, addressed under the highest sense of responsibility in a grave ecclesiastical emergency, to the Church of the provincial capital of Achaia. It is difficult to imagine a document, not actually apostolic or inspired, which could take higher rank in respect of authority. Moreover, this solemn remonstrance of the Church of Rome is entirely concerned, from the first page to the last, with a question of ecclesiastical order. A faction in the Corinthian Church, under the influence of two or three individuals, had displaced its regularly constituted presbyters, some or all, from their office. The dishonour, the danger, and the sin herein involved, constitute to the mind of the Roman Church a crisis of the utmost possible gravity. If the Roman letter does not tell us all we should like to know, it is obvious that such a document, under such circumstances, must yet be, for our present purpose, of capital importance.

Now in one respect the evidence of the Roman letter exactly corresponds with the usage both of the *Didache* and of the New Testament. By St. Clement the word ἐπίσκοπος is still used, without reference to what we call episcopacy, as verbally interchangeable with πρεσβύτερος. In other respects the contrast with the *Didache* is amazing, and shows conclusively, either that the state of things pictured in the *Didache* belongs already, by the year 96, to a practically forgotten antiquity, or else

question. It may be well, however, to point out that it knows nothing of the 'prophet and apostle' nomenclature of the *Didache*. The prophets mean the writers of the Old Testament (ch. v.); and the apostles are twelve in number, according to the number of the tribes of Israel (ch. viii.). The Church is a 'Kingdom of the Lord' from which even 'the called' are liable to be driven out (iv. 11). There is a distinct—though in no way emphasized—note of warning against any separation of, or seclusion from, the common life and unity of the body (ch. iv 10 and xix. 12); and, finally, there is a certain interest in the concluding appeal to the heads of the Church (οἱ ὑπερέχοντες, whose position is regarded as involving counsel, legislation, government, with the necessity of sincerity, of understanding, of wisdom, of insight, of patience, and the inspiration and guidance of God (ch. xxi.).

that, however things may have appeared to the eye in some 'out of the way district' of Palestine or Syria, it was never a fair description of the general aspect of the Catholic Church. Christian prophets or prophecy nowhere appear at all in St Clement's letter. This is especially remarkable when we remember that the letter is addressed to the Corinthian Church, the very place in which they are most conspicuous (and perhaps we may add most threatening to order) in the time of St. Paul. The word 'prophets' occurs indeed in the letter more than once, and in connexion with apostles. But the word refers—and seems to be used as if it could only refer —to the prophets of the Old Testament; 'prophets and apostles' stand together, as it seems, quite naturally, for the Old revelation and the New.

It has been conjectured indeed[1] that the whole revolt against the presbyters was a prophetic revolt; that it is a climax of the old contrast and antagonism between 'bishops' and 'prophets' (in the sense of the *Didache*); and that the one or two individuals who chiefly inspired it were the leaders of the class or order of prophets. This view, if true, would be certainly interesting, and would work together for us some indications which at present remain rather fragmentary and unharmonized But if this is the secret of the matter, we should certainly have expected St Clement to give some more explicit indications of it. It is true that when we last saw below the surface of the Corinthian Church, there was a dangerous tendency to make too much of individual spiritual gifts, a tendency which threatened to destroy both the spiritual balance of their possessors, and the peace and order of the Church. It is true that we might expect *à priori* that the antithesis between this self-inflating sense of spirituality on the one hand, and the self-subjecting orderliness of submission to constituted office on the other, would develop until it came to a head in the form of a sharp antagonism between the two.

[1] See Dr. Salmon's *Introduction*, &c., p 585.

It is true that a disorderly outbreak against constituted office, as represented by the local presbyterate, is the one fact conspicuously certain about the Corinthian Church at the moment. It is true moreover that such inferences as we can draw from the epistle about the character of those who were in revolt against the presbyterate, quite agree, as far as they go, with what we should expect as the development of unbalanced 'prophecy.' This movement of theirs is a headstrong wilfulness (ch. 1); it is a characteristic example of the jealousy which has ever led to the death of martyrs (5); it is fed by vain and empty imaginings, worshipping self rather than God—whose revelation in Christ was the self-sacrifice of Calvary (7); it is puffed up with pride and hot feeling (13), running recklessly into estrangement and feud (14); not afraid to have made, aye and perpetuated, a manifest schism (46); it is self-exalting, in contrast with the self-repression of the ministry of Christ (16); it plumes itself on the sense of special faith, knowledge, discernment, wisdom, energy, holiness (48, cp. 13 and 38); it is immoderate of tongue, and knows not the moral value of silence (21); it is self-confident, daring, pleasing and praising itself (30)

Considerations like these may not carry us so far as Dr. Salmon's suggestion. But when we raise, as we cannot help raising, the question, 'what has come of prophecy and prophets in the Church of Corinth since the time of St. Paul?' I think there are two things which will occur to us in this connexion as elements which a full answer would contain. First, that whatever may have been the *better* development of προφητεία, its *worser* tendencies, if they had a development at all, must have gone to swell (even if it were in a subordinate degree) the un-Christlike temper which culminated in the schism against the presbyters. And secondly, that however much its main development may be conceived by us, if we please, to have been religious and orderly, yet still, just so far as it is characteristically a matter of personal spiritual endowment, as distinct from orderly ecclesiastical appointment, it is, by St. Clement, unreservedly set aside and disallowed as a formal ministry of the Church. If he sets it aside without once referring to it, such ignoring is only a more emphatic form of disallowing. I need not repeat what I said in a former chapter about St Clement's extreme insistence upon the principle of subordination to ministerial authority, or upon the principle of orderly succession of appointment from the apostles as constitutive of ministry. It would be, I think, impossible to read his letter and to suppose either that side by side with presbyterate and diaconate (still less as superseding them) he equally recognized a valid ministry of merely individual spiritual endowment; or that, if he recognized in Corinth or elsewhere such a class as gifted 'prophets' in the Church of Christ, he considered a discussion of their endowments to be so much as seriously relevant at all, in a crisis about Church order, and the constituted authority of Church ministers.

Before leaving St. Clement's letter we can hardly fail to ask the question, however hard it may be to answer quite certainly, what, if anything, can be gathered from it as to the existence, in Rome or in Greece, of 'episcopacy'? That the *name* Ἐπίσκοπος has not yet emerged, has already been stated, are there any traces of the *thing*?

Or rather, this is not quite the form in which the question should be put. I have insisted that, within the New Testament, presbyterate and diaconate always presuppose a background of higher apostolical authority. The *Didache* bears, in its own way, abundant witness to this assumption of an apostolical background. In the letters of St Ignatius it is plain that the apostolical background, though changed in form, is no less present still. It has become the localized 'episcopate.' The question then should rather be whether St Clement's letter so far differs from these documents which precede and which follow it, that in it alone, for the first time (perhaps also for the last), the presbyterate *has no background behind it at all.* To me it seems that there can be no hesitation in answering, first that the letter certainly gives no kind of warrant for such a negative conclusion as this; and secondly, that the evidence of the letter, though obscure, makes not for, but against, the conclusion.

The argument from silence is no doubt in itself a precarious argument. The mere possibility of using it, throws us back upon general presumptions from history. What, then, upon such general data as we have had before us, should we expect episcopacy at this date to mean? It is to be remembered that, at the date of this letter, St. John, the last of the Twelve, has, at the most, only very recently passed away. Bishop Westcott explicitly holds, that St John was still alive in the province of Asia. Now the sense of the withdrawal of the background of the apostolate would hardly be complete in the Christian world so long as St. John was still, or had only just ceased to be, living and accessible. The episcopal substitute for apostolic government would still, at such a time, retain something of its old provisional and relative character. It would not be forced into the sharpness and stiffness of prominence which, when it stood alone as the highest form of government in the Church, it could by no possibility afterwards avoid. The silent modesty, which to St Ignatius is plainly one of the best characteristics of the bishop, would come perhaps more naturally and easily to those whose office still seemed to have something almost tentative about it. The real authority of the governing presbyter who, in the place of apostles, had become the symbol and centre and mouthpiece of the unity of the Church's corporate life, the *de facto* ordainer and governor even of presbyters, might well be a most unostentatious authority. If it be urged that this would be chiefly true of the bishops of Asia where St. John was, but not of Achaia or of Rome, whence apostolate had long been practically absent, we may well hesitate to accept the argument. The persistent reference to St. John of the formal organization of 'episcopacy' would appear to mean that no one realized so clearly as the last of the apostles what the definiteness, the permanence, and the importance of the 'episcopate' was to be We can hardly doubt that the use of the distinctive title grew up under his influence. We should quite consistently suppose that he set himself to formulate and extend, to nurse and to educate, the episcopate, *eo nomine*, as such The bishops who felt his personality would be thereby not dwarfed so much as strengthened and encouraged as bishops. They would be (if anything) less tentative, more definite, than those in other parts of the Church, who had not as yet even a separate title; whose position might therefore in many respects be still very imperfectly defined, even while they felt their commission to represent and to rule.

This brings us more immediately to the question, what was St. Clement's own relation to the Church community in Rome? The leading fact is that when the Church of Rome solemnly addressed the Church of Corinth, it addressed them through St. Clement as its mouthpiece. The only two quite natural explanations of this are either that Clement was a mere secretary, or that he was the representative 'persona ecclesiae.' The very fact that his name is not mentioned in the text, as the name of St. Paul's amanuensis is frequently mentioned in his epistles, would be some presumption against the first. The reference of Hermas[1] is much more than a presumption. Stronger than either, and conclusive as deciding between the two alternatives, is the testimony of tradition. 'The reason for supposing Clement to have been a bishop,' says Bishop Lightfoot, 'is as strong as the universal tradition of the next ages can make it[2].'

But if Clement wrote rather as the representative

---

[1] Πέμψει οὖν Κλήμης εἰς τὰς ἔξω πόλεις, ἐκείνῳ γὰρ ἐπιτέτραπται. Vis. II. 4. Compare Polycarp's οὐκ ἐμαυτῷ ἐπιτρέψας λέγω ὑμῖν περὶ τῆς δικαιοσύνης, as below, p 209

[2] Phil. p. 219.

'persona' than as a mere amanuensis, how much does this carry? This first, that the arguments of the letter are Clement's arguments. Now there is nothing which St. Clement emphasizes more than the appeal to apostolical order, based upon apostolical succession; and he speaks of this as no accidental fact, but as part of the foresight of the apostles, and their careful provision for perpetuity of ministerial office by devolution from themselves. Did this include—with or without a name, with or without ostentatious assertion of pre-eminence—what we understand to be the essential substance of diocesan episcopacy? From the text of the letter we can hardly perhaps decisively reply. But suppose for a moment that to the mind of Clement it did *not*. In that case, of course, we reach no merely neutral or indefinite, but a positively negative result. With so strong a theory about provision for apostolical succession, St. Clement must either have included (what we call) episcopacy, or he must have excluded it. Either he must have believed that presbyters *as such* were the final rulers and ordainers, or he must have believed that in the last resort they ruled and ordained only with and through one who, if he was in any sense apart from or over them at all, could only conceivably (on his principles) have been so by virtue of being apostolically commissioned to be so. And if he were himself, according to the universal tradition, the leading and official figure of his Church, he must himself have acted, as matter of fact, *either* in such a way as illustrated substantially the principle of an apostolic unity embodied in a single representative persona, *or* in such a way as to negate and exclude it, and, so far as in him lay, to stamp it, if ever after him the idea should be introduced, with the brand of unapostolic novelty and falsehood. His theory of apostolic devolution, as the essential condition of any authorized ministry, is too definite and too peremptory to admit of the subsequent insertion of a new ecclesiastical office, behind and above the highest which he recognized himself. We cannot in fairness approach the consideration of his phrases without such presuppositions as these. But if we look at them in the light of any such considerations, we can hardly doubt that, indefinite and ambiguous as they seem to be, even his actual phrases do agree better with the assumption of the presence than of the absence of a government in the Church beyond the merely presbyteral; while their verbal mistiness will perhaps, on second thoughts, seem rather a natural than a strange result of a condition of things in which realities were in advance of words, in which the inner substance of episcopacy had an existence without a title, and therefore also as yet without perfectly adequate definition and distinction of thought.

Such are the passages in chapters 1 and 21 in which Clement exhorts the Corinthians 'to obey (chapter 21 'to reverence') such as bear chief rule over them,' and 'to honour their presbyters.' The word for chief rulers (ἡγούμενοι) is a familiar word either for secular[1] or for ecclesiastical[2] rulers. It would not be impossible to understand it in chapter 1 of the imperial magistrates, but in chapter 21 the compound form τοὺς προηγουμένους ἡμῶν does not lend itself to this very easily, and its place in the context, between the worship of the Lord Jesus Christ and the honour to the presbyters, almost excludes it[3]. Bishop Lightfoot, on the ground that in each passage the context goes on at once to νέοι and γυναῖκες, interprets προηγούμενοι of the spiritual rulers, i. e. the presbyters, and denies that the word πρεσβύτεροι means presbyters at all. It is only 'seniors,' in relation to the juniors, who follow next in thought. Now, without denying the verbal possibility of this translation, I must submit that it does not at all well agree with the probabilities of the letter. From the first page to the last the motive of the letter is to protest against

---

[1] As in ch. 37, 55, 61.
[2] As in Heb xiii 7, 17 ; Herm Vis II ii 6, &c.
[3] For, of course, if προηγούμενοι means magistrates, πρεσβύτεροι cannot but mean the presbyters.

dishonour to the presbyters, and to persuade the Corinthians into repentance and reparation to them. There is not a shadow of doubt what he means by factious opposition against the presbyters in chapter 47[1]; or being at peace with the duly constituted presbyters in chapter 54[2]; or obedience to the presbyters in chapter 57[3]. If, then, he opens such a letter as this by recalling the time when they were lowly-minded and orderly, obeying their ἡγούμενοι and rendering the honour which was due to their πρεσβύτεροι, the fact that the thought goes on to the training of the young and modesty of the women does not seem to me to suggest anything so paradoxical as that he uses the word πρεσβύτεροι without the slightest reference to the presbyters. The truth, as it seems to me, is that as yet he partly veils the directness of his rebuke by deliberately letting *the other* possible meaning and reference of the *word* emerge for a moment upon the current of his sentence[4]. Upon this view it is natural that there should be some ambiguity. The word does retain, in part, its double reference; and it is part of the ἐπιείκεια of the writer to intend that (for the present) it should. It is really a strong argument against Bishop Lightfoot's translation that it shuts out all ambiguity, and with it the characteristic mental trait which the ambiguity, just because it is ambiguous, delicately represents. According to the Bishop, the meaning 'presbyters'

---

[1] Στασιάζειν πρὸς τοὺς πρεσβυτέρους
[2] Εἰρηνευέτω μετὰ τῶν καθεσταμένων πρεσβυτέρων
[3] Ὑποτάγητε τοῖς πρεσβυτέροις.
[4] Compare the language of 1 Pet v. 1, 5, where πρεσβύτεροι would almost certainly be pronounced to mean merely 'old men,' if the intermediate verses did not make this impossible. Dr. Hort, writing of that passage (*Ecclesia*, p 222), says 'The first four verses of chap. v. must be addressed to "elders" in the usual official sense, for they speak of "the flock of God" and of "the chief shepherd," and lay down instructions for the right tending of the flock. But St Peter seems to join with this the original or etymological sense when he calls himself a fellow-elder, apparently as one who could bear personal testimony to the Christ's sufferings, and when (v. 5) he bids the younger be subject to the elder. (For a similar combination see Polycarp, 5, 6, where νεώτερος comes between deacons and elders.)'

is so 'exhausted in τοῖς ἡγουμένοις' that we are to understand that such a phrase as 'τιμὴν τὴν καθήκουσαν ἀπονέμοντες τοῖς παρ' ὑμῖν πρεσβυτέροις' in the opening thought of St. Clement's grand remonstrance about dishonour to presbyters, contains no allusion to presbyters at all. Far truer to life is the view which recognizes that St. Clement's thought is here really upon the presbyters, though (as yet) he half veils his thought by deliberately accepting the semi-unconsciously suggested verbal antithesis between πρεσβύτεροι and νέοι[1]. And, if so, the phrase ἡγούμενοι remains, not perhaps as a title which could, with any reasonableness, be directly translated 'bishops,' but at all events as a word which, both in itself and in its place in the context, is suggestive of a conception of Church government such as, to say the least, is imperfectly exhausted in the technical 'presbyterate,' taken alone.

There is again an ambiguous expression in chapter 44. The apostles, St. Clement says, in perfect orderliness, gave mission to 'bishops and deacons' under themselves. Foreseeing, moreover, that there would be jealousies about this office of bishopric, they made permanent provision for the due succession of others if those first appointed should die. Those then who have been duly constituted either by apostles, or, since the apostles, ὑφ' ἑτέρων ἐλλογίμων ἀνδρῶν κ.τ.λ., are presbyters indeed. Who are these ἕτεροι ἐλλόγιμοι ἄνδρες who since the times of apostles, have 'constituted presbyters and deacons,' as the apostles did before? Our not unnatural inclination to lay emphasis in this passage upon the word ἐλλόγιμοι, as though it meant men of exceptional eminence, is indeed, as it seems, entirely prohibited by an examination of its use in the 57th, 58th, and 62nd chapters of the same epistle[2]. But when we have reduced the word ἐλλόγιμοι

---

[1] In ch. III. I should certainly infer from the phrase οἱ νέοι ἐπὶ τοὺς πρεσβυτέρους that the presbyters were felt to be in fact elderly men.

[2] Ἄμεινόν ἐστιν ὑμῖν ... μικροὺς καὶ ἐλλογίμους ὑμᾶς εὑρεθῆναι ἢ καθ' ὑπεροχήν, κ.τ.λ.

to a colourless meaning, something equivalent (say) to 'other faithful men,' the question essentially remains unchanged. Who are these 'other faithful men' who, in the apostles' place, when apostles were gone, so 'constituted' presbyters and deacons that the men whom they 'constituted' could no more be removed than if they had been constituted by apostles themselves? And by what authority did these 'other faithful men' presume so far to enact the part of apostles, in a Church whose first principle was that the one essential condition of any lawful ministry was delegation, by orderly succession, from the apostles? Either they were simple presbyters, in which case St. Clement presents us with a theory of succession through presbyters, so formal, exact, and complete, as to leave no room for that system of episcopacy which at this very moment was already, on any showing, quite completely formulated and organized—distinctive title and all—throughout Asia Minor and Palestine, under the immediate superintendence of St. John[1]; or if there is not to be this sharply antithetical—nay irreconcilable—contradiction of principle between the formulated episcopacy of Asia, and the formulated presbyterianism of Greece and Italy, then these men of whom St. Clement speaks represent, through whatever vagueness of phrase with whatever uncompleted definiteness of thought, the essential substance of episcopacy already in existence and working in the Western Church, while it was only in the full sense articulate and self-conscious in the East. It is said by Bishop Lightfoot that 'the recognition of

Ὁ ποιήσας ἐν ταπεινοφροσύνῃ . . . τὰ ὑπὸ τοῦ Θεοῦ δεδομένα . . . οὗτος ἐντεταγμένος καὶ ἐλλόγιμος ἔσται εἰς τὸν ἀριθμὸν τῶν σωζομένων, κ.τ.λ.

Σαφῶς ᾔδειμεν γράφειν ἡμᾶς ἀνδράσι πιστοῖς καὶ ἐλλογιμωτάτοις καὶ ἐγκεκυφόσιν, κ τ.λ

[1] In which case it is difficult to see how the Roman Church polity could have been superseded by the Asiatic without a controversy which would have shaken the Church to its foundation; and impossible to believe that to Hegesippus in the middle of the second century the full list of bishops of Rome, *from the Apostles,* should have been complete matter of course.

the episcopate as a higher and distinct office must have synchronized roughly with the separation of meaning between bishop and presbyter.' His suggestion is that those who have not the name cannot have the thing. A more exact inference, I submit, would be that those who have begun to have the thing before they have acquired the name must be expected to show meanwhile not only that their language about that which they have is inarticulate, but that even their idea of it is indistinct. So it is in Rome and in Corinth. Whilst we recognize dim traces of a more than presbyteral authority without separation from the presbyteral name, we are not perplexed if the distinction which the language has not yet defined seems often imperfectly present—though yet present imperfectly—even to the thought

When we turn from the letter of St. Clement to those of St. Ignatius we may seem at first sight to have crossed a wide interval. But if the Ignatian letters be genuine at all, the interval of time can be but short. According to Bishop Lightfoot, St Clement's letter was written in 96. The martyrdom of St. Ignatius is 'within a few years of 110, before or after.' Thus the interval in time would be only about, not improbably within, 15 years. Ignatius, Bishop of Antioch in Syria, is on his way to martyrdom in Rome. He writes four letters while detained in Smyrna, three more before leaving Troas. From Smyrna he writes to the Ephesians, Magnesians, Trallians, and then to Rome. The first three letters we may consider first. It is to be remembered that they are written practically together; and it is not to be supposed that what his mind is full of in any one of them, can be far from his mind in either of the other two. The letter to the Magnesians is coloured by the earnestness of his warning against Judaizing error. That to the Trallians is no less emphatic against Docetism. To the Ephesians he is more general, as to those who had rather refused than been infected by specific forms of heresy. But whether on general grounds, or by way of remedy against Judaic or against Docetic heterodoxy, that which he positively urges in all three letters is the same. His great theme is, in a word, unity, the corporate unity of a Church which is ever one, in body and in spirit. His mind is full of the living glory and power of the one life, one faith, one love, one bread, one altar. The one altar is perhaps the culmination, on the earthward side, of the thought. But the one altar primarily involves one ministry, and the unity of the ministry is most concretely expressed in the bishop who is its culmination, and in closeness of adherence to him. Thus it is that though there is no indication that he is setting himself to preach 'episcopacy' as such, and certainly no consciousness whatever of preaching anything novel or unusual, the maintenance of the unity which the bishop represents, and adherence to the bishop as the expression of the unity which is vital to the Church, becomes the distinctive thing upon which his earnest endeavour practically turns.

Nothing indeed can exceed the earnestness of his appeal, but it is, as I read it, though fervent, though enthusiastic, yet fervent with the enthusiasm of an assured, and therefore ultimately even a tranquil, conviction, deep and joyous and confident—not passionate with anything like the wildness of a partisan. 'Let no man be deceived. If any one be not within the precinct of the altar, he lacketh the bread of God. For if the prayer of one and another hath so great force, how much more that of the bishop, and of the whole Church. Whoever therefore cometh not to the congregation . . . let us therefore be careful not to resist the bishop.[1] . . .' 'Do your diligence therefore to meet together more frequently for thanksgiving to God (εἰς εὐχαριστίαν Θεοῦ[2]), and for His

[1] Lightfoot's translation—Ephes v.
[2] Eph. 13 It may be doubted whether the word εὐχαριστία could be used in such a context without a consciously direct, even if secondary, verbal reference to the 'Eucharist.'

glory. For when ye meet together frequently the powers of Satan are cast down, and his mischief cometh to nought in the concord of your faith.' This, in fact, is no less than the difference between real and nominal Christianity. 'It is therefore meet that we not only be called Christians (μὴ μόνον καλεῖσθαι Χριστιανοὺς ἀλλὰ καὶ εἶναι), but also be such; even as some persons have the bishop's name on their lips, but in everything act apart from him.[1]' . . . 'Therefore as the Lord did nothing without the Father, being united with Him, either by Himself or by the Apostles, so neither do ye anything without the bishop and the presbyters, and do not try to persuade yourselves that anything is right or proper which you do by and for yourselves; but let there be one prayer in common, one supplication, one mind, one hope, in love and in joy unblameable, which is Jesus Christ, than whom there is nothing better. Hasten to come together all of you as into one temple of God, as to one altar, even to one Jesus Christ, who came forth from One Father and is with One and departed unto One.[2]' 'Be obedient to the bishop and to one another, as Jesus Christ was to the Father according to the flesh, and as the Apostles were to Christ and to the Father, that there may be union both of flesh and spirit.[3]' "He that is within

---

[1] Magn. iv
[2] Magn. vii. I have thought it wise to follow Bishop Lightfoot's translation in almost every instance In this particular sentence I have merely substituted the translation given in his commentary, because his continuous translation hardly explained itself completely.
[3] Magn. xiii. '"Both in flesh and spirit" is a very favourite phrase of Ignatius, and he uses it with more applications than one. But if we remember that his main yearning is for fullness of corporate unity, when we read in Magn. i. how he prays for the Churches that they may realize the "oneness of flesh and spirit of Jesus Christ" (ἕνωσιν σαρκὸς καὶ πνεύματος Ἰησοῦ Χριστοῦ), and again in Magn. xiii. hear him preaching the spirit of obedience, both to the bishop and to one another mutually, that their oneness may be of flesh as well as of spirit (ἵνα ἕνωσις ᾖ σαρκική τε καὶ πνευματική), it is difficult not to think that the phrase does, in these cases, express the idea of "unity of *outward order* as well as of inward spirit." And if this is so at the beginning and end of the Magnesian letter, it seems probable that the phrase εἰρηνευούσῃ ἐν σαρκὶ καὶ πνεύματι, in the superscription to the letter to Tralles, along with

the sanctuary (ὁ ἐντὸς θυσιαστηρίου) is clean, but he that is without the sanctuary is not clean; that is, he that doeth aught without the bishop and presbytery and deacons, this man is not clean in his conscience.[1]'

I think these passages will sufficiently show that Ignatius' main thought is the priceless value of unity, corporate and sacramental; and that the strong things which he says about the ministry, strong as they are, are yet secondary and as it were incidental to this. This fact by itself would at once suggest the inference that the constitution of the ministry—viz. as bishop, presbyters, and deacons—was neither to St. Ignatius' own mind a novelty, nor such as he would expect to be challenged, as novel or as doubtful, by others. And this inference is fully confirmed by his phrases in Ephes. iii. where he speaks of the bishops as 'settled in the farthest parts of the earth' (οἱ ἐπίσκοποι οἱ κατὰ τὰ πέρατα ὁρισθέντες), and in Trall. iii., where after exhorting that all should 'respect the deacons as Jesus Christ,' the 'bishop as being a type of the Father,' and the 'presbyters as the council of God and as the college of the Apostles,' he adds, 'apart from these there is not even the name of a Church' (χωρὶς τούτων ἐκκλησία οὐ καλεῖται).

It will be noticed also that emphatic as is his language about the bishop, when viewed from the lay side as the concrete symbol of Church unity, it is still characteristically the bishop *along with the presbyters and deacons*: —'The presbytery is attuned to the bishop, as its strings to a lyre,' Eph. iv.; 'the presbyters are the type of the council of the apostles,' Magn. vi.; 'be united with the bishop and with them that preside over you,' Magn. vi.; 'your bishop with the fitly-wreathed spiritual circlet of your presbytery,' Magn. xiii.; 'the presbyters as the

its more immediate reference to freedom from persecution, would also refer to a unity of Church order which (despite some schismatic tendencies) was not really broken by schism.'

[1] Trall. vii.

council of God and the college of the apostles,' Trall. iii.; nor is there anything in these letters to indicate the nature or conditions, or indeed (strictly speaking) even the existence, of a jurisdiction over presbyters exercised by the bishop. So far are they from being a polemic to enhance episcopal jurisdiction or dignity, that—except in respect of the one fact that adherence to the bishop, presbyters and deacons, or (more shortly) adherence to the bishop, is the concrete test of reality of proper Church fellowship—the letters are not as they stand incompatible with a working theory of episcopacy in which jurisdiction over presbyters could hardly be said to exist. I do not mean to suggest that there was no such jurisdiction, but that it certainly need not have been the full-fledged thing that is sometimes supposed. The letters are compatible with its being still inchoate and undefined to almost any degree. Indeed it is from the New Testament, or from the nature of the case, or from the subsequent history, from anything rather than the Ignatian letters themselves, that such a jurisdiction is to be inferred at all.[1]

There are two points more to be noticed in connexion with this thought. The first of them is the remarkable value which Ignatius attaches to silence and modesty on the bishop's part. 'In proportion as a man seeth that his bishop is silent, let him fear him the more,' Eph. vi.

---

[1] Perhaps the phrases in Smyrn. viii. (μηδεὶς χωρὶς τοῦ ἐπισκόπου τι πρασσέτω τῶν ἀνηκόντων εἰς τὴν ἐκκλησίαν. ἐκείνη βεβαία εὐχαριστία ἡγείσθω, ἡ ὑπὸ τὸν ἐπίσκοπον οὖσα, ἢ ᾧ ἂν αὐτὸς ἐπιτρέψῃ), especially the last five words, might seem to be as strong a passage as any But after all it is really taken for granted in such a passage that the bishop and presbyters are one whole. The words do not necessarily imply in the bishop any more authority than would be possessed among us by any chairman or president of any authoritative council. The 'authority of the chair' means in fact the authority of the council as a whole. But it is compatible with the existence of almost nothing that can be properly called 'jurisdiction' over the other members of the council. All the statements about 'nothing without the bishop' are addressed, it is to be remembered, to the general community, not to presbyters or deacons specifically. These are always assumed to be an essential part of the unity which is emphasized. In fact, 'the bishop' in such contexts is only a short formula for (what is always implied) 'the bishop and presbyters and deacons.'

This sentence should be taken in connexion with two remarkable passages, not about the bishop, which occur later in the same Epistle 'It is better to keep silence and to be, than to talk and not to be. It is a fine thing to teach, if the teacher practise. Now there is one teacher who spake and it came to pass, yea, and even the things which He hath done in silence are worthy of the Father. He that truly possesseth the word of Jesus is able also to hearken unto His silence (ἡσυχίας), that he may be perfect; that through his speech he may act, and through his silence he may be known' (ch. xv.). 'Hidden from the prince of this world were the virginity of Mary and her child-bearing, and likewise also the death of the Lord—three mysteries to be cried aloud—the which were wrought in the silence of God' (ch. xix.) (τρία μυστήρια κραυγῆς ἅτινα ἐν ἡσυχίᾳ Θεοῦ ἐπράχθη). Compare what he says about the bishop of Philadelphia in Philad i.: 'And I am amazed at his forbearance; whose silence is more powerful than others' speech (οὗ καταπέπληγμαι τὴν ἐπιείκειαν, ὃς σιγῶν πλείονα δύναται τῶν λαλούντων). For he is attuned in harmony with the commandments, as a lyre with its strings[1].' The second point is that Ignatius, being bishop of Syria (Rom. ii. and ix.), has no sense whatever of incongruity in describing himself as the last of all the members of the Syrian Church, and unworthy to be even reckoned amongst them[2]. There is of course nothing unusual in his language, which is, in this connexion, clearly Pauline. But it would hardly be—at that date—the language of autocratic pretension.

When we turn to the Epistle to the Romans we pass at once to a document of an entirely different kind. There are no exhortations, no perils, no warnings, no local conditions, or colourings, of any sort. There is no approach

---

[1] Cp. also his commendation of the Magnesians, both presbyters and people, for their respect to their bishop Damas, in spite of his obvious youthfulness.
[2] Eph. xxi, Magn. xv, Trall xiii. Cf. Eph. xii., Magn. xi.; Rom. ix.

to any 'pastoral' note at all. He does not urge unity. He does not urge anything. It is all about himself. There is therefore, and there could be, no reference whatever to the ministry of the Roman Church. From the first line to the last the one object is to beg the Roman Christians not to use their influence to prevent his martyrdom. This being the character of the letter, it would seem to be somewhat absurd to argue negatively from it that there was no bishop in Rome. From a letter so markedly different in scope and tone from the others, which never so much as approaches the topics in connexion with which he had been in the habit of emphasizing episcopal unity, and never glances in any way at the conditions of the Church he is writing to, save to deprecate the exercise of their political power, we can simply draw no presumptions about the Roman Church at all. The nearest approach to such a presumption would point (as far as it goes) the other way. It is plain from the superscription that the Roman Church is, to Ignatius, an august model of Christian eminence, wholly One, in flesh and spirit[1], with every ordinance of Christ, and free from the least tinge of irrelevant colouring This it is to be observed is the language of a man who from the very same place, and as it were at the same moment, is writing to the Ephesians that as Jesus Christ was, or is, 'the mind of the Father,' so are the bishops *established to the ends of the earth* 'within the mind of Jesus Christ'; and to the Trallians that 'apart from these' (bishop, priests, and deacons), 'there is not the name of a Church' I must certainly submit that the presumption which these phrases suggest that Ignatius regarded the Roman Church as episcopal, or, at the least, that he did not regard it as, even in the faintest degree, unepiscopal or anti-episcopal, is of far more effective

---

[1] Κατὰ σάρκα καὶ πνεῦμα ἡνωμένοις πάσῃ ἐντολῇ αὐτοῦ, πεπληρωμένοις χάριτος Θεοῦ ἀδιακρίτως καὶ ἀποδιυλισμένοις ἀπὸ παντὸς ἀλλοτρίου χρώματος On the first of these phrases compare the note on p 192

weight than any negative inference that can be drawn from his not urging the subject of episcopal unity in a letter which urges nothing, save about himself personally, at all[1]. Meanwhile it is certainly to be remembered, first, that the whole strain of the letter takes absolutely for granted that the Roman Christians know all about himself, who and what he is, and whence and under what circumstances he is being brought to Rome, takes for granted, that is, a degree of knowledge about persons and things in Asia Minor which would quite exclude the idea that the episcopacy so fully established there, could be otherwise than *in full view*, to say the least, of Rome; and, further, that Ignatius assumes, quite naturally and of course, that the Roman Church will be ready to sing praise to God for the martyrdom of the 'bishop of Syria,' and also that they will condole with and intercede for the Church of Syria, on the ground that it is deprived of its bishop or pastor, and therefore, under Jesus Christ[2], dependent for episcopal care on the love of other Churches[3]. In other words, he clearly assumes as of course their full intimacy and full sympathy in Christ with that which he means by episcopacy. In passing from the letter I cannot but ask once more in what possible manner either this or the full tradition of episcopacy, only one generation later, in Rome, can be reconciled with the stringent theory of apostolic devolution and succession as set forth in the Roman letter of St. Clement, except on the one supposition that the

---

[1] If it be said that he would have surely saluted, or at least mentioned, the bishop, it is to be noticed that in *none* of his letters does he *salute* the bishop, as though this were—or were a necessary accompaniment of—the salutation to the Church; and that in writing to the Smyrnaeans he does not so much as *mention* Bishop Polycarp at all

[2] Who, with the Father, is ever the true, invisible Bishop. Cf. Magn. iii. with the superscription and concluding words of the letter to Polycarp.

[3] Μνημονεύετε ἐν τῇ προσευχῇ ὑμῶν τῆς ἐν Συρίᾳ ἐκκλησίας, ἥτις ἀντὶ ἐμοῦ ποιμένι τῷ Θεῷ χρῆται. μόνος αὐτὴν Ἰησοῦς Χριστὸς ἐπισκοπήσει καὶ ἡ ὑμῶν ἀγάπη, ch. ix. In ch. iii. he had called himself τὸν ἐπίσκοπον Συρίας.

episcopal office was *de facto*, with whatever indeterminateness of style or name, already contained in St. Clement's principle, and already in operation in St. Clement's person?

It is not necessary to dwell at any length upon the three remaining letters, which were written from Troas, because the phenomena are in no important respect different from those of the first three. The letter to the Philadelphians is like a more emphatic version of that to the Magnesians. In it he speaks for the first time as to a Church in which he is personally known; and for the first time also as in the face of a systematized heterodoxy which schismatically refuses the unity of the Church. Similarly the letter to the Smyrnaeans re-echoes that to the Trallians. As to the Magnesians and Philadelphians, it is Judaism so to the Smyrnaeans and Trallians it is Docetism, which is the enemy[1]. In each case the later letter shows the more organized schism. The schism does not in either case appear to be primarily of the nature of a revolt against episcopacy It is primarily doctrinal But the doctrinal heresy organizes itself as schism. Thus it is that 'unity' is preached as the remedy for false doctrine. 'As many as are of God and of Jesus Christ they are with the bishop; and as many as shall repent and enter into the unity of the Church, these also shall be of God, that they may be living after Jesus Christ. Be not deceived, my brethren. If any man followeth one that maketh a schism, he doth not inherit the kingdom of God. If any man walketh in strange doctrine, he hath no fellowship with the Passion. Be ye careful therefore to observe one Eucharist (for there is one flesh of our Lord Jesus Christ and one cup unto union in His blood; there is one altar, as there is one bishop, together with the presbytery and

---

[1] Bishop Lightfoot would make it a 'Docetic Judaism,' and in all four cases the same. This may be so but considering how closely all the letters are connected together, we could hardly draw this inference from the fact that when he is writing against Judaism incidental phrases show that Docetism too is in his mind, and *vice versa*. *This* phenomenon could hardly fail to appear anyhow.

deacons my fellow-servants), that whatsoever ye do, ye may do it after God¹.'

The 'strange doctrine' which destroys 'fellowship with the Passion' is a phrase which becomes much clearer in the light of what he says to the Smyrnaeans about Docetism. 'They believe not in the blood of Christ.' 'Far be it from me even to remember them, until they repent and return to the Passion.' 'They abstain from εὐχαριστία because they allow not that the Eucharist is the flesh of our Saviour Jesus Christ. . . . Shun divisions as the beginning of evils. Do ye all follow your bishop, as Jesus Christ followed the Father, and the presbytery as the apostles; and to the deacons pay respect, as to God's commandment. Let no man do aught of things pertaining to the Church apart from the bishop². Let that be held a valid Eucharist which is under the bishop, or one to whom he shall have committed it. Wheresoever the bishop shall appear, there let the people be; even as where Jesus may be, there is the universal Church. It is not lawful apart from the bishop either to baptize or to hold a love-feast; but whatsoever he shall approve, this is well-pleasing also to God; that everything which ye do may be sure and valid.' The foundation of the evil is a heresy which destroys the reality of the Atonement, and therefore of the Christian Eucharist, and which therefore systematically substitutes something else, on principle, for the true valid eucharistic Life and Oneness of the Church.

The Epistle to Polycarp of Smyrna echoes the general teaching of the two letters before it, though without direct reference to heresy. It suggests also that contracts of marriage should be made with the knowledge and consent of the bishop, and that private resolutions of celibacy should on the one hand be consecrated by being made known to him, and, on the other, preserved from carnal pride by being made known to no one else; a suggestion

---

¹ Philad. iii, iv.   ² Smyrn v., vi, vii., viii.

which would only seem to cohere with a very early condition of Church life.

The testimony then of St. Ignatius' letters to the threefold ministry needs no sort of emphasizing. But in passing from them I cannot but repeat, what I have endeavoured to indicate above, that there is, in their portraiture of episcopacy, nothing whatever that is inconsistent with its earliest, and even (in a sense) most tentative stage. It is only as the symbol of unity that the bishop is magnified. If St. Ignatius' expressions are compatible with an episcopally autocratic jurisdiction, they are no less compatible with an episcopacy which wields no jurisdiction save as chairman and symbol of the presbyteral body. Whatever more there was, or was to become, must be looked for elsewhere than in these letters[1].

It is difficult to dissociate the Ignatian Epistles as a whole from the Epistle of Polycarp to the Philippians, which is, in time and circumstances, almost of one piece with them[2]. The interest of considering them together is not diminished but enhanced by the fact that they seem at first sight to bear the most diverse testimony on the point which is now immediately before us, the episcopal constitution of the Church. The mention of a bishop, or episcopacy, in respect of the Philippian Church is conspicuously absent from St. Polycarp's Epistle. The fact is indisput-

---

[1] In view of the very wide variations of apocalyptic interpretation, I have not introduced the 'angels of the churches' (Rev. ii. and iii.) into the argument of this chapter. It is impossible, however, not to notice that the whole imagery which the language implies is closely bound up with the Ignatian conception of corporate unity summed up in an individual personality; of an individual personality as the symbol and the guardian and the expression of corporate unity. Unlike the 'princes' of Dan. x. and xii., the 'angels' appear not only to be the spiritual champions, or to represent the spiritual idea, of their churches, but also to have, vested in themselves, the duty, and the responsibility which is involved in the duty, of a personal jurisdiction.

[2] Polycarp has not yet heard, and begs the Philippians to let him hear, any exact tidings of what actually befell Ignatius and his companions in Rome; ch. xiii.

able Does it point to any inference that the Philippian Church was non-episcopal? I think that it does not. And it may be worth while to try and explain why.

In the first place there is no doubt that Polycarp who writes the letter, writes himself as bishop of Smyrna. We need not go for this to the letters of Ignatius to his Church or himself, recent and decisive as they were. His own opening words, 'Polycarp and the presbyters who are associated with him,' are sufficient[1]. But of course these cannot be read without the Ignatian comment; especially as Ignatius' own letters—that is, it is to be presumed, at least those to the Smyrnaeans and to Polycarp personally —are (at the Philippians' request) actually enclosed by Polycarp with his own letter, and strongly commended by him as 'comprising every kind of edification which pertaineth unto our Lord' (ch. xiii.). When it is remembered what these letters, thus enclosed and commended, contained, and what moreover was the geographical nearness and frequency of intercourse between cities like Smyrna and Ephesus and Philippi, it is clear at least both that the letter itself comes in all respects out of the full completeness of the atmosphere and assumptions of the Ignatian letters, and also that this atmosphere and these assumptions must have been thoroughly and intimately familiar to the Philippian Church.

But did the Philippian Church, though familiar with Asiatic episcopacy, and its relation to St. John, remain itself deliberately non-episcopal? that is to say, had it gone on, since the practical withdrawal of the background of apostolate, with a presbyterate which, without background, was itself ecclesiastically final or supreme? Perhaps the apostolic background can hardly have been said to have been lost by such a city as Philippi, so long

---

[1] Πολύκαρπος καὶ οἱ σὺν αὐτῷ πρεσβύτεροι. Cp. also ch. xiii.: ἐγράψατέ μοι καὶ ὑμεῖς καὶ 'Ιγνάτιος, ἵνα ἐάν τις ἀπέρχηται εἰς Συρίαν, καὶ τὰ παρ' ὑμῖν ἀποκομίσῃ γράμματα· ὅπερ ποιήσω, ἐὰν λάβω καιρὸν εὔθετον, εἴτε ἐγώ, εἴτε ὃν πέμψω πρεσβεύσοντα καὶ περὶ ὑμῶν.

as St. John still lived in the province of Asia. But of course so far as Philippi fell in this way under the guidance of the last of the apostles, there is a strong presumption that it would not have been left out of the episcopacy which his old age so strongly shaped and watched, and finally left in full and articulate completeness. On the other hand, if Philippi is regarded as having had no background behind its presbyters for a quarter of a century, I must submit that the principle of presbyterism would have become so stereotyped, that the evolution of a higher order, having inherent supremacy and jurisdiction over presbyters, would have involved not development but 'dislocation' and 'reversal[1].' Here, as in Rome (where Clement's theory of apostolic devolution must either have contained, or have been overthrown by it), such a change could only have been the stormy change of a revolution, not a merely silent and imperceptible growth.

But to come to the Epistle. I admit not only that there is no hint of a Philippian bishop, but that this is so in spite of the fact that the circumstances and topics of the letter seem, at first sight, specially to call for some reference to him. But this is only a part of the fact For what is the letter itself, and what is the occasion of it? 'The Epistle of Polycarp,' says Bishop Lightfoot[2], 'was written in reply to a communication from the Philippians. They had invited him to address words of exhortation to them (§ 3); they had requested him to forward by his own messenger the letter which they had addressed to the Syrian Church (§ 13); and they had asked him to send them any Epistles of Ignatius which he might have in his hands.' Of course these statements are true; but are they an adequate account of the letter which he wrote? The most characteristic thing about it, as it seems to me, is that it is not of the nature of a letter of general friendliness, or

---

[1] See Bishop Lightfoot, *Apostolic Fathers*, Part II vol. i. p. 475.
[2] Part II vol. iii. p. 313.

moment of orphanhood, to Jesus Christ and to God, the supreme invisible bishop, and, on earth, to the prayer and the love of other Churches[1]. It is then a quasi-apostolic or episcopal attitude in which Polycarp writes. And this seems to me to be expressed in his own words in ch. iii. It is not he who has taken on himself so to write. Neither he nor any one like him is really fit to claim the wisdom or wield the place of the apostle St. Paul. St. Paul taught them face to face; St. Paul wrote them letters when absent, and by such letters they were built up indeed in the faith. Does not all this reference to St. Paul and his apostolic letters imply in itself that Polycarp's letter was something far more than a neighbourly courtesy? So perhaps does his rather curious phrase when he describes it not as a letter about them, or the things they had asked of him, but as about 'righteousness[2].' Thus then it is not his own assumption but their reference to him that causes Polycarp to stand for the moment as the concrete representative of the 'intercession and love of other Churches,' bishoping them, when their own bishop was lost. I cannot but say that this view seems to me to account for the actual phenomena of the letter far more exactly than any view which simply sees in it a witness to the non-episcopal character of the Philippian Church, and a sharp antagonism, unconscious indeed but none the less difficult to reconcile, between the Asiatic and European Church theories[3].

[1] Μόνος αὐτὴν Ἰησοῦς Χριστὸς ἐπισκοπήσει καὶ ἡ ὑμῶν ἀγάπη. Rom ix.

[2] Οὐκ ἐμαυτῷ ἐπιτρέψας γράφω ὑμῖν περὶ τῆς δικαιοσύνης, ἀλλ' ἐπεὶ ὑμεῖς προεπεκαλέσασθέ με. ch iii.

[3] If Philippi, like Syria, has just lost its bishop, one is naturally tempted to ask whether the words of ch. xi. do not contain a still more explicit reference to the fact. The Church at Philippi has just seen before its eyes—as of old in St. Paul and the other Apostles, as since then in many of its own confessors—so at this moment in the persons of the blessed 'Ignatius and Zosimus and Rufus,' a model of the discipline of Christian character Who were Zosimus and Rufus? It is almost certain that they were sharers in Ignatius' martyrdom. It is probable (from the total absence in his own letters of reference to them, or to *any* fellow prisoners) that they were not sharers in his journey, sooner than at Troas; perhaps not until Philippi.

neighbourly interchange, or encouragement, or even warning, but of a 'pastoral' or 'episcopal' letter. It takes just the place and tone that their own bishop's letter would have taken. For the moment, its writer is himself in the attitude of pastor to the Philippians. In this respect there is a marked contrast between it and any of the letters of Ignatius. Its specific exhortations to the different classes in the Church—the general community, the women, the widows, the deacons, the young men in general, that is, all up to presbyters, culminating in an emphatic exhortation to submissive obedience to the presbyters and deacons 'as to God and Christ'; then the vigorous address to presbyters, as to the exercise of their pastoral discipline, their firmness, their justice, their graciousness and compassionate sympathy; still more his clear statement about the fallen presbyter Valens, the impossibility of his being allowed to continue in the discharge of his office, his own concern for the man himself and his wife, and his prayer that they may be brought to a real penitence; the caution that he adds, withal, against the overstraining of discipline, his pleading for Christian tenderness even towards the culprits and his insistence upon the limitation of Christian anger,—all this is exactly episcopal.

But why should Polycarp write thus to Philippi? Immediately indeed because they had referred themselves to him. This no doubt is why Polycarp of Smyrna, rather, e. g. than Onesimus of Ephesus. But why any other Church, or bishop, at all? Because Philippi knew nothing of episcopate? and had never accepted a bishop? This does not sound at all *probable* as an answer. A Church which had never had a bishop would not be likely to feel that sort of need or desire. A Church which maintained presbyteral constitution, as such, would quit certainly not. But a Church which had just lost i bishop, would. It would stand then exactly in the positi in which Ignatius describes the Church of Syria as sta' ing—looking, that is, for its episcopal oversight, a'

It may be doubted, then, whether anything would adequately explain the letter as it stands, except the theory of an invitation from the Church at Philippi to the Bishop of Smyrna, to take for the moment the position not so much of a friendly Christian neighbour as of a pastoral or episcopal supervisor; and I must repeat that this in itself appears to be an invitation which would not have proceeded from a presbyteral Church, but only, with perfect naturalness, *sede vacante*, from a Church which was accustomed (as of course) both to feel, and to value, episcopal oversight.

It is hardly, perhaps, necessary to add that episcopal oversight at this stage would be far from having all the associations, of pomp or awe, which afterwards belonged to it. But it did mean that one who was chief amongst and behind the presbyters—with distinct title or without, but always on the principle, and by the right, of apostolic devolution and empowerment—did exercise *de facto* the same sort of apostolic functions of government which Titus and Timotheus had exercised, for the absent St. Paul, half a century before. The apostolic pedigree, the first place in whatever functions or rights were involved in presbyteral office, and especially in the Eucharist, the right and practice of 'constituting,' and (if need were) of exercising discipline over, even presbyters and deacons, as well as the general representative leadership and care of the community — these are the points which seem to be directly involved or implied in the actual evidence about bishops which has been before us.

Had either of these been 'bishop of Philippi'? Had either name been put before that of Ignatius or specifically distinguished as ὑμετέρῳ, the positive probability would have seemed very strong In this case, moreover, inasmuch as the see would not actually be vacant, we should see at once why it is treated as vacant practically, and yet no reference is made to the fact—or to the filling—of the vacancy. No doubt, both here and in ch. xiii., the name of Ignatius is treated as being, even to the Philippians, the name that is clearly pre-eminent. Perhaps if we knew the circumstances more exactly, we should see at once why this was. But of course the serious considerations urged in the text are wholly independent of any suggestion so utterly precarious as this.

When we turn to the *Shepherd* of Hermas, the first thing in relation to the present subject which can hardly fail to impress us is the position occupied in the writer's thought by the Church. The Church is the great primal, fundamental, and final unity. The Church was before the world, and the world was created for the sake of the Church[1]. So in the third Vision, the Tower foursquare, founded upon the baptismal water, is the Church. It is everything to be built into the Church, to be rejected from the building is death. This is elaborated in great variety of detail both in the third Vision and in the ninth Sim. (a city to be entered by a single gate, p. 200). Nothing could be more alien from any theory of Christian individualism, or a gradual coalescing of Christians, more or less, towards oneness. That the Church is 'one Body' is hardly urged at all; it is rather an underlying postulate of thought[2]. Thus such exhortations as there are towards unity never appear even to contemplate anything like disunion on schismatic principle, but exclusively the natural tendency, on the part of the Christians who were rich and respected in society, to withdraw themselves in selfish isolation from the life and the burthens of the poorer brotherhood. He is constant and urgent about this peril of the disuniting of wealth[3].

[1] Πάντων πρώτη ἐκτίσθη· διὰ τοῦτο πρεσβυτέρα, καὶ διὰ ταύτην ὁ κόσμος κατεστάθη. Vis. ii. 4; cf. Vis. 1. 1

[2] Cp. οὕτω ἦν ᾠκοδομημένος ὡσὰν ἐξ ἑνὸς λίθου μὴ ἔχων μίαν ἁρμογὴν ἐν ἑαυτῷ ἐφαίνετο δὲ ὁ λίθος ὡς ἐκ τῆς πέτρας ἐκκεκολαμμένος μονόλιθος γάρ μοι ἐδόκει εἶναι. Sim. ix. 9; cp. Vis. iii. 2 This, no doubt, is ideal—looking on towards the final consummation, as Sim. ix 17 sqq. But though it is only at the end that it becomes a perfect monolith, it is obviously throughout a compacted building, realizing more or less and representing the 'monolith' ideal.

[3] Αὕτη ἡ ἀσυνκρασία βλαβερὰ ὑμῖν τοῖς ἔχουσι καὶ μὴ μεταδιδοῦσιν τοῖς ὑστερουμένοις. Vis. iii. 9. οἱ πλούσιοι δυσκόλως κολλῶνται τοῖς δούλοις τοῦ Θεοῦ. Sim. ix. 20. μὴ κολλώμενοι τοῖς δούλοις τοῦ Θεοῦ ἀλλὰ μονάζοντες ἀπολλύουσι τὰς ἑαυτῶν ψυχάς Sim. ix 26. οὗτοί εἰσιν οἱ ἐν ταῖς πραγματείαις ἐμπεφυρμένοι καὶ μὴ κολλώμενοι τοῖς ἁγίοις Sim. viii. 8. οὗτοί εἰσιν πιστοὶ μὲν γεγονότες, πλουτήσαντες δὲ καὶ γενόμενοι ἔνδοξοι παρὰ τοῖς ἔθνεσιν ὑπερηφανίαν μεγάλην ἐνεδύσαντο καὶ ὑψηλόφρονες ἐγένοντο καὶ κατέλιπον τὴν ἀλήθειαν καὶ οὐκ ἐκολλήθησαν τοῖς δικαίοις, ἀλλὰ μετὰ τῶν ἐθνῶν συνέζησαν, καὶ

In the second place, we may ask what indications does the book supply on the subject of ministerial constitution or distinctions? To begin with, there are, as it seems, three positive things to be said in answer to this question. First, it is clear that there *are* leaders and governors, sitting in the place of Church dignity. It is largely to them that Hermas' own mission is addressed. The terms by which he describes them, though plainly marking their dignity, are often quite general. They are, 'those who have the rule over the Church[1]'; 'those who have the rule and sit in the chief seats[2].' Secondly, it may probably be said that the word which he instinctively uses of specific office is the word πρεσβύτεροι. Thus the command just quoted, 'Thou shalt say to those who have the chief rule over the Church,' is taken up by the question in the next page, asked by the Church herself, whether he had 'already delivered the book to the presbyters[3]:' and the phrase about the chief seats receives an instructive comment in his exclamation, 'Let the presbyters sit down first[4].' Thirdly, it is nevertheless true that the most nearly formal list of offices or dignities which the book contains is in a passage which declares that the great stones of which the tower is built, four-square, and shining white, and joined

αὕτη ἡ ὁδὸς ἡδυτέρα αὐτοῖς ἐφαίνετο ἀπὸ δὲ τοῦ Θεοῦ οὐκ ἀπέστησαν, ἀλλ' ἐνέμειναν τῇ πίστει, μὴ ἐργαζόμενοι τὰ ἔργα τῆς πίστεως. Sim. viii. 9.
The opposite ideal is sketched in Mand viii.. χήραις ὑπηρετεῖν, ὀρφανοὺς καὶ ὑστερουμένους επισκεπτεσθαι, ἐξ ἀναγκῶν λυτροῦσθαι τοὺς δούλους τοῦ Θεοῦ, φιλόξενον εἶναι (ἐν γὰρ τῇ φιλοξενίᾳ εὑρίσκεται ἀγαθοποίησίς ποτε) μηδενὶ ἀντιτάσσεσθαι, ἡσύχιον εἶναι, ἐνδεέστερον γίνεσθαι πάντων ἀνθρώπων, πρεσβύτας σέβεσθαι, δικαιοσύνην ἀσκεῖν, ἀδελφότητα συντηρεῖν, ὕβριν ὑποφέρειν, μακρόθυμον εἶναι, ἀμνησίκακον, κάμνοντας τῇ ψυχῇ παρακαλεῖν, εσκανδαλισμένους ἀπὸ τῆς πίστεως μὴ ἀποβάλλεσθαι, ἀλλ' επιστρέφειν καὶ εὐθύμους ποιεῖν, ἁμαρτάνοντας νουθετεῖν, χρεώστας μὴ θλίβειν καὶ ἐνδεεῖς, καὶ εἴ τινα τούτοις ὁμοιά ἐστιν.

[1] Ἐρεῖς οὖν τοῖς προηγουμένοις τῆς ἐκκλησίας. Vis. ii. 2.
[2] Ὑμῖν λέγω τοῖς προηγουμένοις τῆς ἐκκλησίας καὶ τοῖς πρωτοκαθεδρίταις. Vis iii. 9.
[3] Εἰ ἤδη τὸ βιβλίον δέδωκα τοῖς πρεσβυτέροις. Vis. ii. 4.
[4] Ἄφες τοὺς πρεσβυτέρους πρῶτον καθίσαι (though it is not πρώτους) in Vis. iii. 1; and so μετὰ τῶν πρεσβυτέρων τῶν προισταμένων τῆς ἐκκλησίας. Vis. ii. 4.

so perfectly as if they were all of one piece, are 'the apostles and bishops, and teachers, and deacons, who have walked in the reverence of God and served the elect in bishopric, teachership, diaconate, holily and reverently—some of them still living, some fallen asleep.'

It will be observed here that after the apostles, who are mentioned first and once only, the other three technical names are given twice over. It seems to me that 'apostles' are regarded herein as all fallen asleep, the three other orders as partly dead and partly alive. It is noticeable also, especially after what we have observed about the word πρεσβύτεροι, that just when he seems to be distinguishing grades of ministry the word πρεσβύτεροι drops out and διδάσκαλοι appears instead. But I cannot but suggest that this verbal change becomes at once wholly natural, if we imagine (what would be perfectly consistent with an ecclesiastical condition intermediate between that of the letters of Clement and of Ignatius) that the title ἐπίσκοπος is beginning more or less to emerge, even in Italy, as the distinctive title of the apostolically governing presbyter, but that he has not yet ceased to be also reckoned as a presbyter amongst, though presiding over, presbyters; and consequently that πρεσβύτερος, *as verbally including both orders*, is not for the moment a distinctive title[1]. So far, however, as this passage may be said to recognize the emergence of 'bishops' (as I believe that it may), it must certainly be taken in connexion with the well-known close of the second Vision,

---

[1] If it is true that πρεσβύτεροι, to Hermas, signifies both bishops and presbyters, διδάσκαλοι would quite naturally be the title of presbyters proper. It is a title which comes familiarly from St. Paul's epistles The διδάσκαλοι of 1 Cor. xii. 29 and Eph. iv 11 connect themselves naturally with the πρεσβύτεροι who, in 1 Tim. v. 17, are distinguished as κοπιῶντες ἐν διδασκαλίᾳ.

It is right perhaps to add the further comment that, if there is real ground for thinking, that, in Hermas, the word πρεσβύτεροι includes both bishops and presbyters, it becomes very difficult to say whether the same may not be true, in a directer sense than is commonly supposed, of the letter of Clement also. Πρεσβύτεροι may, to Clement, include, as of course, the episcopal president, as surely as ἐπίσκοπος, to Ignatius implies as of course, the accompanying presbytery.

where Hermas with a view to the general publication of his Visions, is directed to prepare two written copies, and to send one to Clement and one to Grapte. Grapte represents the instruction of the widows and the orphans, but Clement shall send the Visions to the Churches of other places, 'for that has been entrusted to him[1].' This little clause receives a somewhat significant comment from St. Polycarp's apologetic phrase to the Philippians, when he pleads that 'it is not in virtue of any self-imposed trust' that he ventures to address his Epistle to them[2], and a far more decisive explanation from the actual letter of the Roman Church through Clement to the Corinthians. I need not repeat anything that has been already said about this. But if the things which have been urged are true, it would be difficult not to admit that Hermas does in this phrase implicitly recognize the *de facto* existence of Clement's presiding office.

What was said just now about the use of διδάσκαλοι as the title of the second order of the ministry receives some corroboration in the language of Sim. ix. Three times over[3] apostles and teachers (ἀπόστολοι καὶ διδάσκαλοι) are mentioned together as those through whom the name of Jesus Christ is made known to the world. The third of these three passages is instantly followed by a condemnation of unworthy deacons (διάκονοι). On the other hand, in the first of the three passages, apostles and teachers are 'a second generation' of righteous men, the first generation being God's prophets and ministers (προφῆται τοῦ Θεοῦ καὶ διάκονοι αὐτοῦ). Both these two words are curious but the phrase 'first generation' which is applied to them seems to exclude the idea that they are to be interpreted in any New Testament sense. It is further to be added that the passage about the unworthy διάκονοι

---

[1] Ἐκείνῳ γὰρ ἐπιτέτραπται.
[2] Ταῦτα ἀδελφοὶ οὐκ ἐμαυτῷ ἐπιτρέψας γράφω ὑμῖν περὶ τῆς δικαιοσύνης. ch. iii.
[3] Sim. ix 15, 16, 25

shows clearly that the 'deacons' in Hermas still had, as in the Acts, distinctive functions in respect of distribution to widows[1], and that on the following page it is equally clear that hospitable entertainment of the brethren from other Churches when travelling, and general protection and shelter of widows and others in want, were recognized as specially pertaining to the office of bishops[2].

So far we have observed in Hermas, first the general assumption of a body of ecclesiastical rulers (ἡγούμενοι, &c.); secondly, the apparent identification with these in a general way with πρεσβύτεροι; thirdly, the indications of such distinctions of office after the apostles, as ἐπίσκοποι, διδάσκαλοι and διάκονοι. There are a few things more to add. The first of these is the picture in Mand. xi. of the true and false prophets, a picture which is none the less interesting in itself, though it seems to stand curiously alone in the book. The tone carries us back in some respects to the *Didache*, but it is plain at once that the false prophets are far less numerous, pretentious, or aggressive here than there; that προφητεία altogether plays now a comparatively subordinate part. The points of most importance, as I conceive, on the positive side are, first, that the place of προφητεία and προφῆται is most explicitly recognized; there are false prophets to be eschewed, but there is a true spirit of prophecy to be recognized, and believed, and obeyed; and secondly, that there is no indication of these true prophets being ranged as an order either with, or instead of, the official dignitaries of the Church. I do not say that this follows decisively from the passage. But the indications are at least in complete agreement

---

[1] Οἱ μὲν τοὺς σπίλους ἔχοντες διάκονοί εἰσι κακῶς διακονήσαντες καὶ διαρπάσαντες χηρῶν καὶ ὀρφανῶν τὴν ζωήν, καὶ ἑαυτοῖς περιποιησάμενοι ἐκ τῆς διακονίας ἧς ἔλαβον διακονῆσαι. Sim ix. 26.

[2] Ἐπίσκοποι καὶ φιλόξενοι, οἵτινες ἡδέως εἰς τοὺς οἴκους ἑαυτῶν πάντοτε ὑπεδέξαντο τοὺς δούλους τοῦ Θεοῦ ἄτερ ὑποκρίσεως· οἱ δὲ ἐπίσκοποι πάντοτε τοὺς ὑστερημένους καὶ τὰς χήρας τῇ διακονίᾳ ἑαυτῶν ἀδιαλείπτως ἐσκέπασαν καὶ ἁγνῶς ἀνεστράφησαν πάντοτε. Sim ix. 27.

herein with what the letter of Clement makes practically certain, viz that the existence and functions of προφῆται in the Christian body did not really come into sight or question at all in a discussion about the constituted ministries of the Church.

Before making any comment upon Hermas' conception of the false prophet, it is well to notice at this point the position occupied by Hermas himself. He is favoured with a series of visions in which 'the Church' appears to him and communes with him The things which he sees in vision are fully explained to him, not for his own sake, but for the sake of the brethren generally, to whom he is charged to deliver them. It is 'the Church' who charges him, and he is sent to the members of the Church[1]. It is not for his worthiness—others there are before him, and better than he, but revelations are made to him for the glory of God, and διὰ τοὺς διψύχους —on account of the men of double mind like himself[2]. He is charged to deliver his message to the elect[3], to the chief rulers[4], to the presbyters[5], to Clement[6], to Grapte[7] to all[8]. This was to him a solemn charge and ministry. He is urged to stand fast in his ministry like a man, and to fulfil it, that he may make it a ministry well pleasing to God[9] What then was Hermas' position? He is certainly not a presbyter[10]. He sharply differentiates himself from the Church rulers Yet to them, as to all, he has a divinely revealed ministry and message. These things seem so completely to corroborate, as almost to establish, the theory that Hermas is himself to be reckoned as a 'prophet,' and that in Mand. xi. he is speaking, with earnestness of personal feeling, about

---

[1] Οὐ σοὶ μόνῳ ἀπεκαλύφθη ἀλλ' ἵνα πᾶσι δηλώσῃς αὐτά. Vis. iii 8.
[2] Vis. iii. 4.   [3] Vis. ii 1.   [4] Vis ii. 2.   [5] Vis. ii. 4.
[6] Ibid   [7] Ibid   [8] Sim. v. 5, &c.
[9] 'Permane ergo inquit in hoc ministerio et consumma illud,' Sim x 2. 'Viriliter in ministerio hoc conversare, omni homini indica magnalia Domina, et habebis gratiam in hoc ministerio.' Ibid.
[10] Ἄφες τοὺς πρεσβυτέρους πρῶτον καθίσαι   Vis. iii. 1, &c.

the gift of revelation which he himself claimed, and about the suspicion which he personally felt to attach in his time to the class and to the title. Certainly he as a prophet is as much concerned as any one to guard the title against those who would assume it falsely. It will probably therefore be felt that he is in the main, through this chapter, upon the defensive. Even when he is stigmatizing false prophets, he is still on the whole vindicating from suspicion a class and a claim which are rather unduly suspected than unduly revered [1].

His picture of the false prophet is in the main an ignoble one. A man who shrinks away from the assembly of honest Christians, because their very presence abashes him; who consorts with the empty-minded in a corner, and gives out prophesies for hire in answer to questions, and says nothing unless questioned and unless paid; this is a rather pitiful sort of impostor. There are two touches, however, in the whole picture of a somewhat different kind. In § 12 we see the false prophet exalting himself and claiming to sit on a chief seat [2], and living luxuriously; and in § 1 he is shown in the vision as seated by himself on a *cathedra*, over against the true prophets who sit together on a *subsellium* or bench. In exact parallelism with this language there is the curious explanation in Vis. 3 why the lady personifying the Church first appeared as old, and sitting on a *cathedra*—'because every one who is feeble sits upon a *cathedra* by reason of his feeble-

---

[1] It may not improbably be felt that the view of prophets in this and the preceding chapter is unduly depreciatory. I shall certainly not plead guilty to depreciating the Christian gift of προφητεία. Do we not owe to it the New Testament itself, as well as all Christian literature, and the discernment and proclamation of spiritual truth in every generation, and across the inhabited world? The divine endowment of προφητεία has indeed been manifest in Christians of all classes and kinds, and eminently, as I believe, in the Christian ministry of many generations But professional prophets are a different thing. προφητεία does not involve a class of προφῆται. And it has to be suggested that from the earliest, as well as in later, generations, 'prophets,' as such, have not been much of a success in the Church.

[2] Πρωτοκαθεδρία.

ness¹'; then as younger looking, and standing up; and finally as altogether young and beautiful, and sitting on a *subsellium*, 'because that is the position of strength, because the *subsellium* has four feet and stands strongly, just as the world is made strong through the four elements.'² It has been suggested that this curious representation is really a covert attack upon the new-fangled pretensions of an 'episcopos,' possibly even in the interest of the waning predominance of the 'prophets.' Whether there is any element of such an innuendo, it may be difficult to pronounce with absolute certainty; but I cannot but submit that, even if there be (which is exceedingly doubtful), it would be much more like the playful shaft of a comrade, or perhaps the remonstrance of an anxious friend, than the serious disagreement of an opponent.³ This might probably be inferred from the passage itself. For if any seriously anti-episcopal sense is to be put upon the imagery, if there is more than some sort of passing verbal allusion to the danger of sitting alone upon a *cathedra*, or a faint touch at most of half-amused pique, the picture drawn of the ψευδοπροφήτης will become at once inconsistent with itself. The claim to be bishop and head of the organized presbytery, and the shrinking from the assembly and divining in a corner at the hire of the empty-pated, cannot really be parts together of a single character And it is to be remembered that the phrases which are thought to carry the former meaning are only passing touches in what is mainly the later portrait. Or, if it is thought that the strong feeling of the writer impels him to introduce inconsistent

---

¹ Ὅτι πᾶς ἀσθενὴς εἰς καθέδραν καθέζεται διὰ τὴν ἀσθένειαν αὐτοῦ.

² Ἰσχυρὰ ἡ θέσις· ὅτι τέσσαρας πόδας ἔχει τὸ συμψέλιον καὶ ἰσχυρῶς ἕστηκεν· καὶ γὰρ ὁ κόσμος διὰ τεσσάρων στοιχείων κρατεῖται.

³ Bishop Lightfoot, putting aside as untenable the suggestion that this is a presbyterian protest against episcopacy, quotes the remonstrances of Irenaeus against the tendency to episcopal pride. 'Contumelis agunt reliquos, et principalis consessionis (MSS concessionis) tumore elati sunt.' The words are curiously like those of Hermas. But no one would dream of suggesting that Irenaeus was making an attack upon episcopacy. He quotes also Matt xxiii. 6, &c.

touches into an alien portrait, in order to strike an indirect blow at the bishop, we can only say that a blow so very indirect and indeterminate as this, if it shows some faint possible flavour of personal jealousy, goes in fact much further to establish the *de facto* acceptance, than to suggest any serious suspicion, of an institution which those who by hypothesis disapproved of it, could only glance at so faintly and so indirectly.

This view is indefinitely strengthened when we turn from internal to external indications. When did Hermas write? He describes himself as ordered in Vis. 2 to send his book to Clement, to be sent to other Churches. He is asserted by the wholly unknown writer of the Muratorian fragment to have been the brother and to have written during the episcopate of Pius, Bishop of Rome, i. e. about the middle of the second century. Now personally I should be ready to accept Dr. Salmon's argument that it is useless to try and reconcile these statements[1]. One or other must be in some way a false indication. Personally also I should agree in deciding in favour of the former date, which I believe to be seriously given by Hermas himself, and with which the different internal indications, as I have tried to represent them, seem perfectly to accord But for the present purpose it is enough to say that Hermas *either* wrote about or just after the time of St. Clement's Epistle to the Corinthians; *or else* fifty years later, when his own brother Pius was bishop of Rome, and when episcopacy in Rome was in its own way as much a matter of course as it is now. If any one chooses the later alternative, he is I think bound to admit not only that the vagueness about episcopacy in Hermas' writings is no argument against the completeness of its establishment, but also, as a further corollary, that no similar vagueness in any other writer could constitute adequate ground, in their cases either, for any negative inference. But if he chooses (more reasonably as I believe) the earlier date, I shall still submit that there is too much

---

[1] See *Introduction*, pp 582-4.

indication of Clement's position, both elsewhere and in Hermas himself, to allow of our finding in this curiously vague and isolated passage any serious opposition on the part of the section of the Church to the principle of episcopacy. More than this, I should certainly claim Hermas, on the whole, not only as strengthening the evidence in favour of Clement's own *de facto* episcopate, but also as giving indication that even the title *episcopos* was, as title, less unknown to the Roman Christians of Clement's generation than we could possibly have supposed from Clement's own letter.[1] Clement's occasional use of the word in the older sense, and his omission to use it in the newer, do not seriously conflict with this. Such usage might be more surprising in another, but in the mouth of the bishop himself it has an obvious moral significance of its own.

It may be well to try and sum up the results of this sketch—such as it has been; though in fact the results are already upon the face of it.

It is quite plain, then, that from the earliest apostolic times there were in every Church regularly constituted presbyters. It is plain that, with these, deacons are habitually associated, as inferior ministers. It is, I think, sufficiently plain that prophets, as such, were not at any time a regularly constituted order of ministers; and that, even as a class of 'gifted' men, they passed rapidly into insignificance and even suspicion. It is, however, when we assume the continuity of presbyters and deacons that the question begins. The real question is, what is there behind, or beyond, presbyterate? Within the New Testament, it is certain that presbyterate never was complete or ultimate. Behind and above it, there was always the background of apostolate. It may be taken as equally certain that from the middle of the second century on-

[1] Compare what was said above on p. 197 about the references to episcopacy in the Ignatian letter to Rome.

wards, there is invariably found, behind and above presbyterate, the background of episcopate[1].

The question is then whether, between the close of the New Testament and the middle of the second century, there was an interval in which presbyterate had *no background at all*; and whether, by consequence, the background of episcopacy which we may certainly assume as universal and unquestioned before 150 A.D., was really, without continuous apostolic devolution of authority, invented and evolved from below. Was one background abolished, and, when there was none, was another devised in its stead? Or was the later background, with whatever modifications of condition or title, itself the direct outcome, by lineal descent, from the earlier?

[1] Bishop Lightfoot writes (*Phil* pp. 224-5): 'The notices thus collected present a large body of evidence establishing the fact of the early and extensive adoption of episcopacy in the Christian Church. The investigation, however, would not be complete, unless attention were called to such indirect testimony as is furnished by the tacit assumptions of writers living towards and at the close of the second century Episcopacy is so inseparably interwoven with all the traditions and beliefs of men like Irenaeus and Tertullian, that they betray no knowledge of a time when it was not Even Irenaeus, the earlier of these, who was certainly born and probably had grown up before the middle of the century, seems to be wholly ignorant that the word bishop had passed from a lower to a higher value since the apostolic times. ("The same," he adds in a note, "is true of Clement of Alexandria") Nor is it important only to observe the positive though indirect testimony which they afford. Their silence suggests a strong negative presumption, that while every other point of doctrine or practice was eagerly canvassed, the form of Church government alone scarcely came under discussion.'

Even before Irenaeus, Hegesippus, without any hint or apparent consciousness that he is entering upon ground which could possibly be controvertible, makes a point of drawing up a list of the Roman bishops till the time when he himself visited Rome See Euseb., *H E.* iv. 22. As the visit of Hegesippus to Rome was not very different in date from that of the (now aged) Bishop Polycarp, it would be within the lifetime, and perhaps within the personal knowledge of Polycarp, that this list of the Roman succession was thus carefully made as a perpetual monument of the unity and continuity of the Church. Polycarp was already bishop of Smyrna before the writing of the Ignatian letters To him, if to any one, the great change must have been intimately known, if change there ever was, by which the Church of Clement, with its tenacious hold of the doctrine of apostolic succession of presbyters, became transformed—strange to say, without a word, a hint, a breath even of consciousness!—into a Church in which presbyterate depended for its very being upon apostolic episcopacy.

This question, and the answer to it, are cardinal. Upon the answer that is given it is not too much to say that absolutely everything, in the rationale of Church ministry, depends. If episcopacy is really in its origin evolved, not transmitted, then the orders which it confers, and which depend upon it, are ultimately also not transmitted, but humanly devised. Then the entire belief of Christendom upon the essential character of Church ministry—which was true, in fact, in the New Testament, and during the lifetime of apostles—died to truth when they died, and has been a fundamental falsehood ever since. Then the saintliest bishops and priests in Christian history, whatever they might be in personal endowment, differed not one jot—if we need not quite say, in respect of ministerial character or authority, yet at least in respect of the ultimate rationale of principle which constitutes the divine foundation and security of ministry—from the good men whom the last new sect has chosen to appoint to be its ministers.

It is not irrelevant to emphasize thus the wider effects of such a theory, and the extent to which all Church conviction, and every historical principle of ordination, and perhaps form of Ordinal, would be shattered by it. But it is more in accordance with the scope of the present chapter to insist that this later Church theory must be understood to be already established in the mind of the Church before 150 A.D.; and so established, that there is no glimmer of consciousness that the belief ever had been, or could have been, otherwise. But such a belief follows upon an immemorial tradition of facts. When, then, were the facts really otherwise? Certainly they could not have been otherwise so long as apostolate lasted. Certainly, in Asia Minor at least, episcopacy was most expressly articulate, name and all, before the death of St. John. No loophole appears to be left except the suggestion, itself upon the broad facts not very probable, that in the non-Asiatic Churches at the end of the first and the opening of the second century presbyterate had a final and self-dependent authority. Now this is certainly not at all like the *Didache*. The background which it portrays may be in some ways misty or mystifying, but the presence of a background is unmistakable. Nor is it easy to reconcile with Ignatius's apparent belief as to the universality and indispensableness of bishops. Neither, I must submit, is it really sustained either by the letter of Clement to the Corinthians, or of Polycarp to the Philippians, or by the *Shepherd* of Hermas. These have sometimes been thought to sustain it; but I must submit that every one of these, when weighed broadly and fairly, may be said—to say the very least—to lend itself more conveniently to the opposite view.

I have urged more than once that the evolution of an episcopate upon which the presbyteral office depended for its very being would shatter to pieces the uncompromising theory of apostolical succession in the letter of Clement, if it were not already somehow implied and contained within the system of the Church as Clement understood and intended it. And I must say, finally, that whilst, on the one hand, I do not believe that the European Churches could have become silently episcopal, if episcopacy had involved any real alteration of their constitution at all; on the other, the actual phenomena of the writings of Clement and Hermas seem to point to a real *de facto* existence of quasi-apostolic oversight over Churches and presbyters, which is none the less practically real because it is still perhaps imperfectly defined in title and outline.

As apostolate gradually disappeared, so episcopate gradually stood out into clearness of view. There is a long period of transition, in which episcopacy, *eo nomine*, may be said perhaps gradually to 'emerge'—for that is consistent with the previous existence of what, though there, yet lacked explicitness and recognition; but never to be 'evolved'—for that would imply that it did not, in essential completeness, exist before. That which was to come (between, say, the Rome of St Clement and the Rome which Hegesippus visited) was the stereotyping, by titular contrast, of a difference inherently familiar, not the revolutionary creation of a novel distinction. Meanwhile the indefiniteness of nomenclature (such as it is) is no very unnatural result of what is historically a gradual, and at first semi-conscious, process of transition, from the full and unfettered apostolate, to something which, though (in many respects) far inferior, did yet really represent and perpetuate, as it was essentially derived from, apostolic authority.

CHAPTER VII

WHAT IS PRIESTHOOD IN THE CHURCH OF CHRIST?

THE question now to be raised will seem to carry us across a considerable interval of time. If we have really had the foundations of it even in the earliest generations, it is rather with reference to the sixteenth century, and its controversies and changes, that the question of the definition of priesthood becomes acute. It is from the sixteenth century that our own form of Ordinal dates. We go at once to the heart of the matter, both in respect of the abstract question, and in reference to Anglicanism, by asking what is really the inner truth which the recasting of the Sarum into the Anglican Ordinal represents?

It is not, however, simply a question between Ordinal and Ordinal. The Sarum *Celebratio Ordinum* is itself the climax of a long historical process of accretion. Whatever may be thought of this Ordinal as it stands, or of the history which is represented in it, it is certainly also to be remembered that the sixteenth century Divines, when confronting the question, had to deal not only with an authorized form of service which had (or perhaps had not) grown in some directions gradually out of due proportion, but also with a general atmosphere of popular interpretation and assumption, which—to say the least—certainly outran any tendency towards disproportion which may be found in the text of the Ordinal itself.

There can be in fact no doubt that the sixteenth century

exhibits two currents running in opposite directions, and both alike with most formidable volume and force. On both sides, moreover, there is a ready tendency to extreme, and often most painful, exaggeration.

On the one hand, there is what would sometimes be called the 'Doctrina Romanensium,' by those who understand by that phrase, not so much the doctrine of authorized Roman forms, as the current conception of Romanists, more or less authorized (or unauthorized), more or less truly (or falsely) deduced from, more or less, in a word, interpreting, or misinterpreting, the forms. Now there can I suppose be no doubt that, at least to a considerable section of popular unreformed thought, the Priesthood was mechanical, and the Sacraments material, to an extraordinary degree; that outward observance had constantly taken the place of spirituality; that superstitious formalism, hard, cold, and unintelligent, had proved too often the paralysis of personal religion; that the Mass was too often, much in the heathen sense, or the Old Testament manner at its worst, a completed sacrifice,—that is an outward performance of intrinsic efficacy, to be so many times repeated, with a value arithmetically calculable; and so that the Priest stood as a real intermediary between the *plebs Christiana* and its God,—to make, by sacrifice, atonement for sin. I have already had occasion to insist, in an earlier chapter, that this literalizing and materializing tendency is never wholly absent, and while human frailty remains, will never be wholly absent, from the Church[1]. Man's imperfectness naturally tends towards mechanical formalism in the use and conception even of things most spiritual. It will hardly be denied that in the generations immediately before the Reformation and the Council of Trent, in the age, for instance, of that sale of indulgences which is symbolized for us by the name of a Tetzel, this tendency, never wholly absent, was present in most abnormal and appalling strength.

[1] See above, p 53.

But such exaggeration on the side of mechanical formalism, always and necessarily provokes a reaction on the spiritual side. Too often this reaction, itself caused, and in some measure excused, by the formalism it revolts against, runs headlong into the counter-exaggeration of depreciating all outward forms and observances whatever. Over against, then, the appalling exaggeration of mechanical sacramentalism, stands in the sixteenth century the fierce tide of ultra-Protestant reaction. The one matches the other. Nothing indeed short of the terrible excesses of irreligious churchmanship on the Roman side could fully account for the terrible excesses of virulent antichurchism on the Protestant side. This, protesting in the name of personal religion and of spiritual truth, and genuine enough in its original impulse, but ignorant to an extreme degree, and prejudiced in proportion to its ignorance, was eager to sweep away, in one great destructive flood, all ordinances, outward and historical, whatsoever; as if the inward would best express itself without an outward, or spirit be educated best by annihilation of body. The full force of this eager destructiveness turned itself, most of all, against everything which was connected, in popular feeling, with Purgatory, and the Mass, and Sacrificing Priesthood. Nothing indeed but the hideous exaggerations connected, in popular feeling, with this whole phraseology could fully account for the abiding savageness of the popular instinct against it, seeing that this instinct, whatever carnal passions quickly became involved in it, was certainly in its underlying impulse a religious, not an irreligious, instinct.

Such was the character of the counter influences—no calm academic tendencies, but each embodied as a strong flooding tide of fierce popular enthusiasm—between which the theologians of the sixteenth century stood. Meanwhile on neither side could the great questions be deferred for more peaceful times. They must be met and dealt with in that generation. And in fact they were dealt with

VII] *PRIESTHOOD IN THE CHURCH OF CHRIST* 223

on both sides; by English theologians, in the Anglican Prayer-book; by Romans, in the Council of Trent.

It is of considerable importance for some purposes to remember that the Tridentine definitions are not themselves exactly the Romanism which the Anglican Reformers had in mind. The Council of Trent was itself, as far as it went, a reforming Council Its statements are not a representation in full, but rather a modification, of current doctrines; a toning down and careful defining made by official theologians in full knowledge of, and with reference to, the great 'Reformation' impulses; meaning, however, by that phrase 'Reformation' not so much the Anglican Prayer-book as the General Protestantism—and the Anglican Prayer-book only so far as it was supposed to symbolize with, or be interpreted by, German Protestantism. The sittings of the Council of Trent were in the years 1546-7, 1551-2, and 1562-3; and inasmuch as all the definitions which belong directly to our present subject fall within the last batch of sittings, it is plain that they were none of them yet in existence at the time of the Prayer-books of 1549, or 1552, or 1559. Nevertheless, with this caution premised, I must use the Tridentine statements along with the language of the Sarum Ordinal, not forgetting that they express some modification—or at least a very guarded statement —of what the Reformers regarded as the unreformed position; but because they nevertheless constitute the fairest and most official statement of what that position can be said actually to be.

What then was the teaching on this subject from which the Anglican Ordinal made its departure? Take first the official language of the Sarum Pontifical. There is a sort of initial definition, in six words, 'Sacerdotem[1] oportet

[1] The Pontificals of Egbert and Dunstan, as printed by Martene. contain an exposition 'de septem gradibus Ecclesiae quos adimplevit Christus'; in the course of which the words occur: ' Presbyterum autem oportet benedicere, offerre, et bene praeesse, praedicare, et baptizare, atque communicare; quia his supradictis gradibus senior est, et vicem Episcopi in Ecclesia facit.

offerre, benedicere, praeesse, praedicare, conficere, et baptizare.' There are four standard prayers in the service—all ancient. The *praefatio* ('oremus') is mainly for a blessing on those whom God has called to the 'munus presbyterii.' The *oratio* ('exaudi') asks for them the benediction of the Spirit, and the power of spiritual (or 'sacerdotal[1]') grace. In the great prayer 'Vere dignum[2]' the 'dignitas presbyterii' and 'secundi meriti munus' are asked for them; but the one leading and characteristic idea of the whole is that they are to be assistants, 'adiumenta,' 'cooperatores,' to the episcopal order,—as the seventy to Moses, as Eleazar and Ithamar to Aaron, as the 'doctores fidei' to the Apostles. In the prayer called 'consecratio[3]' the office is called 'honor presbyterii,' and its holders are to prove themselves true 'seniores': it is prayed that, by the blessing of God, they may meditate and live on the Divine law, teach with their lips and show in their lives righteousness, constancy, mercy, courage, and all virtues, maintain pure and undefiled the 'donum ministerii sui[4],' and, 'per obsequium plebis tuae,' transform bread and wine by their benediction into the Body and Blood of Christ, in perfectness of love,—'unto the measure of the stature of the fulness of Christ.'

Now so far we have been following the ancient prayers, in substance wholly unchanged since at least the time

Similarly in the modern form of the Roman Pontifical the short Sarum sentence appears as part of an exhortation to the candidates for Priesthood, but with the omission of the word 'conficere.' The difference between this exhortation and that in the Anglican Ordinal is very significant.

[1] Maskell gives it as 'spiritualis' in Sarum (and so York), but it is 'sacerdotalis' in Winton and Exon, and in Missale Francorum and the Pontificals of Egbert and Dunstan

[2] Which (beginning from 'Domine Sancte') is called 'Consecratio' in the Pontif. of Egbert and the Missale Franc., and is, according to Duchesne, the true old Roman 'consecratio.'

[3] Which appears in Miss. Franc. and Egb as a 'Benedictio,' and in Pontif. Dunstan (cp. possibly Miss. Franc.) as 'consummatio presbyteri'; and which is probably, according to Duchesne, the old Gallican benedictory or consecratory prayer.

[4] *Tui* in the older documents.

when first, as in the Missale Francorum, they stood together as a single, amalgamated form of Ordinal. In them the office is, characteristically, 'presbyterate'; though the word 'sacerdotal' does also, quite simply and naturally, attach to it. In the picture of the office which they present there is nothing whatever that we should desire to challenge; though it may be felt that the phrase 'benedictione transforment' might need some guarding, in view of later controversies, in order to avoid misapprehension[1]. But, as the mediaeval office stands in its completeness, it is plain that the ancient service thus sketched, so far from itself explaining how 'presbyterate' (or 'priesthood') is to be interpreted, remains only as a sort of background, against which the characteristic lineaments of the 'priesthood,' as mediaevally conceived, stand out.

The fact is that the idea of 'assistance to the episcopate' was in earlier days[2] quite clearly the dominating idea about presbyterial office It was so not only in the old 'consecratio,' but throughout the Missale Francorum as a whole. This is strongly illustrated by the ancient usage (which is very marked e. g. in the Apostolical Constitutions) according to which every distinctly 'priestly' title belonged characteristically to episcopate,— though Presbyters also were, to a certain extent, and rather in partnership with, and dependence upon, Bishops than independently or *iure suo*, capable of sharing in the titles As far as the text of the prayers alone is concerned, this conception may be said to have held its ground in the unreformed Ordinal to this day.

[1] See Note, p 300.
[2] I say 'in earlier days'; but it does not at all necessarily follow that it was so in the earliest. The first indications we possess of Ordinal forms seem to belong to times when Bishops were exceedingly numerous, and often perhaps had only an insignificant number of Presbyters under them The position of Presbyters under these circumstances could hardly be for practical purposes the same as it must have been within the first century of Church life, and especially in the times of the Apostles themselves. For that apostolic background, which always existed as behind and above Presbyters, must (to say the least) have been to most Churches, within the apostolic period, rather occasionally than normally present

Now as long as the presbyteral ordination was obviously in this key—admitting into a certain partnership with the 'sacerdotium' of the Bishops—it might fairly be urged that the character of that to which they were admitted was to be ascertained rather from the service of consecration to episcopate, than from the ordination to presbyterate, taken apart. If we are thus referred to the consecration of Bishops for the meaning of 'priesthood,' we shall find, whether in the Apostolic Constitutions or the Missale Francorum, or it may be added the Sarum or the Roman Pontificals to this day, a far more truly balanced teaching about it than in the mediaeval or modern ordination of Presbyters. In the consecration of Bishops the pastoral aspect of priesthood has never been extinguished by a disproportioned insistence upon the truth of 'sacrifice.' But in the unreformed ordination of Presbyters, this earlier relation of the services (itself quite explicable and satisfactory) has not been maintained. The mind is no longer referred to the 'consecratio electi in Episcopum' for instruction about priesthood. On the contrary, there is a very marked and emphatic teaching about 'priesthood' in the ordination of Presbyters. The old prayers, which were themselves in a certain sense colourless just because they made Presbyters primarily *adiumenta* and *cooperatores* to somebody else, have been allowed to continue as a mere background, against, and in front of, which a new exposition of priesthood (itself not so much untrue as most lamentably out of proportion) has gradually grown into more and more of emphasis.

The development of this conception finds expression —not, of course, in the great prayers of the Ordinal, which remain substantially unchanged throughout the centuries, but in the growing complexity of ceremonial actions, each accompanied by its own words of short but significant petition. In the Sarum Pontifical there are six of these[1]

[1] In the *Statuta* ('Carthag. iv.') there had been only one—the laying on

(1) the laying on of hands by the Bishop and Presbyters, before, or during, the *Praefatio* 'oremus'; (2) drawing the stole over the right shoulder; (3) vesting with the chasuble; (4) anointing of the hands; (5) delivery of the chalice and paten; (6) final laying on of hands by the Bishop alone. The last five of these six have their appropriate formulae—four of them in the shape of an 'Accipe.' With the stole it is 'Accipe iugum Domini . . . stola innocentiae induat te Dominus' With the chasuble, 'Accipe vestem sacerdotalem per quam caritas intelligitur.' With the chalice and paten, 'Accipe potestatem offerre sacrificium Deo, missamque celebrare tam pro vivis quam pro defunctis.' With the last laying on of hands, 'Accipe Spiritum Sanctum; quorum remiseris peccata,' &c The formula at the blessing of the hands asks God to sanctify them (a) 'ad consecrandas hostias quae pro delictis atque negligentiis populi offeruntur, et ad caetera benedicenda,' (b) 'ut quaecumque consecraverint consecrentur, et quaecumque benedixerint benedicantur . . .' The same note is struck once more in the final benediction: 'Benedictio Dei Patris et Filii et Spiritus Sancti descendat super vos, ut sitis benedicti in ordine sacerdotali, et offeratis placabiles hostias pro peccatis atque offensionibus populi . . .'

It is impossible not to feel to what an extent these accretions have altered the proportions of the more primitive conception. More and more, the attention becomes concentrated upon a single dominant and differentiating idea.

The one thing which stands out at last so conspicuously that it seems to be the very thing which 'priesthood' distinctively signifies, is the 'potestas offerre sacrificium,' or 'placabiles hostias.'

Unfortunately the developments were in this one

of hands (of Bishop and Presbyters together), in the Miss Franc there had been two—the laying on of hands, and the anointing of the hand; in Pontif. Egb. there were five—the stole, the laying on of hands, the chasuble, the anointing of the hand, and the anointing of the head. By the time of the Sarum Pontif. the anointing of the head is dropped; but there are added (1) the *porrectio*, and (2) the final laying on of hands.

direction only. In the fully developed Pontifical there is no emphasis whatever upon what we mean by service to, or self-sacrifice for, the people. There has been no attempt to develop, by so much as a single word, the correlative idea of priestly 'intercession,' or indeed any form whatever of self-expenditure. There is no solemn responsibility for the flock[1]. The word 'flock' does not occur, nor any equivalent to it. There is personal good character, indeed, and good example; there is something about preaching and teaching, and a good deal about governing; there is blessing and absolving, and, above all, offering of sacrifice; and things like these imply, no doubt, the 'people' (who are mentioned as 'populus' or 'plebs'); but there is no distinct expression of relation to them, there is not a word of anything like what we mean by 'pastoral' devotion, or responsibility, or suffering[2].

Thus it is that with the developed Pontifical we can but feel that the formal definition of Pope Eugenius and the Council of Florence only too naturally corresponds: 'Materia est illud per cuius traditionem confertur ordo· sicut presbyteratus traditur per calicis cum vino et patenae cum pane porrectionem. ... Forma sacerdotii talis est, Accipe potestatem offerendi sacrificium,' &c. Presbyterate is indeed coming to mean, only too simply and precisely, this.

The sacrifice is 'for the quick and for the dead.' This phrase is not interpreted in the service itself. It is a phrase, I presume, which can perfectly well be defended But its defensibleness would seem largely to depend upon its remaining free from attempts at over precise definition. Dogmatic teachings about purgatory, and systems of practice based upon such teachings, had made it, indeed, almost intolerable. At least from all suspicion of these excesses, it needed to be kept scrupulously clear.

[1] Though these had received, and did maintain, their position in the service of the consecration of a Bishop.
[2] See Note, p 300.

But at this point we pass from the Pontifical to the Council of Trent. At Trent, the phrase receives some authoritative definition.

In Sess. xxii. c. ii. it is ruled that the sacrifice of the Mass is offered not only for the quick, &c, 'but also for the dead in Christ, whose purgatorial cleansing is not yet complete[1].' And in the opening of Sess. xxv. it is decreed that there *is* a purgatory, 'and that the souls there detained are assisted by the prayers of the faithful, but most of all by the acceptable sacrifice of the altar[2],' which is expressed in the Catech. ad Paroch. II. cap. iv. Quaest. lxxvii., by saying that it is offered, and is effectual, for the sins of all the faithful alike, whether they be still alive, or dead—with their expiation not yet accomplished ('sive iam in Domino mortui nondum plane expiati sint'). No doubt these are, by comparison, guarded phrases. But it must be noticed that the assertions made are not made simply of the sacrifice of Christ; but of that sacrifice as presented upon earth, in recurring Eucharistic celebrations. And they fasten, with emphasis, upon the *temporal* interval, which the 'nondum ad plenum' represents. Can it then be said that they add nothing to the revelation which the Church has received?

Returning from this special point to the general idea of the sacrifice by which priesthood is defined, it is to be observed that the actual Tridentine canon de Sacramento Ordinis (Sess. xxiii. can. 1) is very carefully expressed. It is aimed most certainly not against the Anglican Prayer-book, but against an ultra-Protestant denial of all sacrifice and all priesthood. It asserts that there *is* a priesthood of visible ministry, and that it does not consist only in preaching the gospel; but that it does possess a real power of consecrating and offering the Body and Blood of the Lord, and of absolving and

---

[1] 'Sed et pro defunctis in Christo *nondum ad plenum purgatis.*'
[2] 'Animasque ibi detentas fidelium suffragiis, fortissimum vero acceptabili altaris sacrificio juvari.'

retaining sins. Meanwhile the first sentence of cap. i. in this session connects, in indissoluble fashion, the two words 'sacrifice' and 'priesthood' 'Sacrificium et sacerdotium ita Dei ordinatione coniuncta sunt, ut utrumque in omni lege exstiterit[1];' while in Sess. xxii. c. i. and the following canons the sacrifice of the Mass is a 'real and proper sacrifice,' and 'really propitiatory,' and (as above), 'for the living and the dead[2].' And in the Catech. ad Paroch II. cap. vii. quaest. xxiv, the 'munus' of the priest is said to be 'To offer sacrifice to God, to administer the Sacraments of the Church[3].' And after reference to the Ordinal, culminating in the 'Accipe potestatem offerendi,' &c., it is added, 'By which words and ceremonies he is constituted a mediator and representative between God and man, which is to be reckoned the principal function of priesthood[4].' Then 'ad extremum vero' the absolving power is added 'Haec sunt sacerdotalis ordinis propria et praecipua munera'

Now I may say at once that it is no part of my object to try and convict the Tridentine statements of being wrong I am quite aware that both on this and other subjects there are statements of more than one kind, which are not always easily reconcilable, and which may perhaps be capable, in more directions than one, of a considerable, and perhaps unexpected, amount of explanation. Neither is it any part of my duty to endeavour to enter upon such explanations, or to determine how

[1] So Morinus, Pt. III Exercit vii. cap 1. p 102 · 'Cum sacerdotio Dei ordinatione sacrificium semper conjunctum fuit, ut nos docet Conc. Trid. Itaque sacerdotium totius religionis Christianae fundamentum esse nemo dubitare potest '—Most true language—though probably not quite in Morinus' sense ' And again, Exercit. ix cap 1. p. 132 : ' Diacono semel et necessario propter sacrificium et sacerdotem constituto, multa alia tribuuntur in quibus praeter sacrificium Ecclesiae ministrat,'—which is a rather audacious way of putting the history.

[2] 'Verum et proprium sacrificium,' 'vere propitiatorium,' 'pro vivis et defunctis.'

[3] 'Deo sacrificium facere, ecclesiastica sacramenta administrare.'

[4] 'Quibus caeremoniis et verbis interpres ac mediator Dei et hominum constituitur, quae praecipua sacerdotis functio existimanda est.'

far explanations, which ought to be satisfactory, could be furnished, either of most, or even of the whole, of the language I have quoted. That which concerns my task is rather to see the impression which language like this was most calculated to produce, and particularly when the Council of Trent is regarded as a Roman Reformation, and its language as either the prudent modification — or at least as the most scientific and guarded statement—of popular doctrines which certainly had stood in need of a guarded expression. I do not forget that in Sess. xxii. c. ii. the Council had declared 'That the victim offered, and the offerer of the victim, are one and the very same, as in His self-oblation upon the Cross, so in the ministry of His priests in the Church, the *method* only of offering being changed [1]'; and that each part of this statement stands somewhat amplified in the Cat. ad Par. II. c. iv. quaest. lxxiv. and lxxv [2]. If the doctrine insisted on were to the effect that the Eucharist is the Church's divinely ordered ceremonial method of self-identification with the sacrifice of Christ, which itself therefore may legitimately be called the sacrifice with which it is divinely identified (not being a sacrifice

[1] 'Una eademque est hostia, idem nunc offerens sacerdotum ministerio, qui se ipsum tunc in cruce obtulit, sola offerendi ratione diversa.'

[2] It will be observed that the Catechismus, going somewhat further, does in fact explicitly deny that the Eucharist is a sacrifice *other than* the sacrifice of the Cross· 'Unum itaque et idem sacrificium esse fatemur et haberi debet, quod in missa peragitur, et quod in cruce oblatum est; quemadmodum una est et eadem hostia, Christus videlicet Dominus noster, qui se ipsum in ara crucis semel tantummodo cruentum immolavit Neque enim cruenta et incruenta hostia duae sunt hostiae, sed una tantum, cuius sacrificium, postquam Dominus ita praecepit: "Hoc facite in meam commemorationem" in Eucharistia quotidie instauratur.' Qu. lxxv.: 'Sed unus etiam atque idem sacerdos est, Christus Dominus; nam ministri qui sacrificium faciunt, non suam sed Christi personam suscipiunt quum eius corpus et sanguinem conficiunt Id quod et ipsius consecrationis verbis ostenditur. Neque enim sacerdos inquit "Hoc est corpus Christi," sed "Hoc est corpus meum"; personam videlicet Christi Domini gerens, panis et vini substantiam in veram eius corporis et sanguinis substantiam convertit.' It would be a fuller expression of the truth to say that it is 'the Church' which 'Christi personam suscipit'; and that the Priests act herein as the divinely authorized representatives and organs of the Church.

directly 'in itself,' but indirectly by virtue of that beyond itself with which it is made one), there would be nothing to criticize. But could there in that case be any emphasis upon the word 'proprium'? At least the *apparent* force of the word 'proprium' seems to be to deny the dependence and to assert an independent character, as though the sacrifice of the Eucharist were a sacrifice *per se*. When, then, the conclusion is repeatedly emphasized, that the Eucharist is a 'verum et proprium sacrificium' and that this 'proprium sacrificium' is 'vere propitiatorium,' alike for the remission of sins of every kind on earth, and for souls in purgatory not yet fully 'purged' or 'expiated,' it must I think be admitted that even the guarded definitions of Trent in 1562 lend only too much of apparent colour to certain popular views of sacrifice and priesthood which (to put it very mildly) had tended not a little to exaggeration [1].

To call the Eucharist 'the Church's sacrifice' (in the sense e. g. of the Church's identification with the sacrifice of Christ) is one thing: to call it *'verum sacrificium'* may point only a most legitimate contrast between it and the Old Testament sacrifices which were certainly not '*vera*': but to call it (under anathema) 'proprium sacrificium' either is, or certainly may seem to be, another [2]. Again to

[1] Compare the exaggerations quoted in the Appendix, p. 312, note.

[2] It may be said, no doubt, that the Eucharist can be called a sacrifice, even when regarded in itself, as the offering of our worship, or of our gifts, or simply of the elements of bread and wine. Without denying the truth of such thoughts, I must still urge that it is really a sacrifice in these subordinate senses, only in dependence upon, and in consequence of, its being the Church's divinely ordained identification with the Atoning Sacrifice of Christ. If it were not, in this far deeper sense, the Church's 'sacrifice,' the word sacrifice, seriously applied to it in these lesser senses only, would be a somewhat misleading overstatement. But when it is realized first as the Church's ceremonial method of identification with the perpetual offering of the Sacrifice of Christ, then every lesser act which, in greater measure or in less, expresses or symbolizes the surrender or homage of men—illumined, as it now is, by the light of the one transcendent reality—becomes itself also, according to its capacity, a true mode or aspect of the spirit of sacrifice in the Church. The Eucharist is a sacrifice, primarily and essentially, in exactly the sense or measure in which it can be said to be the sacrifice of Christ. If in relation

point out that that with which it is identified is the offering of Christ which is the atonement for the sins of the world is one thing, to fortify by anathema the definition of the Eucharistic celebration as a sacrifice '*vere propitiatorium*' is, or at least may seem to be, another. To say that the sacrifice of Christ was indeed for all, for the quick and the dead, '*pro vivis ac defunctis*,' is one thing; to anathematize those who hesitate or decline to lay down that the earthly celebrating of the sacrifice produces an effect upon souls in purgatory, can hardly fail to be felt to be another. In each of these points even Trent may be said to appear, and the Romanism of the Tridentine generation was, without doubt, popularly understood, to identify itself only too completely with the extreme and most doubtful form of assertion, and having thus tied up the idea of 'sacrificium' just to its own most questionable possibilities, then to find in the 'offering of sacrifice,' so explained and defined, the one differentiating conception and definition of 'priesthood.' That, then, which was before the mind of the Reformers was a completeness of view, conceived with only too painful a sharpness of logical precision; a view which the Tridentine fathers either did—or did not —succeed in adequately limiting; a view according to which the 'priesthood,' consisting of the power of offering actual atoning sacrifices (sacrifices which could be indefinitely repeated and arithmetically appraised), constituted a real propitiatory mediation between the lay people and their God. In context with any such conception as this—or the suspicion of it—to say, with the Catechismus, that the principal function of a priest is to be '*interpres ac mediator Dei et hominum*,' or, with Morinus, that, because it means sacrifice, therefore 'no one can doubt that the priesthood is the foundation of the entire Christian religion' (though both phrases in themselves

to that sense the word 'proprium' is a doubtful one, it cannot, in virtue of the subordinate senses taken (as they cannot really be taken) apart, be made to be satisfactory.

may be capable of an excellent meaning), will at least be to open the way to misconceptions of a very serious kind.

What then was the truth? Was all this language about the sacrifice and the priesthood wholly wrong; and, as wrong, to be wholly swept away? Unquestionably this was the view of unbridled Protestantism. Or was it, on the other hand, as Romanism has maintained, not only not wrong, but altogether right, and rightly proportioned?

Beyond all question it is clear that the Anglican Reformers took neither of these two lines. What they did clearly implies (1) that they did not judge it wholly wrong nomenclature, and (2) that its conception and statement had nevertheless, in their eyes, so far fallen out of due proportion as, if not to contradict, yet at least to jeopardize, the right balance of Christian truth.

Take the importance of the retention of the nomenclature. It requires perhaps no slight effort of imagination for us at the present time fully to realize how great the pressure must have been upon reformers who were themselves Protestants, in the midst of the rising tide of destructive Protestantism, to 'abolish priesthood'; and how very much more is meant than might at first sight appear by the deliberate retention, in the reign of King Edward VI, of the three orders of 'Bishops, Priests, and Deacons' as immemorial 'from the Apostles' time,' and therefore perpetually to be retained and revered in the Church of Christ. I say the deliberate retention, for that this was no piece of inattentive conservatism the detail of the circumstances makes abundantly clear. It has been several times pointed out, and it is certainly well to remember, into what exaggerations Archbishop Cranmer had himself been prepared to go some years earlier in the direction of denying the spiritual character of Order[1]. Here again it requires a real effort of imagination to judge

---

[1] 'We know as matter of history that the inadequate conceptions of ordination to which Canon Estcourt alludes were before the Reformers of the Church of England, and had met with considerable countenance among them. But

quite fairly of a tendency which to us at first sight sounds shocking and wanton enough. Those, however, who have seen, in the balance between revealed and rational truth, how easily those disparage reason who cling to revelation, or those undervalue revelation who claim to be rational; or, in the equipoise between spiritual and secular claims, how easily insistence on the spiritual loses sight of the secular, or clear apprehension of the secular obscures the spiritual; those who, in the actual case of the mediaeval rivalry between Pope and Emperor know how hard it was to do justice to the true claims of each at once—will form a more patient, and a fairer estimate. They will not judge too harshly, or with excessive surprise, if in the earlier moments of maintaining the independence of national Churches from an autocracy which because it was spiritual claimed to be secular, the minds of individuals even in high places reacted sometimes quite extravagantly towards asserting the secular and national sanction of what really was spiritual.

This tendency to disparage the true character of Order, into which Cranmer himself had at one time fallen so far,

they regarded the theory not in that timid fashion which might cause them, if they had closed with it, to express it in words and in acts belonging to a different order of ideas. They looked fairly in the face the real and only consistent application of these notions; which is this, the total abolition of any real form of ordination, and the retention of the laying on of hands, if at all, only as a recognition of a previous election In the before-quoted discussions of 1540, which issued in the "Necessary Doctrine and Erudition," and are to be found among Burnet's *Records* (P. 1 B. iii. No. xxi) we find this question proposed, "whether in the New Testament be required any consecration of a bishop or priest, or only appointing to the office be sufficient?" And the answer of Canterbury (that is, Cranmer) is, "that he that is appointed to be a bishop or priest needeth no consecration by the Scripture." .... What we wish the reader to observe is, that if in 1549 Cranmer had still held these opinions about Holy Orders, or, holding them, had found himself able to lead the Ordinal Committee to adopt them, they would have displayed themselves in the Ordinal in some thoroughly unmistakable form. Whereas, what do we really find? .... Bucer's draft is set aside, and words of a totally different character are substituted. It is perfectly manifest that the object must have been to express a wholly different idea upon Ordination.' *Church Quarterly,* Jan. 1878, pp. 281, 282

was present as an immediate challenge to the Anglican divines in the person of Bucer. It is well known how great and how injurious an influence was exercised at this time by Bucer in England, and especially upon the revision of the Prayer-book of 1552. In the Ordinal itself, as published with that book, there are traces of him, for which we have little cause to be grateful. But these facts, however painful in themselves, only bring out into sharper relief the clear decision with which, in their official work, these divines, although led by Cranmer and perilously exposed to the influence of Bucer, yet resisted the Bucerian pressure, and would have none of the tendency which had once been Cranmer's own. Bucer's own draft was before them. He would have made short work of the old language. So much indeed he would have yielded to conservatism, that there should be still three ranks of ministers, that there should be 'some difference made,' and the higher grades appointed 'somewhat more fully and solemnly'; but he proposed to designate them respectively as the 'superintendent,' the 'presbyters of the second order,' and the 'presbyters of the third order,' or 'presbyters who help'; and he proposed the same sentence of ordination in each case, a sentence which, if adopted, would indeed have jeopardized the historical continuity of them all[1]. Is it possible, in the face of

[1] 'In the winter [i. e. in the end] of the year 1549, we find that a Committee was appointed to prepare an Ordinance against the ensuing April 1 Now on April 25 [i. e. in the beginning] of the same year 1549, Martin Bucer had reached England from Strasburg. It is very well known that Bucer exercised a very injurious influence upon the Prayer-book. But little or no notice has been taken of the important work which we find, under the title *de ordinatione legitima ministrorum ecclesiae revocanda*, at p. 238 of his *Scripta Anglicana*. The most cursory perusal of this work will prove its relationship to our Ordinal The selections of Scripture to be read are very nearly identical with those used in our three forms The beautiful exhortation in our Ordinal of Priests stands unmistakably, though in a poor Latin style, in Bucer's work. The questions put to the ordinands are in many cases identical, and of many of the prayers the same may be said. But Bucer's form is only one for all the three orders. The sentence of Ordination is the same whether it is a bishop, priest, or deacon that is being ordained, viz. "The hand of God Almighty, Father, Son, and Holy

all these melancholy proposals, to exaggerate the significance of the deliberate substitution of the clear and strong language of the Anglican Ordinal? 'It is evident unto all men diligently reading the holy Scripture and ancient authors that from the Apostles' time there have been these Orders of Ministers in Christ's Church; Bishops, Priests, and Deacons.... And therefore, to the intent that these Orders may be continued and reverently used and esteemed in the Church of England, no man shall be accounted or taken to be a lawful Bishop, Priest, or Deacon ... except he be,' &c. 'Reverend Father in

Ghost, be upon you, to protect and govern you, that ye may go and bring forth much fruit by your ministry, and that it may remain unto life eternal." But he adds at the conclusion an account of an attempt (of a quite illusory character) to keep up the appearance of Episcopacy in a Church really Presbyterian; proposing this apparently as a model for the Church of England:—

'"Since there are three orders of presbyters and guardians of the Church · the order of bishops, then that of presbyters, whom the ancients call cardinals, who carry on the chief government of the Church in places where there are no bishops; and then that of those presbyters who help the former and are called among us deacons or helpers; thus also ordination is graduated; that when any one is ordained a superintendent, i. e. bishop, all things may be done and accomplished somewhat more fully and solemnly than when a presbyter of the second or third order is ordained. So also there is made some difference between the ordination of presbyters of the second and third orders."'

'Now, regarding this work, only two theories are possible Either it was the Ordinal of 1549 translated into Latin (as the English Prayer-book was) for the information of Bucer, who did not know English, and by him altered and welded into one form and proposed as a "reduction of episcopacy" for the Revision of 1552, or else it was an original draft for the Ordinal of 1549; either drawn up by Bucer himself as an account of the arrangements in his church of Strasburg and proposed as a model for England, or an alteration by him of some draft by Cranmer or some other of the Committee. Various indications, which we have not space to recount, incline us to the first form of the latter alternative. We hold that the document was a draft for the Ordinal of 1549, and moreover, that it is the original work of Bucer himself. But for the purpose which we have at present in hand, it does not make much difference which of these theories we adopt. *Either* the Reformers in 1549 composed their Ordinal on the basis of a draft by Bucer altered by them, *or* the Reformers in 1552 rejected certain proposals by Bucer for an alteration of the Ordinal of 1549.'

From the *Church Quarterly Review*, January, 1878, pp. 269-270. It does not quite appear from the context of the *Scripta Anglicana* why the statement quoted as to the 'three orders' is described as an 'account of an attempt,' &c.

God, I present unto you these persons present, to be admitted to the Order of Priesthood.'

In this matter of retention of titles the chief emphasis will undoubtedly lie upon the continuous use of the words 'Priest' and 'Priesthood,' not only because these were the titles which were thought to have been most deeply misused, and were most savagely attacked, but also, and perhaps even more emphatically, because a close fidelity to the language of Scripture was always to the Reformers a palmary object — it was their great sheet-anchor of safety and truth; and because anything like a superficial following of Scripture in this matter might so easily and naturally have led, whatever might be their views about the *thing*, to their agreeing at least in ruling out the *word*.

On this point no doubt the attitude and language of Hooker, forty years afterwards, will be well remembered. But that the Church of England is not represented herein even by Hooker, the language of the Ordinal and its preface bears perpetual witness.[1]

At the jealousy as to the title 'Priesthood,' and its

---

[1] 'Seeing then that *sacrifice is now no part of the Church ministry*, how should the name of Priesthood be thereunto rightly applied? Surely even as St Paul applieth the name of flesh unto that very substance of fishes which hath a proportionable correspondence to flesh, *although it be in nature another thing*. . . . The Fathers of the Church of Christ with like security of speech call usually the ministry of the Gospel Priesthood in regard of that which the Gospel hath proportionable to ancient sacrifices, namely the Communion of the Blessed Body and Blood of Christ, *although it have properly now no sacrifice*. As for the people when they hear the name it draweth no more their minds to any cogitation of sacrifice, than the name of a senator or an alderman causeth them to think upon old age. Wherefore to pass by the name, let them use what dialect they will, whether we call it a Priesthood, a Presbytership, or a Ministry it skilleth not, although in truth the *word Presbyter doth seem more fit, and in propriety of speech more agreeable* than Priest with the drift of the whole gospel of Jesus Christ.' E. P., V. lxxviii. 2 and 3.

The phrases which I have italicized show clearly that Hooker is misled by the fallacy (commented on below) of conceiving that the *proper reality* of sacrifice is to be found in the Old Testament, instead of in the New. It is, of course, one thing to recognize that the office, while emphatically pronounced to be 'sacerdotal,' was yet, till far down in mediaeval times, *entitled* 'presbyterate':

meaning, which had carried Cranmer off his balance; which was becoming in the ultra-Protestants a simple ferocity; which warped so dangerously in the next generation even the judicial mind and learning of Hooker, and which has proved to this day, so deeply rooted and inveterate, I, for one cannot affect to be surprised. There had been only too much cause to provoke and to justify it. Nevertheless, those who feel how deeply and perilously wrong the change of nomenclature would have been, and how plausibly nevertheless it could be urged as if it alone were the true and exact fidelity to Scripture, are entitled not only to thank God for the firmness of the Anglican language at an infinitely critical time, but also to point to the very urgency of the danger itself, as immensely emphasizing the significance of the language which was then so quietly but so firmly retained. That these perilous tendencies are by no means out of date we are reminded, not only by an immense weight of familiar modern prejudice, but even by the arguments of such a writer as Bishop Lightfoot. He too lends his great authority to the opinion that the abolition of the title 'might have been better.'[1]

It is hardly possible to pass on without lingering a little upon this portion of Bishop Lightfoot's essay. Some of the underlying assumptions of its earlier portions we have had occasion to canvas before.[2] The last twenty-five pages of the essay are given up to a discussion which touches closely our present point. It is in the form of

it is quite another to substitute the title presbyterate for priesthood, *with a view to denying* its sacerdotal character.

[1] 'If therefore the sacerdotal office be understood to imply the offering of sacrifices, then the Epistle to the Hebrews leaves no place for a Christian priesthood. If on the other hand the word be taken in a wider and looser acceptation, it cannot well be withheld from the ministry of the Church of Christ. Only in this case the meaning of the term should be clearly apprehended; and it might have been better if the later Christian vocabulary had conformed to the silence of the Apostolic writers, so that the possibility of confusion would have been avoided'; p. 235 of the *Dissertations on the Apostolic Age*.

[2] See above, pp 43, 75, 117.

a historical sketch of the introduction and development of what he calls the 'sacerdotal' ideas and phraseology; and it is, in effect, a serious argument against the 'sacerdotalism' of which he speaks.

In such a sketch, or argument, everything turns upon the question what exactly is meant by 'sacerdotalism.' And I must submit that that which Bishop Lightfoot is found to understand by it is just that which the sacerdotal language, in its Christian acceptation, does not and cannot really mean. But the misunderstanding, if misunderstanding it be, is one which illustrates, with damning effectiveness, the tendency towards error which is too truly suggested by what I must call the misproportion of the unreformed language.

What does Bishop Lightfoot understand sacerdotalism to mean? He begins by a definition and distinction. 'The word "priest" has two different senses. In the one it is a synonym for presbyter or elder, and designates the minister who presides over and instructs a Christian congregation: in the other it is equivalent to the Latin "sacerdos," the Greek ἱερεύς, or the Hebrew כהן, the offerer of sacrifices, who also performs other mediatorial offices between God and man. . . . The word will be used throughout this essay . . . in the latter sense only, so that priestly will be equivalent to "sacerdotal" or "hieratic";' p. 184; cp 243 n. 'In speaking of sacerdotalism, I assume the term to have essentially the same force as when applied to the Jewish priesthood. . . . Sacerdotal phraseology was certainly so used as to imply a substantial identity of character with the Jewish priesthood, i. e. to designate the Christian minister as one who offers sacrifices and makes atonement.' Compare again the comment upon the word 'sacerdotal' implied in the opening paragraph of the essay: 'Above all, it [the kingdom of Christ] has no sacerdotal system. It interposes no sacrificial tribe or class between God and man, by whose intervention alone God is reconciled and man forgiven.' It is plain from these passages that Bishop Lightfoot has (1) made the capital mistake of taking the Mosaic use of the words 'priesthood,' &c. as the truth and true standard of their meaning, and measuring, by that, their meaning in the Church of Christ: and (2) that he has gone on from this initial—and fatal—mistake, to allow himself to consider (a) the sacrifices so spoken of as things in themselves independent and absolute—as actual offerings of atonement; and so (b) the priests as a class really intervening, as indispensable intermediaries, between Christians and their God. Thus he speaks of priests as a 'sacerdotal caste[1]' 'in some exclusive sense' (to which the idea of his standing to represent the congregation is regarded as antithetical[2]), as 'an exclusive priesthood[3]'; of their claim to 'sacerdotal privileges' and 'sacerdotal sanctity[4]' (phrases which are not explained); of their claim to 'obedience' on pain of profanity and sacrilege[5]; and again, by implication at least, of their being sacerdotal, and the Eucharist a sacerdotal act, 'in the same sense in which the Jewish priesthood and the Jewish sacrifices were sacerdotal[6]'; of their 'vicarial' character—regarded as antithetical to being 'representative[7]', of the interposing of the priest 'between God and man in such a way that direct communication with God is superseded on the one hand, and that his own mediation becomes indispensable on the other[8].' And he not unnaturally concludes by the position that the words themselves can only be retained 'in a wider and looser sense' than that which his argument has treated throughout as if it were the one that most properly belonged to them.

Now I must submit that at least half of the objections which these different statements imply, are at once as mere cobwebs swept out of sight by the conception which it was my endeavour to emphasize in the third chapter, according to which the Christian ministry is not a substituted inter-

[1] p. 260. [2] p 261. [3] p 262. [4] p. 250.
[5] p. 257. [6] p. 264. [7] p. 265. [8] pp 165-6.

mediary—still less an atoning mediator—between God and lay people; but it is rather the representative and organ of the whole body, in the exercise of prerogatives and powers which belong to the body as a whole. It is ministerially empowered to wield, as the body's organic representative, the powers which belong *to the body*, but which the body cannot wield except through its own organs duly fitted for the purpose. What is duly done by Christian Ministers, it is not so much that *they* do it, in the stead, or for the sake, of the whole; but rather that the whole does it by and through them. The Christian Priest does not offer an atoning sacrifice on behalf of the Church · it is rather the Church through his act that, not so much 'offers an atonement,' as 'is identified upon earth with the one heavenly offering of the atonement of Christ.'

In the light of this one great principle, as I conceive, all that the Bishop says about a sacerdotal caste, its exclusiveness, its intervention, its sacerdotal privileges and sanctity, its demand of obedience on pain of sacrilege, almost, or quite, totally disappears. All that is said about atonement, mediation, sacrifice, is, at least, enormously modified. But this is not enough. It is necessary to examine a little further where the truth exactly lies about the fundamental words 'priesthood' and 'sacrifice'; and in so doing to show how hopeless is the position which, assuming that these words have their true and absolute meaning in the Levitical law, makes their meaning in that the measure by which to try the correctness of their meaning elsewhere. I pass then from all thought of the interpretations—or misinterpretations—to which the unreformed language, whether popular or official, have been, in fact, unjustly or justly, liable, to the more fundamental question, what do these words which are consecrated at least by well-nigh immemorial Christian usage—what do 'sacrifice' and 'priesthood' really and rightly mean?

II.

I said just now that it would be a superficial following of Scripture which would lead men to strike out such words as priest, priesthood, and sacrifice, from the familiar vocabulary of the Christian Church. It would not only be superficial; it would be profoundly and fatally wrong. The Church of Christ, as exhibited in the New Testament, is priestly and sacrificial in substance, as the Church of the Old Testament was only in figure. Mosaic priesthood, with its sacrifices, was no more, on the one hand, a non-significant, than it was, on the other, a complete or substantial, thing It sketched out, it led up to, it enacted parabolically, that which transcended itself, that in which alone its detached, external, and symbolic suggestions found their unity and fullness. All priesthood, all sacrifice, is summed up in the Person of Christ.

It is one of the capital mistakes of those who discuss Christian priesthood, a mistake which is answerable for some of the most deplorable conclusions—to go back, for the standard of the 'true' or 'literal' or 'proper' meaning of the words Sacrifice and Priest, to what they meant in the Old Testament, or what they meant in the ancient pagan world, or in the mouths of those who may be supposed to have first devised the terms. Nothing could be more fatally misleading. Not one of these, Pagan or Israelite, ever attained, ever so much as conceived, the true idea of Sacrifice or Priest. They were like prophets, who did not understand what they prophesied. They never adequately realized the import of their own acts or words. Considering where the real meaning of their acts lay, it was wholly impossible that they should have grasped it. No, there is one standard only, and measure, of the reality of the meaning of these words, and that is, their meaning in the Person of Christ.

Now the Person of Christ does not pass away from the Church. The Church is the Body of Christ. The Spirit of Christ is the Breath of the Life of the Church. Whatever Christ is, the Church is; as reflecting, nay, in a real sense even as being, Himself. If we want to see in what the priesthood of the Church consists, or what the word priesthood ultimately means, we must examine first what it means in the Person of Christ.

Wherein, then, is Christ a Priest? The answer perhaps will be that He is a Priest in that He offered sacrifice; and that the sacrifice which He offered was the sacrifice of Himself. This answer of course is correct, as far as it goes. But there are one or two directions in which it seems that, in order to be anything like an adequate presentation of the truth, the answer needs not a little supplementing.

First, then, it is of some importance to ask exactly when, or how, was this priestly sacrifice offered by Him? Does it mean the moment of Calvary? I do not stay now to dwell upon the thought — true and valuable though it is — that His entire life in mortal flesh was a sacrifice, a dying, a crucifying, so that Calvary, however supreme as a culmination, was a culmination of, rather than a contradiction to, what the life before had meant. But assuming that, upon the side of suffering, the sacrifice of His death may be taken to be at least the culmination— perhaps rather the consummation — of the sacrifice of His preceding life; still, is it perfectly adequate to point to Calvary, as, in the fullest sense, the consummation in Him of all that is meant by sacrifice?

It is to be remembered that, even under the Mosaic law, however indispensable death might be to sacrifice, death was not in itself the consummation of sacrifice. The culminating point of the sacrifice was not in the shedding of the blood, but in the presentation before God, in the holy place, of the blood that had been shed; of the life, that is, which had passed through death, and had been consecrated to God by dying. It is not the death itself which is acceptable to the God of life: but the vital self-identification with the holiness of God, the perfect self-dedication and self-surrender which is represented, in a life that has sinned, by voluntary acceptance of penitential or penal death. It is the life as life, not the death as death; it is the life which has been willing to die, the life which has passed through death, and been consecrated in dying, the life in which death is a moral element, perpetually and inalienably present, but still *the life*, which is acceptable to God. That blood means life, and not death, is insisted on, almost paradoxically, in the Levitical law itself. 'For the life of the flesh is in the blood; and I have given it to you upon the altar to make atonement for your souls; for it is the blood that maketh atonement by reason of the life. Therefore I said unto the children of Israel, No soul of you shall eat blood, neither shall any stranger that sojourneth among you eat blood[1].'

Here is the ritual, by which in the sacrifice of the Day of Atonement 'sacrificial' truth was prefigured symbolically 'Aaron shall present the bullock of the sin-offering, which is for himself . . . and shall kill the bullock of the sin-offering . . and he shall take a censer full of coals of fire . . . and his hands full of sweet incense, . . . and he shall put the incense upon the fire before the Lord . . . and he shall take of the blood of the bullock, and sprinkle it with his finger upon the mercy-seat on the east; and before the mercy-seat shall he sprinkle of the blood with his finger seven times. Then shall he kill the goat of the sin-offering that is for the people, and bring his blood within the veil, and do with his blood

[1] Levit xvii 11, 12

as he did with the blood of the bullock, and sprinkle it upon the mercy-seat, and before the mercy-seat; and he shall make atonement for the holy place¹'. . . .

As, then, the shedding of the blood is not itself the consummation, but is the preliminary condition necessary for the consummation, of the symbolic sacrifice under the Levitical law; so when we turn to the essential realities, though Calvary be the indispensable preliminary, yet is it not Calvary taken apart, not Calvary quite so directly as the eternal self-presentation in Heaven of the risen and ascended Lord, which is the true consummation of the sacrifice of Jesus Christ. But of course, in that eternal presentation Calvary is eternally implied. Of that life, the ὡς ἐσφαγμένον², the 'as it had been slain,' is no mere past incident, but it has become, once for all, an inalienable moral element Christ's offering in Heaven is a perpetual ever-present offering of life, whereof 'to have died' is an ever-present and perpetual attribute. If 'Calvary' were the sufficient statement of the nature of the sacrifice of Christ, then that sacrifice would be simply past and done, which is in truth both now and for ever present. He is a Priest for ever, not as it were by a perpetual series of acts of memory, not by multiplied and ever remoter acts of commemoration of a death that is past, but by the eternal presentation of a life which eternally is the 'life that died³.'

But have we come really to an end of the ideas that are involved in the word 'sacrifice' by seeing wherein it culminates in Levitical ritual, and how that ritual corresponds to the sacrifice of Christ? What we see even in Him, is the form which sacrifice took in a world of sin.

---

[1] Levit. xvi. 11-16.   [2] Rev. v 6.
[3] The words 'pleading,' or 'presenting,' in this connexion, must not be understood as describing anything corresponding to specific acts done, or words spoken, by Christ in His glory. His glorified presence *is* an eternal presentation; He pleads by what He *is*. Cp. Westcott on Hebrews viii. 1, 2, and Milligan on the Ascension, lect. III. § 2, pp 149-161.

But to see this hardly explains what is essentially meant by sacrifice. We see how 'sacrifice' found its expression in Him. Whatever sacrifice in Him essentially meant, took the form of crucifixion. Is sacrifice then identical with crucifixion? Or why did it take this form? Or what was that essential reality which uttered itself in this form? The form which it took—the cross—was, we cannot but be sure, the result of human sin. Is then sacrifice a word which has no meaning, except in relation to and as coloured by sin? It will be observed that even if we answer this question in the affirmitive, there must still be something behind, some essential root lower down, some abiding reality, which, having no relation to sin in itself, becomes 'sacrifice' as it passes within the atmosphere of sin. Whether we still call it sacrifice; or reserving the word sacrifice for what sin has characterized, call it only that which becomes sacrifice in the sphere of sin, is in part a verbal question. But what is it? What is that which is in no sense dependent on, or correlative to, the presence of sin? which was from the beginning, and shall be to the end? which, as it passes within the shadow of sin, takes the form and hue of what we call sacrifice, but which, whether it pass beneath the cloud or no, whether tinged or untinged with the gloom and the pain, is itself for ever the same? What is that which must become sacrifice in sin's atmosphere; and which sacrifice, as it passes beyond sin's atmosphere, is found really to be? There can be no doubt of the answer. It is love. Love is not self-contained, but self-expending, and perfected in self-expenditure. The devotion of love in the sphere of Heaven is perfection of joy. But devotion of love to another in conditions of earth—even whilst it touches the highest possibilities of joy—means always more or less of pain. Devotion of self, in a world of sin and suffering, to the spiritual welfare of those who are enmeshed in suffering and sin, is forthwith in external aspect, sacrifice; and, in inner essence, love. There is no essential contrast between sacrifice and love.

Love, under certain disabling conditions, becomes sacrifice; and sacrifice is not sacrifice, except it be love[1].

Thoughts like these are, it seems to me, of primary importance, if we would understand the sacrifice of Christ. It is the aspect which Divine love takes within the sphere of certain conditions, which conditions are *de facto* inseparable from our life on earth as it is. The heart of what it really is, is the holy offering up of life, in love. Apart from sin it would have been all life and all love. But life that has sinned cannot offer itself perfectly to love, without dying to sin. One aspect of love to God is hatred of sin. Man cannot love God without hating sin; nor love Him perfectly without hating sin even unto death; and since the sin is in himself, surrendering himself unto death in detestation of sin, which is the sinner's possibility of devotion to God. Divine love then, in the nature of man, takes the form of self-surrender to death. But so far from being, as death, the final object, this death is only real as a mode of love, and a passage from sin into holiness, which is life. If, verbally, we confine the word

---

[1] See Dr. Milligan on the Ascension, lect. iii. p. 117, and his quotation from Westcott on Hebr. ix. 9: 'Sacrifice, in fact, in the most general form belongs to the life of man, and, in the truest sense, expresses the life of man. It is essentially the response of love to love, of the Son to the Father, the rendering to God in grateful use of that which has been received from Him Language cannot offer a more expressive example of moral degeneration in words than the popular connexion of thoughts of love and suffering with that which is a Divine Service.' Dr Milligan is responsible for the capitals not only to Divine Service, but also to the word Son. Bishop Westcott had printed 'of the son to the Father,' i. e. of man to God, rather than of the Second to the First Person of the Blessed Trinity. It may be doubted, however, whether Bishop Westcott does not go too far on the verbal point: and whether the accidental alteration from son to Son—utterly as it seems, at first sight, to alter the sense—may not really supply a test by which to try the possibility of the Bishop's language Could the word 'sacrifice' ever really have been used, or was it apt for use, in the mouth of fallen man, to express 'offering' save as it is conditioned by the fact of sin, i e. as dependent upon the inherent condition of death? The reciprocity of the Father and the Son is eternal love Could it ever, with verbal propriety, be spoken of as eternal sacrifice? Yet love, under altered conditions, becomes sacrifice; and no sacrifice can be real as sacrifice which is not love.

'sacrifice' to that which love becomes within the sphere of sin, we must recognize at least in doing so that our word, so defined, expresses not the central essence, but what is really a secondary, if inseparable, aspect of that of which it speaks. The essential heart of sacrifice is love; pain and death are, so to say, its acquired conditions.

By sacrifice then we mean Divine love;—yet not Divine love as it is in itself, but as it has become, once for all, by entering within the circumstances of sin and pain: we mean Divine love as it has suffered and died in the nature of man, and as it is offered for ever, in the nature of man, alive from sin to holiness and to God, through the consecration of death.

Such a definition of the sacrifice of Christ carries with it, in effect, a corresponding definition of His priesthood also. Christ is Priest in that He is the eternal offerer of this devotion of love, which, though human, is yet living because it died. Through death His priestly sacrifice is what it is; it is characterized by death; yet it means, and is, not death but living love. The act of death is never dissociable from it; yet what it really is, though inseparably characterized by death, is not death, but is rather that which died and is alive. As in the case of the use of the word 'sacrifice,' I would distinguish that which, because it has passed under certain conditions, has now acquired, and is known by, its character of sacrifice, from that which the same thing in itself essentially is, so that the word sacrifice expresses a conditioned aspect of something which is itself before it is sacrificial: so too with the use of the words priest and priesthood, I wish to recognize that since they are titles relative to sacrifice, they too describe an aspect of something which is what it is before it acquires this relative character to which the priestly language properly belongs. Sacrifice is love, within the sphere of sin, suffering and dying: and priesthood is the function of expressing and exhibiting that love which, once for all, in the person of Jesus Christ, has become, within sin's sphere, self-devoting sacrifice. The priesthood of Christ, then, is Divine love under conditions of humanity. As such, it has at once a Godward and a manward aspect. To manward it is the inconceivable condescension and embrace of love, divinely redeeming; to Godward it is the homage, perfect and perpetual—as, primarily, of human penitential atonement for sin—so also of human sinlessness, and unblemished service, and response of love worthy of God.

It follows very clearly from this that the so-called priesthood of the Old Testament is external and symbolic only. The act of slaying a victim is a merely representative act. It enacts a sort of outward parable of priesthood. It does not touch the essence of what priesthood means. Willingness, love, is of the essence of sacrifice. As the animal does not willingly die, of love, but its death only presents an outward figure of sacrificial dying, so on the part of the offerer, neither the slaying of the animal, nor the sprinkling of its blood, is in itself directly an act of moral import at all. The enactment of the Old Testament is in itself outward only. But true priesthood is an outward that is perfectly expressive of an inward, and is what it is by virtue of that real inward to which the outward does but give utterance. It seems to me of the utmost importance to insist upon this, and upon the truth which corresponds immediately to this, namely, that any definition of priesthood which stands in terms only of what is ceremonial and outward and official is inadequate and misconceived. There is an outward, but it is but the shell or body or symbolic expression of an inward; only an outward that is the outward of an inward is truly priestly, the outward that rests in being outward—whether in the Jewish or in the Christian Church—is only the symbol and shell, not the truth, of priestliness. Certainly in Jesus Christ, the one true and perfect Priest, it will at once be felt that what He did was inseparable from its own meaning—inseparable, that is, from what He Himself was.

Now I have insisted that what Christ is, the Church, which is Christ's mystical body, must also be. If Christ is Prophet, the Church is prophetic. If Christ is King, the Church is royal. If Christ is Priest, the Church is priestly. And if Christ's priesthood is, in relation to men, fundamental even to His royal and prophetic aspects, then whatever tends to suppress or undervalue the essentially priestly character of the mystical body of Christ, obscures a most fundamental conception of the truth[1]. And this is undoubtedly the conception of the New Testament. There priestliness of character is a consequence which outflows upon the Church from the Person of Christ; and the Church's priesthood being in its inner truth the priesthood of Christ, is a substantial reality, and stands therefore in contrast with that 'priesthood' of the Old Testament which did but symbolically represent reality. Priesthood is not abolished, but consummated in Christ's Church 'The priests go in continually into the first tabernacle . into the second the high priest alone . . . the Holy Ghost this signifying, that the way into the holy place hath not yet been made manifest while as the first tabernacle is yet standing· . . but Christ having come a high priest of the good things to come . . .

[1] This thought receives a great deal of very valuable illustration in Dr. Milligan's exposition of 'the Ascension and Heavenly priesthood of our Lord,' particularly the last three lectures. In lect. v pp. 236-7, the principle is thus laid down. 'From these considerations it follows that whatever function is discharged by our Lord in heaven must be also discharged by His Church on earth. Is He, as glorified, a prophet? The prophetical office must belong to her. It may, for the sake of order, be distributed through appropriate members; but primarily it belongs to the Church as a whole, the life of Christ in His prophetical office being first her life, and her life then pervading and animating any particular persons through whom the work of prophesying is performed. In like manner is He glorified Redeemer or King? The kingly office must also belong to the Church; and if it is to be represented in any particular members rather than in the body as a whole, her life must so penetrate and pervade them that they may be kingly. If it be thus with our Lord's offices as Prophet and King, it cannot be otherwise with that priestly office which is the foundation of both of these. All who allow that our Lord is a Priest in heaven must, upon the principles now laid down, acknowledge the priestliness of the Church on earth.'

entered in once for all into the holy place. . . . For the law having a shadow of the good things to come, not the very image of the things, they can never . . . make perfect. . . . Wherefore when He cometh into the world He saith . . . Lo, I am come to do Thy will. . . . By which will we have been sanctified through the offering of the body of Jesus Christ once for all. . . . Having therefore, brethren, boldness to enter into the holy place by the blood of Jesus . . . and having a great priest over the house of God, let us draw near with a true heart in fulness of faith, . . . not forsaking the assembling of ourselves together[1]. . . . Ye are not come unto a mount that might be touched . . but ye are come unto . . . the heavenly Jerusalem . . . and to Jesus the mediator of a new covenant, and to the blood of sprinkling that speaketh better than that of Abel. . . . We have an altar, whereof they have no right to eat which serve the tabernacle. . . . Jesus, . . . that He might sanctify the people with His own blood, suffered without the gate. Let us therefore go forth unto Him. . . For we have not here an abiding city, but we seek after the city which is to come[2].'

Compare all this with the language of St. Peter, 'Unto whom coming, a living stone, rejected indeed of men, but with God elect, precious, ye also as living stones are built up a spiritual house, to be a holy priesthood, to offer up spiritual sacrifices, acceptable to God through Jesus Christ[3] . . . ye are an elect race, a royal priesthood, a holy nation, a people for God's own possession[4];' and the parallel language of the Revelation, 'unto Him that loveth us, and loosed us from our sins by His blood; and He made us to be a kingdom, to be priests unto His God and Father, to Him be the glory and the dominion for ever and ever[5].' . . . 'Thou wast slain, and didst

[1] Cp. also above, ch. i. p. 14. [2] Hebrews ix. 6-xiii. 14.
[3] Οἶκος πνευματικός, ἱεράτευμα ἅγιον, ἀνενέγκαι πνευματικὰς θυσίας εὐπροσδέκτους Θεῷ διὰ Ἰησοῦ Χριστοῦ, 1 Pet. ii. 5
[4] Γένος εκλεκτόν, βασίλειον ἱεράτευμα, ἔθνος ἅγιον, λαὸς εἰς περιποίησιν, 1 Pet. ii 9
[5] Ἐποίησεν ἡμᾶς βασιλείαν, ἱερεῖς τῷ Θεῷ καὶ πατρὶ αὐτοῦ, Rev. i. 6.

VII] *PRIESTHOOD IN THE CHURCH OF CHRIST* 253

purchase unto God with Thy blood men of every tribe and tongue and people and nation, and madest them to be unto our God a kingdom and priests, and they reign upon the earth[1].' ... 'Over these the second death hath no power; but they shall be priests of God and of Christ, and shall reign with Him a thousand years[2].' These passages are explicit, in the use of the priestly as well as royal title; but it may be doubted whether as much might not have been legitimately inferred from such more general statements of the identity of His members with Christ as pervade the teaching of St. Paul. 'In Him ye are made full, who is the head of all principality and power.... in baptism ... ye were also raised with Him.... If then ye were raised together with Christ, seek the things that are above, where Christ is, seated on the right hand of God.... For ye died, and your life is hid with Christ in God[3].' 'God, being rich in mercy, for His great love wherewith He loved us ... quickened us together with Christ ... and raised us up with Him, and made us to sit with Him in the heavenly places, in Christ Jesus ... for we are His workmanship, created in Christ Jesus for good works, which God afore prepared that we should walk in them[4].'

Now it will be observed that all the passages thus referred to are of general application. We need not desire to deprecate, but rather to emphasize with the utmost distinctness, the essential truth that these phrases are not used of apostles or of presbyters distinctively, but of the body as a whole, and of it just because it is the body of Christ; of it because of Him; and therefore of it, the whole, not of a part

---

[1] "Ὅτι ἐσφάγης, καὶ ἠγόρασας τῷ Θεῷ ἐν τῷ αἵματί σου ἐκ πάσης φυλῆς κ. τ. λ. καὶ ἐποίησας αὐτοὺς τῷ Θεῷ ἡμῶν βασιλείαν καὶ ἱερεῖς καὶ βασιλεύουσιν ἐπὶ τῆς γῆς, Rev. v. 9, 10.

[2] Ἐπὶ τούτων ὁ δεύτερος θάνατος οὐκ ἔχει ἐξουσίαν, ἀλλ' ἔσονται ἱερεῖς τοῦ Θεοῦ καὶ τοῦ Χριστοῦ, Rev. xx. 6.

[3] Col. ii. 10, 12; iii. 1, 3

[4] Eph. ii 4–6, 10. Cp Rom. vi 8; viii 9 and 17; 1 Cor. ii. 16; Gal. ii. 20, and ver. 19; 2 Tim. ii. 11, 12; &c., &c.

of it merely. The whole body of Christ is priestly, with Him and in Him 'raised up and made to sit in heavenly places,' 'offering up spiritual sacrifices,' prepared unto 'good works.' But it is just the priestly character of the Church as a whole which I first desire to establish. If this be once conceded and understood, I do not apprehend that much difficulty will remain about the priestly character of the ministry of the Church. If those be right who deprecate the use of the words priest and priestly, all substantial reality in the conception of the priesthood of the layman must go too[1]. The priesthood of the ministry is to be established not through depreciation, but through exaltation, of the priesthood of the body as a whole. And in the long run I do not believe that it is those who enter into the solemnity of the universal priesthood, but rather those who would eliminate priesthood and its solemnity altogether, who will be the really uncompromising opponents of the priesthood of the ministry

In what then does the priestly character of the Church consist? The priesthood of Christ we found in His offering of Himself as a perfect sacrifice, an offering which is not more an outward enactment than an inward perfecting of holiness and of love; an offering whose outward enactment is but the perfect utterance of a perfect inwardness; an offering which, whilst, so to say, containing Calvary in itself, is consummated eternally by His eternal self-presentation before the presence and on the throne of God. The sacrificial priesthood of the Church is really her identification with the priesthood and sacrifice of Christ. With this priesthood and sacrifice she is identified outwardly and inwardly; by outward enactment ceremonially, and by inwardness of spirit vitally. Christ Himself has prescribed for all time an outward ceremonial, which is the symbolic counterpart in the Church on earth, not simply of Calvary, but of that eternal presentation of Himself in

---

[1] 'Sacerdotium laici, id est baptisma,' Jerome, adv. Lucif. 4. Cp. Col. ii. 12, quoted above.

heaven in which Calvary is vitally contained. Through this symbolic enactment, rightly understood,—an enactment founded on and intrinsically implying as well as recalling Calvary,—she in her Eucharistic worship on earth is identified with His sacrificial self-oblation to the Father; she is transfigured up into the scene of the unceasing commemoration of His sacrifice in heaven; or the scene of His eternal offering in heaven is translated down to, and presented, and realised in the worship on earth. Of course the outward ceremonial, as merely outward, is valueless. But its use is solemn and responsible, just in proportion as those who use it do, or might, enter into what it means. This is her identification through outward ceremonial enactment.

The correlative identification in inwardness of spirit will require no doubt, first of all, an intelligence of spiritual apprehension reverently to apprehend the meaning of what is outwardly done, and to adore and love what it apprehends. But I should not at all like to express the meaning of the inward identification only in terms of intelligent apprehension of the outward ceremonial. Or if so, then intelligent apprehension means much more than it seems to mean. For this identification of the Church on earth with the eternal presentation of the sacrifice in heaven, and with Him who presents the sacrifice, means the reproduction in her of the Spirit of Him who sacrificially offered Himself. It is Christ Himself who is being formed in her.[1] It means therefore in her, as in Him, the Spirit of Love which itself, in its outward expression on earth, is self-devoting sacrifice; or conversely, the spirit of sacrifice, self-devotion, self-expenditure, which is, in the sphere of human life and duty, the spontaneous and inevitable utterance of the Spirit of Love, or of God.

The two aspects are inseparable aspects of one life. The Church is priestly because from her proceeds the aroma of perpetual offering towards God. The Church is

[1] Gal. iv. 19.

priestly because her arms are spread out perpetually to succour and intercede for those who need the sacrifice of love. Both aspects are brought into relief when we think of the Church as a small kernel or focus of brightness in the midst of the world. Then the Church is God's priest in the world and for the world, alike as presenting to God on the world's behalf that homage which the world has not learned to present for itself, and as spending and suffering for God's sake in service to the world. I say that the thought of the Church as a spot of light in the midst of surrounding darkness illustrates the conception of her priestliness. But I would not so speak as though the priestliness of the Church depended upon the surrounding presence of the world. If all were baptized and included as members within the Church, still the mutual service of Christians one towards another—each for all, and all for each—would be, both to Godward and to manward, a real corporate priesthood; a priesthood still, in the full sense of sacrifice and suffering, as long as failure and sin, sorrow and death remained, a priesthood still, even when these were gone, only transformed into that pure joy of love which had been the underlying reality of priesthood all through.

The priestliness may be spoken of as essentially towards God: only then this offering to God involves and contains a *manward* devotion also. Or *quâ* priesthood, it may be thought of as immediately to and for man; only then this manward devotion means the presentation of humanity *as an offering to God* The offering to God is an offering of humanity. The service 'for others' is *ipso facto* to Godward. It is this intense 'to Godwardness' which makes the Church in the world—whether surrounded by external contradiction or no—a perpetual aspiration, and offering to the Father; and therefore also, by inherent necessity, a perpetual reflection of what He is, as revealed to the world in the Person of Jesus Christ. It is this intense 'for-other-ness,' this marvellous spirit which—Calvary apart—finds its highest expression historically in the

'Blot me I pray Thee out of Thy book which Thou hast written' of Moses, or the 'I could wish that I myself were anathema from Christ' of St. Paul,—this spirit meanwhile that has been, and still is being, so wonderfully, yet so characteristically exemplified, all the world over, in great things and in small, in the self-sacrificing ministrations of Bishops and Pastors, in the tender, self-devotion of fathers or mothers, comrades or brothers, wives or sisters, or teachers, or nurses, or neighbours, or strangers, yes or even, with a certain reflected fidelity, in outsiders, Samaritans, enemies,—it is this, as well as reverent intelligence of Eucharistic worship—this which in its highest perfectness is itself the corollary and outcome of spiritually intelligent Eucharistic worship—it is this which is the expression in ordinary terms of human life of the true inwardness of the priesthood of the Church. This is sacrifice taking practical form in the protectiveness of pastoral love: and there is no true pastoral love without sacrifice. It is no unique fact only, but an eternal principle which is recorded in the words: 'The good shepherd giveth his life for the sheep.' And where is this *not*, in greater degree or in less, continually going on? Truly it is Christians as such, it is the members of the Body—the partakers of the Spirit—of Jesus Christ, the Lamb of God, who are the real high priestly family on earth[1].

All this is the inherent privilege of the members of the body of Christ What, then, is the priesthood of Christ's ordained ministers? The priesthood of the ministry follows as corollary from the priesthood of the Church. What the one is, the other is. If the priesthood of the Church consists *ceremonially* in her capacity of self-

[1] It is not unfair to apply to this thought the expression of Justin Martyr, οὕτως ἡμεῖς ἀρχιερατικὸν τὸ ἀληθινὸν γένος ἐσμὲν τοῦ Θεοῦ But it is, far more exactly, the very thought which Clement of Alexandria is upon in the passages quoted by Bp. Lightfoot; see above, ch iii. p 83. It is the echo of this thought which, in spite of all its disproportions and negations, gives so much of nobleness to the effort of Dr. Hatch's fifth Bampton Lecture.

identification, through Eucharistic worship, with the eternal presentation of Christ's atoning sacrifice, and *spiritually* in her identification of inner life with the spirit of sacrifice which is the spirit of love uttering itself in devoted ministry to others, so it is by necessary consequence with the priesthood of the ministry. For the priesthood of the ministry is nothing distinct in kind from the priesthood of the Church. The ordained priests are priestly only because it is the Church's prerogative to be priestly; and because they are, by ordination, specialized and empowered to exercise ministerially and organically the prerogatives which are the prerogatives of the body as a whole. They have no greater right in the Sacraments than the laity · only they, and not the laity, have been authorized to stand before the congregation, and to represent the congregation in the ministerial enactment of the Sacraments which are the Sacraments—and the life—of both alike. I need not go over the argument of the third chapter again. Any one who cares to read that will understand that it is no part of the present object to draw an essential contrast between the priesthood of the Church and of the ministry. The powers, the privileges, the capacities, are the powers and privileges and capacities of the body as a whole. Only here, as there, we utterly protest against the unauthorized *sequitur* which would conclude that therefore the powers of the whole can be ministerially exercised by any, or by all. It is not given to the eye to hear, nor to the ear to see. Those who actually celebrate do but organically represent, and act for, the whole. But the executive right, the power to represent, and act for, and wield ministerially the capacities of the whole, is not indiscriminate Those who stand before the congregation, either as its representative organs to Godward, or as the accredited ministers of God to it, must be authorized and empowered so to do We shall I believe approach the truth in this matter, neither on the one hand by exalting the ministry at the expense of the laity, nor on the other—and even less—by dropping the distinctive words priestly and priesthood; but by insisting, in no metaphorical sense, upon the sacred character and the solemn responsibility of the priesthood of the Christian Church as a whole, and (apart from its ministerial and executive sense) of every individual lay-member of the Church [1].

But to return to the priesthood of the ministry. They are Priests because they are personally consecrated to be the representatives and active organs of the priesthood of the Church And they represent it emphatically in both of its directions. In the ceremonial direction they represent it as divinely empowered to be themselves its leaders and instruments And from this representative leadership in all external enactment of worship and sacrament — itself no mean privilege and responsibility — I apprehend that it follows also, on the inward and spiritual side, that those who outwardly represent the priesthood of the Church must no less specially represent it in its true inwardness. The priest is not a priest in the act of divine worship only. His personal relation to the priestliness

[1] Cp the Tridentine Catechismus ad Parochos, P II. cap. vii. qu. 23. 'Sed quoniam duplex sacerdotium in sacris literis describitur, alterum interius, alterum externum, utrumque distinguendum est, ut, de quo hoc loco intelligatur, a pastoribus explicari possit. Quod igitur ad interius sacerdotium attinet, omnes fideles, postquam salutari aqua abluti sunt, sacerdotes dicuntur; praecipue vero iusti, qui spiritum Dei habent, et divinae gratiae beneficio Iesu Christi summi sacerdotis viva membra effecti sunt, hi enim fide, quae caritate inflammatur, in altari mentis suae spirituales Deo hostias immolant, quo in genere bonae omnes et honestae actiones, quas ad Dei gloriam referunt numerandae sunt [Then follow quotations from Rev 1 5, 6, 1 Pet ii 5; Rom. xii. 1; Ps. li 17.] Quae omnia ad interius sacerdotium spectare, facile intelligitur Externum vero sacerdotium non omnium fidelium multitudini, sed certis hominibus convenit. . Hoc sacerdotii discrimen in veteri etiam lege observari potest; nam de interiori Davidem locutum esse paulo ante demonstratum est, [sc. Ps. li. 17] externi vero nemo ignorare potest, quam multa Dominus Moysi et Aaroni praecepta dederit . Quia igitur eandem sacerdotii distinctionem in lege evangelica licet animadvertere; docendi erunt fideles, nunc de sacerdotio externa agi, quod certis hominibus attributum est; hoc enim tantummodo ad ordinis sacramentum pertinet.' It is only fair to bear this passage in mind; but it may be doubted whether it gives us all that we ought to ask, so long as the priesthood of the layman is interpreted without reference to any thought of care, or responsibility, for others.

of the Church is something which has been conferred on him once for all, and which dominates everything that he does, or is. It does not cease when he leaves church. Only its external opportunities are altered—not its essential character—when he is withdrawn from parochial office altogether. Wherever he is, he still, in his personal life, bears the same relation to the Church, and to the world. He cannot but be a representative *persona*. He is always, in his own spiritual attitude and effort—to Godward for man, to manward for God—called to realize, and (as it were) to personify, the characteristic priestliness of the Church. This is not because he is an intermediary between Christ and His Church; it is not because he is something which the Church is not, but because he is set to represent, in his own personality, with an eminent distinctiveness, that which the whole Church cannot but essentially be. If she is priestly because from her proceeds the aroma of a perpetual offering—her mystical identity with the perpetual self-offering of her Lord—before the Majesty of the Father's presence; if, in corresponding necessity of spirit, she is priestly because her arms are perpetually lifted up to intercede for, and to succour, those who need the sacrifice of love; ever presenting to God on their behalf the homage which they have not learnt to present for themselves, and spending and suffering for God in service to them; so is it with him, as by God's will and act specially ordained to be her ministerial representative.

The inwardness, then, of priesthood is the spirit of sacrifice; and the spirit of sacrifice is the spirit of love in a world of sin and pain, whose expression in the inner soul is priestly intercession, and whose utterance in the outward life is devotion of ministry 'for others':—for others, from the Christ-like point of view, as for those for whom Christ died. The Levitical priesthood belonged distinctively to the side of ceremonial function, and might be both adequately fulfilled and adequately defined in terms of ceremonial enactment only; but a Christian priesthood misapprehends itself which can be content to find the beginning and end of its definition or meaning in terms only of what is outward and ceremonial, or in any sacramental service, however intelligent it may be or reverent in itself, which does not sweep in the whole heart, and action, and life. There are not only priestly functions, or priestly prerogatives there is also a priestly spirit and a priestly heart—more vital to true reality of priesthood than any mere performance of priestly functions. Now this priestly spirit—I must repeat it once more—is *not* the exclusive possession of the ordained ministry; it is the spirit of the priestly Church. But those who are ordained 'priests' are bound to be eminently leaders and representatives of this priestliness of spirit, and they have assigned to them an external sphere and professional duties which constitute a special opportunity, and a charisma of grace which constitutes a special call and a special capacity, for its exercise. Such opportunity and call are inseparable from the oversight of the life of the Christian body to Godward, and they are as wide as is the life of the Christian body. Leadership in Eucharistic worship, truly understood, is its highest typical expression, the mystical culmination of its executive privilege; but Eucharistic leadership, truly understood, involves many corollaries of spirit and life—the bearing of the people on the heart before God; the earnest effort of intercessory entreating; the practical translation of intercession into pastoral life, and anxiety, and pain. Things like these are necessary elements in that inwardness of spirit which should correspond to and explain the outward dignity of executive function; and apart from which the outward dignity of executive function, even in its highest point of mystical reality, is as the shell or the shadow, the outward presentment and image, the technical enacting —not the true heart—of Christian priesthood.

It is necessary, then, to emphasize unreservedly the

truth that the priesthood of ministry and of laity are not really antithetical or inconsistent, but rather correlative, complimentary, nay, mutually indispensable ideas[1]. Magnify first the solemnity of ministerial priesthood, and then from that expound the dignity and power of the priesthood of the laity, or, if you will, magnify lay priesthood first, and mount from thence to its concentrated meaning in those who are set apart personally to represent the collective priesthood, and to wield it ministerially: in either case your exposition will lead to results which will be no less true than they may well be felt to be amazing. But use the phrases 'priesthood of the laity' (or 'priesthood of the body') in order to discredit the idea of ministerial priesthood, and from ministerial priesthood thus explained away turn to draw out what the universal priesthood practically means; and you will have succeeded, with admirable skill, in conjuring both realities into empty air. It will only remain to toss the whole nomenclature aside, as an unmeaning or misleading metaphor.

[1] I have thought it convenient, upon the whole, to leave in this place the phrase 'priesthood of ministry and of laity.' But it has been pointed out to me—and the observation is of some importance—that there is a certain inexactness in the collective phrase 'priesthood of the laity,' which cannot be alleged against Jerome's '*sacerdotium laici.*' The laity, collectively as laity, have no distinctive priesthood. There is a collective priesthood of the ministry; and there is a collective priesthood of the body as a whole. In this all members of the body, whether ministers or laymen, share. But though there is assuredly a priesthood in which every layman should claim part, yet any phrase which seems to imply that the laity corporately, as laity, have a priesthood in which the ministry does not share, or which may be set over against the priesthood of the ministry, is, so far, misleading.

III.

It will be observed that if the present contention be true, if the Church of Christ is, because Christ is, inherently priestly, and the ministry of the Church is the ministerial presentment of the Church's priestliness, and priestliness, to be real, must be the perfect outward expression of correspondingly perfect inwardness, there will follow a principle of considerable importance. It will follow that the 'priestly' aspect of the ministry, whose executive culmination is Eucharistic leadership, and its aspect as guiding and governing with general oversight (ἐπισκοπή), or as ministering pastorally to, the Body and its members, are not things substantially different: they cannot be properly sundered: each in its reality requires and implies the other: they differ not as two things, or as three, but as several aspects of one The true priestliness necessarily carries with it the pastoral character: the real pastoral character is but an expression, in outward life, of priestliness. And if they thus, of inward necessity[1], contain and imply each other, then of course they must always have done so, from the very first. 'Sacerdotalism' may have acquired some disproportionate exposition, or been linked to exaggerated claims: but if sacerdotalism, *name and thing*, be in any true sense a later accretion to the idea of Christian ministry; if it did not, in essence, belong to it inherently from the first; if oversight of the Christian body had not always this inner

---

[1] It is not denied, of course, that either can be—and often has been—artificially taken apart, in injurious and un-Christlike isolation from the other. Only in its proper richness of Divine power can neither of them be realized without the other.

character, and this inner character did not always imply the spirit and activities of pastoral oversight—then indeed we must sorrowfully admit that our entire interpretation is at fault, and with it, the mind and language of the Church as a whole, for at least some seventeen centuries.

But were the two things ever separate? Think first of the Scripture. Now I shall admit that in the words of Scripture, both the connexion of Christian ministry with Eucharistic leadership, and the application to Eucharistic worship of sacrificial and priestly language, is less explicit than we might perhaps at first sight have expected. One or two reasons, however, suggest themselves which constitute a perfectly sufficient answer to any question on this score. First and foremost, Christian life and Christian worship are essentially spiritual. If the spiritual expresses itself by material means, the material means are to be only expressions of the spiritual. Any approach to very strong insistence, in the Scripture itself, upon the means, as such, would almost inevitably have resulted in an exaggeration of the intrinsic sanctity of what was outward and mechanical. Considering the extreme readiness of human nature to take refuge from spiritual reality in mechanical observance; considering the extent to which this has been done, and (one may almost say) the daily difficulty of preventing its being done, in this very matter of the materializing of sacramental worship—we can hardly, on second thoughts, feel any surprise if, in the scriptural picture of the Apostolic Church, we find a marked and most impressive reserve from any such emphasis on the external ordinances of religion. But if there is, in the Acts and Epistles, less direct emphasis than mere men might have laid upon sacramental outwardness, it remains none the less—but rather the more—emphatically to be remembered, first, that to the Church and her life the atoning Blood of Christ (including in that word not its shedding only, but its offering in heaven) is *everything*; secondly, that Jesus Christ bequeathed, when

VII] *PRIESTHOOD IN THE CHURCH OF CHRIST* 265

parting from this life, an ordinance, universally prescribed to Christians, as the symbolic embodiment and realization of that atonement in its fullest inclusiveness; and thirdly, that since this command remained, and remains unmodified and unmodifiable, the reserve of the New Testament can never be taken as throwing a doubt upon, but as assuming, this: and this being assumed as the basis of distinctively Christian worship and life, all that it does say belongs to the exposition of the spiritual inwardness which is to be expressed and contained in this. If there is one case more than another to which Dr. Dale's half-paradoxical canon would apply—viz. that the fundamental importance of any element in Christianity is almost in inverse ratio to the frequency of its mention in the New Testament —it is this.

And the second reason is this, that both Acts and Epistles were written at a time when sacrificial and priestly language were *de facto* identified with the symbolic, ceremonial, and unreal priesthood and sacrifices of the Mosaic law. To have simply taken over the language while the Temple was standing and its worship in full force, *then* to have called Christian ministers, as such, ἱερεῖς, and the breaking of the bread simply θυσία, would have led to inextricable misunderstanding and confusion What was possible without confusion, and what was necessary for apprehension of the truth, was to explain that that priesthood and those sacrifices were symbolic only and unreal; that Christ only was the true Priest, and His sacrifice the only real sacrifice; which, coupled with the basal Christian principle, that the bread and the cup are the Church's ceremonial identification with Christ in His sacrifice, and that a real identification[1] with him in His sacrifice is the one *essentia* of the Church's life, constitutes the whole essence of

---

[1] The real identification is very complete, and covers the whole range of life. It involves, according to Scripture, con-crucifixion, con-burial, cor-resurrection, co-ascension, con-session in heaven. Gal. ii. 20; v. 24; vi. 14. Rom vi. 2-11 Col ii 12; iii. 1 Eph. ii. 5, 6.

sacrificial and priestly doctrine. All this the New Testament does emphatically teach.

It follows, I think, that when all this came to be more and more completely apprehended, and when, with the passing away of Judaic priesthood and sacrifice, the pressure of immediate ambiguity died away from the words, it was, on New Testament principles, quite inevitable that the terms priest and sacrifice should be more and more current in the Christian Church. Of course such a growth into terms (however inevitable) which at first were, with good cause, restrained, was not, and was not likely to be, a sudden thing. It was, in fact, a perfectly natural growth, not a break or a change. The analogy with the old order was impressively felt, as analogy, before it was realized that the old order itself became real only in the new. The terms were used as highly instructive metaphors before they came to be familiar titles. Titles, indeed, they could hardly be with any completeness, until not only the Temple service had come to an end, but the conception of the Temple service had ceased to furnish the normal and regulative standard by which the direct significance of the terms would be measured[1].

If it be once admitted that the 'breaking of the bread' was the essential Christian service from the first, and that

---

[1] Canon Gore says (*The Church and the Ministry*, p. 196): 'Irenaeus and Clement do not speak of the Christian ministers as priests, while Tertullian and Origen do' But he is speaking of the 'regular' use of the words as titles Long before Tertullian and Origen, the familiar use of θυσιαστήριον for the Christian altar in the letters of Ignatius; the terms in Clement of Rome, προσφοραί, δῶρα, θυσία αἰνέσεως for the Eucharist, ἀρχιερεὺς τῶν προσφορῶν (of Christ), προσενεγκεῖν τὰ δῶρα, λειτουργεῖν τῷ ποιμνίῳ (of presbyters); in the *Didache* the use of θυσία (of the weekly Eucharist), and the suggestion of οἱ ἀρχιερεῖς ὑμῶν (of the prophets); the θυσιαστήριον of Hebr. xiii. 10 (on which see more fully below, p. 269); even St Paul's ἱερουργεῖν (of his own ministry), Rom. xv. 16—are at the least instructive metaphorical suggestions, and many of them stages beyond mere suggestiveness or metaphor, on the road towards the simple titular use of θυσία and ἱερεῖς, as correlative terms, in relation to those who enact on earth the Church's celebration of the Sacrament of the Sacrifice, and to that which the Church so celebrates through them. But all these are spoken of more fully below.

VII] *PRIESTHOOD IN THE CHURCH OF CHRIST* 267

it meant, and was, the Church's identifying with the offering of the Body and Blood of the Lord, everything follows in order from this one fact. When was the Eucharist administered? or how? or how often[1]? or by whom? If not, in the absence of Apostles, by those who had been constituted by the Apostles as elders and heads of the Church in every place, then by whom? If it were not implied of course as part of the leadership of the presbyteral office, then we must needs have good evidence[2] of the existence of some other distinct and necessarily higher stratum in the spiritual order for the breaking of the bread. But if it were implied in the presbyteral office, then it could not but characterize the presbyteral office, seeing what a place it necessarily had in the life and life's meaning of the Church. To those who governed the flock, who watched for souls, and taught them and fed them, and should 'give account' for them, was not the Eucharistic offering an element, and if an element, then of inherent necessity the culminating element—in a sense even, if spiritually apprehended in its full inwardness, the all dominating, all inclusive element — in their official prerogative? 'Take heed unto yourselves,' cries St. Paul to the elders of Ephesus, 'and to all the flock, in the which the Holy Ghost hath made you bishops, to feed ($\pi o \iota \mu a \iota \nu \epsilon \iota \nu$) the Church of God, which He purchased with His own blood.' How much of the awful allusiveness is taken out of these words if he is not, in fact, speaking to those who week by week, at least, were indeed as pastors feeding the Church of God with the very blood by which they had been bought! And if he is—and on the most general view of the facts as a

---

[1] As to the question 'how often,' see further below, p 269, note 5.
[2] Perhaps the 'prophets' of the *Didache* will be offered as evidence. But in face of the assumptions and terminology of Clement of Rome, Ignatius, Polycarp, and Barnabas, it is impossible to rely on the 'prophets' of the *Didache*. [See above, ch. vi. p. 176 sqq.] Moreover, the *Didache* itself, with singular directness, connects the local $\epsilon \pi \iota \sigma \kappa o \pi o \iota$ with the local weekly necessity of the celebration of the 'Sacrifice.'

whole it is difficult even to conceive that he is not—how idle to argue either that the connexion of presbyterate with Eucharist or of Eucharist with thoughts, if not terms, fundamentally sacrificial—and priestly in a sense far transcending Aaronic priestliness — are unknown to, and alien from, the Church of the Apostles! When St. Paul says of himself, 'We are a sweet savour of Christ unto God, in them that are being saved, and in them that are perishing. to the one a savour from death unto death; to the other a savour from life unto life. And who is sufficient for these things[1]?' and again, 'Our sufficiency is of God, who also made us sufficient as ministers of a new covenant, . . . the ministration of the spirit, . . . the ministration of righteousness,' by reason of the surpassing glory whereof the dazzling glory of Moses was outdazzled—it is clear that he is speaking of Christian ministry as such. In order to make a plausible argument for excluding from the idea of such Christian ministry the great Christian sacrament, it would be necessary to show something more than the merely negative fact that the New Testament does not emphasize the specific connexion. It would be necessary to show *either* that, in the New Testament, the life of the Church does not centre in 'fellowship with the Father, and with His Son Jesus Christ'; *or* that the Holy Communion is not the characteristic Christian service; *or* that,—though both these things in themselves be true,—yet the New Testament has expressly made severance between the solemnly appointed ministerial methods of the Church's spiritual life, and that executive ministry of the Church which was, as ministration of Spirit, so surpassing in glory. It is needless to say that there is no shadow of justification for conclusions such as these.

All this seems to me to be implicitly contained in every part of the New Testament. When we come to the

[1] 2 Cor. ii. 15, and iii.

Epistle to the Hebrews, we have an elaborate exposition of the Levitical priesthood as both transcended[1] by, and consummated[2] in, the priesthood of Jesus Christ; we have, based immediately upon this Christian priesthood, a solemn exhortation to keep fast to the Christian assembly, the divine access to God through the Blood and Flesh of Jesus Christ,[3] the sanctifying 'Blood of the Covenant,' which not to reverence is to 'tread under foot the Son of God' and 'do despite unto the Spirit of grace.'[4] There follows (in ch. xi.) the noble outburst of enthusiastic glorification of the spirit of faith, and (in ch. xii.) the *a fortiori* contrast of the Divine revelation of the earthly Sinai and the spiritual Zion, 'the heavenly Jerusalem,' 'Jesus, the mediator' of the 'new covenant,' the 'blood of sprinkling' that transcendeth Abel. And so, passing to the close of the whole Epistle (xiii. 10 sqq.), we come to the emphatic claim to 'an altar,[5]'

---

[1] Hebr. iii.-viii.   [2] Hebr. ix., x.
[3] Hebr. x. 19-25. Cp. also above, p. 14.   [4] Hebr x. 26 sqq.
[5] The alteration of Bishop Lightfoot's interpretation of the θυσιαστήριον of Hebr. xiii. 10 is very remarkable. In the dissertation as originally published he wrote: 'The sacrifices are praise and thanksgiving and well-doing, the altar is the congregation assembled for Christian worship.' In its ultimate form the last clause has become 'the altar is apparently the Cross of Christ.' Now as to the real outcome of either of these interpretations, or the word in the original, or any similar hints in the New Testament, it hardly seems to be sufficiently realised how largely a true exegesis must depend upon the historical question what was, and what was not, the practical thought and life of the Apostolic Church. Was the Eucharist the climax of their distinctive worship? the regular symbol and channel of their spiritual life? There are several indications in the New Testament which would most naturally suggest (as in the *Didache*) a weekly, there is a phrase which seems to assert a daily, Eucharist. Into the question between these two we need not enter. I am not aware that any other alternative can be plausibly suggested. Now either they did, or they did not, live, and work, and suffer, and adore, in the continual habit of a regular Eucharistic celebration, which was to them, verily and indeed, the κοινωνία τοῦ σώματος—the κοινωνία τοῦ αἵματος—of Christ. If they did not do so, then no doubt we may look right and left, when we meet such a phrase as that of Hebr. xiii. 10, for whatever analogical or symbolic meaning may satisfy our religious fancy most. But if they did, then such phrases must, in all reason, be interpreted in the light of this, their liturgical practice. In this case it does not follow that θυσιαστήριον is the direct name for the piece of wood or stone on which the bread and wine stood, as 'altar' with many of us is the name which stands as a label for a

as the distinctive prerogative of Christians. 'Through Him, then,' thus it proceeds in ver. 15, 'let us offer up a sacrifice of praise to God continually, that is, the fruit of lips which make confession to His Name.'[1] I do not suggest that the phrases of this verse have what would be called a literal or direct—far less an exclusive—reference to the Eucharistic celebration, but can any one suppose that to those who were living, in fact, in the fellowship of the breaking of the bread, and finding in it their communion with the Body of Christ, the Eucharistic celebration could ever have been less than the palmary meaning of the Christian 'sacrifice of praise and thanksgiving'? When the writer goes on to exhort his hearers, 'But to do good and to communicate forget not, for with such sacrifices God

---

particular piece of historical church furniture; on the contrary, it may be of considerable importance to insist that this was a secondary, not a primary usage of the word (cp Bp. Westcott *in loco*), but it does seem to me altogether to follow that, however much more inclusive or indefinite may be, to thought, the entire connotation of the word, the Eucharistic celebration must, after all, be that among concrete things which it most directly signified, and which most fully embodies and expresses its meaning. If the main principle be once granted, *both* the meanings given by the Bishop—and others, perhaps, besides them—may be readily allowed. The 'Cross of Christ' (which seems to me essentially to concede the whole point at issue) may be directer and fuller than 'the congregation assembled for Christian worship'; but both are true, and, on analysis, both will mean the same thing. Either, in its highest culmination of earthly enactment, can only be the celebration of the Christian Eucharist.

[1] Θυσίαν αἰνέσεως, from Psalm 1 ('Will I eat the flesh of bulls, or drink the blood of goats? Offer unto God the sacrifice of thanksgiving; and pay thy vows unto the Most High,' vv. 13, 14; and 'Whoso offereth the sacrifice of thanksgiving glorifieth Me; and to him that ordereth his conversation aright will I show the salvation of God'; ver. 23) · so Clem. Rom ch xxxv; see below, p 273. Both here, and in the passage of St Clement, and everywhere else (as in the prayer of oblation in the Prayer-book), it is, I conceive, quite inevitable that any such phrase as this, our 'sacrifice of praise and thanksgiving,' describing the distinctively Christian offering of service, should have its supreme reference as well to the outward celebration, as to the inward and spiritual character, of the sacramental Eucharist. not (as I have said above) exclusively, nor always directly, but as the highest embodiment, at least, and symbol of what *Christian* thanksgiving and praise mean. To a distinctively Christian experience, θυσία αἰνέσεως could no more ultimately fail to express the aspiration and joy of 'Holy Communion,' then εὐχαριστία to find its consummating significance in 'the Eucharist.'

is well pleased,' he is still upon the expression in act of that inwardness of spirit which is itself the result—not of the typical, and external, sacrifices of the law, but of spiritual union with the Body and Blood of Christ. And how near topics like these bring him to the thought of their regularly constituted Christian ministry is, to say the least, strongly suggested by the words which immediately follow: 'Obey them that have the rule over you, and submit to them; for they watch in behalf of your souls, as they that shall give account; that they may do this with joy, and not with grief: for this were unprofitable for you.' He goes on to ask their prayers for himself, and ends with a form of solemn blessing, the very terms of which echo still, as in the language of the twentieth chapter of Acts, the implicit thought of the shepherds feeding the flock which was purchased with Christ's Blood: 'Now the God of peace, who brought again from the dead the great Shepherd of the sheep with the blood of the eternal covenant, even our Lord Jesus, make you perfect in every good thing to do His will, working in us that which is well pleasing in His sight, through Jesus Christ; to whom be the glory for ever and ever. Amen.'

The only thing that seems still to hesitate at all is the directness of nomenclature. I have already given reasons why this could not but hesitate at the time of the New Testament, but have also noticed already that even in the New Testament the Christian Church is to St Peter a new ἱεράτευμα, to offer up spiritual sacrifices,[1] and Christians are to St. John ἱερεῖς: to which we must add that St Paul, in a strain which is no doubt for the moment largely figurative, begins to use hieratic language of his own ministry: 'The grace that was given me of God, that I should be a minister of Christ Jesus unto the Gentiles, ministering the gospel of God, that the offering up of the Gentiles might be made acceptable, being sanctified by the Holy Ghost.'[2] It is

---

[1] 'Ανενέγκαι πνευματικὰs θυσίαs εὐπροσδέκτους τῷ Θεῷ διὰ 'Ιησοῦ Χριστοῦ, 1 Pet. ii. 5.

[2] Εἰs τὸ εἶναί με λειτουργὸν Χριστοῦ 'Ιησοῦ εἰs τὰ ἔθνη, ἱερουργοῦντα τὸ

certainly true that 'ministering in sacrifice' (see R. V. margin) and 'offering' are not in this passage used directly of the Eucharist. Once grant, however, that the Eucharist was what it surely must be allowed to have been to the writer of the tenth and eleventh chapters of 1 Cor., understood in harmony (at least) with the tenth chapter of Hebrews, i e. was at once the Christian 'proclaiming' and the Christian 'communion of' the only one real sacrifice of the only one real priest—which every Levitical sacrifice did but outwardly and unreally symbolize—and it is hard to see how hieratic language used of Christian ministry could fail to have ultimate reference to the Eucharist. Often indeed it may not be spoken of the Eucharist quite directly; but however little it is to be confined to any outward enactment whatever, it is hard to see how such language can fail to find at least its crowning exemplification and expression ceremonially in that Sacrament of the Sacrifice which constituted the distinctive worship and characterized the distinctive life of the Christian Church.

When we pass beyond the Scripture it is plain, even from the very earliest moments, that such a strain of thought was taken for granted. The earliest writers do not dream of arguing it. If in some ways they are a little more explicit than Scripture, they are like Scripture in this, that the proportion of the truth in this matter is not so much a thesis insisted on as a hypothesis assumed.

So it is with the writers of the *Didache*. The Christian congregation must not fail in the perpetual sacrifice as prophesied by Malachi Week by week, every Lord s day, it must be offered with regularity—in purity; and *therefore* must the Church in every place provide itself with its own bishops (i. e. presbyters) and deacons.[1] Could there be a

εὐαγγέλιον τοῦ Θεοῦ, ἵνα γένηται ἡ προσφορὰ τῶν ἐθνῶν εὐπρόσδεκτος, ἡγιασμένη ἐν Πνεύματι Ἁγίῳ, Rom xv 16.

[1] Κατὰ κυριακὴν δὲ Κυρίου συναχθέντες κλάσατε ἄρτον· καὶ εὐχαριστήσατε προσεξομολογησάμενοι τὰ παραπτώματα ὑμῶν ὅπως καθαρὰ ἡ θυσία ἡμῶν ᾖ . . ἵνα μὴ κοινωθῇ ἡ θυσία ὑμῶν αὕτη γάρ ἐστιν ἡ ῥηθεῖσα ὑπὸ Κυρίου ἐν παντὶ τόπῳ καὶ χρόνῳ προσφέρειν μοι θυσίαν καθαράν ὅτι βασιλεὺς μέγας εἰμί, λέγει

more striking testimony than this, which, coming out so incidentally in a context which can hardly be called either sacerdotal or episcopal, shows quietly, without emphasis or self-consciousness, what was at least a characteristic and leading thought of the meaning of presbyteral office.

St. Clement's letter to the Corinthians is certainly not occupied with special or pointed insistence upon this aspect of the ministry. And yet it is unmistakably there. The thought is learning to fix itself upon Christ as High Priest, and as High Priest in relation to the 'offerings' of the Christian Church, and upon the Christian service as 'the offerings,' and upon the presbyteral office as the office chiefly characterized (as far as outward routine of office goes) by the presentation of the offerings. Thus, to put a few passages together, after quoting the last eight verses of the fiftieth Psalm, verses which immediately follow upon a denunciation of merely external sacrifice in comparison with 'the sacrifice of thanksgiving,' and which themselves culminate in the words 'the sacrifice of thanksgiving (αἰνέσεως) shall glorify me, and therein is a way which I will show to him, the salvation of God' (LXX), St. Clement goes on, 'This is the way, beloved, in which we found our salvation—Jesus Christ, the High Priest of our offerings, the defender and helper of our weakness.' Put this with the forty-first chapter, where after emphasizing the discipline, order, and precision of the offerings and services (προσφοραὶ καὶ λειτουργίαι) of the old covenant, of high priest, priests, Levites, and layman (ὁ λαικός), he goes on, 'Let each one of you, brethren, make his thanksgiving (εὐχαριστείτω) to God in his own ordered place (ἐν τῷ ἰδίῳ τάγματι), being in a good conscience, not overstepping the appointed line of his service (μὴ παρεκβαίνων τὸν ὡρισμένον τῆς λειτουργίας αὐτοῦ κανόνα), in awe[1].' After this we are prepared for the terms in

Κύριος· καὶ τὸ ὄνομά μου θαυμαστὸν ἐν τοῖς ἔθνεσι. χειροτονήσατε οὖν ἑαυτοῖς ἐπισκόπους καὶ διακόνους ἀξίους τοῦ Κυρίου, κ. τ. λ. Chap. xiv., xv.

[1] The parallelism between the phrases and ideas used of the Levitical and

which he speaks of the presbyters and their office in chap. 44. The Apostles, he says, had carefully provided for a perpetual succession, that when those died whom they themselves had ordained, others from them might take up their ministry (τὴν λειτουργίαν αὐτῶν) 'Those, then, who were constituted by them or by their successors with the assent of the whole Church, and who have ministered blamelessly to the flock of Christ (λειτουργήσαντας ἀμέμπτως τῷ ποιμνίῳ τοῦ Χριστοῦ) in lowliness of spirit, quietly and modestly, receiving for many years universal testimony, these men cannot righteously be thrust out from their ministry (ἀποβάλλεσθαι τῆς λειτουργίας). For we shall incur no light sin if we thrust out from their presbyterate (ἐπισκοπῆς) men who have blamelessly and reverently presented the gifts. Blessed are the presbyters who have finished their course before ... for they fear not lest any should remove them from the place to which they have been appointed (ἀπὸ τοῦ ἱδρυμένου αὐτοῖς τόπου). For we see that there are men of good Christian lives whom ye have removed from the service which they had served in

the Christian offerings respectively is, throughout these chapters, very close. Thus —

1 To offer the Levitical service is ποιεῖν τὰς προσφοράς; ἐπιτελεῖν τὰς προσφορὰς καὶ λειτουργίας. To offer the Christian service is εὐχαριστεῖν; προσφέρειν τὰ δῶρα; λειτουργεῖν; λειτουργεῖν τῷ ποιμνίῳ τοῦ Χριστοῦ

2 It is of necessity that the Levitical offerings must be οὐκ εἰκῇ ἢ ἀτάκτως; κατὰ καιροὺς τεταγμένους; ὡρισμένοις καιροῖς καὶ ὥραις; ποῦ τε καὶ διὰ τίνων ἐπιτελεῖσθαι θέλει αὐτὸς ὥρισεν

So in the Christian offerings, though there is no single place or moment for them, yet each member of the Church must abide in his own τάγμα, not overstepping τὸν ὡρισμένον τῆς λειτουργίας αὐτοῦ κανόνα.

3 Those who thus conform to Levitical order are εὐπρόσδεκτοί τε καὶ μακάριοι τοῖς γὰρ νομίμοις τοῦ Δεσπότου ἀκολουθοῦντες οὐ διαμαρτάνουσιν.

So the Christian presbyters who have done their part aright have served an ἀμέμπτως τετιμημένη λειτουργία Μακάριοι are they who have been allowed to live and die in that service

The Levitical phrases are chiefly in ch. 40. The Christian in 41 and 44. It is to be added that the intervening ch 43 contains a solemn reminder to the Corinthians how peremptorily God had vindicated the Aaronic priesthood from such as presumed to invade it without authority.

All this, it is to be remembered, is a *first century* comment upon the character of the Christian presbyterate

honour without reproach (ἐκ τῆς ἀμέμπτως αὐτοῖς τετιμημένης λειτουργίας).' We may notice also the phrases of chap 59, 'God the creator and bishop of every spirit', and of 61, 'We acknowledge Thee through the high priest and defender of our souls, Jesus Christ'; and 64 again, 'through our High Priest and defender, Jesus Christ.'

To me it seems plain that the actual form taken by the Corinthian insubordination and sin against the unity and order of the Church[1] was an intrusive transgression, by those unauthorized because unordained, beyond their appointed place and line in the Christian service (ὡρισμένον κανόνα τῆς λειτουργίας): and that this intrusion into the presbyteral office meant specifically an intrusion into the 'offering of the gifts,' which was itself a sin against the true high-priesthood of Jesus Christ, who is called both the 'High Priest of the souls' and the 'High Priest of the offerings' of Christians. It is plain also that this revolt of which he thinks and speaks with such exceeding gravity, was to the mind of the writer unreservedly parallel with the great revolt against the Aaronic priesthood in Numbers xvi., xvii. In all this, both in his assumptions and in the silent unconsciousness with which he makes them as of course, St. Clement seems to me to re-echo and to illustrate, precisely in the way we should most have expected, the essential position and meaning, as I have tried to interpret it, of the Scripture itself.

It is not of course meant that to St. Clement any more than to St. Paul this one aspect of what was implied in presbytership swallowed up all the others. To describe a presbyter simply as a 'sacrificer,' or ordination to presbytership as the 'conferring of power to offer sacrifice,' would have probably been as surprising to the one as to the other. Immediately, no doubt, the presbyteral office made demands

[1] Cp. 54: Τίς οὖν ἐν ὑμῖν γενναῖος; τίς εὔσπλαγχνος; τίς πεπληροφορημένος ἀγάπης; εἰπάτω· Εἰ δι' ἐμὲ στάσις καὶ ἔρις καὶ σχίσματα, ἐκχωρῶ, ἄπειμι οὗ ἐὰν βούλησθε, καὶ ποιῶ τὰ προστασσόμενα ὑπὸ τοῦ πλήθους μόνον τὸ ποίμνιον τοῦ Χριστοῦ εἰρηνευέτω μετὰ τῶν καθεσταμένων πρεσβυτέρων.

upon its holders of very varied and anxious responsibility, and therefore presented a *prima facie* appearance in which no ceremonial observance, however far-reaching or profound in significance, would be the one thing that first would meet the eye. But what is contended is that, nevertheless, the idea of Eucharistic leadership, with all the corollaries that were in fact contained and implied therein, was present inherently from the very first as one necessary aspect of the office It might seem almost incidental to the general conception of spiritual oversight and government, and responsibility for teaching and for life. It might be thought of just as the culminating instance of the executive duty and prerogative of an office which was characteristically *not* made up of executive duty and prerogative. But however incidental it may have looked to the eye, the point is that it always was—with all the meanings that really belonged to it—assumed as an inherent property of presbyteral office. That it must have been so of *some* office in the Christian Church seems to be a necessary corollary from the Epistles to the Hebrews and to the Corinthians. That it was so of presbyterate seems to be implied with sufficient clearness by St. Paul, and, without argument, tacitly taken for granted alike by the writers of the *Didache* and by St. Clement.

We find in Ignatius, as we might expect, the same strain of thought with a somewhat accentuated clearness. It will be remembered that he does not take the presbyteral office apart. The presbyterate to him is always as a council or a 'coronal' of which the Bishop is the culminating point. But what concerns us immediately is that, to St. Ignatius, the unity of the 'bishop with the presbyterate' means always, as of course, Eucharistic unity. Ἱερεῖς is still distinctively a Jewish title ; but the relation of Christianity to the Jewish ἱερεῖς is not that of a novelty which supersedes in the sense of abolishing, but rather of an inclusiveness which supersedes in the sense of absorbing them : for the presence of Christ is characteristic of the Church , and if they claim to be priests, the Christian claim outdoes theirs, on their own ground; for the one real High Priest is Christ. And so the unity of the Eucharist is the unity of 'the altar.' 'Let no one be deceived. Except a man be within the altar, he is deprived of the bread of God. For if the prayer of one or two is of so great force, how much more that of the bishop and the whole Church together[1]?' 'He that is within the altar is pure, that is to say, he that does anything apart from the bishop and the presbytery and the deacons, he is not pure in conscience[2].' 'That ye may be obedient to the bishop and the presbyters with a mind that cannot be moved, breaking one bread, which is the medicine of immortality, the antidote against death[3].' 'One prayer, one supplication, one mind, one hope in love. . . . Come ye all together as to one temple of God, as to one altar, to one Lord Jesus Christ' (Lightfoot, 'as to one temple even God, as to one altar, even to one Jesus Christ, who came forth from One Father and is with One and departed unto One')[4]

'Be dutiful then to use one Eucharist · for there is one flesh of our Lord Jesus Christ, and one cup unto union of His blood: one altar, as there is one bishop with the presbytery and deacons[5]' 'The priesthood [i. e. of the Jews] is good; but better is the High Priest to whom was entrusted the Holy of Holies, to whom alone were entrusted the hidden things of God—Himself the door of the Father through which enter in Abraham and Isaac, and Jacob, and the prophets and the Apostles and the Church. These things all of them work towards the oneness of God. But the Gospel has somewhat peculiarly its own, the presence of the Saviour, Jesus Christ our Lord, His passion, and His rising again. For unto Him the beloved prophets in their teaching looked on; but the Gospel is

---

[1] Eph. v [2] Trall vii [3] Eph. xx.
[4] Magn. vii See also Magn ix. μηκέτι σαββατίζοντες ἀλλὰ κατὰ κυριακὴν ζῶντες ἐν ᾗ καὶ ἡ ζωὴ ἡμῶν ἀνέτειλεν Compare the phrase 'living according to the Lord's day' with *Didache*, ch. xiv.
[5] Philad. iv.

the perfecting of immortality. All things together are good, if ye believe, in love[1].' In Smyrn. viii. no Eucharist is valid except it be under the bishop or one appointed by him[2].

When all these passages are put together and dispassionately viewed, it seems to me impossible to deny that every essential conception of the priestliness of the Christian ministry, as of the priestliness of the Christian Church, as I have endeavoured to expound it above, is present—implicitly at least and essentially—within the New Testament; and with increasing explicitness and familiarity to the thought and in great part to the speech of the Church, by the close of the first or the opening of the second century.

That the view here given is a true reading of the history on this matter seems to me to be abundantly corroborated when we look at the passages which Bishop Lightfoot has himself cited in his essay in respect of the intervening time from Ignatius to Cyprian Thus he quotes Justin Martyr as arguing against an unconverted Jew, 'We who through the name of Jesus have believed, .. having divested ourselves of our filthy garments ... are the true high-priestly race of God, as God Himself also beareth witness, saying that in every place among the Gentiles are men offering sacrifices well-pleasing unto Him and pure. Yet God doth not receive sacrifices from any one except through His priests. Therefore God anticipating all sacrifices through this name which Jesus Christ ordained to be offered, I mean those offered by the Christians in every region of the earth with the thanksgiving ($\epsilon\pi\grave{\iota}$ $\tau\eta$ $\epsilon\dot{\upsilon}\chi\alpha\rho\iota\sigma\tau\acute{\iota}\alpha$) of the bread and of the cup, beareth witness that they are well-pleasing to Him, but the sacrifices offered by you and through those your priests He rejecteth[3]...' Now for what

[1] Philad. ix.
[2] Observe that $\pi o\iota\mu\acute{\eta}\nu$ is equivalent to bishop in Ignat Rom. ix., Philad. ii.
[3] *Dial. cum Tryph.* 116, 117. The prophecy of Malachi is reminding of the *Didache*, 14, and the antithesis $\epsilon\dot{\upsilon}\alpha\rho\acute{\epsilon}\sigma\tau o\upsilon\varsigma$ . . . $o\dot{\upsilon}$ $\pi\rho o\sigma\delta\acute{\epsilon}\chi\epsilon\tau\alpha\iota$, of the $\epsilon\dot{\upsilon}\pi\rho\acute{o}\sigma\delta\epsilon\kappa\tau o\varsigma$ of Rom. xv. 16 and 1 Pet. ii. 5.

purpose does the Bishop cite this passage? It is in order to show on the one hand that Justin does 'lay stress on sacerdotal functions'; on the other, that these 'belong to the whole body of the Church, and are not *in any way* the exclusive right of the clergy' [the italics are mine]. But is this really a self-consistent theory? If the Church performed 'sacerdotal functions,' by whose instrumentality did she perform them? It is quite clear that by the Christian sacrifices Justin means the celebrations of the sacramental Eucharist. It is also quite clear that in Justin's own well-known description this 'sacrifice' is celebrated in fact by the one 'president' of the congregation. But might it have been celebrated equally by any other Christian? Of course this is not suggested by Bishop Lightfoot. But ought it not to have been suggested, if the position is to be really a consistent one? If the Christian Church is a 'priest,' offering 'sacrifice' in the perpetual Eucharist; if the function of representing the Church in this her priestliness, and ministerially celebrating the Eucharistic 'sacrifice,' is not indiscriminate, but confined to instruments by ordination specially set apart, then it would seem to be simply misleading to say that the 'sacerdotal functions' are not *in any way* the exclusive right of the clergy. The sense in which they are 'the right of' the clergy may be less important than, and may be wholly dependent upon, the sense in which they are 'the right of' the body as a whole; but whilst the clergy constitute an order empowered to be, in this matter, the Church's representative instruments or *personae*[1], there certainly is 'a way' in which the functions may be said to belong, even 'exclusively,' to the clergy.

Bishop Lightfoot has previously said (p. 244), 'A separation of orders, it is true, appeared at a much earlier date, and was in some sense involved in the appointment of a special ministry. This, and not more than this, was originally contained in the distinction of clergy and laity.'

---

[1] Compare the remarks on the same passage above, pp. 87, 88.

I do not desire 'more than this.' But, read with this, the outcome of the passage of Justin will be that whilst only certain ministers, authorized as such, could ministerially exercise the 'priesthood' and offer the 'sacrifices,' yet the sacrifices which they offered and the priesthood which they exercised were the sacrifices and priesthood of the Church as a whole, and of her ministers rather as the representative organs of her power, than as a power apart, standing outside of her, or between her and God. This of course is exactly the view which I have been interpreting. But how is it relevant to the Bishop's argument? That argument seems to me to fall to the ground, if it be once conceded that the ministerial celebration of the Eucharist was the right of some and not of others, according as they were, or were not, ordained to ministry.

Must it not then be said that the Bishop has been misled by a false antithesis? Is not his argument really based upon the assumption that the priesthood of the Church as a whole, and a ministerial priesthood within the Church, or at least a ministerial priesthood divinely authorized and delimited, are mutually incompatible ideas? He is bound therefore to use the passage in Justin in a way which will only lead to contradictions. But the passage fits at once perfectly to our view, and confirms it in every particular.

Again, when he comes to Irenaeus and Clement of Alexandria, I cannot but submit that there is another false antithesis underlying his argument. He writes as if men who recognized that the true heart of Christian priesthood was in inward and spiritual reality were *ipso facto* excluded from acknowledging an outward and ministerial priesthood at all. Upon this pseudo-antithesis I have dwelt sufficiently in an earlier chapter. But if it be swept away, there is nothing left in his citations from these two fathers. They both, in fact, believed in an episcopal succession continuous from the Apostles; and Clement shows explicitly that he recognizes the *de facto* 'presbyter and deacon and layman,' or, elsewhere, the 'bishop, presbyter, and deacon,' none the less distinctly because he knows that reality of presbyterate—inwardly, ultimately, in the presence of God — depends not on earthly rank but on spiritual character. The same two fallacies completely undermine what he says of Tertullian and Origen. But I need not repeat what I have said of these before, and particularly of the use which he makes of the Montanist position of Tertullian[1]

Whilst therefore I do not believe that Bishop Lightfoot's position is true in this matter even of the apostolic epistles themselves, I certainly cannot admit that he has made it good in respect of either the sub-apostolic writers, or those who intervene between these and St. Cyprian. From St. Cyprian onwards he would admit that this 'sacerdotal' language has been the received language of the Catholic Church. It has been, then, in admitted possession for at least 1,600 years I must submit that its essential reality is plainly discernible for over 200 years more. Even the very completeness of its acceptance from the middle of the third century might well suggest that it was rather in implicit agreement than in any real contrast with that universal sense of the Christian Church, into which, upon any showing, it fitted so easily and so completely We may do well to separate ourselves from all language which would fairly imply a belief in the existence of a distinct caste, of higher holiness or strictly mediatorial power, as if by any right of its own to offer sacrifice, or in any proper sense of the word to 'atone', but I must venture to think that the theological judgement — or instinct — of the Anglican reformers, who, in the face of the destructive flood of Edwardian and Bucerian Protestantism, retained with deliberate emphasis the Christian 'priesthood' as apostolic and perpetual in the Church of Christ, is at once more consistent, more scriptural, and more profound, than any considerations which have been or can be urged

[1] See above, pp. 78-86.

to palliate a modification in this respect of the wellnigh immemorial language, expressive as it is of the wholly immemorial meaning, of the Christian Church. Had Bishop Lightfoot's argument been directed, not (as it is) against the whole association and language of 'sacerdotalism,' but rather against a certain misconceived and disproportioned idea of sacerdotal association and language, the outcome—and we must add, the value—of his dissertation would have been very different.

IV

Now I have dwelt for some time upon the interpretation and vindication of this 'sacerdotal' and 'sacrificial' phraseology. It will, however, be obvious that it is, after all, precisely in this respect that the Anglican Ordinal does make deliberate and decided departure from the unreformed language and thought. All direct language about the power to 'offer sacrifice,' which, by a process of gradual accretion, had come to be at last so continually and so emphatically reiterated in the Sarum Pontifical, is removed, and other things are emphasized in its place. What is the nature and meaning of this crucial alteration?

Now the answer seems to me as simple as it is important. It is one thing to admit the reality of sacrificial language; it is quite another to make it the one definition and measure of Christian ministry. We have seen something of the progress of gradual development, by which this one aspect or thought—not merely colours so far the office of the Christian presbyter as to justify the instinct of the Church in stamping upon the word 'presbyter' whatever associations rightly belong to its shortened form 'priest,' but itself—becomes the characteristic essence, the one differentia, the adequate definition of 'presbytership.' But if we go back to the really early indications, still more if we go back to Scripture itself, it is impossible not to be struck with a wide difference of *proportions* in this respect. Whatever we may, by perfectly just constructiveness, infer and understand about Christian ministry, it seems to be perfectly undeniable that, in the New Testament, (*a*) the 'sacerdotal' idea of the ceremonial offering of Eucharistic sacrifice is nowhere obviously upon the surface, as the one constitutive idea of Christian ministry, whether apostolic or presbyteral, and (*b*) certain other conceptions emphatically are.

Take the sketch of apostolate through the whole of the fourth chapter of 1 Cor ; or again the second and four following chapters, or again the eleventh chapter, of the Second Epistle. The first of these is a picture of inconceivable outward contemptibleness culminating in 'the filth of the world, the offscouring of all things'; the second expressly combines inconceivable glory in spiritual work upon souls with the same paradoxically extreme depression, contempt, dying upon the earth; the third is, to the end of time, a most marvellous picture in detail of humiliation and endurance, culminating above all in 'that which presseth upon me daily, anxiety for all the Churches.' Turn from these again to presbyterate as indicated in the Pastoral Epistles or in the solemn words of St. Paul in the Acts, 'I hold not my life of any account . . . so that I may accomplish . . . the ministry which I received from the Lord Jesus, to testify the gospel of the grace of God.' . . . 'Take heed unto yourselves and to all the flock in the which the Holy Ghost hath made you bishops, to feed the Church of God which He purchased with His own blood;' words which in more ways than one recall our Lord's own picture of the true Pastor: 'The good shepherd layeth down his life for the sheep.'

I was myself arguing, not long ago, that the thought of the Christian 'sacrifice of Eucharist,' the 'sacrament of the Christian sacrifice,' is in some of those passages very near at hand But it is not upon the actual surface of any one of them. What then is really the foreground of the picture? Whatever may be by just inference implied and contained, what is that which stands forward as the dominant idea of the whole? It is something far more general, and more inclusive of all vital activities and meaning, than anything, however mysterious and far-reaching, in the form of ceremonial observance. It is the unreserved offering, the total self-dedication, of what is, on the one side, wise oversight, anxious forethought and rule, an unwearied guidance, preaching, teaching, discipline, and on the other side withal boundless endurance, joy only in completeness of utter sacrifice. It is the care of an utterly loving pastor, a shepherd who tends, feeds, nurses, rescues, and is ready to die for the souls of his flock. All this belongs exactly to that inner reality of the spirit and the life which, as I urged just now, should be the true inwardness of the outward representation of the sacrifice of Christ. This is in no sort of antithesis with ceremonial Eucharistic leadership. But this is its true reflection, in spirit and life,— the inward which should correspond with that outward so perfectly, that that outward should be just its true utterance.

In Scripture then it is this vital inner aspect which is dwelt upon so prominently; the mode of its official enactment in ceremony is rather implied than expressed. But by the sixteenth century the official performance of sacraments had come to be more and more the entire definition of the office; the inwardness of which that should be the outward, the pastoral self-surrender, had practically ceased to be mentioned at all. It is a striking fact, but in the unreformed office for ordaining Priests—with all this emphasis upon the outward and ceremonial celebration of mysteries—you will search in vain for anything like a corresponding recognition of this pastoral inwardness of priesthood. The word 'praedicare,' the word 'caritas' (neither of them enlarged upon), and such phrases as 'exemplum conversationis suae,' are some of the nearest approaches (see above, pp. 224-8) Of the pastoral responsibility for the flock, expressed so awfully in the twentieth chapter of the Acts, there is not one word. It is, then, not the sacerdotal idea or language in itself, but this disproportioned emphasis upon the outward aspect of the sacerdotal idea, from which the Anglican Ordinal clearly departs. It was felt that this emphasis at the least seriously jeopardized the proportionate apprehension of the truth. Every overemphasized truth is itself, in another aspect, untruth; and the untruth which was bound up with this over-emphasis made itself obvious in the more and more absolute overshadowing of the whole pastoral ideal[1].

Here then is the point of a real and characteristic shifting of conception. And what is it that the Anglican Ordinal does? It fixes the eye, first and foremost, just as St. Paul in the New Testament does, upon the thought of the self-dedication and surrender, the pastoral responsibility, the service of the flock, the cure of souls—the life-absorbing inner and spiritual relation—in which, and of which, 'administration of sacraments' comes in as the highest method, the culminating point of executive privilege and power. Whatever is true in fact 'sacrificially' or 'sacerdotally,' comes in as a necessary aspect, or element, or part, of the Church's spiritual government and leadership. In so far as these things are really contained and implied in a true interpretation of Christian 'priesthood,' they are given to those to whom the Christian 'priesthood,' is deliberately given, with whatever it contains or means. The formal celebration of the Eucharist may be the very highest of its administrative methods, the most glorious and wonderful of its executive privileges; yet priesthood itself is something more vitally inclusive than any mystery of formal executive privilege. Eucharistic leadership inheres in Christian priesthood rather as the supreme method of priestly executiveness than as a thing quite apart, a sort of separate magic, in which the whole width of the priestly idea is merged. Say what you will of the stewardship of the Divine mysteries; of the ghostly prerogatives of pronouncing forgiveness, or retention of sins; of Eucharistic celebration as the culmina-

---

[1] Of course, in making this criticism on the 'unreformed' Ordinal, I am making no assertion as to the actual unreformed Ministry. Aspects which are far from adequately represented in the official documents may receive much more justice in practical life. No doubt there have been, and are, vast numbers of most admirable Roman pastors.

tion and crown of what these things mean; though every one of these things can be materialized, degraded, vulgarized,—yet in its true setting every one of these things is true, and in their truest reality one and all are necessarily contained in the priesthood of the Church. But, however august, all these things belong to the executive machinery and method of a Christlike 'cure of souls,' whose meaning can never be exhausted by anything in the sphere of ceremonial method. Neither does any dignity of ceremonial method, though divinely prescribed, stand over against the 'care of all the Churches' as a separate or a higher thing. It is then this central meaning, this spiritual inwardness of the office of Church leadership as a whole, which stands in the forefront of the Anglican Ordinal, as that upon which the thought is primarily centred. Throughout that most solemn exhortation addressed to all candidates for priesthood the ring of St. Paul's words in Acts xx. is never absent. It is to a 'high dignity,' to a 'weighty office and charge' that they are called; 'to be messengers, watchmen, and stewards of the Lord; to teach and to premonish; to feed and provide for the Lord's family, to seek for Christ's sheep that are dispersed abroad, and for His children who are in the midst of this naughty world, that they may be saved through Christ for ever. Have always therefore printed in your remembrance how great a treasure is committed to your charge. For they are the sheep of Christ, which He bought with His death, and for whom He shed His Blood. The Church and congregation whom you must serve is His Spouse and His Body... Wherefore consider with yourselves the end of your ministry towards the children of God, towards the Spouse and Body of Christ...' All this is cardinal and primary. But the solemn administration—and discipline—of sacraments, 'the binding and loosing,' are also emphasized, if no longer as the one thing which Christian priesthood means, yet in their place, in perfect order, as the supreme and typical summing up of all ordinances of outward administration[1]. 'Will you give your faithful diligence always so to minister the Doctrine and Sacraments, and the Discipline of Christ, as the Lord hath commanded, and as this Church and Realm hath received the same?' . . . 'Receive the Holy Ghost [for the office and work of a Priest in the Church of God, now committed unto thee by the imposition of our hands[2]]. Whose sins thou dost forgive, they are forgiven; and whose sins thou dost retain, they are retained. And be thou a faithful dispenser of the Word of God and of His holy Sacraments.' . . . 'Take thou authority to preach the Word of God, and to minister the Holy Sacraments.' . . .

Now I do not feel in the least bound to maintain that in every patricular the Anglican Ordinal represents the highest perfectness of proportion or expression that is ideally possible. I do not feel in the least concerned to deny that some traces of the great influence of the Protestant reaction are discernible in it too; that the excision, for instance, of the formal delivery of the chalice and paten and of all direct mention of Eucharistic 'offerings,' or 'sacrifice'

---

[1] Compare the *proportion* of these thoughts in *Apost. Constitutions*, VIII. xvi.: δὸς δύναμιν πρὸς τὸ κοπιᾶν αὐτοὺς λόγῳ καὶ ἔργῳ εἰς οἰκοδομὴν τοῦ λαοῦ σου . . . τοῦ ἀντιλαμβάνεσθαι καὶ κυβερνᾶν τὸν λαόν σου . . . καὶ νῦν Κύριε παράσχου ἀνελλιπὲς τηρῶν ἐν ἡμῖν τὸ πνεῦμα τῆς χάριτός σου· ὅπως πλησθεὶς ἐνεργημάτων ἰατικῶν καὶ λόγου διδακτικοῦ, ἐν πραότητι παιδεύῃ σου τὸν λαὸν καὶ δουλεύῃ σοι εἰλικρινῶς ἐν καθαρᾷ διανοίᾳ καὶ ψυχῇ θελούσῃ, καὶ τὰς ὑπὲρ τοῦ λαοῦ ἱερουργίας ἀμώμους ἐκτελῇ διὰ τοῦ Χριστοῦ σου. . . .

[2] I have put these words in brackets in recognition of the historical fact that they were inserted in this place in 1662. In spite, however, of the emphasis which has often been laid on this fact, and which the Pope has been sufficiently misinformed to re-emphasize, I must confidently assert, not only that the addition of the words made no difference at all to the sense, but that no one who should read the Ordinal of 1552 as a whole, with a judicial mind and with adequate historical knowledge, could doubt for one moment—either what was the character of the office for which the ordinands were bidden 'Receive the Holy Ghost,' or by what name the office, which the Ordinal intended, was, in the Ordinal, uniformly called.

That Canon Estcourt, twenty-five years ago, should seriously have argued that the inserted words themselves clinch finally the unsacramental intention of the Anglican Ordinal, is a paradox perhaps worth remembering.

is a result of reaction going further than really was necessary; and that the restoration of a somewhat richer and more generous fullness in some of these respects would enhance the beauty of the Anglican service alike from the historical and from the theological points of view[1]. But, after all, these are trifling matters comparatively, questions only of a little more or less of richness and beauty of expression. On the other hand, I cannot withhold my conviction that the Anglican Ordinal has gained something far more vital and substantial than anything that it can be supposed to have lost; it has restored, in the main, what had been gradually lost in the accretions of the mediaeval Ordinal, the true *proportion* between the outward and the inward; it has restored the essential relation and harmony between Eucharistic leadership—with all that it involves—and a right conception in Christ's Church of the meaning of ministerial priesthood as a whole. If upon some of these points its expression is less rich and full (for obvious historical causes) than one might desire, I do not undervalue the loss which necessarily accrues from this—as from every other—incompleteness of statement, but putting this loss even at its highest, I cannot admit that its deflection from the most perfect proportions of truth is so much as seriously comparable, either in itself or in its unfortunateness of effect, with that disproportion of the unreformed office from which it none the less rightly reacted, even if its reaction may be thought to be in some details unnecessarily complete. Thoughtful men will not be greatly attracted by any claim, from whatever side, to absolute perfection of achievement; but if, on the one side, the retention of the old word 'offer,' and a richer emphasis, in symbol or otherwise, upon the large significance which belongs to Eucharistic offering, *if fully and spiritually*

---

[1] Of course this was not a really ancient rite (cp. above, p 227, and not as the Reformers well knew. Yet it was venerable and, when rescued from its disproportion, valuably expressive. The omission of it, in 1552, is real matter for regret.

understood, might have constituted a somewhat more generous expression of a great truth, which is far from being really suppressed or disowned; on the other side, I must hold that everything which goes to emphasize very pre-eminently in 'priesthood,' still more to define 'priesthood' altogether by, the power 'offerre sacrificium' or 'offerre placabiles hostias pro vivis ac defunctis'—does tend directly, in spite of all denials, to separate unduly between the outward and the inward of priesthood, as well as (perhaps) between the priestly organ of the Body, and the Body of whose priestliness he is the organ, just as every assertion that the Eucharistic celebration on earth is a 'sacrificium *proprium*' and '*vere propitiatorium*,' both 'pro fidelium vivorum peccatis, poenis, satisfactionibus et aliis necessitatibus,' and 'pro defunctis in Christo nondum ad plenum ⸺ ⸺gatis' does, in spite of all disclaimers, directly tend to an undue separation between the ever-repeated sacrifice of the Eucharist and the one sacrifice of Jesus Christ.

Now upon the general position which the last few pages have been trying to set forth I rather anticipate one or two comments, which it may be worth while to consider. It may be urged then that whilst it is perfectly true that the pastoral disposition is needed in Christian ministers as well as the priestly character, and whilst it is obvious enough that the Anglican Ordinal dwells with quite a new emphasis upon pastoral ideals, it is nevertheless a mistake to speak of the pastoral aspect as an aspect of *priesthood*, or to suppose that the fullest or most admirable emphasis upon it would compensate for any defect in the priestly character, or constitute an answer of any relevancy to those who doubt whether Anglican ministers are, after all, really 'priests' Thus it may be urged that the 'priest' language means one thing, and the 'pastoral' another, that both are good, both necessary; but that it is a confusion, in thought, of things which language has historically kept distinct, to try to read the one into the other, or make them in any direct sense the same thing.

Now there is a certain truth in this plea. It is true that within the office of the Christian minister we do, both in language and thought, make a certain distinction between the 'priestly' and the 'pastoral' aspects. It is impossible not to speak in detail—as I have repeatedly spoken above—of the 'priestly' or 'sacerdotal' in particular reference to certain specific functions. It is also true that no amount of emphasis upon the 'pastoral' character would confer 'priesthood,' if all those things were effectually set aside which have reference to the sacramental presentation of the Blood of the Atonement. It is certainly possible so to distinguish between priesthood and pastorate, as in continuing the second to deny and to drop the first. Nor, if the question rises whether this has been done or no, in any particular case, does it constitute any answer to argue that the 'priest' associations have *ipso facto* been maintained—or the loss of them compensated—by the extra emphasis upon pastoral care, unless the pastoral care has itself a very particular significance and method The loss, or the maintenance, of that whole range of administrative prerogative which St. Clement would have summed up as the 'offering of the gifts' depends upon the abandonment, or the reverent conferring and use, of the Christian sacraments.

But though, in this sense, I admit that a particular aspect of the Christian ministry is that to which the peculiar associations of the words 'priest' and 'priesthood' specially belong, and though I claim that the ancient Church in so for as she called her ministers 'sacerdotes' or ἱερεῖς, and the Church of England in her refusal to abandon the title 'priests' (by that time identified verbally with sacerdotes and ἱερεῖς), did emphasize the truth that all the true associations of ancient priesthood had so far, through the High Priesthood of Jesus Christ, a direct place within the functions of Christian ministers, that the new office might rightly inherit the old name, and *to deny the admissibleness of the old name would involve a misunderstanding of the new office;* yet it is to be remembered that it was only very gradually, and at a comparatively late time, that the sacerdotal title became the exclusive title of the second order of the ministry, and that, as it became so, there was, or ought to have been, a corresponding widening of the signification of the word. In the *Apostolical Constitutions*, in the 'Statuta antiqua' (Carthag. iv.), in the *Missale Francorum*, the Pontificals of Egbert and Dunstan, in the more ancient portions of the Sarum, and even (it may be added) of the modern Roman *Celebratio Ordinum*, the most natural and spontaneous title is 'presbyter.' If 'sacerdos' is also *true* sacerdos is certainly by no means the one and only title of the office Now so long as 'priesthood' is *a* title of the 'presbyterate,' the connotation of the word may well be limited to that particular aspect which its own associations specially suggest; if the word 'priesthood' tends towards superseding 'presbyterate,' it does so because it is felt that there is a spiritual sense in which the 'priest' associations may not uninstructively constitute the dominant element in the thought of the office; but from the moment when it becomes, simply and exclusively, the one formal and official title of the office as such, it is necessary to insist that the word which designates the office must no longer be confined to any one—however dominant—aspect of the office, but must connote and contain whatever the office contains and means as a whole. Even on these grounds then it is only with considerable reserve that we can admit that the word 'priest' now has one meaning and 'pastor' another. It is, unhappily, true if the two aspects of one thing are wrongfully divorced. But while they remain what they ought to be, two aspects of one thing, it is, even as matter of words, not properly true. When the Church is clear that from the Apostles' times there have been 'these Orders of Ministers, Bishops, *Priests*, and Deacons'—or when she has constituted any one among us a *Priest* in the Church of God'—what has she done? or what is the meaning of this title in her mouth? I must answer that the title of the whole office means the whole office, not a part of it. If priesthood were still a thing distinct from pastorate, then priesthood and pastorate ought to be separately conferred. But the Church ordains men to be 'priests' —not 'priests,' and 'pastors', even whilst, in ordaining them 'priests,' she stamps with so solemn an emphasis the 'pastoral' aspect of their 'priesthood[1].'

But this contention, though true, is not the whole truth. If the 'priest' associations become prominent in the title of the 'presbyteral' office, and to deny that 'presbyter' does legitimately mean 'priest' would be to deny some fundamental truths in the Christian faith; yet the 'presbyteral' office must not so be explained as to mean nothing but the distinctively 'priest' associations,—not only because, for purposes of practical use and need, we require to have included in the ministry all the things which belong to pastoral care; but also because, as has been pleaded above, the conception even of the 'priest' functions themselves will become attenuated and externalized if they be not the outward of an inward; which inward will never have its complete development without involving the pastoral character. I do not say that the priest who merely celebrates is not a priest validly ordained   I am not discussing the question of 'validity.' But I do say that he who finds the whole meaning of his priesthood in the act of celebrating does not at all understand what Christian priesthood truly means; and that if any Church should teach that Christian priesthood simply meant this, she would teach the meaning of priesthood definitely amiss. The 'inwardness' of a true priesthood requires the dedication of the inner life to Godward[2]; of which again a necessary aspect or corollary is dedication of self on behalf of 'the others'

---

[1] In connexion with this thought, the *verbal* identity of 'priest' with 'presbyter' has its own significant suggestiveness.

[2] Cp. Rom. xii. 1, 2.

—interceding for them, thinking for them, living for them, enduring for them. It is not that this 'for other-ness' will always take the same form. Plainly the priest who is permanently invalided may illustrate perfectly the priestly spirit in his intercession for his brethren, which is perhaps the directest correlative of his right to present before them their ceremonial 'offering.' It may be in preaching, or in writing; in counselling or teaching; in organizing or visiting; or just in maintaining an integrity, and, in love, suffering for doing so; in any average parochial sphere it will probably be in some measure of every one of these things · but however opportunities and conditions may differ, some correlative measure there must be of the utterance of that inwardness which is as the breath of every priesthood that is not self-condemned as merely official and formal; and which, however indirectly, is itself already an illustration of the meaning of pastoral love. I do not think it is anything like a fanciful analogy to say that the perfect outward and the perfect inward, the ideal pastorate and ideal priesthood, are blended together as one indivisible reality in the words of St John, ch. x., 'I am the good shepherd: the good shepherd layeth down his life for the sheep'

But there is another form which criticism may probably take. It may be admitted that external functions in themselves are merely formal and official things; that they are, in God's sight, unreal and only condemnatory, except there be in the officiants an inward corresponding to the outward; and that the inward, in priesthood, does contain much of the things which have been said. Nevertheless it may be urged that when we are engaged in distinguishing an office from not an office, we must needs differentiate function from non-function in respect of its outward performances. It is a question of doing or not doing, of having a right or not having a right to do, certain things. The things done, as such, are external things of course. But the defining distinction cannot but be made in terms of such things as these. Thus if you distinguish the office of a lieutenant from that of a midshipman, you do it in terms of what a lieutenant does, or has to do, or may do—and a midshipman does, or may, not: you say nothing about the qualities which go to make him do it well. In either case the difference is assumed to exist between a good, or a bad, midshipman or lieutenant: and the nature of the difference between good and bad will in either case be approximately the same. But when you are defining the difference between office and office, you are dealing exclusively with external duty of action. So, whatever may be the inward truth of priestliness, it is both right and inevitable that its distinguishing definition should be in the sphere of ceremonial function, and that its formal conferring should be just a conferring of official prerogative.

There are two points in this statement; and it may be useful to comment upon each. There is the question of the terms in which the office ought to be, or can be, defined; and there is the question as to the ceremonial method and interpretative language with which it is appropriate that the office shall be conferred First as to definition. The immediate reply, then, will be that the contention described is only perfectly true in respect of pursuits (if any such there be) which are wholly outside the personal character. It may be true, approximately, of different sets of mechanics, doing different works in detail, in a huge factory But the more complex and responsible the work, and the more inclusive it is of the whole life and mind and character, the less can it be defined by its outward operations How far the statement is true of midshipmen or lieutenants I leave it to others to say. But I have no doubt at all that the higher you go in the grade of responsible office, the less is it true. It is less true of a captain than of a lieutenant; less true of a commander-in-chief than of the colonel of a regiment. When you turn from things like these to what is no longer an office primarily of external duty, though involving vital or spiritual qualities; but an office essentially spiritual, though expressing itself in certain external duties; there is hardly any truth left in the contention at all. The character is no longer a moral condition valuable because it leads up to the right discharge of practical duties: but the duties—though in the practical sphere they are duties, and have to be done—can only be done, even as duties, aright, in so far as they produce and express the right moral character. To condescend to define such an office as this simply by the ceremonial functions which are involved in it, is not only to depose from their proper relative position the qualifications and duties which are *not* ceremonial, but is to misinterpret the true meaning and character even of the ceremonial functions themselves.

Indeed I must maintain that no inconsiderable fallacy underlies—and has historically throughout these controversies underlain—this assumption that the definition of an office is to be found in the methods, even in the most characteristic and highest methods, of its exercise. Take for instance the case of a great viceroyalty. What is the truth of the office which a viceroy receives? If he thinks and plans for the people, and tries to direct and arrange, by upright administration and wise legislative provision at home, by prudent direction of policy abroad, there is no element in this general responsibility, forethought, fatherly anxiety and care, which is not also shared, though in somewhat different degree, by a host of others, councillors, and lieutenant-governors, judges, and commissioners—his subordinates in a vast variety of spheres and degrees. It is at least conceivable that the only things which could be found which the viceroy could do, and no one but the viceroy, might be such things as signing death-warrants or free pardons, subscribing assent to statutes, or heading the most august ceremonials of state. Moreover, I should certainly not deny that the power of life and death, represented by the prerogative of signing death-warrants or free pardons, might—if largely enough understood—be said, with considerable truth, itself to symbolize and represent the whole range of sovereign responsibility. But would any one dream of really defining the sovereignty as the prerogative of signing pardons, or of subscribing statutes, or anything whatever of the kind? Is it not manifest that even though things like these might conceivably be the only functions which externally differentiated the office—in the sense that these, and these alone, could be performed by no one but by the viceroy himself, yet these never could describe what his entrusted sovereignty really meant? And on the other hand, is it not manifest also that the real nature of the meaning of his mighty office could only be described, with any approach to adequacy, by emphasizing responsibilities and duties which were *not* strictly distinctive of the personal sovereignty, because they were shared with the viceroy (of course in very varying degrees) by every one of those who, under him, were responsible for the welfare of the country? It is, after all, the general responsibility, the undefinable width of all inclusive anxiety and care—it is this, which may indeed be symbolized here and there by certain specific prerogatives of royalty, but which no specific prerogatives come near to expressing or defining —in which the truth of the viceroy's great commission lies.

So in the case of St. Paul, 'that which presseth upon me daily, anxiety for all the Churches,' approaches far more nearly to a definition of what he understood by apostolic ministry, than could any amount of enlargement either upon preaching, or celebrating, or anything else whatever in the way of specific ministerial prerogative or duty. Whatever difficulty, then, there may be in framing, in brief form, an adequate definition of what ministerial priesthood means in Christ's Church; I must submit that the true idea of its essence is to be found, not so much by picking out and exclusively emphasizing the things which Christian lay priesthood may not do, as rather by discernment of the quickened intensity and more representative and responsible completeness which characterizes ministry in qualities that are *not* altogether distinctive of ministry, but belong, or ought to belong, alike to the body as a whole, and, in a measure, to every individual member of the body. This concentrated demand on the personal character and activity is indeed accompanied, nay (if all be understood) is consummated, in the priestly office, by distinctive outwardnesses of sublime function and prerogative; yet even these rather illustrate, and give a crowning expression to, the true essential meaning of the office, than constitute its essence in themselves.

It is indeed one of the things which the Church has to be perpetually on her guard against, this inveterate tendency of the natural mind to measure a spiritual and living whole by its own objective forms of outward expression; to define, for example, Christian life by its moral achievements, or Christian priesthood by the acts it is authorized to perform. It is so much easier to be mechanical than to be spiritual! The externalizing and stereotyping of the conception of priesthood—that large and living reality—by making it simply identical with authority to perform certain ceremonies, when the ceremonial authority itself should be but as the necessary utterance of that which is the essential reality of priesthood, is a danger which is never far away, a danger which it is easier to discern than wholly to avoid; a danger which too much of Western Christendom appears to have forgotten even to discern. Has it not run too often, almost greedily, into the external and mechanical definition, as if it were the adequate exposition of the truth? It is so much easier to the natural mind to make the outward the simple measure of the inward, than to keep it in its place as an outward which is only ultimately real because it is *the outward of an inward* reality!

If considerations like these are of weight in reference even to a definition of what ministerial priesthood means, they will assert themselves still more emphatically when the question is not of a scientific summary of the meaning of the office, but of the structure and contents of the special service in which it is to be conferred. The service of ordination to priesthood as a whole will, after all, constitute the fullest teaching of the Church as to what she means by priesthood Of the Ordinal service then I must submit that it is most emphatically true that it ought to reflect and express this larger fullness of the real truth of priesthood. Priesthood is a relation—to God, to the Church, to the world—which touches and consecrates the whole range of the personal life, so that its own technicalities, however precious, its own executive possibilities, however august, either must be understood to include the essential pastoral relation and responsibility to the 'Spouse and Body of Christ,' or else will fall far short of that deep and vital and mysterious reality into which those have really been admitted who are sent out as 'priests' in the Church of God. But if priesthood is essentially this, then it is just the full expression of the text and ceremonial of the Ordinal which should make this width of interpretation transparently obvious, in its full proportion, and with ringing clearness, and should impress it with the profoundest solemnity upon those who, approaching priesthood, yet remaining most human, are in any case naturally liable—in proportion as they grasp the unearthly greatness of their office at all—to the peril of conceiving of it too mechanically. In the text of the Ordinal, if anywhere, it should be plain, that to the ideal meaning of the Church the outward of administrative priestliness must be in perfect correspondence with the inward; that objective and subjective are but conterminous aspects of one living reality; that true priesthood is pastorate, and true pastorate based on priestliness; that 'cure of souls' is itself so really a sacrifice, and intercession an Eucharist, that the very ministry of the Eucharistic sacrifice fails to understand itself, if it find no corresponding utterance, in the secret chamber at least, as divine love and 'cure' of souls.

NOTE, p. 225

BUT over this particular phrase (as has been truly pointed out to me) there hangs an ambiguity historically. In the codex Rotomagensis (Morinus, pt. ii. p. 230) it is the presbyter who is 'transformed' into love. The words run 'per obsequium plebis tuae corpore et sanguine filii tui immaculata benedictione transformetur ad inviolabilem caritatem et in virum perfectum,' &c. In another text 'ex manuscripto codice bibliothecae S. Germani in suburbio Parisiensi' (Morinus, pt. ii. p. 243) they are 'per obsequium plebis tuae vel corpus corpore et sanguine filii tui immaculata benedictione transformentur et inviolabilem caritatem, et in virum perfectum,' &c. This last is unconstruable as it stands, but its mixed condition is suggestive of a gradual transformation of a sentiment like that of Rotom. into one like that of the Missale Francorum. No doubt the Missale Francorum is itself the most ancient of the three. It looks rather as though the later documents had in this case preserved traces of an earlier version of the words, a version which (it can hardly be denied) gives in the immediate context a much smoother and more natural continuity of meaning. But whatever the original text may be thought to have been, there is no supposition so improbable as that the present text of the Missale Francorum could have been afterwards corrupted into that of the other documents referred to.

NOTE, p. 228.

IN the exhortation to candidates for priesthood in the *Roman Pontifical* (referred to in note 1 to p. 223) there are one or two phrases of a more pastoral character; 'Agnoscite quod agitis, Imitamini quod tractatis; quatenus mortis Dominicae mysterium celebrantes, mortificare membra vestra a vitiis et concupiscentiis omnibus procuretis. Sit doctrina vestra spiritualis medicina populo Dei. Sit odor vitae vestrae delectamentum Ecclesiae Christi; ut praedicatione atque exemplo aedificetis domum, id est, familiam Dei'... But these are not part of what is before the Reformers; nor indeed do they go very far.

APPENDIX

UPON THE RECENT ROMAN CONTROVERSY AS TO THE VALIDITY OF ANGLICAN ORDERS

It will have been observed that the discussion just concluded has not been a discussion as to what does, or what does not, constitute a valid transmission of Holy Orders. The fact is that the discussion has been directed to a deeper issue than that of validity. Those who discuss the validity of what purports to confer 'priesthood,' must assume, as the basis of their discussion, an understanding of what priesthood in itself means. Confusion about this will make a necessary confusion in the discussion of validity. But, fundamental as it is to the discussion of validity, a real inquiry into the nature and true scope of priesthood is itself of deeper and more significant interest than any question of validity only.

It is, however, perfectly true that for certain purposes it is necessary to take the outward apart from its inwardness, the mere shell apart from all that gives it meaning. If the question is whether this man is, or is not, viceroy; we do not for the purpose begin to ask what viceroyalty means, we ask rather whether the instruments of his appointment are in order. If the question is whether this 'bishop' is *capable* of ordaining, or that 'priest' of celebrating; it is not immediately to the point to say whether the one has any rationally Christian conception of what his episcopate, or the other of what his priesthood, means. The one may be materialistic, to the point of paganism; the other may be rationalistic, to the point of atheism. Neither may realize, even remotely, the true nature of his office; neither may be able, in the least degree, to exemplify its mystery or its dignity to others. And neither — it is possible — may be recognized, in the day of the revelation of Christ, as Christian minister or as Christian believer, at all. And yet for the technical purposes of external order, the sole question will be, 'were they duly ordained?' Though the pagan bishop or the atheistic priest is an outrage to the idea of priesthood or bishopric; though it is worse than useless to look to them in order to see what priesthood or bishopric means; yet in the merely outward order of things it has certainly to be admitted that, if untried and undeposed, they are 'bishop' and 'priest.' This is part of the essentially imperfect identity, in human things, between the outward and the inward —between discernible expression and the meaning which it only exists to express. It belongs to the failure of the ordinance, not to what it means. It does not touch us in the least, so long as we are trying to interpret the true meaning of priesthood. We dare not frame our exposition of priesthood with a view to including those whose priesthood is the denial of what priesthood means. If, as mere symbols and channels, we cannot deny that they have been accredited, and can be made use of; yet, so far from expressing or interpreting, they only belie, and are themselves belied by, all that their own office signifies.

On the other hand, if the ordained priest may be a priest without exemplifying any one of the graces or meanings of priesthood, it is no less true that even the most splendid exemplification, in mind and life, of the things which priesthood ought to mean, would not of itself confer on any man the right to stand before the congregation to Godward in the ministry of priesthood.

There is then an outward, unhappily distinguishable, as mere outward, from all the inner realities which it ought to symbolize. Perhaps it may serve to clear the position taken in these pages, to formulate at once the requirements which seem, in the outward and technical sphere, to be necessary for a valid ordination.

They may be stated as four. First, the ordination must be conferred by those who themselves have received authority to confer it. This, as a principle continuous from the beginning, is what is called Apostolical succession. There seems to be absolutely no warrant whatever, in the New Testament or in the history of the Church, for supposing that Christian ministers can either commission themselves, or be commissioned by any who have not themselves been commissioned to commission. That a layman or a gathering of laymen could consecrate a bishop, is an idea which would find no warrant whatever in the theology or history of the Church. Now those who are commissioned to commission are what we call bishops. It may be admitted that this is a point which it would have been difficult to lay down with confidence from the very earliest evidence of all. That succession from Apostles was a cardinal principle is quite clear from the epistle of Clement of Rome. It may not be quite clear at first through whom the succession was transmitted. But even from Apostolic and sub-apostolic times there are data enough to make it exceedingly improbable that the transmission would have been by presbyters only, apart from the apostolic or episcopal background. And when such data are interpreted in the light of the universal assumption of every subsequent century, we may lay it down, quite as a certain principle of the historical Church, that a valid ordination must be performed by those who as 'bishops'—or, if any one prefers it, as 'episcopal presbyters'—have received a commission, from those duly commissioned before them, which includes the apostolic faculty of commissioning ministers.

Secondly, the ordaining bishop must have the intention to ordain. He may be a bad theologian—full of misconceptions about the doctrines of the Church and the ministry; but at least he must be dealing dutifully according to his conceptions (or misconceptions), that is, he must have the purpose of exercising a power committed to him of constituting men as ministers (bishops, priests, or deacons) in the Church of Christ. In the absence of unmistakable evidence to the contrary, the fact that he acts in the matter just as others, with serious intention, would and do act, is sufficient presumption that he means as they mean. This, as a general principle, is intelligible enough. Cases can probably be imagined, in which there might be a reasonable ambiguity on this head. But such cases have probably rarely, if ever, occurred.

Thirdly, we may ask to be assured that the bishop has signified his purpose by solemnly laying his hands on the head of the ordinand. There is no controversy about the laying on of hands, and I do not desire to suggest one. Whether, however, it is as literally indispensable as e. g. the divinely commanded elements of water in Baptism, or bread and wine in Holy Communion, is a point about which we may hesitate to speak with confidence. Laying on of hands has been practically the universal method in the Church of Christ; and no one who affects to ordain is likely to dispense with it. But it hardly seems necessary for the present purpose so dogmatically to assert its indispensableness (if all that it expresses were in other ways made unmistakably manifest) as to decide, quite absolutely, that a bishop consecrated according to the description of the eighth book of the *Apostolical Constitutions* (supposing the words to be taken *ad pedem literae*) could not possibly be held to be consecrated at all.

And fourthly, this manual blessing must be an act of prayer. This means, I presume, that the ordaining bishop, if on the one hand he makes use of a ceremonial action, must obviously, upon the other, refer his ceremonial action to God. It is this Godward appeal which gives the significance to what would otherwise be a mere outward act. Whatever mode or utterance of prayerfulness has the effect of thus interpreting his act, may be said to meet the literal requirement. Of course the prayer must not be wholly irrelevant to the act, nor out of all discoverable relation with the act. But whatever it be, so that it has the intelligible character of interpreting before God and man the meaning of the act, and thereby uplifting it as an aspiration to God, it is such prayer as can make the otherwise merely physical act of laying a hand upon a head into the symbolical act of blessing for ministry.

Where these four things are, there is the technical, outward, verifiable requirement. Where any of these four things can be shown to be absent, there the material outward, which men who fear God dare not dispense with, is lacking.

A discussion which turns upon the evidence, in particular cases, as to things so far material and external as these, can hardly be a very elevating discussion. Those who have to conduct it need to be always on their guard against confounding the real meaning of 'priesthood'—which has a material aspect and is (in a sense) materially conveyed—with the things which thus represent it on the material side.

Still there are times when these are the things which have to be discussed. And there are occasions, no doubt, in which there is a perfectly genuine ambiguity about one or more of them. In any case of such ambiguity we must be content to lay aside for the moment all deeper thoughts as to the significance of priesthood, and address ourselves to the points (however material or narrow) which are really in doubt.

But in truth in the so-called controversy about Anglican Orders there is not really any such ambiguity at all. It is no question really of evidential details The question, such as it is, is theoretical or theological. It turns upon such matters as e. g. (1) the precise content of the Roman definition of priesthood; (2) the right of Rome to provide such a definition authoritatively; (3) the logic of the Roman inference, that those who do not accept her definition or acknowledge her authority to define (whatever ministry they may have, or by whatever title they may call it), cannot at all events have the priesthood *which she means* Often, of these three things the first and the second being assumed as postulates, the discussion is found to move only within the narrow compass of the third. For underlying all argument, the assumption is apt to be made obvious, that the words 'Rome,' 'the Catholic Church,' 'the Church of Jesus Christ,' are synonymous and conterminous words.

Now if this assumption be justified, the question of the validity of Anglican Orders has no importance or meaning whatever in itself. It comes in only at the moment when Anglicans give in their surrender to Rome; and then only as determining the precise manner in which she is to receive their penitence. For, upon the assumption, until they make their submission, all Anglicans are simply outside of the Church of Christ.

On the other hand, if the assumption be not justified, the Roman arguments about Anglican Orders are, for the most part, emptied at once, not of cogency only, but of meaning.

Thus it is that the recent discussion about Anglican Orders, though in some ways, as a phenomenon, of remarkable interest, was nevertheless to Anglicans, for the most part, a singularly unreal dialectical exercise. The real issue was never so much as raised at all. Perhaps it was hardly possible that it should be. The question discussed was rather, *on the assumption that Anglicanism was of course contumacious and heretical*, whether that heresy and contumacy amounted to just so much, or to just not so much, as to make transmission of orders impossible.

Now whatever motive any Anglican may conceivably have for consenting under circumstances to argue upon such a hypothesis, it is plain that the character of the hypothesis must prevent the argument, to an Anglican who believes his position to be right and true, from having in it any touch of vital reality at all.

If a question were really to be raised between Romans and Anglicans on the subject of priesthood; if there were to be a serious scrutiny as to what exactly Romans mean by the word, and what Anglicans mean; what is the structure and rationale of the Roman Ordinal, and what of the Anglican; if both were to be impartially tried and compared, not only with each other, but with the true history and theological significance of 'presbyterate' from the time of the Apostles onwards, no one could possibly be more ready than we may claim to be to enter upon such an inquiry; nor should we be able to entertain a shadow of doubt as to the character of the result.

But if the question be merely whether the Anglicans do, or do not, intend exactly what the Romans intend, and do exactly what the Romans do, the discussion is a mockery upon the face of it. It is closed before it is begun. There is literally nothing whatever to discuss. It is demonstrably plain, upon the very surface of the history, that we hold that their meaning and practice had fallen out of due and balanced proportion, that into a meaning and practice once expressive of truth they had imported exaggerated interpretations and symbolisms, that the exaggerations, more or less seriously, distorted truth, and therefore that we, correcting their disproportions, emphatically did *not* mean *exactly* what they meant; and that the detail of what they did in practice we varied, not a little, on the express ground that it had lost by degrees, and needed to have restored to it, the balance and harmony of truth. That Anglicans are not in practice, because they are not in doctrine, precisely and identically Roman, the very existence of the Prayer-book is incontrovertible proof.

What is a priest? why is the Church priestly? wherein or how is Christian ministry a priesthood? We hold that it is part of the inveterate tendency, particularly of the Western mind, to treat these questions, and to answer them, in too cut-and-dried, too external and too material a fashion, to treat them so as to deprive them of their mystery, so that their outward and material meaning no longer represents, no longer as it were shades off into, a significance spiritual and infinite; but as if their whole meaning not only were easily, exclusively, and exactly intelligible, but were understood and exhausted in the sphere of outward and visible distinctions. Answers sharp, and crude, and positive, and logical, are, we feel, *ipso facto*, as perilous as they are fascinating to the mind that is spiritually untrained. 'Oh! it is exceedingly simple. Ministry is priesthood just because it offers sacrifice, the Eucharist is a sacrifice, and he who may celebrate the Eucharist has the power of sacrificing. This is what to be a priest means.' However profoundly such words may be representative—as indeed they are—of truth, who does not feel the risk that there always is to spiritually in the whole region to which such off-hand answers properly belong? It argues a certain intellectual—and specially a spiritually intellectual—defect, to be too easily satisfied with clear-cut externalities like these. That this defect was conspicuous, and that it carried with it a fatal train of externalizing and materializing consequences *de facto* in the sixteenth century, is indeed, as matter of history, not open to question.

Whatever peril there was of this kind was enhanced by the great complication and consequent ambiguity of mediaeval Ordinals, and by that which was a further result of ambiguity, the discussions technical and pedantic, and the over-defined definitions, as to the 'materia' and 'forma' of each several Ordinal service. No doubt 'materia' and 'forma' are quite legitimate, and up to a certain point illuminative, words. There must be an inward and an outward, a ceremonial and an interpretation of the ceremonial; but a discussion of these things will have always to be on its guard against over-pressure of sharp logical distinctions; the words are not on the whole recommended by the associations of their own history, and should be used for argumentative purposes only with considerable care. It may be doubted whether, even now, the minds of theologians have shaken themselves quite free from the assumption that the 'forma' must mean one particular sentence, or one particular prayer, *in detachment from* the total service of dedication and prayer of which it forms a part, whilst even as to the 'materia' it is possible that the usual assumptions may be made a little too absolutely [1].

[1] I am not prepared to concede that the eighth book of the *Apostolical*

Now against all these forms of rigidity and over-pressure and over-definition the Reformation was intended to be, and was, an unmistakable protest. Priesthood, to the conception of the 'Reformed,' however truly it might mean Eucharistic offering, was no longer defined exclusively by Eucharistic offering Eucharistic offering, however essentially it might be both supernatural and sacrificial, was expressly not defined by the crude mediaeval theory of 'transubstantiation,' and was, to say the least, less exclusively regarded in its sacrificial character; whilst the conception of it as 'sacrifice' was emphatically not tied up to such defining, but highly debatable, words as 'proprium,' 'vere propitiatorium,' 'pro vivis et defunctis nondum ad plenum purgatis.' On all these points the Anglican Reformation involved a real loosening of bonds which had been by degrees too tightly tied and knotted up, the bonds of over-exact, and therefore narrow, and therefore inexact, definition.

Now if any one is willing to argue with us squarely on points like these, and to examine whether our attitude in respect of them —with the criticism which of course it involves upon mediaeval theology — is itself theologically right or wrong, no doubt Anglicans would be more than ready to join issue with him. But it is obvious that for the purposes of such an argument the appeal to Scripture, to Catholic (not Roman) theology, and to Church history must be free and untrammelled. To propose to conduct such an argument on the basis of the assumption that every practice which had been sanctioned, and every explanation that had been offered by the Roman Church, ancient, mediaeval or modern, was not only absolutely right, but was itself the ultimate standard and norm of right and truth in all others, would be obviously absurd. It would be at least as reasonable to try and argue in defence of infant baptism against Baptists, on the avowed hypothesis that everything they have ever said or done in protest against baptism of infants is itself, alike in principle and in detail, the infallible standard of truth.

It would not be true to say that this false hypothesis has been intentionally assumed for controversial purposes by every writer

Constitutions intends that a bishop should be consecrated without literal laying-on of hands. But it is undeniable that there is something to be said even for this See the Rev T. A. Lacey's paper in *Revue Anglo-Romaine*, Jan. 4, 1896, vol. i. p 193.

APPENDIX

on the Roman side. But it is extraordinarily difficult for a Roman controversialist, with the most liberal intentions, to get free from it. And whatever justice may be done to individual efforts of the kind, it must still be said that the controversy, as a whole, exhibits in the first place what we must regard as pathetic efforts, and in the second place a no less pathetic failure, to argue the case on its merits, apart from these incapacitating presuppositions. This failure, it need hardly be said, has been clinched, and—so far as that can be done—made final for all time by the authority of the Bull 'Apostolicae curae.' The hypothesis of their own infallible correctness at every point has defeated, and for the present at least will continue to defeat, all attempt at argument. It may here and there be disguised. But it remains in fact as the wall of adamant which really fences round the Roman position from all intrusive approach of intelligent reasoning.

There are two forms in which this hypothesis appears in the sphere of controversy upon our subject. The first is briefly represented by the word 'schism.' It may be stated nakedly thus. The Papal obedience *is* the Catholic Church. Anglicans have repudiated the Papal obedience. Therefore Anglicans have repudiated, and are contumaciously outside of, 'the Church.' There is therefore no need to examine particularly what they hold, or why they hold it. Whatever they hold, even if it resembles the truth, cannot *be* the truth, until they submit to the Church which enshrines the truth.

The other is represented by the word 'intention.' In its barest form it might perhaps stand thus. It is of no use to consider the 'materia' or the 'forma' of the Anglican Ordinal. Even if both were adequate in themselves, they would not confer Orders unless administered with the right intention. The necessary intention is the intention of the Catholic (i. e. of the Roman) Church. That Anglicans have not precisely the Roman intention may be probably shown without difficulty, at least on examination of their Ordinal services and the service of Holy Communion. But *even if it could not be shown* from any of these, the presumption of right intention can only be pleaded by those who at least *do* what the Catholic (i. e. the Roman) Church does. Now Anglicans do not follow, they have deliberately altered, the Roman Pontifical. Such a *de facto* alteration of the Roman Pontifical—whatever might be the intrinsic value of their substituted Ordinal—is of itself palpable and final proof, not only of an imperfect intention to do and mean, but of a positive negation, an ostentatious intention not to mean, nor even to do, what the Church does. The fact therefore that they have separated themselves from Rome is proof demonstrative of an 'intention' which would invalidate the most perfect form of Ordinal in the world.

Once concede that 'Roman' and 'Catholic' are convertible terms, once assume that whatever Romans mean by Priest, Sacrifice, Sacrament, is the true norm and standard of the meaning of the words, and these consequences, sweeping as they are, may logically follow. But those who are clear that Rome has pushed these true words far out of their proportion; and who can only regard with amazement the audacity of her claim to be the whole and only Church of Christ, are not greatly moved by pretensions which rest upon no basis at all. They are but part of the audacity of an audacious major premiss; which major premiss, fairly challenged, dissolves like a tyrannous dream in the morning-waking, and leaves the fair world once more in the fresh air and open freedom of nature, and reason, and faith,—of man undistorted and of God unbelied

For some time past the stress of Roman attacks has been directed not so much against the inherent adequacy of the Anglican Ordinal, as against the sufficiency of Anglican 'intention'; and only in the second instance against the Ordinal, as supposed to bear witness to, or to become defective because it is vitiated by, this defect of 'intention.' Thus the volume published by Canon Estcourt[1], nearly twenty-five years ago, may be said to treat as impossible the view of the *intrinsic* inadequacy of the Anglican forms. For him this impossibility is clinched by the decision pronounced in respect of Abyssinian Orders in 1704. He therefore (besides suggesting as many historical 'doubts' as could be raised, probably or improbably, about Bishop Barlow's consecration, about Archbishop Parker's consecration, &c.), builds an elaborate structure of argument, out of manifold details, with a view to showing (1) that Anglican reformers made deliberate changes, in order to eject the sacramental idea from their services, and (2) that Anglicans therefore cannot possibly have, what they

---

[1] pp. 188-193.

not merely do not intend, but protestingly deny. Such an argument would no doubt be formidable if it were to be assumed that the sacramental idea and the detailed exactness of the Roman interpretation of sacraments are one and the same thing. But if it be conceived for a moment to be possible that there was a disproportion in the Roman theology, the argument falls at once to the ground That Anglicans do not accept but protest against the precise Roman proportions of sacramental doctrine, it was never worth while to write a volume to prove.

But Canon Estcourt is perhaps out of date. It is more important to pass to the controversial experiments of the last two years.

The paper published in 1894, *Les Ordinations Anglicanes*, 'par Fernand Dalbus,' was in many ways a remarkable document. Perhaps the most striking thing about it, to an Anglican reader, was the rare appreciation which it showed of the general Anglican standpoint. With more than usual fairness and skill it exhibited the argument, from the Anglican point of view[1], on the following points, viz. First, the Anglican Ordinal does not (as had been said on the other side) exclude, but bases itself upon, the sacramental reality of the $\chi\acute{a}\rho\iota\sigma\mu a$ given in ordination. In this connexion the *contrast* is emphasized between the official language of the Ordinal on the one hand, and on the other (1) the words used at an earlier date by Cranmer personally, and (2) the formal proposals of Bucer, which the Ordinal set aside. This argument is concluded with the words: 'Les compilateurs rejetèrent donc de propos délibéré les suggestions de Bucer, pour garder fidèlement l'enseignement traditionnel de la distinction des ordres et de leur réalité sacramentelle' (p. 24). Secondly, the Communion Office in the English Prayer-book does not contradict the *truth* about Eucharistic sacrifice. What it *is* afraid of is rather the gross exaggeration and materialistic superstition with which this doctrine was in fact held and taught Thus we read: 'Il est nécessaire, avant tout, pour comprendre ce que répudie l'église anglicane, et juger sa manière d'agir avec impartialité, de se rappeler quelles étaient les opinions des théologiens et des docteurs touchant le sacrifice de la messe, à l'époque où cet article [article 31] a été

---

[1] Referring to the *Church Quarterly Review*, Jan. 1878, pp. 269, 270. See above, pp. 234 n. and 236 n.

rédigé, c'est-à-dire, au xvi° siècle. A ce moment, des opinions bien extraordinaires, insoutenables aujourd'hui aux yeux de tout le monde catholique, étaient défendues par certains théologiens non dépourvus d'autorité. On supposait, par exemple, que le sacrifice eucharistique était un sacrifice absolu, complet en lui-même, fournissant une expiation indépendante de l'expiation accomplie par Notre Seigneur sur la Croix. On osait dire que Notre Seigneur, par le sacrifice de la Croix, avait expié le péché originel ainsi que les péchés commis sous l'ancienne loi et ceux commis par les individus avant le baptême ; tandis que la messe expie les péchés commis après le baptême. On disait aussi que par le sacrifice de la messe les péchés mortels étaient effacés, *ex opere operato*[1].'

[1] It may be worth while to quote in full the statements which the pamphlet contains in justification of this last paragraph (pp 27, 28).—
'Notre première citation est empruntée à Vasquez*. "Notat igitur Catherinus† in eodem opusculo superius citato (De veritate incruenti sacrificii) ‡ *Primum igitur*, duo esse genera peccatorum expianda per sacerdotium et sacrificium alterum est originalis peccati, et eorum quae cum eo conjuncta sunt et haec vocat ipse peccata, quae erant sub priori testamento nempe sub veteri, juxta modum loquendi Pauli ad Hebraeos ix. Alterum vero peccatorum quae post Baptismum committuntur, et haec vocat ipse peccata quae sub novo testamento admittuntur, et pro quovis genere suum assignat sacrificium : quia putat fore, ut sine suo peculiari sacrificio sacramenta pro quovis illo genere peccatorum expiando non consisterent, sicut ait in ‡ *Cum ergo peccata*. Pro peccato itaque originali, et aliis cum eo conjunctis, quae ipse vocat peccata sub priori testamento, assignat Christum, et sacramentum Baptismi quod virtute illius sacrificii ea remittat et quia haec omnia reputantur (inquit) unum peccatum ratione unius originalis, a quo oriuntur, et cum quo conjuncta sunt, ideo pro illorum remissione satis fuit una ipsius oblatio, quae nunquam esset repetenda Atque hoc modo explicat Paulum ad Hebraeos x cum ait. *una enim oblatione consummavit in sempiternum sanctificatos* ubi reddit causam, ob quam antiqua sacrificia in dies repeterentur, sacrificium autem crucis semel tantum fuerit oblatum At vero pro peccatis commissis post Baptismum pro quibus inquit non relinqui hostiam Christi cruentam quod voluntarie committantur, juxta illud ad Hebraeos x., *voluntarie enim peccantibus nobis post acceptam notitiam veritatis jam non relinquitur pro peccatis hostia*, nempe, ut ipse intelligit, cruenta, quae iterum repetatur, assignat sacrificium incruentum missae, quod ideo asserit quotidie repeti et iterari, quia offertur pro peccatis, quae jam sub novo testamento committuntur · nam cum haec, inquit, plura sint neque ab uno originali derivata, sed singula per se considerentur, quodlibet etiam suam expiationem sacrificii postulat, ac

* Vasquez *Comment in tert part* tome 3, quest 83, art I ch iv Edit Anvers, 1621, tome vii p. 479 —Vasquez combat Catharin
† Catharin naquit à Sienne en 1487, entra chez les Dominicains en 1521 et se distingua au concile de Trente. Il occupa l'évêché de Minori en 1547, l'archevêché de Conza en 1551, et mourut en 1553
‡ *Les Indulgences et la Messe*

The statement is concluded in the following sentence: 'Le lecteur a déjà conclu avant nous, ce que l'église anglicane réprouve et condamne : ce sont ces doctrines qui aujourd'hui nous paraissent extraordinaires, mais qui, alors, étaient admises par quelques théologiens et parfois même prêchées au peuple chrétien. L'article XXXIe, par conséquent, au lieu d'aller contre la vraie doctrine catholique, a pour but de la défendre'

Passages like these are interesting, as showing a somewhat unusual attempt to do justice to the Anglican position. They belong, however, only to a statement of the Anglican contention as such; and themselves, as arguments, are neither expressly accepted nor denied.

Meanwhile, upon an examination of the English Ordinal, M Dalbus has come to the unhesitating conclusion that, in itself at least, it fulfils all the conditions, of ceremonial and of language, which can fairly be asked. Confuting the Père Monsabré, who had supposed that the Orders were vitiated by the absence of

proinde sacrificium incruentum repetendum est pro his peccatis, quae sub novo testamento committuntur, quocirca in * *Denique considerandum*, addit ad expiationem horum peccatorum non applicari nobis cruentum Christi sacrificium sed incruentum per sacramentum Poenitentiae."

'Quand un évêque, un théologien renommé, malgré la singularité bien connue de ses opinions, parle ainsi, on peut imaginer facilement que des ecclésiastiques moins instruits et des prédicateurs populaires devaient parfois enseigner d'étranges choses

'Il est encore une autorité très souvent invoquée par les auteurs de l'époque, celle d'Albert la Grand Voici le passage qu'ils lui empruntent, tout en l'attribuant parfois à Saint Thomas · "Secunda causa institutionis hujus sacramenti est sacrificium altaris, contra quamdam quotidianam delictorum nostrorum rapinam Ut sicut corpus Domini semel oblatum est in cruce pro debito originali , sic offeratur jugiter pro nostris quotidianis delictis in altari, et habeat in hoc ecclesia munus ad placandum sibi Deum super omnia legis sacramenta vel sacrificia pretiosum et acceptum †" Les évêques d'Angleterre, en particulier Gardiner du parti romain, et Latimer du parti d'Henri VIII, protestent contre cette doctrine prêchée parfois au peuple Dans un discours prononcé le 9 Juin 1536, à l'ouverture d'un synode de la province de Cantorbéry, Latimer disait, "Il en est qui déclament les idées des hommes à la place de la parole de Dieu, prêchant en même temps au peuple que la Rédemption accomplie par la mort du Christ ne doit profiter qu'à ceux qui sont morts antérieurement à son Incarnation , et que, conséquemment, le pardon des péchés et la rédemption * achetée avec l'argent et inventée par les hommes est la seule efficace, et non la Rédemption qui nous a été procurée par le Christ."'

---

* *Les Indulgences et la Messe*
† Albert le Grand, *Serm de Euch* tom xii p 250 Edit Lugd,

special mention of 'sacrifice' and of 'sacerdotal powers,' and quoting the Abbé Duchesne as having demonstrated that nothing was required for ordination in the early Church beyond 'laying-on of hands' and 'prayer [1],' he repeatedly [2] formulates the conclusion that the Anglican is, in itself, an undoubtedly adequate rite.

And yet the main conclusion, apparently almost reached, is set aside, and Anglican Orders are, after all, disallowed. This is done upon two grounds. The first is that though Barlow consecrated Parker by a rite in itself adequate, yet Barlow had not adequate ideas about the rite. It is true that he meant to do what was done by the primitive Church But he did not regard what he was doing as the 'conferring of a sacrament.' Not indeed that this inadequacy of Barlow's inner mind can itself be pronounced to be a certainty · 'Mais les doctrines de Barlow sur le sacrement de l'Ordre suffisent pour rendre cette intention positivement douteuse et, dès lors, rendre incertain l'acte sacramentel. La consécration de Parker serait donc douteuse, selon nous, par un vice d'intention' (p. 31) This was a sufficiently surprising ground for the negative conclusion. But the second was more astonishing still. It was nothing less than a deliberate theory that what Pope Eugenius wrote to the Armenians in 1439 constituted a formal erection of the 'Porrectio instrumentorum,' by the solemn authority of the Pope, and the Council of Florence behind him, into an indispensable 'materia' for ordination to priesthood. It had not been so before. At that moment the Church in her discretion made it to be so It is of course sufficiently obvious that the words of Eugenius themselves betray no shadow of consciousness of thus creating for the first time a new, and from thenceforth immutable and imperative, 'materia' for ordination. Quite the reverse. His avowed object is to sum up in a *breve*

---

[1] Notice particularly his insistence, 'Ce ne sont donc pas les mots plus ou moins clairs de cette oraison qui la rendent apte à être la forme de la consécration, mais sa nature de prière'; p 13.

[2] 'Il semble donc que nous sommes en droit de conclure très légitimement que le rite anglican pris en lui-même pourrait être suffisant . . . Comme on le voit, non seulement la nature de la forme a été respectée, mais la pensée générale a été empruntée à une ancienne prière usitée en France, en Angleterre, et dans bien d'autres pays Nous croyons donc devoir regarder comme certain que le rite anglican, pris en lui-même, pourrait être suffisant'; pp. 13, 14.

compendium what is the actual teaching of the Roman Church upon the points in question: and he does so, naturally enough, by giving—in the words, as M. Dalbus shows, of St. Thomas—the then received (but mistaken) theory on the subject [1]; and all this, in order that he might succeed in making it perfectly clear for the future, for ever—not to the Roman but to *the Armenian* communities.

The authority however which affirmed the decree is, to M. Dalbus, overwhelming. Pope and Council had declared that 'porrectio' was the indispensable 'materia.' Henceforth nothing less than a similar authority could dispense with it [2].

Incidentally there is here another very curious point. The *decretum Eugenii ad Armenos*, whatever be its value, would certainly appear to be addressed, not to Romans as such, but to Armenians. Curiously enough, it appears to be maintained that its effect was to impose, as indispensable, a new 'materia' upon the whole Western, *but not upon the Eastern*[3], Church. This, however, is by the way.

[1] 'Expedire judicavimus, ne ulla in futurum de fidei veritate apud ipsos Armenos haesitatio esse valeat, atque idem per omnia sapiant cum sede apostolica, unioque ipsa stabilis et perpetua sine ullo scrupulo perseveret, ut sub quodam brevi compendio orthodoxae fidei veritatem quam super praemissis Romana profitetur ecclesia, per hoc decretum, sacro hoc approbante Florentino concilio, ipsis oratoribus ad hoc etiam consentientibus, traderemus'; pp 31, 32.

[2] 'Si le sens de ce décret est parfaitement clair, l'autorité n'en est pas contestable non plus'; p. 32 —'Pour les catholiques romains, l'autorité du Pape dans ce cas suffirait, mais nous avons, de plus, l'autorité du Concile de Florence qui se continuait.'—'Un concile a donc approuvé un décret dans lequel il est dit que la matière du sacrement de l'Ordre est la porrection des instruments'; p 33.

[3] 'Voilà donc approuvés deux rites sacramentels différents: une matière pour les Grecs, et une pour les Latins; une matière pour les dix ou douze premiers siècles, et une autre pour la suite des âges' (p. 33); and on p. 35 he quotes Billuart thus: 'Ecclesia itaque hac potestate sibi a Christo tradita utens, determinavit, seu saltem consensit, quod impositio manuum cum forma illi respondente pro ecclesia Graeca, et forte etiam in prioribus saeculis pro ecclesia Latina, esset signum legitimum utriusque potestatis traditae ad consecrandum et ad absolvendum. At postea determinavit pro ecclesia Latina quod porrectio instrumentorum cum his verbis, Accipe potestatem &c., esset signum legitimum potestatis consecrandi, impositio autem manuum cum his verbis, Accipe Spiritum sanctum &c., signum potestatis absolvendi: ita quod Graecus ordinatus ritu Latinorum aut Latinus ritu Graecorum sine dispensatione summi Pontificis invalide ordinaretur.'

What then the whole Church had solemnly ordained, at least for the West, could not be abrogated by any province, or kingdom, taken apart. Granting, then, even that the English Bishops had the most unimpeachably excellent intentions; granting that their one desire was to recover again primitive forms and apostolical usages; yet they could not, on these lines, establish an adequate rite, because they had no power to suppress a ceremony which, brought in by custom at first, had been decreed to be essential, in the West, by the authority of Eugenius IV., with the approval of the Council of Florence.

So the whole claim falls to the ground. The argument is summed up by M. Dalbus, in these words : 'Nous croyons avoir démontré : (1) que le rite de l'ordinal anglican, pris en lui-même, pourrait être suffisant ; (2) que la consécration de Parker doit être regardée comme certaine quant au fait, mais qu'un doute subsiste au sujet de l'intention du consécrateur ; (3) que, par le fait des altérations introduites dans les cérémonies de l'ordination des prêtres, les ordinations anglicanes sont nulles'

In the *Bulletin Critique* of July 15, 1894, there appeared a short criticism of M. Dalbus' work by the Abbé Duchesne.

The first objection made to Anglican Orders—the doubt as to Barlow's sacramental orthodoxy—M. Duchesne puts quietly aside as irrelevant. The question is, he says, what *the Church* means by Ordination. The heterodox teaching of an individual bishop, or even, if it be so, of the Anglican Church collectively, would not invalidate their act, if by a rite adequate in itself they sought to confer the Orders of the Church : 'Il y a eu, en dehors de l'Angleterre, des évêques incrédules ; n'oublions pas qu'une partie du clergé français dérive son ordination de M. de Talleyrand'—'Le baptême peut être conféré validement par une personne qui sait seulement que c'est un rite sacré par lequel on devient chrétien De même, les ordinations anglicanes ont toujours été célébrées par des personnes qui voulaient faire des évêques, des prêtres, et ainsi de suite. Il n'en faut pas demander davantage.'

Neither does he admit M. Dalbus' objection about Pope Eugenius and the Porrectio Instrumentorum to be admissible. Granting, in theory, that the Church has power to make a solemn alteration even in the essential 'materia' of a Sacrament, where is the evidence, he asks, that she has ever determined so to do, or been conscious of so doing, at all¹?

He adds that the objection, even if valid, would be valid only against ordinations to priesthood, and not against consecrations to episcopate. Inasmuch therefore as there are abundant historical instances of the consecration to episcopate of those who were not in priest's Orders, the argument, even if true, would make nothing against the recognition of the English *episcopate*.

His practical conclusion is that English ordinations² *might be* recognized as valid. The contrary opinion prevalent in Rome is accounted for by the necessity which Rome is under to be very tender to the scruples of Catholic consciences. As things stand, there are few who would accept the Sacraments from a Priest who had only been ordained as an Anglican: 'En ces matières, il est naturel de multiplier les garanties.'

The fact that public prejudice is as it is, is, he says, an inheritance from the sixteenth century, when scholastic (but erroneous) views about the 'porrectio' were in possession; and the prejudice was fostered and maintained by the 'legends' published about the consecrations of Parker and of Barlow.

Some day, he concludes, it is possible that the feeling may improve, and the present attitude of authority on the subject may be changed: 'Rien n'empêche de croire que, par la suite des temps, cette opinion se corrige, et que l'autorité ecclésiastique elle-même n'en vienne à modifier son attitude.'

Now it may be said that to reopen the details of this controversy is to go back to things which belong already to a remote past. In a sense, perhaps, they do. But this past, if already remote, is certainly pregnant with instruction.

No one will deny that the two gentlemen whose writings have been quoted are eminent among Roman ecclesiastics, for their large-minded effort to be fair. Assuming this, I must ask for a little further attention to the intellectual difficulty in which they found themselves placed. M. Dalbus had disposed of all

---

[1] 'Où est (1) l'acte officiel, public, explicite, par lequel l'Eglise s'est reconnu le droit dont on parle? (2) l'acte officiel, public, explicite, par lequel elle a déclaré user de ce droit pour les rites essentiels de l'ordination? J'ajouterai que l'on pourrait demander aussi dans quel intérêt elle aurait introduit un changement aussi considérable.'

[2] 'Peuvent être considérées comme valides.'

the natural presumptions against the Anglican Ordinal. Yet he disallowed it upon considerations (1) of intention, and (2) of the overruling authority of an utterance (generally supposed to have been an exceptionally unfortunate one) of a Roman pontiff. Now what did he really mean by the difficulty of intention? It is hard to believe that he ever really supposed that the private heterodoxy of an individual bishop would invalidate his pontifical actions, or that he would have felt his objection fully met by the reference which Duchesne made to M. de Talleyrand. But if the gist of his objection never really lay in the greater or less probability that Barlow, individually, performed a sacramental act with an unsacramental conception of what he was doing, wherein did it lie? Must not the underlying suggestion be this—that Barlow not only, whilst consecrating, individually held, but that, in and by the very method and (taken with all its surroundings) admitted significance of his consecrating, he did officially and representatively express, an inadequate doctrine of what priesthood and episcopate were? I am not suggesting that this gloss would make his charge of inadequate intention effectual; but at least it would make it more intelligible. But if it is Barlow representatively and publicly, rather than Barlow individually and privately, whereby is that which Barlow represented to be judged? His own writings may, under the circumstances, be an item in the evidence; but only so far as he and his writings may, under the circumstances, be supposed to be representative of reformed Anglican doctrine. It is reformed Anglican doctrine that is really in question—not the vagueness of mind of an individual bishop[1]. But if this is true, then the doubt which really underlay and was disguised by this complaint about intention was really a doubt not how far Barlow's own 'unsacramentalism' may privately have gone, but how far that corporate doctrine, which Barlow may be supposed for the moment to have personified, was or was not adequately 'sacramental.' By the time we get as far as this, it is plain that what the question will come to, on analysis, will be, whether 'sacramental' in an Anglican context is, or is not, all that 'sacramental' from a Roman standpoint may be required to mean. It becomes,

---

[1] This suggestion is somewhat fortified by M. Dalbus' reference in this connection to Gasparri. For the passage quoted from Gasparri, see below, p. 322.

though indirectly, an instance of testing Anglican meanings by their coincidence with Roman.

But if this is, as I believe, indirectly true of what M Dalbus says of defective intention, there can be no doubt that it is true quite directly of his argument about Pope Eugenius and the 'porrectio.' This is nothing but an invoking of the supreme authority of the Roman pontiff. The argument depends upon the assumption that Rome always was, and always must have been, right. Suppose for a moment that Roman theology may have fallen into disproportion, or made a mistake; and the argument would be no argument at all. It depends, in other words, on the assumption that, Rome being absolutely right, everything in Anglicanism must be wrong, if, or just so far as, it definitely differs from Rome But, as I have urged already, as long as Roman infallibility has to stand in the major premiss, the most learned and large-minded efforts made on the Roman side, to do justice to the Anglican standpoint, are made necessarily in vain It can hardly be said too plainly that if the Roman Church has, at every point, been right, then the Anglican Church has been, of necessity, wrong. We have condemned the proportions and altered the expressions of her doctrine. The question is, which is right? It might be held indeed, without any defect of logic, that whilst each was in many points right—perhaps even right in the main—yet each had made mistakes and was in some points open to correction: but if either is *absolutely* right, it follows, by inexorable consequence, that the other—just so far as she really differs—must be absolutely wrong. Neither can really argue with the other so long as her own infallibility is a postulate in the argument.

When we turn from M. Dalbus to M Duchesne, the fetters which forbid free discussion are not removed. It is difficult to see how a loyal Roman Catholic could really go further than M. Duchesne went. Every argument against Anglican Orders was set aside. There remained in the field not one. But what was the resulting position? That the Orders might be acknowledged as valid, if Rome chose to acknowledge them. Perhaps Roman prejudice might die away; perhaps Roman authority might pronounce their validity. Nothing was really lacking but the will. If on one side this may look like the extreme of concession, on the other it is, no less, the extreme assertion of the infallibility and autocracy of Rome.

Of course I am not finding fault with either of these gentlemen. Towards themselves there can be no feeling but the most hearty and respectful sympathy They did not make their position, or the conditions of it But I believe that it is worth while to point out that, unless tacit concessions were allowed to them, incompatible with the real nature of the position, the position itself was one which made any real appreciation of Anglicanism impossible Would such concessions—*could* such concessions—be either expressly, or even tacitly, allowed?

Some months later, in the early part of 1895, there appeared a much more elaborate criticism of M. Dalbus—an 'Étude théologique sur les ordinations anglicanes,' by 'A. Boudinhon, Professeur de droit canon à l'Institut Catholique de Paris.' M. Boudinhon was a much more hostile writer. He, at least, had no doubt, from the beginning, that English Orders were null. His argument, however, is of no slight interest to us. In the first place, he, like M. Duchesne, only much more elaborately, pulled to pieces the reasons alleged by M. Dalbus against Anglican validity. As to the 'porrectio instrumentorum,' he warned M. Dalbus of the danger to which the rest of his position becomes liable, if he ventured to rest upon that—the danger of being ultimately driven to admit that the Orders are real[1]!

For to M. Boudinhon it was perfectly clear that the view that the 'porrectio' was essential could not be maintained, He argued that, whereas the modern Roman Pontifical is, in fact, an amalgamation of early Gallican and Roman Ordinals, together

[1] 'Je commence par lui signaler le danger qui résulterait inévitablement pour sa thèse, si sa troisième conclusion se trouvait fausse. Car si l'ordinal anglican est suffisant, en lui-même, pour la consécration épiscopale, il doit l'être aussi pour l'ordination presbytérale si l'on admet que celle-ci ne requiert pas comme élément essentiel la porrection des instruments. Que s'il reste seulement un doute sur la valeur de la consécration de Parker, par suite de l'intention peut-être vicieuse de Barlow, les ordinations anglicanes seraient tout au plus douteuses et on ne pourrait dire qu'elles sont nulles. Que si enfin l'ordination anglicane est suffisante, en lui-même, pour la consécration épiscopale, il suffira de montrer que l'épiscopat pourrait bien être valide sans le presbyterat, pour être obligé d'admettre la valeur au moins probable de la hiérarchie épiscopale anglicane', p. 37.

with added ceremonies of later date, what is essential must necessarily be looked for, not in the added ceremonies, but in the original rites. It would be absurd to maintain that Ordinals once valid in themselves were emptied of their validity because new rites were added which took over, and monopolized, the 'essential' character. Ordinations to episcopate, priesthood, and diaconate, are essentially all of one type; their essence consists in the consecratory prayer—with imposition of hands. Only that can be essential which is universal. To call the 'porrectio' essential is out of the question[1].

As to the other difficulty—at least in the form in which M. Dalbus had stated it—that Barlow's 'unsacramental' intention nullified Parker's consecration, M. Boudinhon is no less clear and trenchant. If the rite which he used was adequate, and he used it seriously, the private heterodoxy of the consecrating bishop, evidenced by his teaching or preaching elsewhere, could have no power to nullify or neutralize what he did. Th s M. Boudinhon gives not as his private opinion only, but ; s the universal judgement of theologians — 'leur enseignemer t est absolument uniforme, souvent même conçu en termes ident ques. Le minimum requis, suivant l'expression du décret *ad Armenos*, reproduite par le concile de Trente sess. vii. can. 11, est l'inten-

[1] 'On est bien obligé de reconnaître que les rites anciens de ces ordinations comprenaient les éléments essentiels, ou, si l'on veut, la matière et la forme ; d'autre part on ne saurait soutenir sérieusement que l'efficacité essentielle des ordinations a été déplacée et attachée à des rites d'accession postérieure', p 39.

'... et consistent essentiellement dans la prière ou préface consécratoire, accompagnée de l'imposition des mains C'est dans ce rite, le seul qui existe dans toutes les liturgies, orientales et occidentales, romaine et gallicane, anciennes et récentes, qu'il faut chercher la matière et la forme des trois ordinations sacramentelles. La tradition des instruments, comme matière essentielle, est définitivement écartée.

'Le célèbre décret *ad Armenos*, sur lequel M. Dalbus s'appuie peut-être trop, n'a pas empêché, on le sait, la diversité des opinions parmi les théologiens. Jamais, que je sache, l'Église n'a positivement réprouvé aucune de ces opinions, pas plus qu'elle n'en a fait aucune sienne. Les décisions qu on peut alléguer visent surtout la pratique, et en pratique l'Église est tutioriste' ; p. 40.

'Pour motiver sa conclusion, M. Dalbus est dans la nécessité de faire de son opinion la seule certaine ; il doit prouver que la porrection des instruments est non seulement obligatoire, ce que personne ne conteste, mais encore seule essentielle, ce qui ne résulte ni de l'enseignement commun des théologiens, ni des décisions de l'Église' ; p. 41.

X

tion de faire ce que fait l'Église' (p. 30). That is, he must do what the Church does, meaning to produce the effect which the Church means. He need not understand what the Church means. He may be in serious error in respect of it. He may think most unsacramentally of the sacrament which he performs. Still, whatever his errors, if he has but the purpose, virtual and implicit, to use the Church's forms for the Church's purpose, his act is a valid and effectual one. In support of this position he quotes a passage from le P. Lehmkuhl—embodying a quotation from Suarez—and a definition laid down by Mgr. Gasparri.

Before turning to the definition of Mgr. Gasparri, upon which both Dalbus and Boudinhon rely, it may be well to say that the position just laid down—the need of an intention 'facere quod facit ecclesia'—an intention which may be presumed, in the absence of evidence to the contrary, from the mere fact of an apparently serious performance of the Church's ceremony—is stated, so far as the terms themselves are concerned, much as Hooker stated it in fact, on behalf of Anglicans three hundred years ago, and as it would be generally accepted in all parts of the Church. But it is no less manifest that there is on the face of the terms an ambiguity which must be cleared away. 'Facere quod facit ecclesia' by all means. But if to half of those who use the phrase, 'Ecclesia' is simply identical with 'Ecclesia Romana,' the definition would be obviously valueless; for those who might have agreed to use it would mean, in using it, incompatible things. It is plain, then, that there must be a definition of the word. What, for the purpose of the argument, is meant by 'Ecclesia'?

With this question, then, we approach the somewhat singular ruling of Mgr. Gasparri. The first half of it indeed sounds studiously liberal: 'Ex dictis sequitur ordinationem valere, si minister intendit quidem facere quod facit Ecclesia Christi, sed simul putat illum ritum non esse sacramentum, non esse ritum sacrum, nullam conferre potestatem, Ecclesiam Romanam non esse veram Ecclesiam Christi,' &c. After a statement so liberally conceived as this, particularly after the words of its final clause, it is no small surprise to find a proviso appended, as indispensable condition, that he must not have any positive purpose to differ, in what he does, from the Church *of Rome*· 'dummodo actu positivo voluntatis non dicat. Nolo facere sacramentum, conficere ritum sacrum, conferre potestatem, facere quod facit Ecclesia Romana, &c. Sane in casu unicus est actus voluntatis, nempe faciendi quod facit Ecclesia Christi, quem non destruit error concomitans, de quo supra At e contrario ordinatio foret nulla prorsus, si minister intendit quidem facere quod facit Ecclesia Christi sed simul actu positivo et explicito voluntatis, non vult conficere sacramentum aut ritum sacrum, aut facere quod facit Ecclesia Romana, aut conferre potestatem ordinis, aut imprimere characterem, &c Nam in casu forent duo voluntatis actus positivi et contrarii, quorum posterior priorem destruit, vel qui mutuo eliduntur, et ideo minister revera non vult facere quod facit Ecclesia Christi' (pp. 31, 32). Now this is a ruling which certainly itself requires further explaining How much is meant by not intending to do what Rome does? Rome for instance intends to celebrate the Eucharist and, in doing so, conceives that she performs a certain peculiarly defined miracle, the technical name of which is 'transubstantiation' Is it a deliberate disbelief in 'transubstantiation,' involving a positive disclaimer of doing what Rome conceives that she does in celebrating the Eucharist, or is it only a purpose *not* to 'celebrate the Eucharist,' which would fall within Gasparri's meaning? So in respect of Ordination—is it the intention 'not to make a priest,' or the disclaimer of the Roman definition of a priest and the Roman theory as to the precise mode of making one, which would make the Orders null? The difference is enormous. But in either case the introduction of the word 'Romana,' and the assumption that he who does not wish to do as the 'Ecclesia Romana' does not really wish to do as the 'Ecclesia Christi,' has the effect of completely destroying the value of Gasparri's statement. It comfortably re-establishes Romanism, as a whole, in the major premiss, and therefore sweeps every conclusion necessarily into Romanism

It will be anticipated, then, that M Boudinhon's repudiation of the argument as to Barlow's 'intention' was a repudiation only of the form in which M. Dalbus had stated it—with a view to its more confident restatement in another form. He restates it much in the form which I ventured just now to suggest as really underlying M. Dalbus' thought. Barlow is no longer an accidentally 'heterodox' individual; he is officiating as the public representative of 'heterodoxy.' That which clinches the proof that he is so, is the Ordinal form which he uses[1]. Had he continued to use the Roman Pontifical, no question as to his 'intention' would, according to M. Boudinhon's argument, have been relevant. But he used a form which—whether it could or could not have been adequate 'in itself,' on the impossible hypothesis that the Church (i. e Rome) had adopted it[2]—was in fact drawn up as the overt and deliberate expression of dissentience from Rome. The open and representative use of such a form, under such circumstances, is the demonstrative conviction—nay is the defiant proclamation—of a positive intention not to mean or do what the Church does and means. If 'Ecclesia' and 'Ecclesia Romana' are terms, for all purposes, simply convertible, the argument of course is complete. But if this is, after all, what is meant, was it really worth while to construct an argument at all?

Such seemed to be the nature of M. Boudinhon's comment on Mgr. Gasparri's text. It is true that a considerable section of the 'étude' had been devoted to showing the inadequacy of the Ordinal as reformed, and that this inadequacy of the Ordinal is then alleged as evidence of the inadequate intention of those who used it; but it is difficult to attach much importance to an argument which is so very apparently circular. For the objections in the Ordinal really turn upon the plea that it is an unauthorized departure from the Ordinal forms of 'the Church[3]!'

---

[1] 'Il est bien difficile, pour ne pas dire impossible, de conclure à la nullité de la consécration de Parker par suite de l'intention hérétique de Barlow, abstraction faite du rite. En revanche, l'emploi du rite de l'ordinal ne permet pas d'admettre que Barlow ait pu avoir l'intention suffisante de faire ce que fait l'Église', p. 30

[2] 'Quelle que soit la valeur de l'assertion de M Dalbus que l'ordinal anglican, pris en lui-même, pourrait être valable, c'est-à-dire aurait pu être valable, si l'Église l'avait choisi au lieu de celui qu'elle a établi, je crois pouvoir dire, sans témérité, qu'en réalité il n'est pas valable . .'; p 21.
He had said before, 'J'espère avoir dissipé la confusion dissimulée dans l'assertion de notre auteur. Il n'est pas logique d'argumenter ici de l'hypothèse à la réalité, et s'il est possible de dire, avec M. Dalbus, que l'ordinal anglican, pris en lui-même, pourrait être suffisant, il n'est pas permis d'en conclure qu'en réalité il soit suffisant'; p. 17

[3] 'Son premier vice est donc de manquer d'autorité. . . . Toute détermination faite sans autorité ou par une autre autorité que celle de la véritable Église semble donc contraire au droit divin, et, par suite, dépourvue de l'efficacite sacramentelle'; p. 13.

It is obvious that nothing can be added by an argument like this.

Before leaving the 'étude,' it may be worth while to quote one word of a different kind—its final word—addressed plainly, though not by name, to M. Duchesne. 'Si l'Église pouvait accepter les ordinations anglicanes comme valables, elle devrait le faire; d'abord parce que ce serait son intérêt, puisque cela rendrait ainsi plus facile le retour de cette Église depuis si longtemps séparée, retour qui est un de ses plus chers désirs; ce serait plus encore son devoir, puisqu'elle enseigne que les rites catholiques de l'ordination, employés par un ministre hérétique avec l'intention requise, confèrent le sacrement de l'Ordre, lequel ne peut sans sacrilège se réitérer.'

It is unnecessary to comment further upon the argument of the 'Étude.' For not the least remarkable fact about it is that, within the year, a great part of it was publicly withdrawn by M. Boudinhon himself. Christmas Day, 1895, is the date of the preface to a new pamphlet, larger than the first, in which he has materially reconsidered his position.

In this brochure, 'De la Validité des Ordinations Anglicanes,' he devotes his whole effort to bring the argument for their nullity away from all considerations of 'intention' (herein pointedly separating himself from English Roman Catholics[1]) and to base it altogether on the inherent inadequacy of the Anglican rite.

He lets go the argument which had seemed to be so conclusive in the Étude—alike against the possibility of the adequacy

'*A priori*, et avant la détermination légitime faite par l'Église, toute forme est suffisante, dès lors qu'elle indique l'effet de l'ordination; mais, en réalité, après la détermination compétente, les formules imposées par l'Église sont nécessaires'; pp. 16, 17.

'Ou plutôt, pour conclure ainsi, il faudrait autre chose: il faudrait démontrer, suivant ce que j'ai dit plus haut, qu'il n'existe pas de différences entre l'Ordinal anglican et le Pontifical latin, si ce n'est des différences purement accidentelles Or la comparaison entre les deux textes—comparaison que chacun peut faire—ne permet pas de réduire les différences entre l'un et l'autre à n'être qu'accidentelles'; pp 17, 18.

[1] 'Les catholiques anglais se font illusion, ce me semble, en s'attachant presque exclusivement aux motifs de nullité tirés du défaut d'intention des ministres de l'ordination, et des hérésies professées par eux et par l'Église Anglicane, particulièrement sur l'Eucharistie et le sacrifice Tout cela est presque complètement en dehors de la question', pp. 17, 18.

of the rite, and the possibility of the adequacy of the intention —drawn with charming simplicity from the obvious fact that Anglicans had altered the Ordinal of the [Roman] Church. Putting 'intention' aside, he admits that, as far as the rite is concerned, its inadequacy does not instantly follow. There is still one chance [1]. Though they had deliberately varied the form of 'the Church,' it is still to be asked whether in varying they had or had not lost the *essential* elements in the forms of 'the Church.' The animus implied in the fact of altering at all does not settle the matter by itself.

He is good enough to remind us that such a testing of the Anglican rite by 'legitimate' rites is only necessary because the Anglican rite is itself schismatic and illegitimate. Had it existed within 'the Church,' or even been recognized by 'the Church,' that would suffice. But being schismatically 'without,' it can only justify itself by its conformity with that which is 'within'; pp. 23, 24.

This is delightful. The whole of the major premiss, then, which he is about to construct, avowedly depends, for its relevancy to the argument, upon the fundamental assumption that Anglicans, their principles, their ceremonies, their service books, have no place in, but are wholly outside of, the history and the life of 'the Church.' So frank a begging of the only question really worth arguing of course considerably clears the ground.

But to return to M. Boudinhon. He grants that the Anglican Ordinal fully possesses, in the laying on of hands, the one and only essential materia. Everything therefore turns on the question of the 'forma,' which to him is a term synonymous with the 'canon consécratoire.' What then is essential for a consecratory forma?

Of the answer to this his new premiss consists. Examine, he says in effect, all the constitutive 'formae' which have ever in fact been recognized by 'the Church.' Observe what features are common to them all These features constitute the essential

---

[1] 'Il ne reste donc qu'une seule hypothèse—mais il en reste une— . . . si elles avaient conservé ce qu'il y a d'essentiel dans les prières des Pontificaux catholiques légitimes'; p. 24

'J'avais conclu, je l'avoue, trop rapidement à l'insuffisance des formules anglicanes, ayant un peu trop vite admis une différence substantielle entre ces prières et celles des formes catholiques', p 5b

'form.' A 'form' which has these is adequate. A form which lacks any one of these is not.

I cannot but point out that in this new major premiss there are tacitly contained no less than three assumptions, every one of which is gratuitous and inadmissible. The first is (as always) that 'the Church' and 'Rome' are simply synonymous terms. He goes on no doubt to examine the Ordinals of many ages and of many countries. But he examines them on the basis of their having been authorized or acknowledged by Rome. And for this reason he of course, by hypothesis, omits the Anglican. This means at once that between him and Anglicans there is no real community of ground.

The second assumption is that the essential 'forma' in Ordination is one single separate prayer, which can be and must be detached from that whole service of prayer of which it forms part; so that it is, and the service as a whole is *not*, before God and man, the devotional and interpretative accompaniment of the laying on of hands. If St. Paul laid hands on Timothy in a service of prayer which lasted (say) half an hour, it was not the uplifting of heart through that half hour in Godward aspiration and request—it was the words of some one single, short, separate moment of prayer, in immediate juxtaposition with the manual act which, taken quite apart and alone, constituted in that case the 'prayer' which (as all theologians allow) must accompany the laying on of hands for Ordination. I am not now to discuss this point in full, but must at least express my conviction that theologians (too ready, as often, materially to externalize and logically to define!) have been misled in their theories on this point by an analogy falsely drawn from the sacrament of Baptism; for in Baptism there is, as there is not in any other sacrament or sacramental rite whatsoever, a single formula (itself not in the shape, though with the implications, of a prayer) which, because prescribed *as a formula* by the lips of the risen Lord Himself, can and does stand alone and apart from everything besides in the full ceremonial of Baptism. So completely, however, is this idea of the technical 'forma' detached by Boudinhon (as by many others in their definition of sacraments) from the service of which it can only *at the most* be a significant climax, that, when he has settled which of the elements in the service is to be taken as the 'forma,' he demands to have, *within the limits of that one detached prayer*, whatever he has laid down to be essential for the 'prayer' that shall accompany and interpret the laying on of hands.

The third assumption is that the Ordinal 'forms' which have ever been used in the Church (i. e. recognized by Rome) have been in such sense under Divine guidance as to warrant not only the negative conclusion—that nothing can be essential to ordination which they do not all contain; but also the much more doubtful positive—that nothing can possibly have been present in fact in them all without being so indispensable in the sight of God, that, if it were not mentioned, the grace of Order would not be given.

It is obvious that M. Boudinhon is here on very dangerous ground historically. We do not know all the forms which existed within the area that Rome is not prepared to condemn; at any moment a new discovery might modify the received belief, and show that under this rule forms had been condemned as inadequate which were really well within the terms of the rule[1]. It is

---

[1] A striking illustration of the probabilities in this direction is supplied by Father Puller [see *Guardian* for Sept. 30, 1896, p. 1474]:—

'The Abbé Boudinhon, by a comparison of the various forms in his collection, has put together all those elements which are common to all of them, and, arranging them in the form of a prayer, he has thus composed a formula which he thinks contains the *minimum* which can be admitted if a valid ordination is to be secured. There is one point in his formula which seems to me to be open to criticism, but I will first quote it as it stands in his treatise *De la Validité des Ordinations Anglicanes*. It occurs on p. 50, and runs thus:—

'"Deus qui . . . respice propitius super hunc famulum tuum, quem ad diaconatum (*respective* presbyteratum *vel* episcopatum *seu* summum sacerdotium) vocare dignatus es; da ei gratiam tuam, ut munera huius ordinis digne et utiliter adimplere valeat."

'Mgr. Gasparri (*Revue Anglo-Romaine*, tom. i. p. 545) accepts this formula as giving satisfactorily those elements which are common to all the recognized precatory ordination forms. The point in the formula which I should criticize is the express mention of the order conferred. Unfortunately M. Boudinhon did not take into account the very old Roman rite given in the Canons of St. Hippolytus. If he had, he would have noticed that in the prayer for the ordination of a deacon in that rite there is no mention of the diaconate. The prayer runs as follows (Achelis' edition of the *Canons of St. Hippolytus*, can. v. sections 39-42, pp. 66, 67):—"O Deus, Pater Domini nostri Iesu Christi, rogamus te nixe [? enixe], ut effundas Spiritum tuum Sanctum super servum tuum N. eumque praepares cum illis, qui tibi serviunt secundum tuum beneplacitum sicut Stephanus; utque illi concedas vim vincendi omnem potestatem dolosi

APPENDIX 329

probable also that this third assumption would be of no value to M. Boudinhon, except as read in conjuntion with the second. But even apart from the second, and apart from the grave historical risks to which it exposes him, it is necessary to insist that this third assumption—the very marrow of M. Boudinhon's major premiss—is a mere assumption, more or less reasonable, no doubt, for ordinary purposes, but of no real cogency.

Proceeding, however, with his scrutiny upon this principle, M. Boudinhon concludes that the 'prayer' (which is to be recognized detachedly as the 'forma') must express three things, (1) petition to God for grace for the ordinands (generally, but not always, expressed as the gift of His Spirit to them); (2) the name of the order to which they are to be ordained; and (3) (with great variety of detail) some reference to the functions to be fulfilled and the endowments required for their fulfilment, but *not* necessarily any specification of the powers conceived to be conveyed in the ordination (pp. 45-47). By

signo crucis tuae, quo ipse signatur; utque concedas ipsi mores sine peccato coram omnibus hominibus, doctrinamque pro multis, quâ gentem copiosam in ecclesiâ sacrâ ad salutem perducat sine ullo scandalo. Accipe omne servitium eius per Dominum nostrum Iesum Christum, etc. Amen." Attention was called to this formula by Mr. Lacey, in the *Supplementum* to the *De Hierarchiâ*, and the Abbé Boudinhon, when reviewing the *Supplementum*, frankly admits that, in view of this formula, his previous result must be modified. It is evident that in this formula there is no mention of either deacon or diaconate, and therefore it cannot be maintained that there is any necessity for the mention of the order, which is being imparted, in the precatory form No doubt, in some way or other, the fact that the ordinand was going to be ordained deacon and not priest was made manifest when the rite contained in the *Canons of St. Hippolytus* was performed; but the ordination formula itself is simply a prayer that God would pour out His Holy Spirit upon the ordinand, so that by his holiness and learning he may draw many souls to salvation. The Abbé Boudinhon (*Revue Anglo-Romaine*, tom. ii p. 674), speaking of this Hippolytean formula, says:—

'"Neither the word 'deacon' nor the word 'diaconate' is found in it. The fixing of the intention of the prayer [to the bestowal of the diaconate] is sufficiently secured either by the allusion to Saint Stephen, or by the other prayers and ceremonies, however summary they may have been at that primitive epoch, or even simply by the will and intention of the bishop who was ordaining."'

Father Puller adduces this as a modification, in detail, of M. Boudinhon's result. It is, in fact, more than this. It is a striking illustration of the precariousness of his principle.

this last statement he pointedly overthrows the letter of the Dutch Old-Catholics[1].

He then finds—curiously enough[2]—that each of the three services of Anglican ordination possesses a prayer which contains these three requirements. They are all adequate then? Not at all. For he nevertheless rules—and we, in our turn, are inclined to see herein 'une très curieuse observation,'—that in each of the three services this prayer can neither itself be the 'forma,' nor even can contribute, in any degree, to make the service as a whole into an adequate 'forma'; because it is not sufficiently close to the laying on of hands. The manual action is accompanied and interpreted only by that fraction of the service which coincides with it (not *quite* indeed, for that would overthrow most Ordinals, but *almost*) when measured by minutes or seconds. The prayer then, which does fulfil all the conditions, being according to this ruling—for purposes of a 'forma'—exactly as if it were not in the service at all, is there any prayer in juxtaposition with the manual act which might serve for a forma? There are indeed interpretative words which accompany the action directly, 'Take thou authority,' &c., 'Receive the Holy Ghost,' &c. But these again, being not in the precatory but the imperative form, cannot *be* the 'forma'; and not being the forma, cannot contribute anything whatever towards bringing the total service into such a relation, of interpretation and supplication, with the laying on of hands, as would be necessary to make that laying on of hands effectual. So these also are—for the purpose—as if they were not there *at all*. Once more, then, is there anything which could possibly serve as a 'forma'?

In the Ordering of Deacons there is nothing left to suggest. Then the Ordering of Deacons is hopelessly invalid. It is invalid, observe, because there is laying on of hands *with no accompanying or interpretative form*. It is a service of laying on of hands *without 'prayer.'* Could anything be more external, more pedantic—to speak seriously as amongst grown men, more childish?

In the ordination of priests, there is a prayer at the required

---

[1] 'C'est ce qui doit faire entièrement rejeter l'opinion de R. P. Tournebize, et des vieux catholiques de Hollande', p 50

[2] 'Nous devons commencer par une très curieuse observation'; p 51

moment; but—when it is petitioning God it is not *exactly* for grace to the ordinands, and when it is speaking to God about His grace to the ordinands, the form of petition is transcended and translated into the form of grateful adoration and praise [1], and therefore it is uncertain whether it is quite a prayer of the character required; and therefore — since of course all the contents of all the rest of the service put together count for nothing as constituting, or as contributing to the constitution of, a forma—the judicial conclusion must be 'que le presbytérat ainsi conféré est douteux, sinon invalide'; p. 57.

It is a controversy full indeed of surprises. Perhaps few surprises will be much greater, after the extraordinary processes by which the diaconate and the priesthood have been practically disallowed, than to find ourselves met with the astonishing phenomenon of an acquittal in respect of the service for consecration of bishops: 'Il faut avouer qu'ici la trame de nos prières catholiques est fidèlement suivie', 'l'épiscopat ainsi conféré, *à ne considérer que le rite*, peut bien être regardé comme valide'; p. 57.

The italics in the last sentence are M Boudinhon's own. But in truth it is not quite easy to see what points, other than the rite, he wishes to have considered. There are indeed two points more which he proceeds to examine—the kind of intention which may be required, and the heretical meaning which the Ordinal by its omissions is said to imply, but on both these points he disallows the arguments of objectors. As to 'intention,' he quotes a passage at considerable length from the dissertation *De hierarchia Anglicana* by Messrs. Denny and Lacey (which chiefly seems to have occasioned his second brochure), a passage which goes very far beyond the contradictory dictum of Mgr. Gasparri; and he quotes it with apparent acceptance, if not even with some degree of enjoyment of the directness with which it refutes a position that Cardinal Vaughan had attempted to occupy. It may be well to give it as quoted by M. Boudinhon:—

'La *Dissertatio* accumule des citations de théologiens catho-

---

[1] 'C'est une prière, sans doute, il y est question des ordinands, sans doute encore; mais je n'y retrouve pas, du moins pas assez clairement, la trame et la construction des prières catholiques, pour oser y voir une forme valable d'ordination au presbytérat'; p 55

liques pour bien déterminer la nature de cette "intentio generalis faciendi quod facit ecclesia" dont parle le Concile de Trente (sess. vii. can. 2). "Quod Ecclesia *facit*, dit d'abord Tournely, non quod Ecclesia *intendit*." Et Bellarmin· "Non est opus intendere quod facit ecclesia *Romana*, sed quod facit *vera* ecclesia, quaecumque illa sit . . . non tollit efficaciam sacramenti error ministri circa ecclesiam, sed defectus intentionis." Et après un long passage de Lehmkuhl, que j'ai reproduit moi-même pour la plus grande part, la *Dissertatio* cite des textes absolument concluants de Liebermann et de Franzelin. Le premier surtout est *ad rem*: "Non requiritur ut minister sacramenti effectum intendat" . . . car les textes qui font autorité dans l'Église ne contiennent aucune mention "aut *finis* quam minister sibi proponit, aut *effectus* qui ex sacramento profluit." C'est ce qui a permis à l'Église de tenir pour valide le baptême conféré par des hérétiques ou des infidèles "quamvis illi effectum sacramenti negarent, aut id tantum intenderent facere quod sua, non quod Romana, facit ecclesia." Cette conclusion peut être corroborée par de nombreux textes des théologiens et par de très claires décisions romaines. J'en citerai deux seulement. Innocent IV. (comme auteur privé; cité par Franzelin, *Dissert*. n 145) dit en parlant du baptême: "Non est necesse quod baptizans sciat quid sit Ecclesia, quid baptismus, vel unde sit, nec quod gerat in mente facere quod facit Ecclesia, immo si contrarium gereret in mente, scilicet non facere quod Ecclesia, sed tamen fecit, quia formam servat, nihilominus baptizatus est, dummodo baptizare intendat." Une récente décision du Saint Office est tout aussi explicite; je l'emprunte à la *Collectanea* de la Propagande, n. 539. "S C. S. Officii, 18 Decem. 1872; Vic. Ap. Oceani Centr.—In quibusdam locis nonnulli (haeretici) baptizant cum materia et forma debitis simultanee applicatis, sed expresse monent baptizandos ne credant baptismum habere ullum effectum in animam: dicunt enim ipsum esse signum mere externum aggregationis illorum sectae . . Quaeritur: utrum baptismus ab illis haereticis administratus sit dubius propter defectum intentionis faciendi quod voluit Christus, si expresse declaratum fuerit a ministro, antequam baptizet, baptismum nullum effectum habere in animam?—R. *Negative*; quia non obstante errore quoad effectus baptismi, non excluditur intentio faciendi quod facit Ecclesia."'

Such is the condition in which he is content to leave the statement of the doctrine of intention, on the hypothesis that the form used is adequate, and in such condition we may be content to leave it too. For himself, he thinks that he has shown the inadequacy of the form. But, if the form sufficed, he holds that no objection about intention could invalidate it [1]. Nor, again, is he willing to allow that doctrinal omissions in the Ordinal itself, even on the assumption that their motive and meaning was heretical, could invalidate the Ordinal, so long as those facts of the Ordinal were still preserved, which had been ruled to constitute the 'essentials.' To omit 'essentials' is to destroy the whole. But if the 'essentials' are maintained, their validity cannot be invalidated by the omission, however wrong in itself, of points which are admitted to be non-essential [2].

Such is the position to which, after so mature a reconsideration, he finally brings his argument upon these points.

Now how do we stand? The position is surely a very curious one. M. Dalbus had got rid of the *prima facie* objections to Anglican validity, but had put forward two reasons nevertheless for disallowing it. Both of these M Duchesne put quietly aside,

[1] 'Les erreurs, les hérésies, de Barlow ou de l'Église Anglicane, qu'elle qu'en soit Pétendue ; la négation de la Présence réelle, et du pouvoir de consacrer, dût-on la regarder comme certaine, ne sont pas un obstacle à la suffisance de l'intention des évêques anglicans, à commencer par Barlow Et si, professant ces mêmes hérésies, ils avaient employé les rites de l'ordination catholique, il n'y aurait même pas lieu de poser la question : on leur appliquerait sans hésiter les règles de la théologie relatives aux sacrements administrés par les hérétiques' ; p 64

[2] 'Une omission de cette nature modifie-t-elle la valeur d'une prière, en restreint-elle la portée et l'efficacité? Il est permis de le nier Le sens et l'intention externe demeurent les mêmes, et de plus, comment une omission, même coupable, d'éléments non essentiels, pourrait-elle être nuisible ? Une omission est chose négative ; si ce qui est omis n'est pas requis, pourquoi ce qui reste deviendrait-il inefficace ?

'Car l'intention personnelle des auteurs de l'Ordinal ne pouvait influer sur la validité des ordinations que dans la mesure où elle se produirait dans l'Ordinal lui-même Ils n'étaient pas, eux, les ministres de l'ordination, et c'est l'intention du ministre qui est requise et peut compromettre l'ordination, si elle est viciée ; or, elle ne peut l'être par une hérésie de prétermission.

'En résumé, les arguments tirés du défaut de l'intention de Barlow et des évêques anglicans contre la validité des ordinations anglicanes ne sont valables que dans la mesure exacte où ils impliquent l'objection principale, l'insuffisance du rite' ; p 67.

—implying that there were no others to take their place, but that the matter waited in simple dependence upon the unfettered discretion of the majesty of Rome. The first M Boudinhon pulled M Dalbus' objections completely to pieces; and with a somewhat solemn word to M. Duchesne ('si l'Église pouvait accepter les Ordinations . . . elle devrait le faire') built up a fatal case against our Orders, which combined inadequacy of form with inadequacy of intention—the inadequacy of the form clinched by the 'heretical' surroundings and purposes—the 'heretical' character of the surroundings and purposes made fatal in the fact of unauthorized alterations of form. The second M Boudinhon (whilst refuting by the way the Dutch Alt-Katholiks, and the English Romanists in general, and Cardinal Vaughan in particular) knocks quietly away all the substance of the argument of the first M. Boudinhon, setting aside all arguments about 'intention' or heresy—not as untrue, but as irrelevant; but trying instead to consolidate anew, by means of a new major premiss (itself on examination quite untenable), a case against the adequacy of the Anglican services as they stand.

Such phenomena are strangely significant. The writers are all able men, and are all in earnest. But if not a shadow of a suggestion is hinted against them, what do the phenomena mean? They mean that these gentlemen, for all their ability and earnestness, are not free. Consciously or unconsciously, they work with the fetters of certain presuppositions—slender it may be in seeming but adamantine in constraining force—upon their minds and consciences. It is the working of the Nemesis which must follow upon submission, intellectual and moral, to a primary untruth. They are paralyzed by the hypothesis of the infallibility of Rome.

There is yet one more brochure that I wish to refer to. The argument is taken up, still in 1895, by the Abbé Delasge. To begin with, he cannot but be struck with this aspect of the controversy: 'Une chose curieuse à noter, c'est que la question a souvent été déplacée . il est bien rare que les adversaires des ordinations anglicanes aient donné, suivant les temps et même aussi suivant les personnes, les mêmes raisons d'invalidité. On paraît surtout s'être préoccupé d'une seule chose, la non-validité, sans trop se soucier de la valeur des preuves fournies. Peu importait d'ailleurs la raison pour laquelle elles seraient invalides, pourvu qu'elles le fussent C'est ce qui explique pourquoi on allégua dans le passé tant de raisons diverses, sérieuses parfois, le plus souvent futiles'; p. 6. For himself he believes that this over-ruling prejudice had its origin in mere errors, based on the proved falsehood of the 'Tête de Cheval,' and that no generation, until the present, has been fully in possession of the data for a true decision. In the very fact that opponents based their objections so long on an incredible fable, he finds a proof that they dared not take up other ground. Driven from this at last, they began to raise doubts of Barlow's consecration. Such doubts he says never crossed the mind of man so long as it was still possible to impugn the consecration of Parker, and for himself he treats them only with eloquent scorn.

There is some touch of scorn still in his treatment of objections on the score of intention · 'Notons tout d'abord que l'intention requise chez le ministre pour qu'un sacrement soit valide n'est pas l'intention de faire ce que fait l'Église romaine, mais bien celle de faire ce que fait *la vraie Église et ce qu'a voulu Jésus-Christ* en instituant ce sacrement. Or, je ne crois pas que l'on puisse refuser aux évêques anglicans l'intention de faire ce qu'a fait Jésus-Christ, lorsqu'ils ordonnent des prêtres ou sacrent des évêques. Qu'on lise dans l'Ordinal d'Edouard les cérémonies du sacre, et tous les doutes à ce sujet seront certainement dissipés'; pp. 14, 15. 'Soutenir, en effet, que les évêques anglicans n'ont pas l'intention d'administrer le sacrement de l'Ordre parce qu'ils professent quelques erreurs relatives au saint sacrifice de la messe c'est dire que l'erreur du ministre, touchant les effets du sacrement, détruit en lui l'intention de faire ce que fait l'Église de Jésus-Christ' (p. 15). . . . 'Si donc Barlow a pris les moyens de faire un évêque, pourquoi lui refuser l'intention d'atteindre le but pour lequel il avait mis tout en œuvre, et qui, d'ailleurs, ressortait le plus naturellement du monde de la cérémonie du sacre de Parker? Peu importe que le rite employé soit ou ne soit pas suffisant, cela ne saurait nuire à l'intention de faire ce que fait l'Église, et Barlow avait cette intention'; p. 18 [1].

---

[1] He cites amongst other things, on pp 17, 18, the decision of Dec. 18, 1872, and the quotation from Cardinal Bellarmine, both given by M Boudinhon above, and offers them (as Boudinhon did) to Cardinal Vaughan ' Un raisonne-

He goes on to speak in much the same tone of objections to the rite: 'Il serait bien facile en effet d'affirmer que le rite employé est insuffisant—et d'ailleurs on l'a dit—mais dire aussi en quoi consiste cette insuffisance, et surtout la corroborer de preuves inéluctables, est certainement moins aisé.' 'Quant aux raisons, elles varient selon les auteurs. Les uns affirment que l'unique fait d'avoir modifié la formule du Pontifical romain suffit pour enlever toute efficacité sacramentelle à la formule tirée de l'Ordinal anglican. Pour d'autres, la raison n'en est pas là : elle se rencontre dans la porrection des instruments supprimée par les réformateurs du Pontifical D'autres invoquent le sens hérétique de la formule. D'autres, enfin, pensent que le rite employé est simplement trop court'; pp. 19, 20. Every one of these reasons is, on examination, set aside. He thinks of course that the Reformers spoilt the beauty and dignity of the Pontifical[1], but he denies that they touched the essentials; and as for the objection of 'heresy,' those who make it do not understand what heresy, in a form of ritual, means. 'Pour qu'une formule soit hérétique, il est nécessaire qu'elle contienne une erreur nettement exprimée et non seulement sous-entendue : Dum-modo error non exprimitur in formula tanquam explicita vel implicita conditio, non excludere intentionem faciendi quod facit Ecclesia, ac proinde non obstare validitati sacramenti[2],' p. 25.

ment bien simple nous permet d'appliquer au cas qui nous occupe cette décision de la Propagande. Supposons, pour un instant, qu'au lieu d'un calviniste administrant le sacrement du Baptême et déclarant qu'il ne croit point à l'acte régénérateur qu'il accomplit, nous soyons, en présence d'un évêque anglican conférant les Ordres et déclarant au sujet qu'il n'en veut pas faire un prêtre sacrifiant. Quelle différence existe-t-il dans la manière d'agir, de ces deux personnages ? Est-ce que l'un et l'autre ne professent pas solennellement une erreur monstrueuse contre la vertu du sacrement ? S'il existait une différence, elle serait certainement en faveur du dernier Si donc vous reconnaissez à l'un l'intention de faire ce que fait l'Église de Jésus-Christ lorsqu'elle accomplit un acte identique, pourquoi la refuser à l'autre qui se trouve dans les mêmes conditions ? Si vous tenez pour valide le baptême administré par les protestants, pourquoi rejetez-vous, comme invalides, les ordinations des anglicans ? Il y a là un manque, de logique que je ne puis admettre, une partialité choquante qui ne mérite pas notre crédit'; p 17.

[1] 'Ils l'ont bouleversé . . . ils l'ont découronné, ruiné, renversé, pour mettre à sa place quoi ? une formule sèche, qui ne parle plus au cœur, qui n'a plus cette attirance mystérieuse, si goûtée des fidèles,' &c. ; p. 21. This is M. Delasge's opinion.

[2] Quoting Gury de Sacram. He adds in a note, 'Non seulement il faudrait

APPENDIX

He not unnaturally demurs to the width of M. Dalbus' phrase, which had appeared to require for the 'forma' of ordination anything, whatever its irrelevancy of context, which could be said to be a prayer; but on the other hand has no difficulty in accepting, as essentially adequate, any such prayers as express and interpret the purpose to ordain. He therefore concludes, without reserve, that Anglican ordinations are not invalid.

What then are we to say of the Abbé Delasge? There is much indeed about the whole atmosphere of his argument which is unusually cogent, as it is unusually bold. Can we, in view of this, be called upon to unsay what has been said about the limitations which imprison and disable Roman controversialists? Does he disprove them? Or rather, though he may illustrate them in a different way from his more guarded compeers, does he not in the total result, passively, if not actively, illustrate them?

But in justice to M. Delasge, it must be remembered that his admissions, at their most, are strictly limited. He began by distinguishing between 'lawfulness' and 'validity': and if he wished to admit the validity, he of course denied the 'lawfulness' of Anglican ministries. To him, as to his brethren, Anglicans were never better than schismatics, who, holding heretical opinions upon many points of essential doctrine, had, of heretical pravity, disfigured and destroyed the venerable beauty and mystery of the Pontifical. If he thought on the whole that these heresies and disfigurements just did not, while most of his brethren thought that they just did, make the transmission of orders impossible to Anglicanism, the distinction between them herein was not, after all, so considerable as it might appear to be. In either case Anglicans were contumacious and schismatical, in either case their Orders were unlawful and irregular; in either case they were without jurisdiction.

The discussion, then, has not carried us very far. Could it

que l'erreur fût exprimée dans la formule en termes non équivoques: il faudrait de plus que son auteur en ait fait la condition *sine qua non* de l'intention du ministre (toujours d'après Gury). condition qui devrait être explicite ou implicite. La condition serait explicite si la formule disait en propres termes qu'elle entend en faire la condition de l'intention. Elle serait implicite si (l'erreur étant nettement exprimée) la formule laissait facilement comprendre qu'elle a voulu faire de cette erreur une condition *sine qua non*. Dans l'un et l'autre cas, l'erreur doit être exprimée en toutes lettres et non seulement sous-entendue'; p. 26.

carry us further? Has it not, upon its hypothesis, gone already as far, or more than as far, as was logically possible to it? Was there ever, from the beginning, any reality in the question whether Anglican Orders could be admitted upon the Roman hypothesis? If 'the Roman hypothesis' merely meant the technical Roman teaching on such points as 'materia' and 'forma,' then all might have been simple enough; but those who boldly set out, upon ideas like these, to carry conviction to Romanists that they ought, on their own hypothesis, to acknowledge English Orders, forgot how much the 'Roman hypothesis,' involved. They forgot that, in fact, 'the Roman hypothesis' includes the whole circle of *her* theory, includes, above all, the postulates—first, that Rome is herself the only and the whole Church, in the sense, at least, that Roman acknowledgement is the one and only test of even the most precarious kind of membership in the Church; and secondly, that whatever at any time Rome has really done or said is in such sense absolutely right, that any deliberate criticism of her doctrine, or intentional divergence from her ways, whether it be more pardonable or less, must be, in every case, absolutely wrong. Be it in things of graver or of lesser moment, she has never by exaggerating or by minimizing, made a mistake. No one, therefore, who has differed from her judgement, ever has been, or can ever be, justified.

But at this point discussion is superseded by the action of the Papal authority itself. And it is impossible not to feel that the intervention of the Papal authority at this point—in a spirit, apparently, of devout piety, Christian love, and fervent yearning for unity—as in any case it had an interest strangely dramatic, so was calculated to raise in thoughtful minds aspirations, at least, if not expectations, which transcended the barriers of difficulties, momentary and technical, in a longing for the vital realities of Divine truth. What could this authority effect if it would?—what would this authority have the heart or the will to desire? Considering the nature of the barriers by which private Romanists were bound, it was clear, at the least, that, whether by authoritative explanation, or authoritative direction, the supreme authority could itself do much more if it had but the heart and the will—than any other but the supreme authority could dare to attempt.

No wonder that unusual feelings, of interest and of kindliness, were aroused. Whilst, from across the Channel, there comes back the memory of almost the final words of Boudinhon: 'L'attitude de la curie Romaine, qui laisse librement discuter le probléme, est à son tour un indice pratique que ces conclusions ne sont pas téméraires', and of Delasge, ' Au lieu de se cantonner dans les préjugés injustifiables d'un côté et de se retrancher dans une indifférence quelque peu dédaigneuse de l'autre, les catholiques et les anglicans ont certes mieux à faire c'est de répondre à l'appel paternel que Léon XIII nous adressait naguère lorsqu'il nous conviait tous à la prière'; and of Duchesne, 'Rien n'empêche de croire que, par la suite des temps, cette opinion se corrige, et que l'autorité ecclésiastique elle-même n'en vienne à modifier son attitude': in England it is of historical interest to recall the sort of feeling to which Mr Gladstone gave his own free and sanguine utterance [1]. ' It is to the last degree improbable that a ruler of known wisdom would at this time put in motion the machinery of the Curia for the purpose of widening the breach. . . .' 'The information which I have been allowed through the kindness of Lord Halifax to share, altogether dispels from my mind every apprehension of this kind, and convinces me that if the investigations of the Curia did not lead to a favourable result, wisdom and charity, would in any case arrest them at such a point as to prevent their becoming an occasion and a means of embittering religious controversy. . . . When therefore it came to be understood that Pope Leo XIII had given his commands that the validity of Anglican Orders should form the subject of an historical and theological investigation, it was impossible not to be impressed with the profound interest of the considerations brought into view by such a step, if interpreted in accordance with just reason, as an effort towards the abatement of controversial differences. . . . What courage must it require in a Pope, what elevation above all the levels of stormy partisanship, what genuineness of love for the whole Christian flock, whether separated or annexed, to enable him to approach the huge mass of hostile and still burning recollections, in the spirit, and for the purpose of peace ! And yet that is what Pope Leo has done. . . .

[1] In a letter published by the Archbishop of York in the *Guardian* of June 3, 1896, p. 873.

Be the issue what it may, there is in my view no room for doubt as to the attitude which has been taken by the actual head of the Roman Catholic Church in regard to them. It seems to me an attitude in the largest sense paternal. . .'

But if, in any such ways, the situation seemed at the time to be rich with the sense of untried possibilities,—what was it, in fact, which the supreme authority in the Roman Church did? There are, I conceive, two strains of description, by no means obviously identical, yet both alike true, which may be applied to the Papal action as a whole. The Pope, it may be said, adopted in effect no new decision · he only made articulate what the whole previous history and circumstances implied, he only formally expressed as conclusion, what was unmistakably contained, on their most natural interpretation, within the premisses. This is true. But that it should be true is the heart of the pathos. It is the very admirableness of the protagonist, it is the moral excellence of his purposes coupled with what seems the logical inexorableness of a perverse setting of preassumptions or preconditions, which is the familiar secret of living tragedy. For on the other hand, it would be no less true to pronounce of the Papal action as a whole, that, basing itself upon the lines of a warped continuity of tradition and theory, it reaffirmed every disproportion of the older conception, re-emphasized every externalizing and materializing tendency, and deliberately riveted, on the struggling intellect and conscience, every paralyzing fetter afresh. At a moment singularly rich with possibilities for the future, it made after all no new effort; it saw no glimpse of newly harmonizing or interpretative insight; it simply sank back—as it were exhausted and defeated—within the rigidities which had suited, which perhaps had sufficed for, a cruder and a rigider age. It was all most human, and most natural. It is just how tragedies happen, for lack of the transcendently creative genius—shall I say the divine inspiration —of some great master-mind. It is no case for censure—hardly even for disappointment, but it is infinitely sad. Not as a blow to 'Anglicanism'—for that, in fact, it is not—but as a blow to human effort of love and insight into Truth; as a blow, above all, to the identification with divine working of love and divine insight into truth of the organization of the Roman communion, it is strangely sad to read this last utterance of authoritative Romanism.

First came the Encyclical, dated on St. Peter's Day. After much that is true and beautiful on the subject of the Church, it passes on to such teaching as this. 'From this text' (Matt. xvi. 18) it is clear that by the will and command of God the Church rests upon St. Peter, just as a building rests upon its foundation.' '[God] invested [Peter] therefore with the needful authority, since the right to rule is absolutely required by him who has to guard human society really and effectively,' . . . 'and since all Christians must be closely united in the communion of one immutable faith, Christ the Lord, in virtue of His prayers, obtained for Peter that in the fulfilment of his office he should never fall away from the faith.' 'It was necessary that a government of this kind, since it belongs to the constitution and formation of the Church, as its principal element—that is as the principle of unity and the foundation of lasting stability—should in no wise come to an end with St Peter, but should pass to his successors from one to another.'. 'For this reason Jesus Christ willed that Peter should participate in certain names, signs of great things which properly belong to himself alone, in order that identity of titles should show identity of power' . . . 'For this reason the Pontiffs who succeed Peter in the Roman Episcopate receive the supreme power in the Church *jure divino*' . . 'But if the authority of Peter and his successors is plenary and supreme, it is not to be regarded as the sole authority. For He who made Peter the foundation of the Church also *chose twelve whom He called Apostles* (Luke vi. 13), and just as it is necessary that the authority of Peter should be perpetuated in the Roman Pontiff, so by the fact that the Bishops succeed the Apostles they inherit their ordinary power, and thus the Episcopal order necessarily belongs to the essential constitution of the Church.' . . . 'But since the successor of Peter is one, and those of the Apostles are many, it is necessary to examine into the relations which exist between him and them according to the Divine constitution of the Church. Above all things the need of union between the Bishops and the successors of Peter is clear and undeniable.' . . . 'It is necessary, therefore, to bear this in mind, viz that nothing was conferred on the Apostles apart from Peter, but that several things were conferred on Peter apart from the Apostles' . . . 'From this it must be clearly understood that Bishops are deprived of the right and power of ruling if they deliberately secede from Peter and his successors, because by this secession they are separated from the foundation on which the whole edifice must rest. They are, therefore, outside the *edifice* itself, and for this very reason they are separated from the *fold*, whose leader is the Chief Pastor; they are exiled from the *kingdom*, the keys of which were given by Christ to Peter alone.' . . . 'The Episcopal Order is rightly judged to be in communion with Peter, as Christ commanded, if it be subject to and obeys Peter; otherwise it necessarily becomes a lawless and disorderly crowd. It is not sufficient for the unity of the faith that the head should merely have been charged with the office of superintendent, or should have been invested solely with a power of direction But it is absolutely necessary that he should have received real and sovereign authority which the whole community is bound to obey' . . 'It is opposed to the truth, and in evident contradiction with the Divine constitution of the Church, to hold that while each Bishop is *individually* bound to obey the authority of the Roman Pontiffs, taken *collectively* the Bishops are not so bound.' . . 'As the Bishops, each in his own district, command with real power not only individuals, but the whole community, so the Roman Pontiffs, whose jurisdiction extends to the whole Christian commonwealth, must have all its parts, even taken collectively, subject and obedient to their authority. Christ the Lord, as we have quite sufficiently shown, made Peter and his successors His *vicars*, to exercise for ever in the Church the power which He exercised during His mortal life.'

Such are the statements which the Pope thought fit to reemphasize for the illumination of those who had ventured to discuss the validity of Anglican Orders; and of such nature, it must be added, are the considerations which, in the face of an intelligent Christendom, he seriously puts forward as proofs of his claim to a sovereignty unconditional and absolute. The claim, thus sharply articulated, is indeed as hopelessly irreconcilable alike with the theology of the Incarnation and even the broad truth of the history of Christendom, as it is with the picture of the Church community, the Apostolate in general, or St. Peter individually, within the pages of the New Testament. But it is no part of my present task to analyze either the assumptions or the arguments of the Encyclical. That such teaching was really part of the Roman system was, of course, known to all the world. That individual Romanists could not venture to seem to contravene it was the main cause of the unreality of the previous stages of the controversy. But that it should, at such a moment, be re-emphasized to the world, with all its unmeasured exaggeration, and in sharp dogmatic trenchancy, was for those who loved not the make-believe of the twilight but the openness of the day, with its freshness, its light, and its truth—a most melancholy symptom indeed.

There followed in the early days of September, the long promised Bull. It is not particularly kind to the French theologians. After reciting 'previous decisions,' the 'invariable practice of the Holy See,' and, as specially crucial, the degree of Clement XI in the matter of John Clement Gordon, it proceeds: 'Hence it must be clear to every one that the controversy lately revived had been already definitely settled by the Apostolic See, and that it is to the insufficient knowledge of these documents[1] that we must perhaps attribute the fact that any Catholic writer should have considered it still an open question.'

Such a mistake, so far as infallibility can prevent it, shall never be made by a Roman writer again. 'We decree that these Letters and all things contained therein, shall not be liable at any time to be impugned or objected to by reason of any fault or any other defect whatsoever of subreption or obreption or of Our intention, but are and shall be always valid and in force, and shall be inviolably observed both juridically and otherwise by all of whatsoever degree and pre-eminence; declaring null

[1] It is possible that the phrase 'these documents' in this context may be intended to refer—not to the 'previous decisions,' &c., above recited, but rather to certain 'documents of incontestable authenticity,' to which the Bull vaguely refers as proving its contention that the decision of Clement XI about Gordon was wholly uninfluenced by the [faulty] arguments put forward by Gordon himself. This, no doubt, would soften the snub to the French divines. If there are such documents, they would be of real, though certainly not decisive, interest. But as the two Archbishops have pointed out, the Pope's reference to them is very uncertain; and they 'ought to be made public if the matter is to be put on a fair footing for judgement.'

and void anything which in these matters may happen to be contrariwise attempted, whether wittingly or unwittingly, by any person whatsoever, by whatsoever authority or pretext, all things to the contrary notwithstanding.' There is something magnificent, if melancholy, in the pretension of this final clause, to those who have any conception of what nature the 'all things to the contrary' will have to be.

Certainly no one can complain that the Pope has not been explicit. 'Ordinations carried out according to the Anglican rite have been and are absolutely null and void.' No 'Catholic' ever ought to have doubted this before No 'Catholic' ever shall make any question about it again.

But 'these Letters and all things contained therein' mean not only a decision, but an argument. As a mode of showing 'the greatest consideration and charity,' the Pope has both re-examined and authoritatively restated the argumentative grounds upon which his decision rests. We know exactly now on what Romanists are to rely. The invalidating defects are entirely to be found in the Prayer Book. There is no longer a breath of doubt about Barlow's consecration, nor about Parker's either, if only the Edwardine form could have conferred consecration The defect is in the Prayer Book wholly

This defect in the Prayer Book appears to be described as twofold. It is partly in 'form' and partly in 'intention'[1]. Let

---

[1] The section of the Bull in question stands, in full, as follows :—

'In the examination of any rite for the effecting and administering of Sacrament, distinction is rightly made between the part which is *ceremonial* and that which is *essential*, usually called the *matter and form*. All know that the Sacraments of the New Law, as sensible and efficient signs of invisible grace, ought both to signify the grace which they effect, and effect the grace which they signify. Although the signification ought to be found in the whole essential rite—that is to say, in the matter and form--it still pertains chiefly to the form; since the matter is the part which is not determined by itself, but which is determined by the form And this appears still more clearly in the Sacrament of Orders, the matter of which, in so far as We have to consider it in this case, is the imposition of hands, which indeed by itself signifies nothing definite, and is equally used for several Orders and for Confirmation But the words which until recently were commonly held by Anglicans to constitute the proper form of priestly Ordination—namely, "*Receive the Holy Ghost*"— certainly do not in the least definitely express the Sacred Order of Priesthood, or its grace and power, which is chiefly the power "*of consecrating and of offering the true body and blood of the Lord*" (Council of Trent, Sess. XXIII,

us try to take the alleged defect in 'form' by itself first It may be stated in these propositions, viz (1) 'The grace and power of' 'the sacred order of priesthood' 'is chiefly the power of consecrating and of offering the true body and blood of the Lord.' (2) This being what the sacrament ought essentially to signify, must not be omitted in the form of the conveyal of the sacrament. (3) This *was* omitted in the Edwardine formula 'Receive the Holy Ghost: whose sins thou dost forgive. . . . And be thou a faithful dispenser of the word of God, and of His holy Sacraments'

de Sacr. Ord., Can. 1) in that sacrifice which is no "*nude commemoration of the sacrifice offered on the Cross*" (Ibid Sess. XXII, de Sacrif Missae, Can. 3). This form had indeed afterwards added to it the words "*for the office and work of a priest,*" &c ; but this rather shows that the Anglicans themselves perceived that the first form was defective and inadequate But even if this addition could give to the form its due signification, it was introduced too late, as a century had already elapsed since the adoption of the Edwardine Ordinal, for, as the Hierarchy had become extinct, there remained no power of ordaining. In vain has help been recently sought for the plea of the validity of Orders from the other prayers of the same Ordinal For, to put aside other reasons which show this to be insufficient for the purpose in the Anglican rite, let this argument suffice for all : from them has been deliberately removed whatever sets forth the dignity and office of the priesthood in the Catholic rite. That form consequently cannot be considered apt or sufficient for the Sacrament which omits what it ought essentially to signify.

'The same holds good of Episcopal Consecration. For to the formula "*Receive the Holy Ghost,*" not only were the words "*for the office and work of a Bishop,*" &c , added at a later period, but even these, as we shall presently state, must be understood in a sense different to that which they bear in the Catholic rite.

'Nor is anything gained by quoting the prayer of the preface "Almighty God," since it in like manner has been stripped of the words which denote the *summum sacerdotium* It is not here relevant to examine whether the Episcopate be a completion of the priesthood or an Order distinct from it, or whether when bestowed, as they say, *per saltum*, on one who is not a priest, it has or has not its effect But the Episcopate undoubtedly by the institution of Christ most truly belongs to the Sacrament of Orders, and constitutes the sacerdotium in the highest degree—namely, that which by the teaching of the Holy Fathers and our liturgical customs is called the "*summum sacerdotium, sacri ministerii summa*" So it comes to pass that, as the Sacrament of Orders and the true sacerdotium of Christ were utterly eliminated from the Anglican rite, and hence the sacerdotium is in no wise conferred truly and validly in the Episcopal consecration of the same rite, for the like reason, therefore, the Episcopate can in no wise be truly and validly conferred by it ; and this the more so because among the first duties of the Episcopate is that of ordaining ministers for the Holy Eucharist and sacrifice '

It is necessary to say a few words about these propositions.

As to the first of them, any one who has been able to read, with the least sympathy, what was said above in the discussion upon the meaning of priesthood, will anticipate the comment that must be made now. The meaning of the proposition appears to be this, that the constitutive essence of priesthood is to be described as the power of consecrating and of offering the true body and blood of the Lord. (So far as the word 'chiefly' qualifies this statement, it apparently does so only as reminding that the power of consecrating, &c. is not an *exhaustive* account of all priestly functions, but not as meant to suggest that the specific mention of other things is a *sine qua non* for ordination to priesthood; far less as modifying the importance of the definition by 'sacrifice' so far as to suggest that priesthood could, perhaps, be otherwise conferred.) Assuming that this is what the proposition means, I must submit that the proposition is a perilous one,—at once true, and not true. It is true that the 'power of consecrating' is the outward sign which marks characteristically the distinction between a priest and not a priest. It is not true that the priesthood to which a man has been ordained can be summed up as the power to consecrate. The prerogative of sacramental leadership, august though it be, is not so much the constitutive essence, as (rather) itself an effect inhering in, and outflowing from, that representative status in the body of Christ, that divinely authorized relation to souls, which is the real core and heart of priestly ministry. In a merely external and conventional sense, the proposition might pass for ordinary purposes as true. But it is untrue if intended as a solemn definition of the inner reality. It might pass as true in the sort of sphere in which it might be said that a 'Bishop' means 'one who can confirm,' or 'can ordain.' But it is equally untrue with that statement if alleged in serious theological exposition. Again, as to say that Episcopate means the 'potestas ordinandi' might represent the truth (which, immediately, it travesties) to those who could catch and spiritualize the implications interpretatively contained in it; so to say that priesthood means the 'potestas offerendi' might, to those who could interpret it spiritually with a width of significance rarely dreamed of in controversy, symbolize the wide truth which immediately it so narrows as, in fact, to belie. The proposition is untrue, in short, as the basis of an argument like the papal; even while there is a popular kind of truth in its literal words, and while that popular truth, spiritually reinterpreted, might be found to represent the very conception which it now is designed to refute.

As to the second proposition, I must point out that two somewhat different statements seem in it to be slurred. Does it mean that a form which fully characterized the priesthood that it meant to convey, would not omit the 'power of consecrating,' &c., or does it mean that any (technically so-called) 'form' for ordaining, to priesthood which did not specify the 'power of consecrating, &c would be *ipso facto* null and void? If it means only the first of these (or indeed if it means anything less than the second) then the argument of the three propositions falls to the ground. But if it means the second, it is a proposition which every (even Roman) theologian knows to be untenable[1]. As to the third proposition, whilst I shall of course admit, that neither the Edwardine nor the Caroline Ordinal speaks explicitly of 'consecrating and offering,' I shall no less certainly claim that they both do, by true and necessary and direct and intentional inference, imply and involve whatever is truly contained in the full doctrinal exposition of the 'Holy Sacraments.'

As a real argument against the adequacy of the form of the Ordinal, there is nothing here that can seem, for a moment, to be substantial. The objection dissolves at a touch. It could only hold if priesthood never *could* have been conferred without a formal conferring of the 'power to offer.'

But of course I anticipate that a rejoinder will at once be ready to this. It will be said that the papal condemnation of the Ordinal turns on the fact that certain things were not only not emphasized

[1] The statement that the words 'for the office and work of a priest,' &c. were added because the 'Anglicans themselves perceived that the first form was defective and inadequate' is, no doubt, a very serious historical blunder. It is an evidence, moreover, of the artificial and pedantic character of thought on the subject that any one who was at all familiar with the service (of 1552) as a whole, should ever have seriously imagined that the presence or absence of these words, apt and solemn and desirable as they are, could have affected, in the slightest measure, either the meaning, or the effect, of the total rite. Considering the resources at the command of the Pope, that a slip like this should have been allowed to appear in a document of such a character, and for such a purpose, is—quite apart from 'infallibility'—altogether surprising

but 'deliberately removed,' 'utterly eliminated.' Quite so. But I wish to point out that the argument in this shape, is not really so much an argument against the 'form' as against the 'intention' of the Ordinal, against the form, not in itself, but as at once the outcome and the evidence of 'intention', as the outcome of the vicious 'intention' of those who constructed it, and as an overt evidence of intention at least inadequate in those who consent to make use of it. By all means let us give full weight to the argument But do not let us be deceived as to the character of it. It is hardly correct, after all, to speak of the argument as twofold. It is not an argument *both* against the form, *and* the intention of the Ordinal. The real argument, and the only real argument, is against Anglican 'intention' It is this which vitiates the form. Apart from this it is not certain, after all, whether the form is really condemned or no The Bull is not guilty then of constructing an argument against the form, by adopting outright the proposition that ordination to 'presbyterate' must specify 'sacrifice,' the proposition which every theologian knows to be untenable. But it must be owned that the way in which the Bull is arranged does give a strong *prima facie* appearance of this And I have purposely taken first the apparent argument against the form, without reference to intention, for the purpose of making it transparently clear that the Bull, whilst it seems to do so, does not really contain an argument against the intrinsic validity of the form at all M. Boudinhon, in his second pamphlet, had essayed to prove that the Anglican form as it stood was incapable of conferring priesthood The Bull makes no such attempt. All that it says about the form, even all that it says about the 'power of consecrating,' becomes effective argumentatively only in proportion as it emphasizes the inherently defective 'intention' of Anglicanism. If it is laid down in the Bull that 'that form consequently cannot be considered apt or sufficient for the Sacrament which omits what it ought essentially to signify,' we find, on second thoughts, that the whole emphasis is upon 'omits,' in the sense of omitting deliberately. For 'omits' in that sentence substitute 'does not express,' and you will have a form of proposition upon which the Bull has not ventured. No, the Ordinal is defective because of the 'spirit' which is behind it History is 'eloquent as to the animus' of its authors. 'Every trace' of 'the sacrifice, of consecration, of sacerdotium,' was 'deliberately removed and struck out' Thus it is that 'a new rite has been initiated in which' 'the Sacrament of Orders is adulterated or denied,' and 'from which all idea of consecration and sacrifice has been rejected.' And thus it is that words which were valid before are now emptied of their validity—'the formula *Receive the Holy Ghost*, no longer holds good,'—because the whole conception behind them is wrong. The very titles, bishop, priest, to the spirit of Anglicanism 'remain as words without reality which Christ instituted.' All this is quite irrespective of any question whether, on another hypothesis, the forms of the Ordinal might, or might not, have been adequate. 'By this same argument,' says the Bull, 'is refuted the contention of those who think that the prayer *Almighty God, giver*, &c. . . might suffice as a legitimate form of Orders, *even on the hypothesis that it might be held to be sufficient in a Catholic rite approved by the Church.*' These last words, which I have ventured to italicize, conclusively show that —intention apart—the Bull makes no real attempt to prove the inadequacy of the Anglican rite.

It is not indeed in itself any object to Anglicans to show that the Bull does not try to prove the invalidity of their form. The considerations against their form which the Bull does contain are so manifestly inadequate for that purpose, that it could only serve their cause to be impugned on such grounds. But unless the Bull wishes to be interpreted as taking up a position notoriously impossible, it is certainly not entitled to use the phrase with which section 9 begins, 'with this inherent *defect of form* is joined the *defect of intention* which is equally essential to the sacrament.' Unless the Papal authority is prepared to maintain that, without mention of sacrifice, no ordination to presbyterate ever has been, or could have been effectual, it has not proved—has not even alleged—against the Prayer Book, anything that can possibly be called an 'inherent' defect of form

But if the real weight of argument in the Bull is, as I must submit that it is, *exclusively* against the general animus, or spirit of Anglicanism, and against forms in detail as results or expressions of this, it would seem to be important, for clearness of thought, to grasp the significance of this fact [1].

[1] 'The Church does not judge about the mind and intention in so far as

What is the nature or the evidence of this hopelessly invalidating animus? There are two ways, if we may gather from the Bull, in which it has expressed itself in the matter of the Ordinal. The one is the fact that Anglicanism has presumed to alter the Roman Pontifical. The other is the fact that, in altering, it has suppressed the explicit mention of the 'potestas offerendi.' Now these two facts show conclusively,—the one that Anglicanism ventures to challenge, and does in fact, separate herself from, the precise proportions of the Roman definition of priesthood,—the other, that Anglicanism makes overt refusal of obedience to the paramount authority of Rome. And this is the whole matter. There is, as of course, not a thought of any such question as whether, in criticizing or disagreeing with Rome, we are affirming or denying the truth of God. There is no attempt to *justify* the Roman definition which we criticize, or to show that the premisses of our criticism are *wrong*. To criticize Rome *is* to swerve from the truth of God. To adopt practices based on independence of Rome *is* to take a position outside of the Church of Christ. Principles like these are assumed as self-evident. The only *argument* necessary is to show that Anglicans do so differ from the Roman—which presumes to call itself the Catholic—Church.

This is all. We do not, in practice, implicitly obey, we do not, in doctrine, perfectly symbolize with, Rome. Therefore we are outside the Church. Therefore nothing that we believe, define, or practise, comes anywhere into the history, or the evidence, of what has been practised, defined, or believed, within the Church of Christ. Rather, therefore, our whole animus or spirit, being intentionally antagonistic to 'the Church,' is so wrong as to vitiate

---

it is something by its nature internal, but in so far as it is manifested externally she is bound to judge concerning it . . . If the rite be changed, with the manifest intention of introducing another rite not approved by the Church, and of rejecting what the Church does, *and what by the institution of Christ belongs to the nature of the Sacrament*, then it is clear that not only is the necessary intention wanting to the sacrament, but that the intention is adverse to and destructive of the Sacrament.' The question-begging words which I have ventured to italicize, and the introduction, in the preceding clause, of 'the [Roman] Church,' entirely neutralize the words, apparently reasonable, which my citation has omitted, 'When any one has rightly and seriously made use of the due form and the method requisite for effecting or conferring the Sacrament, he is considered by the very fact to do what the Church does.' These words therefore do not mean what they seem to say.

in detail everything, however inherently justifiable or effectual in others, which we do or attempt. It is the naked claim, after all, to infallible perfectness, and to absolute autocracy.

The real position, then, of Anglicanism, historical or theological, is never for a moment so much as glanced at. It is, to the Bull, unknown, or unimaginable. Possibly it may be said that this is only a logical result of Romanism. The fundamental hypothesis of Romanism may make, perhaps, any effort of approach to an independent inquiry into the truth of Romanism —and therefore into the truth of any position which challenges the truth of Romanism—little other than an impossible contradiction. For the present, and on present hypotheses, yes. This is but to say that, in the providence of God, the time is not yet ripe, when any such independent effort after truth can be made with seriousness in the name of Rome.

Let any one, even for a moment, make the mental effort to imagine that, owing to a certain intellectual rigidity and hardness, the mediaeval conceptions as to priesthood, though dealing with truth, had lost something of the perfect symmetry and proportion of truth; that they leant over much to a materializing of the spiritual; that their 'outward' was not quite perfectly harmonized as the outward of an 'inward'; that to call a presbyter bluntly a 'sacrificing priest[1],' without being literally untrue, was yet a coarse

[1] A form of statement in which Cardinal Vaughan appears to revel. At the beginning of Nov., 1896, if rightly reported in the daily papers, he shaped his public challenge to the Anglican bishops thus.—'Not one of them had dared to say that he was a sacrificing priest, and that all the clergy of the Church of England were sacrificing priests' In commenting again in March upon the letter of the Archbishops, he asked: 'Did they claim the power to produce the actual living Christ Jesus by transubstantiation upon the altar according to the claim of the Eastern and Western Churches?' He went on to argue that the Anglican 'Eucharistic sacrifice' was 'an essentially different sacrifice' from the Roman, because the Anglican priesthood 'claimed no miraculous, supernatural, sacrificial powers such as were exercised by the Eastern and Roman Churches.'

I need not comment upon his reference to the Eastern Church. The Eastern Church will, no doubt, take excellent care of itself. Meanwhile, the Cardinal has certainly done his best, on behalf of Romanism, to make the two conceptions of sacrifice 'essentially different.' He has done his best to reduce the spiritual mysteries of Christian Eucharist and priesthood to the level of a merely vulgar thaumaturgy; and many a thoughful Romanist must have writhed under the naïve recklessness of his polemics. Unhappily, since the Bull, it seems that even Cardinal Vaughan is justified.

and grating representation of what was only true, after all, in the sphere of things spiritual and mystical let him try to make all the mental effort necessary to such a hypothesis,—and add to it a recognition of the bare possibility that it may *not* be the ordinance of our Lord Jesus Christ that the Bishop of Rome should wield despotic power over the consciences of mankind: and behold! in a moment the whole of the alleged case against Anglicanism and Anglican Orders has vanished into thin air. There is absolutely not a shred of suggestion left. From end to end of the Bull there is not one syllable of argument, or even of suggestion, which is not wholly dependent, for very existence upon the two fundamental Roman assumptions,—that Roman definitions or practices are infallibly right, and that the Roman autocracy is Divine.

Though, then, it takes the form of argument, it is not in any sense really argumentative against Anglicanism. For argument between me and another must rest on some better basis than the simple assumption that I am inherently right, and that he, in precise proportion as he differs from me, must be wrong. If it is to be argument, it must, for the purpose, treat the case of either side as arguable, as deniable, as needing to be made good by evidence. In this sense it will hardly be said that the Bull is argumentative.

All this is much to be deplored. It will not, indeed, injure Anglicanism, for truth is not apt to be injured by insult or contempt, and Anglicanism herein represents the very spirit and truth of the Catholic Church, untrammelled by concealing and distorting overgrowths. Anglicanism is Catholicity, unperverted and rational. It has not stereotyped, as a part of its vital faith, mediaeval rigidities or misconceptions of spiritual truth. It has not woven itself in and in with a polity—too obviously neither apostolic nor primitive—whose impossible pretensions succeed only in opposing a barrier impassable to every such generous yearning after wider truth, every such impulse of conscientious and candid self-scrutiny, as might otherwise have borne fruit in reform and recovery. The true Catholic spirit, the spirit of the Apostolic and primitive Church, alive and expansive, without fossilizing overgrowth, in Anglicanism, appeals to, consecrates, and harmonizes, the whole nature of man. It is natural, not the less, but so much the more consistently, because the 'natural' for it, is of one piece with, and is perfected in, the 'supernatural.' It is thoroughly at home in all the complex workings of the history of man—which, nevertheless, it has, in a perfectly real sense, revolutionized. It cannot really fear, or be alien from, any truth of criticism or of science—which are but subordinate aspects of itself. It is philosophical through and through, while it is like nothing so little as a product of philosophy. Because it is rational, reason can be wholly at home in it. Because it is spiritual, reason can in it be transfigured—can learn to partake of the nature of complete and divinely luminous intelligence. The Spirit of Jesus, which is the life of the Church, the theology of the Incarnation, which is the ordered apprehension of the fundamental truths of the Spirit in the spiritual intellect, is not alien from any of these things, but includes and transfigures them all.

The latest position of Rome will not injure Anglicanism. But its injury must needs be grave to the cause of truth and the rational harmony of religion in the churches of the Roman obedience. The impulse to be too crudely logical in definition and two bluntly material in ceremony; the inherent tendency to externalize and to petrify whatever is set to represent or consecrate the hidden movement of the mysteries of the spiritual life; to smother the inward by over-assertion of outward; to emphasize the objective and material till that immaterial subjective, which is its heart of reality, sickens unto death; this always has been a temptation naturally fascinating to the Western mind. We know it very well among ourselves—often in the more Roman form as exuberant externalism; often in the correlative extreme, as an attempt to trample on legitimate outwardness; an attempt which ends only in making of the very negation of the outward, a new fossil or fetish of outwardness—the outwardness of unauthorized ministries, unseemly ill dress, and irreverent gesture and tone. But the heart of Anglicanism is too conscious of mystery to be itself either Puritanical or material. If some element of either peril is well-known to us within—certainly neither is vital to the being of—Anglicanism.

But it seems that the Papal authority has adopted without reserve this spirit of rigid externalism, which the Western mind loves. The full conception of realities like Sacrifice and Priesthood, which, while having an aspect indeed that is material and definable, are nevertheless themselves large with the undefined mystery of spiritual life, is tightly tied up and up into just what is most questionable, because most clearcut, most dogmatic, most external, least living and large. The universal jurisdiction and the infallibility of the Pope, the explicit doctrine of Purgatory, and the direct work wrought by earthly Celebrations upon souls therein, the technicalities of transubstantiation, and the crudest statements about a sacrificing and a miracle-working priesthood; all these, it seems, are to be necessary ingredients in the 'Catholic' meaning of the word, so that those who demur to any one of these are, *ipso facto*, incapable of apprehending or believing in the 'Priesthood of the Church.' That Rome should once more have identified herself herein with the mental attitude about her own mysteries, that is least large, or balanced, or rational, or true; and should have re-emphasized with all her power the disproportioned corollaries to which it has led in the past; cannot but be matter of profound concern to those who desire the truth and peace of Christendom. She has made, as it seems, one more supreme effort of emphasis to stamp and perpetuate the identity of her very being with ideas and methods such as can only serve to stereotype more and more to the minds and consciences of her own most intelligent children, the divergence—amounting to a contrast—between, on the one hand, the truths of experience and intelligence, of reason and love; and on the other, the definitions and the practices, the expressions and the theories, of (so-called) religious faith.

It might be feared that so tragic a failure as this would be likely to expose Christian thought, at a terrible disadvantage, to the reactionary prejudice of those who would cut short all mystery by explaining away, if not by denying outright, such truths as the Christian Sacrifice, and the Ministerial Priesthood, and the being and order of the visible Church. But perhaps it is not for the first time that the duty is laid by God's providence, on the Anglican Church, of making manifest the true relation between 'inward' and 'outward'—in this world where all spiritual is bodily, and all bodily meant to be spiritual; and so of conserving that true harmony (rational at once and mysterious) of spiritual realities, which the disproportion of a materialistic overstatement, upon the Roman side, had overlaid almost to death.

INDEX

Administration of the Holy Spirit (Dr. Moberly), 69.
Agabus, 160.
Anglican Orders, Roman controversy as to validity of, 301-354; technical questions, 301; four requirements, 302; Roman claim, the real question, 305: recent writers on, 311-338; Papal intervention, 338; the Encyclical, 341; the Bull, 343-351, grave prospect on Romanist side, 353.
Anglican Ordinal, 220, 223; its aim and merits, 286, 289.
Anglican Reformers, retain the priestly title, 234.
Antinomians, 49.
Apostles, the, their method of propagating Christianity, 8; their idea of unity, 34; Christ's commission to the Twelve, 100.
Apostolate, based on Christ's solemn selection, 126; St. Paul's case, 127, 131-134; its fundamental character and warrant, 127; its tremendous authority and power, 128, 133; basis and background of everything in the Church, 135, 145; the *Didache's* view of, 176.
Apostolic authority, a witness to unity, 31.
Apostolic Constitutions, 172, 225, 307.
Apostolic Fathers (Dr. Lightfoot), 202.
Apostolic men, or delegates, 146; instance of St. James—persona ecclesiae Hierosolymitanae, 146, 147, 150; functions of Timotheus and Titus—ruling, teaching, control, jurisdiction, 151-158.
Apostolic Succession, 113; Clement of Rome on, 114 et seq.; a question of the immediate present, 123; its abstract detachment, 124; how distinguishable from episcopacy, 124.
Aristotle's φύσει πολιτικόν, 4.
Article XXIII, 113.
Ascension of our Lord, The (Dr. Milligan), 72, 97, 129, 246, 248.
Ascension and Heavenly Priesthood of our Lord, The (Dr. Milligan), 251.
Athanasius, 172.

Bampton Lectures (Dr. Hatch), 9, 68, 112, 257; (Dr. Moberly), 69; (Canon Curteis), 55.
Baptism, Hooker on, 62; the *Didache* on, 171; its single formula, 327.
Barlow, Bishop, 314, 318.
Barnabas, 16, 140, 178.
Basis of Ministry—Divine Commission, 99-125.
Bellarmine, Cardinal, 335.
Bishop and Presbyter, interchangeable terms, 142, 144, 179; the *Didache's* view of, 175.
Bodily, and spiritual, unity, 31, 35, 39, 57.
Body, the method of Spirit, 39; Church of Christ, is the, 66; oneness of the whole, 67; its specific actions through specific organs, 68; a fallacious inference, 69.
Boudinhon, A. (*Étude théologique sur les ordinations anglicanes*), 320.
Bucer, Martin, 236, 311.
Bull, the Papal, 343.
Bulletin Critique, 316.
Burnet's *Records*, 235.

Cathann, 312
Celebratio Ordinum (Sarum), 220.
Χάρισμα, 103.
Christ, His high-priestly prayer, 7 ; His commission to the Twelve Apostles, 100 ; priesthood in the Church of, 220-299, His priestly sacrifice, 244-248 ; His priesthood, 249; is the Church, 251.
Christian and Levitical offerings — a parallel, 273, 274
Christian and saint, one personality, 38.
Christian Creed, unity of the, 2, 21.
Christian Ecclesia (Dr. Hort), 22, 24-29
Christian Ministry (Dr. Lightfoot), criticised, 43 et seq. ; his initial position, 46.
Christian Ministry, its conceptions dependent on Church unity, 1 ; Dr. Lightfoot's view of, 43 et seq. ; according to the *Didache*, 173 ; priestly executive privilege and pastoral self-devotion—two aspects of one reality, 285 ; objections answered, 290-299
Christian ordinances, efficacy of, 60
Christian Year, quoted, 84.
Christians, the corporate ideal, 9.
Church, The, universally inclusive, 5 ; Militant and Triumphant, 36, 37 ; the visible body of, is the spiritual, 40-42, a Temple and a Body, 66 ; of Christ, priesthood in, 220-299 ; Christ is, 251
Church and the Ministry, The (Canon Gore), 19, 71, 90, 112, 119, 129, 170-172, 266
Church and Dissent, The (Canon Curteis), 55.
Church Quarterly Review, 235, 237, 311.
Church Unity, Nature of, 1-29 ; its conceptions and meaning, 1, 6, 9 ; its ideas and forms, 2 ; outward circumstances, abstract conception, theological idea, of, 3-8 ; its theory, human and politic, 4, 8 ; transcendental and divine, 6, 8, 34; Dr Hatch on higher and lower conception of, 11; only spiritual? 31 ; St. Paul's struggle for, 32 ; apostolic conception of, 34.
Clement of Alexandria, 40, 83, 85, 257, 280
Clement of Rome, on Apostolic Succession, 114 et seq ; authority and character of his Letter · its contrast with the *Didache*, 179 ; its silence about prophets and prophecy, 180 ; his position episcopal, 184 ; his view of presbyters, 185 ; Dr. Lightfoot's translation of his Letter, 186 ; supplemented by Hermas, 209, 211, 214; on the Eucharist, 273.
Clementine writers, The, 49.
Corinthian Church, The, 180, 275.
Council of Florence, 228
Council of Trent, 223 ; regarded as a Roman Reformation, 231.
Cranmer, Archbishop, 234
Curteis, Canon (*The Church and Dissent*), on George Fox, 55 ; on means and end, 56.

Dalbus, Fernand (*Les Ordinations Anglicanes*), 311.
Dale, Dr , 265
Delasge, Abbé, 334, 337.
Diaconate, 136 ; Dr Lightfoot's view of, 136-139 ; its secular work · its spiritual character, 137 ; according to the *Didache*, 175
διάκονος, meaning of, 140.
Didache (διδαχή), 108 , its Jewish character, 171 ; on Baptism and the Eucharist, 171, 267, 272; its questionable authority, 172 ; on Church unity, 173 ; on Church polity, 175 ; like and unlike the New Testament, 177 , its limited insight, 178 ; contrasted with Clement of Rome's Letter, 179
Dissertations on the Apostolic Age (Dr. Lightfoot), 118, 119, 239.
Diversity and Unity, their relation, 31.
Divine Commission—the basis of ministry, 99-125 ; essential to the priesthood, 101 ; *see also*
Divine Designation—three alternatives·
—(1) Individual aspiration—arguments against, 106 , three points for, 107-109 (2) Church appointment, 110; denies ministerial principle, 111; must be established by history, 112 (3) Apostolic succession, supported by 23rd Article, 113 ; Clement of Rome a strong witness, 114 ; its crucial importance, 116
Divine Love, 247, 248
Divine Unity of the Church, 34.
Docetic Judaism, according to Dr. Lightfoot, 198.
Docetism, 190, 198
Doctrina Romanensium, 221.
Duchesne, Abbé, 316, 319.
Dunstan's Pontifical, 223.

Ebionism, 49
Ecclesia (Dr. Hort), 22, 127, 140, 156.

INDEX

Ecclesiastical Polity (Hooker), 103, 238, 239.
Egbert, Archbishop, Pontifical of, 223
Encyclical, The, 340.
End, and means, 56.
Episcopacy, how distinguishable from Apostolic Succession, 124; Dr. Lightfoot on, 216
ἐπίσκοπος, Clement's Letter on, 182; and πρεσβύτερος, interchangeable terms, 141, 144, 175, 179.
Essential, and of the Essence, 58-60.
Estcourt, Canon, 234, 288, 310
Étude théologique sur les ordinations anglicanes (M. Boudinhon), 320.
Eucharist, The, Dr Lightfoot on, 77; Justin Martyr on, 87, 278; the Didache's liturgy of, 171; sacrifice of, 231, 232, 279, 284, 290; when, how, and by whom administered, 267 et seq , writers of the Didache on, 267, 272; Clement of Rome on, 273; Ignatius' views, 276
Eucharistic leadership, the culmination of the priestly aspect of the ministry, 261, 263
Eugenius, Pope, 228, 314.
Eusebius, 172.
Evangelists, a missionary term, 163
Excommunication, a witness to unity, 31.
Expositor, The (Prof R Harris), on Montanism, 47; (Dr Sanday), 142

Florence, Council of, 228
Fox, George, his central aspiration, 55

Gasparri, Mgr., 322.
Gladstone, W E , 339
God, Unity of, what it is, 6
Gore, Canon, his theory of the Church, 2; Church and Ministry quoted, 19, 71, 90, 112, 119, 129, 170-172, 266; quotes Dr Milligan, 34 , on relation between ministry and laity, 71; on Tertullian's Montanism, 80; on Origen, 83; on the universal priesthood, 95; ἐπιμονήν, 115; on the apostolic office, 119, 122
Gradations of Ministry, in New Testament, 126-169, in sub-apostolic times, 170 219.
Grapte, 209, 211.
Guardian, The, 328, 339.
Gury, M., 336.

Harris, Professor Rendel, on Montanism, 47.
Hatch, Dr., his theory of the Church, 2; his Bampton Lectures, 9, 68, 112, 257; on higher and lower conceptions of unity, 11 , his arguments for Ignatian Epistles, 11, 17; on Christian faith and practice, 12 ; on Christian failure, 14-16, 20; refuted by Dr. Hort, 22; on Montanism, 47, 51-54, 74, relation between ministry and laity misconceived by, 73-75; his protest, 94, on methods of ordaining, 112.
Hegesippus, 189, 216.
Hermas, Shepherd of, 15, 172, 184; on Church unity, 206; on ministerial grades, 207-210; true and false prophets, 210, 212; his own position, 211; date of his work, 214, supplements Clement of Rome, ibid.
Hooker, on Baptism, 62; his Ecclesiastical Polity, 103, 238, 239
Hort, Dr. (Christian Ecclesia), 22; on apostolate, 127, 135; on diaconate, 138, 140; on 'elders,' 187; on Timotheus' designation for consecration, 156.

Ignatian Epistles, the, 11, 17, 49, 190; value of unity, corporate and sacramental, 193; a bishop's position, 193, bishop should be silent and modest, 194; Roman Church a model of Christian eminence, 196; references to author's martyrdom, ibid , contrasted with Polycarp's Letter, 203.
Ignatius, his chief aim, 11 ; doctrine of unity, 17, his vehement appeals, 49; on Eucharistic unity, 276; see also above.
Incarnation, vital fact of the, 106.
Individual inspiration, 107-109
Individuality, conditions of, 4
Introduction to the New Testament (Dr Salmon), 170, 180, 214.
Inward and outward, relation between, 30-63.
Irenaeus, 86, 213, 216. 280

Jerusalem, St James, first Bishop of, 150.
Judaic Christianity, 32; its bearing on St Paul's ideal of unity, 35.
Justin Martyr, 87, 257, 278.

Keble's Christian Year, quoted, 84.
Kingdom of Heaven, the, 37.

Lacey, Rev. T. A., 308, 328.
Laity and ministry, relation between, 64-98.
Latham, Mr. (Pastor Pastorum), 127.
Law, Mosaic, 244, 265; Levitical, 245.
Layman, spiritual dignity of the, 98.
le Grand, Albert, 313.

Levitical Law, 'blood means life, not death,' 245.
Levitical and Christian offerings—a parallel, 273, 274.
Liddon, Dr. (*University Sermons*), on the universal priesthood, 96; an apostolic office, 119.
Lightfoot, Dr. (Bishop of Durham), his *Christian Ministry* criticised, 43 et seq., his initial position, 46, on Montanism, 48, on means and end, 56; essence and essential, 58-60; his basis of Church polity, 71; on Sacerdotalism. his misconception, 76; on the Eucharist, 77; his misuse of Tertullian, 80; of Origen, 82; of Clement of Alexandria, 83; on Irenaeus and Justin Martyr, 86; on delegates and representatives, 90; his imperfectly Christianized Gentile, 93; ἐπιμονήν, 115, 116; ignores question of apostolic succession, 117-121; on the diaconate, 136-139; on St. James as principal presbyter or bishop, 146, 149, on Clement's episcopal position, 184; his translation of Clement's Letter, 186-190; his translation of Ignatian Letters, 191; Docetic Judaism, 198; Polycarp's Letter, 202; his *Apostolic Fathers*, ibid., Hermas, 213; on Episcopacy, 216, his *Dissertations on the Apostolic Age*, 238, 239, mistakes sacrificium and sacerdotium, 240, his interpretation of θυσιαστήριον, 269; quotes Justin Martyr, 278; misled by false antitheses, 280

an, his individuality, 4; his personality, 5; flesh and blood · a spiritual being, 39.
Maskell, 224.
Mason, Canon (*The Relation of Confirmation to Baptism*), 93
Mass, sacrifice of the, 221, 229
Means and end, 56.
Media, divine use and moral indispensableness of, 57, 61, 64; Naaman's leprosy an instance of God's essential, 60-62.
Methods, *see* Media.
Milligan, Dr., *The Resurrection of our Lord*, 34; *The Ascension of our Lord*, 72, 97, 129, 246, 248; on Church's prophetical office, 72; on priestly function, 97; Christ, the Prophet, 251;
Ministerial authority, must proceed from God, 100, 102; evolved or devolved, 120.

Ministers, not *delegates* if representatives, 90.
Ministry, relation between laity and, 64-98; how and why indispensable, 65; is it a sanctified intermediary? ibid.; Divine Commission the basis of, 99-125; gradations of, in New Testament, 126-169; gradations of, in Sub-Apostolic times, 170-219; *see also* Church Ministry, and Priesthood.
Missale Francorum, 225, 300.
Missionaries, evangelists were, 163.
Moberly, Dr. (Bishop of Salisbury) (*Administration of the Holy Spirit*), 69.
Monsabré, Père, 313.
Montanism, its spiritual aspirations, 47-49, Dr. Hatch's view of, 47, 51-54, 74; Professor R Harris on, 47, Dr. Lightfoot on, 48; its effect on Tertullian, 79.
Morinus, 230, 233, 300.
Mosaic Law, 244, 265.
Mozley, Dr. (*Ruling Ideas in Early Ages*), 110.

Naaman, his leprosy an instance of God's essential media, 60-62.
Nature of Church Unity, 1-29
New Testament, Gradations of Ministry in the, 126-169, compared with the *Didache*, 175; 'sacrificial' language of, 268-272.
Nicene Creed, its assertion of unity, 2, 20

Old Testament prophecy, 107.
Ordinal, for candidates for priesthood, 102, Anglican, 220, 223, 286, 289; Sarum, 220.
Ordination, even what is divine in it conferred through the Church, 89
Ordinations Anglicanes, Les (F. Dalbus), 311.
Origen, 81, 83

Pastor Pastorum (Mr. Latham), 127.
Pastoral Epistles, the, 142, 152.
Pearson, Bishop, 119.
Personality of man, 5
Philip the Evangelist, 138, 164.
Philippian Church, the, 200, 205.
Πνευματικά, 160.
Polycarp, Letter of, 184; silent about episcopate, 200; Dr Lightfoot on, 202; its episcopal character: contrasted with Ignatian Epistles, 203
Pontifical, Dunstan's and Egbert's, 223;

INDEX 359

Sarum, 220, 223, 224; Roman, 224, 226.
Porrectio instrumentorum, 314, 316, 320.
Praeparatio Evangelica, 9.
Prayer Book, revision of the, 236.
Πρεσβύτερος and ἐπίσκοπος, used interchangeably, 141, 144, 175, 179
Presbyterate, its institution unnoticed, 140 · titles presbyter and bishop interchangeable, 141, 142, 144; presbyter must be of blameless life: ruling, teaching, deeper implications, 141-145; a local leadership with the background of apostolate, 145; a local community, 163; the *Didache* on, 175, 182; Dr. Lightfoot's view of, in Clement's Letter, 182, 186-190; Ignatian Epistles on, 193.
Priesthood, of the Ministry, does not alter personal character or right and wrong, 92; of a layman, ibid. ; vicarious ideas of, 93; Gore and Liddon on the universal, 95, 96; in the Church of Christ, 220-299; exaggerations and extreme tendencies of sixteenth century, 221; work of Reformation, 222; Tridentine definitions of, 223; Sarum Pontifical, 224; *Missale Francorum*, 225; developed in one direction, 227; Council of Trent, its caution and failure, 228-233; Anglican Reformers retain priestly title, 234; jealousy as to title, 239; Dr. Lightfoot mistakes sacerdotium and sacrificium, 240; what it is, 254; specializes and personifies priesthood of the Church, 257; its inwardness and outwardness, 260; inseparable from priesthood of the laity, 262.
Prophecy, an inspiration rather than a ministerial status, 161, 166.
Prophets, and teachers, who and what they are, 159; two notable passages, 160; a personal endowment, 161, 166; three pertinent inferences from St. Paul's picture of, 164; not an 'Order,' 167; summary of arguments, 167-169.
Puller, Father, 328.
Puritans in sixteenth century, 222.

Quakerism, 54.

Relation, between Inward and Outward, 30-63; unity only spiritual? 30; spirit and body, 31; always a contrast, 35; between Ministry and Laity, 64.

Relation of Confirmation to Baptism (Canon Mason), 93.
Resurrection of our Lord (Dr. Milligan), 34.
Revue Anglo-Romaine, 308, 328, 329.
Romain controversy as to validity of Anglican Orders, *see* Anglican Orders.
Roman Pontifical, 224, 226, 300.
Romans in sixteenth century, 221
Ruling Ideas in Early Ages (Dr. Mozley), 110

Sabatier, 171.
Sacerdotalism, according to Dr. Lightfoot, 75, 240; discussed, 263.
Sacerdotium, 130; Dr. Lightfoot's mistaken relation to, 240.
Sacrifice (sacrificium), 228, 230 et seq ; Dr Lightfoot on, 240; its true character, 247-249.
Saint, the, one personality in imperfection or in beatitude, 38.
St. Cyprian, 281.
St. Hippolytus, Canons of, 328.
St. James, 131, persona ecclesiae Hierosolymitanae, 147; his relations to the Apostles, ibid.; 'the Lord's brother,' 148; probably first Bishop of Jerusalem, 150.
St. Jerome, 95; his 'sacerdotium laici,' 262.
St. John, 8, 133, 177, 183, 189.
St. Jude, 14.
St. Matthias, 126, 130
St. Paul, his struggle for corporate unity, 32; consequences of his enthusiasm, 49; on the Eucharist, 71; his theory of inspiration, 107; on the apostolate, 127, 131-134; on the diaconate, 138; presbyters, 140; Timothy, deacon and evangelist, 157, 158; on 'apostles, prophets, and teachers,' 161, his protest against selfish individualism, 162; on excellence of prophecy, 164; preaches self-restraint, 165; on St. James, 147, 148; warns the Ephesus elders, 267; his hieratic language, 271; his words as an exhortation to all candidates for priesthood, 287.
St. Peter, his claim as a presbyter, 121; working of God's judgement in, 133; his message to St. James, 147; a holy priesthood, 252.
Salmon, Dr. (*Introduction to the New Testament*), 170, 180, 214.
Sanday, Dr., 142.
Sarum Ordinal, 220, 223, 227.
Scripta Anglicana (M. Bucer), 236.

INDEX

Sixteenth century, Anglican Ordinal dates from, 220; Roman and Puritan excesses in, 221, 222.
Socialism, 4.
Solidarity of humanity, 4
Speaker's Commentary, 116.
Spirit, the, and the Body, 39-41, 57, 58, 106; character of the Church as, 42
Spiritual, and bodily, unity, 31, 35, 39, 57, Church of Christ the Body, 66
Sub-apostolic times, gradations of ministry in, 170-219.

Taylor, Bishop, on *Episcopacy*, 83, 170, 172
Tertullian, his exaggerations, 48, 49; his false inferences, 78; a result of his Montanism, 79; layman and priest, 112.
Tetzel, 221.
Θυσιαστήριον, 266; Dr. Lightfoot's interpretation of, 269.

Timotheus, 134, 142; at Ephesus—his functions, 151-158, his 'ordination,' 157, deacon and evangelist, 158
Titus, 134, 142; at Crete, 151; his functions, 151-158
Tournebize, R P., 329.
Trent, Council of, 223, 231
Tridentine, definitions of priesthood, 222; Canon de Sacramento Ordinis, 229.
Truth, grades of, 38

Unity of Spirit—unity of Body, their contrast not scriptural, 31 et seq., 56.
University Sermons (Dr. Liddon), 96.

Vasquez, 312.
Vaughan, Cardinal, 331, 345, 351

Westcott, Bishop, 116, 183, 246, 248, 269.

THE END

www.ingramcontent.com/pod-product-compliance
Lightning Source LLC
Chambersburg PA
CBHW052138300426
44115CB00011B/1431